AI-Assisted Language Development for Children with Autism and Disabilities

Nayef Jomaa
https://orcid.org/0000-0001-8952-5812

University of Technology and Applied Sciences, Salalah, Oman

IGI Global
Scientific Publishing
Publishing Tomorrow's Research Today

Vice President of Editorial	Melissa Wagner
Director of Acquisitions	Mikaela Felty
Director of Book Development	Jocelynn Hessler
Production Manager	Mike Brehm
Cover Design	Jose Rosado

Published in the United States of America by
IGI Global Scientific Publishing
701 East Chocolate Avenue
Hershey, PA, 17033, USA
Tel: 717-533-8845 | Fax: 717-533-7115
Website: https://www.igi-global.com E-mail: cust@igi-global.com

Library of Congress Cataloging-in-Publication Data

LCCN: 2026002306 (CIP Data Pending)
ISBN13: 9798337377247
Isbn13Softcover: 9798337377254
EISBN13: 9798337377261
British Cataloguing in Publication Data
A Cataloguing in Publication record for this book is available from the British Library.

Table of Contents

Detailed Table of Contents

Educational robotics can provide predictable and consistent interactions that may benefit children with autism spectrum disorder (ASD). However, many existing interventions focus on either social communication or science, technology, engineering, and mathematics (STEM) learning rather than integrating both. This chapter reviews research on social robots, educational robotics, adaptive learning, language development, and inclusive STEM education for children with ASD. It proposes an integrated curriculum using Buddy for social communication, Marty V2 for coding and embodied STEM learning, and Raspberry Pi for hands-on physical computing activities. The chapter introduces a five-phase framework that combines communication, guided language, STEM activities, debugging, reflection, and assessment into a unified instructional process. The framework emphasizes structured learning, scaffolding, skill generalization, and teacher assessment to support inclusive classroom instruction.

Dyslexia is commonly viewed as a reading and phonological disorder, but it also affects numerical reasoning and mathematics learning. Children with dyslexia often face persistent difficulties in calculation, symbol recognition, sequencing, and problem-solving. In traditional classrooms in Kerala, mathematics instruction is largely language-based, which disadvantages these learners. This chapter reports findings from a study of 25 dyslexic and 25 typically developing children, highlighting poor mathematical performance and emphasizing the need for AI-supported, innovative educational interventions to promote inclusive learning.

Artificial IntelligenceI (AI) is changing the face of therapeutic and special needs education for kids with autism and other disabilities. There are a variety of ways that AI is being applied to support language development in both expressive and receptive terms (through the use of conversational AI and adaptive learning technologies). This chapter will explore the theoretical foundations and technological frameworks that support the use of AI-assisted language systems, as well as how they are implemented. A structured approach for developing and evaluating a model of conversational AI to be used for children with autism and related communication disorders will be proposed. The ethical concerns associated with developing and implementing this type of technology will be discussed, as well as how personalization mechanisms and collaborative human-AI interaction models are possible. In addition, potential future research directions will be discussed, including longitudinal validation, inclusive design, and interdisciplinary integration.

The chapter analyses how the intersection of artificial intelligence (AI) and language development and communication may positively impact the experiences of children with autism and related disabilities. It argues that AI is most effective partner when it complements human caregiving and with empathy, inclusiveness, and ethical considerations. AI can foster expressive, emotional, and social development through learning environments and provision of adaptive feedback and emotional assessment. The author asserts that human dignity and diversity demand technological retrofitting, whereby ethical designed innovations prioritize the values of transparency, equity, and active participation. The author posits that the ideal intersection of AI and human caregiving is the embodied data, bridge of compassion AI. The author ultimately proposes a construct of the future designed relationship with AI as one that redefines inclusion as the future of technology. The author envisions a construct of relationship with AI as one that redefines inclusion as the future of technology.

This chapter per the authors aims to design an ethical, game-based AI framework that supports personalized language development pathways for children with autism spectrum disorder and related developmental communication challenges. The primary target groups include neurodiverse children, caregivers, therapists, and researchers in AI-enabled education. The chapter adopts a design-based research approach, integrating rule-based AI, adaptive game mechanics, and human-in-the-loop dashboards to personalize learning while ensuring transparency and accessibility. Findings demonstrate improved engagement, sustained interaction, and adaptive responsiveness as indicators of potential language development support. The chapter concludes that interpretable, game-based AI systems offer scalable and inclusive opportunities for augmenting language interventions, while highlighting the need for future empirical validation and real-world clinical evaluation.

This chapter was a systematic review of AI-enhanced virtual and augmented reality (VR/AR) interventions that were aimed at enhancing communication and social skills in children with autism spectrum disorder and other related developmental disabilities. After the screening of 1,639 records in key databases using the PRISMA, 23 empirical studies were included. Two reviewers performed the extractions of study design, participant profiles, type of technology, AI features, outcome measures, and usability indices; synthesis was done through deductive content analysis and cross-code triangulation. Results showed that there was a dominance of HMD-based immersive VR, recurrent application of adaptive feedback and emotion-recognition AI, reliable short-term improvement in joint attention and emotion recognition, and inconsistent long-term generalization. The chapter concluded that AI-enhanced VR/AR promised content earnestness upon the condition of larger RCTs, standardized outcome organizations, and comparable scaling ways.

Natural Language Processing (NLP) drives the seamless interaction between humans and machines via speech recognition and text-to-speech (TTS) technologies. Speech recognition systems convert spoken language into text using acoustic modeling, language models, and deep learning, enabling applications like voice assistants and healthcare dictation. Conversely, TTS systems generate natural-sounding speech from text through linguistic analysis, prosody modeling, and neural vocoders like WaveNet. Recent advances, such as transformers and self-supervised learning, have dramatically improved accuracy and voice quality. This study comprehensively explores the core architectures, evaluation metrics (WER, MOS), real-world applications, critical challenges (accents, bias, low-resource languages), and future directions like zero-shot models and personalized emotional synthesis for these transformative AI systems.

Autism spectrum disorder (ASD) and speech delays need to be identified early since children can get better with an earlier intervention. Conventional forms of diagnosis are slow, subjective, and rely on clinical observation. Artificial intelligence (AI) provides a more objective and quicker means of identifying early warning signs through verbal and non-verbal communication and behaviour. It is possible to detect atypical speech patterns by using machine learning and language processing, and facial expressions, gestures, and differences in eye contact can be detected with the help of computer vision. It is also possible to monitor in real-life environments with the help of mobile apps and wearable devices. AI can be used to enable professionals to make earlier referrals and tailor therapy plans. The topics of concern are the privacy of data, equity, access, and cost. Better results in children can be attained through the enhancement of explainable and ethical AI systems.

This chapter critically examines the intersection of artificial intelligence, language development, and inclusive education through a decolonial lens. While AI technologies offer promising tools for supporting children with autism and disabilities, their design and implementation often reflect Western-centric assumptions about language, cognition, and pedagogy. This chapter seeks to challenge these assumptions by proposing inclusive, culturally responsive frameworks for AI-assisted language development, particularly in underrepresented regions such as Africa, Vietnam, and Indigenous communities in Canada. The chapter will explore how AI tools can be adapted to respect linguistic diversity, cultural norms, and local pedagogical practices. It will also highlight the risks of algorithmic bias and data colonialism in AI systems used for speech therapy and communication training. The chapter will offer practical strategies for educators, therapists, and developers to co-create AI solutions that are ethical, inclusive, and contextually grounded

This chapter explores the transformative role of Artificial Intelligence (AI) in enhancing language development among children with autism and developmental disabilities. It integrates insights from neuroscience, pedagogy, and technology to show how tools like Natural Language Processing (NLP), chatbots, social robots, Augmentative and Alternative Communication (AAC) systems, and Virtual or Augmented Reality (VR/AR) can create adaptive, data-driven, and inclusive learning environments. AI facilitates personalized therapy, early detection of language disorders, and continuous progress monitoring through multimodal analytics. However, the chapter also highlights ethical challenges, such as data privacy, algorithmic bias, and the irreplaceable role of human empathy in education. By combining technological innovation with human-centered design, AI becomes

Preface

INTRODUCTION

The rapid advancement of artificial intelligence (AI) is reshaping the way we understand, support, and enhance learning for individuals with diverse educational needs. Among the areas experiencing the most significant transformation is language development for children with autism and other disabilities, where AI-driven technologies are opening new possibilities for communication, literacy, and social engagement. As intelligent systems become increasingly sophisticated, they offer opportunities to complement traditional educational and therapeutic practices by providing personalized, adaptive, and accessible learning experiences. *AI-Assisted Language Development for Children with Autism and Disabilities* has been developed to examine these emerging opportunities while encouraging thoughtful, evidence-based approaches to integrating AI into special education and intervention.

The inspiration for this volume stems from the growing recognition that effective language development requires individualized support that respects the unique strengths, challenges, and developmental trajectories of every child. Recent advances in speech recognition, natural language processing, conversational AI, adaptive tutoring systems, and intelligent communication technologies have demonstrated tremendous potential to improve language acquisition, facilitate social interaction, and empower children to communicate more effectively in educational, clinical, and home environments. At the same time, these innovations raise important questions concerning accessibility, ethics, privacy, equity, and the evolving roles of educators, therapists, families, and technology developers. This book seeks to address these opportunities and challenges through a multidisciplinary collection of scholarly contributions.

The chapters assembled in this volume explore the expanding role of AI in supporting language acquisition, communication development, literacy instruction, and personalized learning for children with autism and other disabilities. Contributors present current research, innovative technological solutions, practical intervention strategies, and real-world implementation experiences that bridge theory with practice. Throughout the book, readers will discover how AI-powered applications can strengthen speech and language therapy, facilitate individualized instruction, enhance inclusive educational environments, and promote meaningful participation across academic and social settings.

A central objective of this volume is to connect technological innovation with educational and clinical practice. While AI offers remarkable capabilities for analyzing learning patterns, adapting instructional content, and providing responsive feedback, successful implementation depends upon collaboration among educators, speech-language pathologists, psychologists, caregivers, researchers, and technology developers. Rather than replacing human expertise, AI serves as a powerful partner that enhances professional decision-making and expands opportunities for individualized support. This collaborative perspective is reflected throughout the chapters, which emphasize practical applications grounded in sound pedagogical principles and clinical evidence.

Equally important is the book's attention to the ethical dimensions of AI adoption. As intelligent technologies become increasingly integrated into educational and therapeutic settings, safeguarding privacy, ensuring equitable access, minimizing algorithmic bias, and designing inclusive systems remain essential priorities. Several chapters examine responsible AI practices and propose frameworks for developing technologies that respect the rights, dignity, and diverse needs of children with disabilities. By highlighting these considerations alongside technological innovation, this volume encourages responsible implementation that benefits learners while maintaining the highest ethical standards.

This reference work has been prepared for a broad interdisciplinary audience. Educators and special education professionals will find practical guidance for incorporating AI into language instruction and classroom practice. Speech and language therapists will gain insights into AI-assisted interventions that complement established therapeutic approaches. Researchers and graduate students will discover emerging directions in artificial intelligence, educational technology, language development, and inclusive education. Parents and caregivers will gain a deeper understanding of how AI can support communication and learning beyond the classroom, while policymakers and educational leaders will find evidence-based perspectives to guide responsible adoption of AI within educational systems. AI developers and educational technology professionals will likewise benefit from discussions that emphasize user-centered design and accessibility for children with diverse developmental needs.

The diversity of perspectives represented throughout this volume reflects the inherently interdisciplinary nature of AI-assisted language development. Advances in this field require meaningful collaboration across computer science, education, psychology, speech-language pathology, neuroscience, human-computer interaction, and disability studies. By bringing together contributions from these complementary disciplines, this book offers a comprehensive examination of current developments while identifying future directions for research, innovation, and practice.

As editors, we extend our sincere appreciation to the chapter authors whose expertise, dedication, and scholarly contributions have made this volume possible. Their work represents a shared commitment to improving educational and therapeutic outcomes for children with autism and other disabilities through thoughtful application of emerging technologies. We also express our gratitude to the reviewers whose careful evaluations strengthened the quality and rigor of each chapter, and to the editorial and publishing teams whose guidance and support were instrumental throughout the development of this project.

We hope this book serves as both a valuable scholarly resource and a practical guide for those working to enhance language development through innovative, ethical, and inclusive AI applications. More importantly, we hope it inspires continued collaboration among researchers, practitioners, technology developers, families, and policymakers as we collectively strive to create learning environments where every child has the opportunity to develop meaningful communication skills and reach their full potential.

ORGANIZATION OF THE BOOK

The chapters in this volume collectively demonstrate the remarkable breadth of artificial intelligence applications that are transforming language development, communication, and learning opportunities for children with autism and other disabilities. Each contribution presents a unique perspective while reinforcing the importance of ethical, inclusive, and evidence-based approaches to AI-assisted intervention.

The opening chapter establishes an interdisciplinary foundation by presenting an innovative AI-assisted STEM curriculum that integrates social robotics, educational robotics, and adaptive learning technologies for children with autism spectrum disorder. By combining communication development with coding, physical computing, and structured STEM instruction, the chapter introduces a comprehensive instructional framework that demonstrates how AI-enabled robotics can simultaneously foster language acquisition, social interaction, and technical skills within inclusive classroom environments.

Building upon the theme of personalized learning, the second chapter expands the discussion beyond autism to examine AI-assisted mathematical interventions for children with dyslexia. Drawing upon empirical research comparing dyslexic and typically developing learners, the chapter highlights the often-overlooked relationship between language-based learning challenges and mathematical achievement. The authors make a compelling case for AI-supported educational strategies that promote inclusive instruction and improve learning outcomes for students with diverse cognitive profiles.

The third chapter examines the growing role of conversational AI and adaptive language systems in supporting expressive and receptive communication among children with autism and related disabilities. It explores the theoretical foundations, technological architectures, and implementation models that underpin intelligent language-support systems while proposing a structured framework for designing, evaluating, and personalizing conversational AI. The discussion is complemented by careful consideration of ethical implementation, interdisciplinary collaboration, and future research opportunities.

The fourth chapter shifts attention toward the human dimension of AI-assisted language learning by emphasizing empathy, inclusion, and ethical responsibility. Rather than positioning AI as a replacement for caregivers or educators, the authors advocate for technologies that strengthen compassionate human interaction through adaptive feedback and emotionally responsive learning environments. Their vision underscores the importance of designing AI systems that uphold dignity, diversity, transparency, and meaningful participation for every learner.

Personalization through engaging instructional design is the focus of the fifth chapter, which presents a game-based AI framework for supporting language development among children with autism and communication disabilities. Integrating adaptive game mechanics, interpretable AI, and human oversight, the proposed framework demonstrates how interactive learning environments can increase learner engagement while providing individualized developmental pathways. The chapter also highlights the importance of transparency, accessibility, and continued clinical validation as AI-based educational games evolve.

The sixth chapter provides a comprehensive systematic review of AI-enhanced virtual and augmented reality interventions designed to strengthen communication and social skills. Synthesizing findings from a substantial body of empirical research, the chapter evaluates immersive technologies that incorporate adaptive feedback, emotion recognition, and intelligent interaction. While documenting encouraging improvements in communication and social engagement, the authors also identify important directions for future large-scale studies capable of demonstrating sustained long-term effectiveness.

Advancing the discussion of foundational AI technologies, the seventh chapter explores the rapidly evolving fields of natural language processing, speech recognition, and text-to-speech systems. The authors explain the architectures that enable increasingly natural human-computer communication while examining recent advances in deep learning, transformer models, and neural speech synthesis. The chapter also considers practical applications, evaluation methodologies, current limitations, and emerging innovations that will continue to improve accessible communication technologies.

The eighth chapter demonstrates the growing importance of AI in the early identification of autism and speech-related developmental delays. By examining machine learning, computer vision, natural language processing, wearable technologies, and mobile health applications, the authors illustrate how intelligent diagnostic systems can support earlier intervention and more personalized therapeutic planning. Equally important, the chapter addresses ethical concerns surrounding data privacy, equitable access, and the development of explainable AI systems within healthcare settings.

The ninth chapter offers a critical and timely examination of AI-assisted language development through a decolonial perspective. Challenging the dominance of Western-centric assumptions embedded within many AI systems, the chapter advocates for culturally responsive and linguistically inclusive frameworks that better reflect the diverse realities of learners across the Global South and Indigenous communities. The authors provide practical guidance for designing AI technologies that acknowledge cultural diversity while reducing algorithmic bias and promoting equitable educational opportunities.

The concluding chapter synthesizes many of the themes explored throughout the volume by presenting a comprehensive overview of AI-assisted language development for children with autism and developmental disabilities. Integrating perspectives from neuroscience, educational practice, and intelligent technologies, the chapter illustrates how natural language processing, conversational agents, social robots, augmentative communication systems, and immersive technologies collectively contribute to personalized learning and early intervention. The discussion concludes by reaffirming that ethical, human-centered AI should complement—not replace—the expertise, empathy, and collaboration of educators, therapists, and caregivers in creating inclusive learning environments.

Together, these chapters provide a comprehensive exploration of the current landscape of AI-assisted language development for children with autism and disabilities. They illustrate not only the remarkable technological advances shaping educational and therapeutic practice but also the ethical, cultural, pedagogical, and human considerations that must guide responsible innovation. Collectively, the contributions offer readers a valuable foundation for understanding both the opportunities and challenges associated with integrating artificial intelligence into inclusive language learning and communication support.

CONCLUDING REMARKS

As artificial intelligence continues to redefine the possibilities of education, healthcare, and assistive technology, its potential to transform language development for children with autism and other disabilities has never been more significant. The contributions presented in this volume demonstrate that AI is not simply introducing new technological tools; it is creating opportunities for more personalized, accessible, and inclusive approaches to communication, learning, and intervention. Collectively, the chapters illustrate how advances in conversational AI, natural language processing, robotics, immersive technologies, adaptive learning systems, and intelligent diagnostic tools can be thoughtfully integrated to support the diverse needs of children across educational and therapeutic settings.

At the same time, this volume reinforces that meaningful innovation extends beyond technological capability. Successful AI-assisted language development depends upon interdisciplinary collaboration among educators, speech-language therapists, clinicians, researchers, caregivers, policymakers, and technology developers. Equally important is a continued commitment to ethical principles that safeguard privacy, promote equity, minimize bias, and ensure that intelligent systems remain transparent, culturally responsive, and accessible to all learners. Throughout this collection, the emphasis remains on AI as a complement to—not a replacement for—the expertise, empathy, and professional judgment of those who support children's communication and development.

As editors, we hope this book serves as both a comprehensive reference and a catalyst for continued research, innovation, and collaboration. The ideas, frameworks, and practical applications presented by our contributors are intended to inspire new investigations, encourage responsible implementation, and foster dialogue across disciplines. As AI technologies continue to evolve, so too must our understanding of how they can be designed and applied to empower every child with opportunities to communicate, learn, participate, and thrive.

We extend our sincere gratitude to all of the chapter authors for sharing their expertise and advancing this important field of study. We also thank the reviewers for their valuable insights and the publishing team for their guidance and dedication throughout the development of this volume. It is our hope that *AI-Assisted Language Development for Children with Autism and Disabilities* will become a valuable resource for researchers, educators, clinicians, technology developers, students, and policymakers, while contributing to a future in which intelligent technologies support more equitable, compassionate, and inclusive educational experiences for children around the world.

Chapter 1
AI-Assisted STEM Curriculum for Children With ASD:
Integrating Social and Educational Robotics

Vennela Akula
http://orcid.org/0009-0003-0152-7170
Auburn University, USA

Nayanika Reddy Rajoli
Auburn University, USA

Sasikiran Reddy Nallapareddy
Auburn University, USA

Daniela Marghitu
Auburn University, USA

ABSTRACT

Educational robotics can provide predictable and consistent interactions that may benefit children with autism spectrum disorder (ASD). However, many existing interventions focus on either social communication or science, technology, engineering, and mathematics (STEM) learning rather than integrating both. This chapter reviews research on social robots, educational robotics, adaptive learning, language development, and inclusive STEM education for children with ASD. It proposes an integrated curriculum using Buddy for social communication, Marty V2 for coding and embodied STEM learning, and Raspberry Pi for hands-on physical computing

DOI: 10.4018/979-8-3373-7724-7.ch001

activities. The chapter introduces a five-phase framework that combines communication, guided language, STEM activities, debugging, reflection, and assessment into a unified instructional process. The framework emphasizes structured learning, scaffolding, skill generalization, and teacher assessment to support inclusive classroom instruction.

INTRODUCTION

There has been extensive use of robots in educational institutions for assisting in the process of learning science, technology, engineering, and mathematics (STEM) subjects, as well as situations of social interaction. Robots can be programmed to help learners make a connection between theoretical information and physical action. In addition, social robots can offer systematic cues, consistent routines, and repeated chances for communication. Furthermore, research that gives an overview of the application of both social robots and educational robots indicates that the success of such robots in classrooms depends on proper interaction design, teacher assistance, and learning task integration (Leite et al., 2013; Mubin et al., 2013).

Autism Spectrum Disorder (ASD) is a neurodevelopmental condition involving differences in social communication, social interaction, behavior, sensory processing, and attention. Learners with ASD can thrive in classroom settings if the class setting offers them structure, predictability of interaction, visual aids, explicit language training, and generalization of skills in terms of interacting with other people, settings, and activities (Diehl et al., 2012; Kewalramani et al., 2024; Pennisi et al., 2016). These characteristics are particularly vital for an inclusive classroom environment.

AI in this chapter is defined as computer techniques that will help the system to detect patterns, give feedback, facilitate communication, adapt prompts, or make rudimentary instructional decisions while learning. In early research about the use of AI in education, the technology was viewed as an aid in personalization, feedback, and teacher decision-making, while more recent reviews about the application of AI in special education highlight not only possible gains but also critical considerations about accessibility, use of data, teacher control, and positioning disabled learners as active learners, not as problems (Luckin et al., 2016; Hopcan et al., 2023; Rice & Dunn, 2023).

Computational thinking refers to the solving of problems through techniques such as decomposition, pattern identification, abstraction, algorithmic creation, and debugging. Computational thinking is an important goal of education in STEM learning in schools due to its association with programming, mathematics, reasoning, and designing (Grover & Pea, 2013; Wing, 2006). For children with ASD, robot-based CT activities may be useful when they are structured, visual, concrete, and connected to communication routines.

Existing literature indicates that educational robots can be used to facilitate STEM education, while social robots can help promote engagement, social interaction, and communication skills (Belpaeme et al., 2018; Benitti, 2012; Darmawansah et al., 2023; Kewalramani et al., 2024; Wang et al., 2023). Nevertheless, the current body of evidence remains imbalanced. Some studies are limited by short intervention durations, small sample sizes, or the use of robots in therapeutic rather than educational contexts. Moreover, other studies focus primarily on coding and STEM skills while overlooking the development of language and communication competence. This chapter aims to address this gap through the proposed curricular framework.

This chapter first defines key terms, then reviews research on social robotics, educational robotics, adaptive learning support, and inclusive STEM education. It then proposes an integrated curriculum framework using Buddy, Marty V2, and Raspberry Pi. The chapter provides a system architecture, a five-phase curriculum model, module tables, worked lessons, a Raspberry Pi sensing activity, illustrative classroom scenarios, an assessment and evaluation plan, implementation guidance, ethical considerations, and directions for future evaluation.

The original contribution of this chapter is not the creation of a new robot and not the report of a classroom study. The contribution is the synthesis of current literature into a proposed five-phase curriculum framework and a Buddy, Marty V2, and Raspberry Pi architecture that can support language development, social interaction, and STEM learning in one classroom sequence.

Learning Objectives

On completion of this chapter, readers will be able to:

- Explain how social and educational robots may support communication, social interaction, and STEM learning for children with ASD.
- Compare the instructional roles of Buddy, Marty V2, and Raspberry Pi in an inclusive curriculum.
- Design a structured robotics activity using predictability, scaffolding, visual support, and reflection.
- Identify practical concerns related to teacher preparation, privacy, access, and assessment.
- Apply the proposed five-phase framework to future classroom planning and research.

METHODOLOGY: REVIEW AND FRAMEWORK DEVELOPMENT

This chapter uses a review-based and conceptual framework approach. It does not include any pilot study, classroom testing, learner data, or pre–post results. This is because the objective of the chapter is to synthesize existing research and develop a curriculum model based on that synthesis.

Relevant literature was obtained from peer reviewed journal articles, conference proceedings, systematic reviews, meta-analyses and selected examples of educational robotics. The sources include IEEE Xplore, ACM Digital Library, Springer Link, Google Scholar, ERIC and publisher databases. Search keywords include a combination of Buddy Robot, Marty V2, educational robotics, social robotics, autism spectrum disorder, ASD, special education, language development, social-emotional learning, computational thinking, STEM education and adaptive tools for special education.

The literature review centered on the sources covering five major topics: Robotics in special education context; social robots and communication assistance for ASD; educational robotics for CT and STEM education; adaptive feedback or personalization; inclusive instructional design. Purely technical papers, product advertisements, opinion pieces without educational grounding, and robotics studies unrelated to school or special education were not used as evidence for pedagogical claims. Vendor sources were retained only for basic hardware or product information.

Thematic analysis was employed on the sources used, not statistical analysis. The primary themes included social communication, emotional regulation, STEM education, embodied learning, coding, teacher practice, access issues, privacy, and research gaps. The proposed architecture, curriculum phases, lessons, and assessment approaches were based on these themes.

LITERATURE SYNTHESIS

Social Robots, Communication, and ASD

Research into social robotics indicates that robots can offer an interaction pattern that can be helpful to some children diagnosed with ASD. Reviews into robot interventions in autism environments highlight promising results regarding engagement, joint attention, imitation, turn taking, and emotion recognition among others, however, there is a caveat that the results depend on the child's individuality, environment, robot itself, and intervention design (Breazeal, 2003; Cabibihan et al., 2013; Diehl et al., 2012; Leite et al., 2013; Kory-Westlund & Breazeal, 2019; Pennisi et al., 2016; Scassellati et al., 2012). These considerations are important in the case of developing a curriculum chapter since the use of robots in classrooms has more value than merely being new and exciting. The key lies in structuring the interaction process, in the way the teacher introduces it, and in the ability of the child to apply the practiced skills in interactions with other children and teachers.

The topic of predictability is a recurring one when discussing robot-assisted interventions for children with ASD. Routines that make it possible to understand the upcoming expectations and actions are very useful for many individuals diagnosed with ASD. However, the robot's ability to repeat the same greeting or a turn-taking sequence without getting tired might make the interaction less exhausting from the social perspective. At the same time, the same predictability can become a limitation if the activity remains scripted and does not lead to flexible communication with people. Diehl et al. (2012) and Scassellati et al. (2012) both emphasize that engagement with a robot should not be mistaken for broad social communication growth unless generalization is measured carefully. This point shapes the proposed framework: Buddy is used to prepare, prompt, and reflect, but the teacher and peers remain part of the lesson.

The research on affective feedback also indicates that robots' reactions influence engagement, although this effect is dependent on how the feedback was designed and explained by the teacher for the task (Błażejowska et al., 2023). A cheerful face, encouragement, and repetition of instructions are helpful in terms of engaging learners in the process, yet it may serve as a distraction from the learning task itself. For this reason, the framework uses Buddy for bounded communication tasks: greetings, emotion checks, vocabulary prompts, help seeking, turn taking, and reflection. These are communication supports attached to a STEM task, not a separate social robotics demonstration.

Buddy specific literature is useful but still limited. Milliez (2018) describes Buddy as a companion robot designed for family and social interaction, while Ramamurthy and Li (2018) present a separate speech-therapy robot prototype also named Buddy for children with cleft lip and palate. Ackerman (2019) provides product-development context for Buddy. These sources support the selection of Buddy as a social communication tool, but they should not be read as evidence that Buddy has already produced measured classroom gains in ASD STEM instruction. The chapter therefore treats Buddy as a plausible instructional support based on its communication features and on the broader social robotics literature, not as a tool with established effectiveness for the complete framework.

Recent work continues to show interest in robotics for social and emotional learning. Kewalramani et al. (2024) identify technologies used in robotics to facilitate social-emotional learning for autistic children, emphasizing the importance of structured interactions. On the other hand, research on teacher perceptions of robot use warns against allowing robots to replace human social interaction or undermine teachers' professional judgment (Smakman et al., 2022). This discussion highlights the need for a balanced perspective in which the robot is viewed as a trigger, model, or mediating tool, while the teacher remains at the center of the learning process.

Educational Robotics, STEM, and Computational Thinking

The literature in the field of educational robotics research has made a consistent association between programmable robots, constructionism, hands-on activities, and computational thinking (Alimisis, 2013; Benitti, 2012; Eguchi, 2014; Matarić, 2004; Mubin et al., 2013; Papert, 1980; Resnick et al., 2009). In constructionist robotics projects, the learners do not just get acquainted with an idea but rather construct, experiment, refine, and explain their product. This is particularly helpful for STEM education since several mathematical and computing concepts remain abstract until implemented into practice. With robots walking, turning, or looping upon receiving certain instructions, the learner can examine the outcome and see how it matches the expected outcome.

Recent studies and meta-analyses have demonstrated the positive impact of educational robotics on learners' success in STEM education, motivation, and problem-solving skills, yet these results are conditioned by the specific teaching methodology used, teachers' assistance, quality of the assessment and duration of the process itself (Darmawansah et al., 2023; Trapero-González et al., 2024; Ouyang & Xu, 2024; Wang et al., 2023). These reviews share one common aspect – the effectiveness of robots lies in their connection with the learning objectives. The robot may help engage learners in a lesson; however, engagement alone does not equate to learning. Marty V2 is relevant to this line of work because it allows learners to connect code with visible movement. For learners who benefit from concrete feedback, robot movement can make sequencing, conditionals, spatial reasoning, and debugging easier to observe. Embodied computing school robotics projects help establish this connection between coding and physical actions, while block-based and text-based programming research demonstrates a possible path from visual coding to Python (Ponticorvo & Dell'Aquila, 2023; Weintrop & Wilensky, 2018). Such a progression is important for inclusive classes, as learners can start with visual coding and shift towards text coding only when the cognitive load is low enough.

However, there are limitations in the educational robotics research. First, some studies are limited by their duration, sample size, or attitude measurements. Second, some reviews show that there is no unified positive result as achievements differ based on learners' age, subjects, robot used, and teacher's qualifications (Darmawansah et al., 2023; Ouyang & Xu, 2024). This chapter therefore does not claim that Marty V2 will automatically improve STEM learning. Instead, it uses the broader evidence to design a framework that makes the instructional role of the robot explicit and testable.

Adaptive Tools in Special Education and Inclusive Learning

Adaptive technology in special education has been found to help learners with disabilities when it is designed to incorporate issues of accessibility, transparency, and oversight by teachers (Hopcan et al., 2023; Rice & Dunn, 2023). Within the presented framework, adaptation would not imply the replacement of the teacher by the adaptive system. Adaptation would simply entail adjusting prompts, choices, timing, and task difficulty based on the learner's performance while still allowing the teacher to observe and understand the actions performed by the adaptive system.

This distinction is important because adaptive tools can create both opportunity and risk. On the positive side, they can provide repeated practice, immediate feedback, and multiple response modes. They can also help teachers track prompt levels, retries, and patterns of error. In terms of risks, they might collect excessive information, prevent teachers from knowing decision-making processes, or view the disability of a learner as something negative which needs to be remedied. Rice and Dunn (2023) state that any AI associated with learners' disabilities should not only be evaluated on its effectiveness but also in relation to its representation of disability, agency, and accessibility.

It means that inclusive education involves more than just adding technology. The principle of Universal Design for Learning implies that educators need to offer learners several ways of engaging, representing, and expressing (Meyer et al., 2014). It includes listening, watching, pointing, speaking, selecting, coding, moving objects, and explaining. The same concept can be shown through Buddy's prompt, Marty V2's movement, a visual card, a learner selection, and a teacher's follow up question. This gives learners more than one path into the activity and more than one way to show understanding.

GAP AND DIFFERENCIATION

One of the major gaps in the literature is that social communication, autism intervention, and STEM robotics are seen as distinct fields. Social robots are generally studied in the context of greetings, emotion detection, turn-taking, mimicry, and communication procedures. Educational robots are generally studied in the context of programming ability, computational thinking, spatial sense, and involvement in STEM. There are some studies that have explored how robotics and coding can be used for social-emotional learning for children with autism; however, it shows that although there are some connections between them, their intersection is still relatively unexplored (Taylor & Glavey, 2024).

This distinction is critical because learning at school is not distinguished in the same manner. While performing the task related to STEM, the learner needs to understand instructions, seek help, describe the sequence of actions, provide an explanation regarding mistakes, take turns, and analyze the situation. In the case of learners with ASD, such communicative and social aspects are often as significant as STEM objectives themselves. Curriculum which distinguishes communication from STEM might fail to provide the opportunity to practice language within a meaningful joint activity.

The proposed model differs from many prior robot ASD interventions in three ways. First, it is dual domain: communication and STEM are taught within the same lesson. Second, it is multi tool: Buddy supports communication and reflection, Marty V2 supports embodied STEM activity, and Raspberry Pi adds sensing and physical computing. Third, it is classroom-embedded rather than only therapist-led. The teacher uses the robot actions, prompts, and learner explanations as parts of ordinary instruction, while future research can evaluate whether this integration produces measurable outcomes.

Language Development Within Robot Mediated STEM Activities

This chapter focuses on not just robots or STEM; it emphasizes robotics as an environment that enables language learning. Lessons involving STEM will inherently entail naming of objects, comparing quantity, describing an action, explaining the cause and effect of something, and reasoning out decisions. These aspects of language learning will come naturally for children who have autism and have similar communication requirements as long as the process involved is predictable, concrete, and visually reinforced.

Robot-mediated STEM lesson allows for language skills of different types to be developed simultaneously. The receptive language will be developed as the learner listens to the prompt from Buddy, understands a direction from it, or associates a verbal instruction with the behavior of the robot. The expressive language will be practiced as the learner names the number, tells which object is bigger, describes the movements of Marty, or explains how a sensor stopped the robot from moving further.

The framework also supports vocabulary development. For teaching number magnitude lessons, words such as greater, less, equal, more, fewer, farther, and shorter are used. Directional lessons use left, right, forward, backward, turn, stop, near, and far. Sequencing lessons use first, next, then, before, after, repeat, and last.

Sensor lessons use if, then, because, detect, trigger, input, and output. These words are used during an action that the learner can see, predict, and discuss.

Narrative and explanatory language are also built into the phases. At the beginning of a lesson, Buddy previews what will happen. During the task, the learner narrates the action or selects a sentence frame. During debugging, the learner compares the expected result with the actual result. During reflection, the learner explains what changed and why. This repeated movement from action to explanation is important because language becomes a tool for reasoning, not only a response to a teacher question.

The generalization should always be carefully planned. It is possible that a learner may apply a word accurately when communicating with a robot, but not when communicating with a teacher, peer, worksheet, or real-life object. The framework therefore includes teacher and peer participation. After Marty V2 walks five steps and three steps, the teacher can ask learners to compare five blocks and three blocks. After a sensor activity, learners can discuss other if then rules in the classroom, such as if the light turns red, then we stop. These bridges help move the language beyond the robot.

Because the chapter does not report a classroom study, these language benefits are proposed instructional possibilities rather than measured outcomes. Future research should test which language targets improve, how much prompting is needed, whether learners generalize words beyond the robot task, and whether peer interaction increases. The value of the framework depends on this careful measurement.

THEORETICAL FOUNDATIONS

This proposed approach is based on a few theories from the realm of education that describe why robots may be helpful when applied within a specific instructional context. These theories do not show how effective this approach is. They offer the reasoning behind the use of such components as communication cues, movement, practice, and reflection.

Firstly, there is Constructionism that stresses the necessity to create and test something meaningful for the learners to learn (Papert, 1980; Resnick et al., 2009). When applying this theory to robotic activities, a learner will not just get an explanation from the teacher but also make something happen, see the outcome, and modify the initial notion. Such devices as Marty V2 and Raspberry Pi are good for constructionist learning since coding, movement, and sensor inputs become a part of one artifact. It means that a learner can check whether a command sequence is correct, a sensor rule has been triggered, and robot actions correspond to the mathematical idea.

According to social learning theory, learners learn behaviors through imitation, observation, and rehearsal of models of behavior (Bandura, 1977). Robots are useful in this kind of imitation process according to Kanda et al. (2004). Buddy can be used as a model for greetings, words of emotions, turn-taking, help-seeking, and reflective language. The goal is for the robot to provide a consistent prompt that the teacher can extend into human interaction. For example, Buddy may model the phrase I need help, and the teacher can then ask the learner to use that phrase with a peer or adult during the debugging phase.

Vygotsky's Zone of Proximal Development supports the use of scaffolding (Vygotsky, 1978). The elements of scaffolding in the proposed curriculum include visual cards, sentence frames, repetition, choice reduction, and step-by-step debugging. For instance, if a learner cannot explain independently why Marty moved farther, they can use a sentence frame as follows: Marty moved farther because five is greater than three. As a learner gains more skills in explaining, a teacher can reduce or eliminate scaffoldings by taking away the sentence frame, reducing the verbal instruction of Buddy, or allowing a learner to explain the same to a peer.

The theory of embodied cognition provides yet another rationale for designing the curriculum. It suggests that cognition should be viewed as closely tied to action and interaction with the environment. In the proposed learning experience, learners use robot movement to represent number, order, direction, pattern, and cause-and-effect relationships. Instead of seeing a symbol on paper, the learner observes the movement through space. This might help learners who need concrete examples, as they get an example to see, point at, and explain. Embodiment helps a teacher to ask questions like "Why did Marty stop?", "Why did the robot move farther?", or "What command changes the pattern?"

Together, these theories justify the five-phase structure. Readiness and guided communication reflect social learning, UDL, and scaffolding. Embodied execution reflects constructionism and embodied cognition. Debugging reflects constructionist revision and computational thinking. Reflection supports language development, metacognition, and generalization. The theories therefore support the design choices in the curriculum while leaving empirical effectiveness as a question for future research.

INSTRUCTIONAL AFFORDANCES OF BUDDY, MARTY V2, AND RASPBERRY PI

The framework uses each technology for a distinct instructional purpose. Buddy is treated as a social communication support tool. Its most relevant classroom functions are greeting routines, emotion prompts, turn taking cues, sentence starters, and guided reflection. Marty V2 is treated as an embodied STEM tool. Its main value is that learners can connect code and mathematics to visible movement. Raspberry Pi is treated as a physical computing extension. It can connect simple sensors, buttons, or classroom objects to robot actions, helping learners observe cause and effect.

This division is important because it reduces overlap. Buddy is not used mainly to teach coding, and Marty V2 is not expected to provide rich social dialogue. Each tool supports the part of the curriculum that fits its instructional strength.

Table 1 summarizes these distinct roles by comparing Buddy and Marty V2 across primary function, interaction style, language use, STEM use, ASD support, and basic hardware information.

Table 1. Buddy and Marty V2 in the proposed curriculum

Area	Buddy	Marty V2	Curriculum role	Evidence base
Primary function	Social communication support	Embodied STEM and coding platform	Connect communication and STEM within one lesson	Belpaeme et al., 2018; Eguchi, 2014; Milliez, 2018; Ramamurthy & Li, 2018
Interaction style	Speech, expression, prompts, routines	Movement, coding, sensors, visible feedback	Provide verbal support and physical demonstration	Kory-Westlund & Breazeal, 2019; Trapero-González et al., 2024; Leite et al., 2013
Language use	Greetings, emotion words, turn taking, reflection	Action words, direction words, sequence language	Support expressive and receptive language during STEM tasks	Kewalramani et al., 2024; Pennisi et al., 2016
STEM use	Previews the task and asks guiding questions	Shows counting, magnitude, sequencing, conditionals, and debugging through movement	Make reasoning visible and discussable	Grover & Pea, 2013; Ouyang & Xu, 2024
ASD support	Predictable prompts and low pressure practice	Concrete movement feedback and repeated structure	Reduce ambiguity and support generalization	Diehl et al., 2012; Smakman et al., 2022
Hardware facts	Useful for social prompts and interaction routines	Useful for block coding, Python, and physical movement	Use vendor sources only for specifications	Ackerman, 2019; Blue Frog Robotics, 2023; Robotical Ltd., 2024

PROPOSED INTEGRATED CURRICULUM AND TECHNICAL ARCHITECTURE

This chapter proposes an integrated curriculum and technology architecture to support a robot-mediated learning environment, which combines language acquisition, socialization, SEL and STEM education. The curriculum uses the robots as instructional mediators that help learners think, communicate, and act within structured STEM tasks.

The curriculum is grounded in predictable routines and flexible expression. Learners may listen, watch, choose, point, speak, code, move objects, or explain. Communication is embedded in STEM activities so that language practice and problem solving occur together rather than as separate lessons.

The proposed system uses four coordinated components in a closed learning loop. A web interface collects learner choices or code. A Python backend validates responses and tracks progress. A Raspberry Pi controls Marty V2 and receives sensor input. Buddy provides prompts, cues, and reflection questions based on the learning state.

Figure 1 shows the proposed four-component technical architecture and learner feedback loop, moving from learner input through backend validation, Raspberry Pi and Marty V2 execution, Buddy-supported prompts, and learner observation and revision.

Figure 1. Proposed four-component technical architecture and learner feedback loop

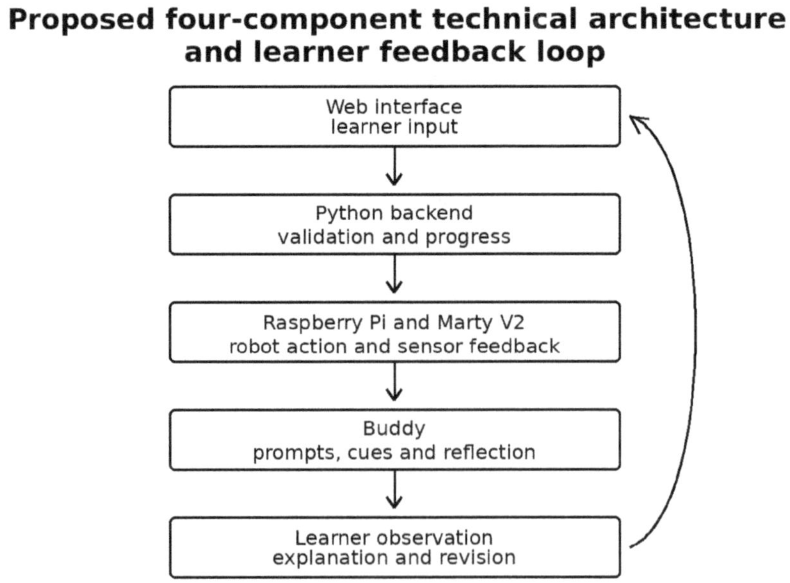

FIVE-PHASE CURRICULUM STRUCTURE

The curriculum is designed around five repeated phases. The same structure can be used across math, coding, language, and sensor-based tasks. Repetition supports predictability, while the content can increase in difficulty over time.

Figure 2 shows the five-phase flow from readiness and guided communication to embodied execution, debugging, and reflection.

Figure 2. Proposed five-phase curriculum flow

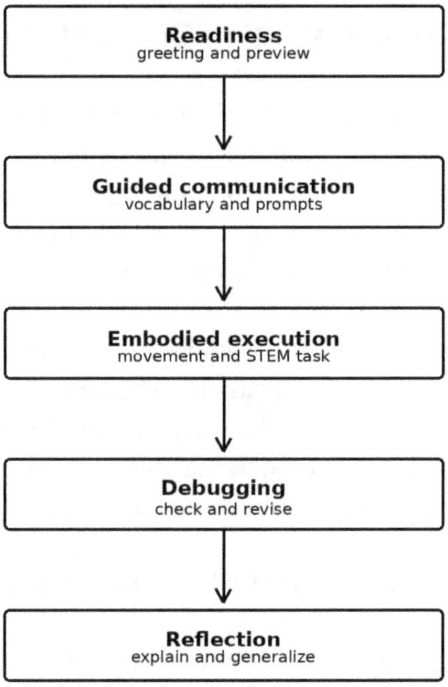

Phase 1: Communication and Readiness Orientation

Each session starts with a well-known greeting procedure and preparation for the task. Buddy can suggest the learners to describe their feelings, select an appropriate picture card or listen to the task introduction. This step serves the purpose of helping learners to focus on the task, prepare for the task and manage their emotions. For most of the learners with ASD, the preparatory procedure is not just a fancy introduction but a necessary scaffolding, which informs the learner about the activity ahead, its duration and what sort of response is required from them.

It is the teacher's responsibility to make the procedure less ambiguous and uncertain. Teacher can demonstrate the schedule, preview the robot's actions, change volume or speed if it is needed, or give the learner the opportunity to respond non-verbally. Teacher is responsible for deciding whether the prompt by Buddy is sufficient or whether the prompt by the teacher should precede it. The success of this phase can be evaluated by observing the learners' readiness behaviors such as orienting towards the task and responding mode selection.

Phase 2: Guided Communication Embedded in Instruction

Then comes language practice related to the STEM activity coming up. This can include verbs, directionals, comparisons, requests for assistance, and sentence starters. Language is integrated into the learning task such that the expressiveness will aid comprehension and performance of the task. Instead of practicing isolated words, the teacher is giving the learners a chance to use those words before, during, and after the robot performs an action.

A limited amount of target words is chosen by the teacher for each lesson. In case of a numbers lesson, the target words can be "greater", "less", "equal", "more", and "fewer". If it is a pathway lesson, the words selected could be "forward", "left", "right", "turn", and "stop". Buddy models the sentence starter, but the teacher allows different modes of response, which can be verbal, pointing, selection, or assistive.

Phase 3: Embodied STEM and Mathematics Execution

Learners then complete a STEM or mathematics task that produces a visible robot action. Marty V2 may walk, turn, stop, or repeat a motion to represent counting, magnitude, sequence, direction, or conditionals. Physical movement gives learners an observable result to discuss. For example, a learner who chooses the number six can watch Marty move farther than when the number three is chosen. The movement becomes a concrete representation of quantity.

The teacher's role is to connect the robot action to the concept, not simply to run the robot. Before execution, the teacher asks for a prediction. During execution, the teacher encourages observation. After execution, the teacher asks learners to explain what the movement showed. At this stage, the phase helps those learners who require visual and kinesthetic information as the same concept will be presented in text form, oral language, selecting and moving.

Phase 4: Error Detection and Guided Debugging

Errors are treated as learning events. If the robot action does not match the expected outcome, Buddy prompts learners to compare, explain, and revise. This phase supports debugging, persistence, and reasoning. It also protects learners from seeing mistakes as failure. The visible robot behavior makes the error easier to discuss because the class can compare what was expected with what happened.

The teacher can guide debugging with three questions: What did you expect? What did Marty do? What should we change? Buddy can repeat a simplified version of these questions, but the teacher decides how much support is needed. Prompt levels can be recorded here because they show progress toward independence. The learner will initially require modeling, followed by a verbal prompt, followed by a visual prompt, and finally, be able to debug independently.

Phase 5: Reflection and Conceptual Consolidation

Each lesson ends with a short reflection. Learners may explain what happened, identify the correct rule, describe the robot movement, or choose a visual response. Reflection helps connect language, movement, and concept understanding. It also gives teachers a chance to check whether the learner understands the idea or only completed the robot action.

Reflection should include generalization. After the robot task, the teacher can ask where the same idea appears without the robot. A number magnitude lesson can move to comparing objects on a table. A direction lesson can move to walking a path in the classroom. A sensor lesson can move to everyday if then examples. Buddy's final prompt should therefore not only ask what happened but also ask where the learner could use the idea again.

Table 2 summarizes sample curriculum modules that apply the same five-phase logic to greeting readiness, counting, number magnitude, directional language, sensor-based cause and effect, group debugging, and reflection.

Table 2. Sample curriculum modules

Module	Language goal	STEM/CT goal	Robot or tool	ASD support	Assessment
Greeting and readiness	Greetings, emotion words, turn taking	Sequence a routine	Buddy	Predictable opening and visual cues	Communication checklist
Robot steps and counting	Action words and first, next, then	Counting and sequencing	Marty V2	Repeated structure and visible movement	Correct sequence completion
Number magnitude	Greater, less, equal, more, fewer	Compare quantities and map number to movement	Buddy and Marty V2	Concrete step counts and sentence starters	Correct comparison and explanation
Direction language	Left, right, forward, stop	Spatial reasoning and path planning	Marty V2	Visual grid and gesture prompts	Path accuracy
Sensor cause and effect	If, then, because, stop, start	Conditionals and sensor input	Raspberry Pi and Marty V2 with Buddy prompts	Simplified choices and immediate feedback	Debugging notes and prompt level
Group debugging	Ask for help and explain an error	Debugging and collaboration	Buddy and Marty V2	Peer roles and sentence starters	Collaboration rubric
Reflection circle	Describe what happened and what changed	Metacognition and generalization	Buddy	Low pressure guided response	Reflection response

WORKED LESSON EXAMPLE: NUMBER MAGNITUDE

The following lesson plan demonstrates the use of five-phase framework for a single target in the field of mathematics. In this case, the target will be number magnitude, and the language targets will include greater, less, equal, more, fewer, first, next and because. The lesson can be taught to a small group where each learner has their own role, such as selecting a number, observing Marty V2, checking the vocabulary card, or explaining the results.

Phase 1, Readiness: Buddy greets the learners and introduces the lesson: Today, we will compare numbers and move Marty. Buddy displays two number cards (e.g., 5 and 3) and prompts the learners to observe both the number cards. The teacher puts these cards on a visual board and tells the learners that the bigger number would move Marty far away. The learners may respond by any means such as speaking, pointing, communication device or selection of two cards.

Phase 2, guided communication: Buddy encourages learners to speak, indicate, or choose a response by asking: Which number is bigger? Learners could employ a sentence starter like "5 is bigger than 3" or "I chose 5 as it is bigger." The teacher highlights the comparative words used and helps construct a sentence. For some learners, the language load can be lowered to choose between greater or less before moving on to a complete sentence.

Phase 3, embodied execution: After choosing the bigger number, the backend triggers a command to the Marty V2 robot to move 5 steps for the big number and 3 steps for the small number. The class watches the difference in distance. The teacher asks learners to compare the two movements: Which movement was longer? Which number made Marty move farther? The physical distance gives learners a concrete representation of magnitude.

Phase 4, debugging: If the learner selects the smaller number, Marty performs the movement and Buddy asks: Did Marty walk more steps or fewer steps? Which number should make Marty move farther? The learner revises the response and runs the task again. The teacher records the prompt level needed for revision. This makes debugging part of the assessment rather than an interruption.

Phase 5, reflection: Buddy asks learners to explain what happened. This can be done verbally by learners, or else using visuals or completing the sentence: 5 is greater than 3 because Marty took more steps. The teacher will then generalize this idea by showing two groups of classroom objects, for instance 5 blocks compared to 3 blocks, and ask which group is greater. The advantage here is that the teacher will connect the idea learned from robot to another setting without the robot.

Some measures could include correctness of the comparison, use of target vocabulary, turn taking, awareness of the robot movement, explaining reasoning, and the number of prompts needed. The teacher will check if the learner provided an answer independently, using a visual prompt, a verbal prompt, or modeling. It is a proposed design example that future research can evaluate.

RASPBERRY PI SENSING ACTIVITY

An example of a simple activity that could use the model for physical computing would be an activity using a Raspberry Pi. This could include, for example, connecting either a distance sensor or button to the Raspberry Pi. When the object is detected, the backend will give instructions to make Marty V2 stop, move forward, or turn. In this case, Buddy can pose cause-and-effect questions such as "What came first?" and "Why did Marty stop?"

Through this activity, learners get a concrete link between sensors' input, condition, robot action, and language. A teacher could start by giving two choices to the learners such as if the object is near, then Marty stops, and if the object is far, then Marty moves. Later on, learners could be asked to change the rule through the block code or Python. Evaluation could involve the learner's ability to recognize the input from the sensor, define the rule, predict the robot's reaction, and change the rule accordingly.

ILLUSTRATIVE CLASSROOM SCENARIOS

The following scenarios are illustrative examples, not evidence from classroom testing. They show how the proposed framework could be used in a classroom after appropriate teacher planning, accessibility review, and school approval.

Scenario 1: Communication Warm Up with Buddy

The class teacher starts her robotics class in a very familiar pattern. Buddy asks each learner to pick an emotion card or an answer from a picture card. The learner can answer the question through verbal response, pointing, using any assistive aid, or even by picking a sentence frame. The teacher then links the response with the lesson, and says, "Today, we shall be comparing numbers and see how Marty moves." Such a situation promotes readiness, shared attention, and helps the learners transition into the academic activity without expecting all of them to follow the same response pattern.

Scenario 2: Peer Collaboration with Marty V2

Learners work in pairs to decide which command sequence should make Marty V2 walk to a target. One learner chooses the number or direction card, while the other checks whether the robot movement matches the plan. Buddy can prompt the pair with simple questions such as What should happen next? and Did Marty move the way you expected? The purpose is to combine turn taking, planning, and visible feedback from the robot movement.

Scenario 3: Sensor Based Explanation with Raspberry Pi

A simple button or distance sensor is connected to the Raspberry Pi. When the sensor is triggered, Marty V2 stops or takes a step. Buddy asks learners to explain the rule using a sentence frame such as If the sensor sees the object, then Marty stops. This scenario links physical computing with cause-and-effect language, conditional reasoning, and guided explanation.

ASSESSMENT AND EVALUATION PLAN

Because this chapter proposes a curriculum rather than reporting a trial, assessment should be described as a future evaluation plan. The framework should not be judged only by whether the robot runs correctly. It should be judged by whether learners demonstrate communication growth, STEM reasoning, independence, and generalization. This requires observation tools that are simple enough for classroom use but detailed enough for research.

Communication indicators can include the learner's use of target vocabulary, response mode, sentence length, request for help, turn taking, and explanation of robot behavior. For example, in the number magnitude lesson, the teacher can record whether the learner uses greater, less, more, or fewer, and whether the learner can explain the comparison after seeing Marty move. The response should not have to be spoken to count as communication. Pointing, selecting a picture, arranging cards, or using an assistive communication device can also show understanding.

STEM and computational thinking indicators can include correct selection, sequence accuracy, ability to predict the robot action, identification of an error, revision of a command, and explanation of the fix. In a sensor lesson, the teacher can record whether the learner identifies the sensor input, predicts the robot action, and explains the if then rule. In a path lesson, the teacher can record whether the learner orders direction commands correctly and revises the route after feedback.

Prompt level is especially important for learners with ASD because it gives more information than a simple correct or incorrect score. A learner may complete a task with full modeling at first, then with a verbal prompt, then with a visual cue, and later independently. Recording this progression allows the teacher to see increasing independence. It also prevents the assessment from overstating learning when the adult or robot provided most of the answer.

Engagement should be measured carefully. Behaviors such as looking at the robot, smiling, or asking for another try are indicators of interest but do not indicate learning. A more effective approach to evaluating engagement includes the amount of time spent on the task, successful completion of the task, prompt responses, and being willing to try again after an error. This framework views engagement as a prerequisite for learning, rather than learning itself.

Generalization should be part of any future evaluation. Following the robot exercise, the learners should be asked to apply their knowledge within another context – either to a peer, the classroom materials, a worksheet, or even a different task that doesn't involve the robot. For instance, having learned that 5 is greater than 3 thanks to Marty walking, the learner should be prompted to compare five blocks to three blocks.

A feasible rubric may include levels of independent, visual cue, verbal prompt, and model required for each objective. Potential categories may include communication, STEM reasoning, debugging, collaboration, and generalization. Such a rubric will enable teachers to assess progress and also provide researchers a standard means of assessment of feasibility and results in future classrooms.

IMPLEMENTATION GUIDELINES AND PRACTITIONER NOTES

The teacher needs to start with short and predictable activities before moving to complex or lengthy ones. Each activity should have an organized beginning, a few options, visuals, and a method of response from the learner which is not pressurized in any way. Buddy should be utilized for communication cues, emotional preparation, and reflection. Marty V2 should be used for visible movement, sequencing, debugging, and STEM reasoning. Raspberry Pi should be used only when the sensor activity directly supports the lesson goal.

Teacher training is the first step in implementing the process. The teacher does not have to be a robotic engineer; however, they must feel comfortable with starting and stopping the robot, loading up the routine that has been prepared in advance, operating the visual interface, and fixing possible connection issues. It is crucial to have a short training session prior to the class. The teacher needs to check the whole process chain, from learner's reaction to Buddy's call.

The classroom setup should reduce sensory and management problems. The robot should have a clear movement space, learners should know where to sit or stand, and materials should be visible. If a learner is sensitive to sound, Buddy's volume should be lowered or replaced by a visual prompt. If a learner is sensitive to movement, Marty V2 can be demonstrated at a slower pace or from a greater distance. The teacher should also have a low-tech backup, such as printed direction cards or a hand moved figure, in case the technology fails.

Pacing matters. Early lessons should be short, with one communication target and one STEM target. For example, a first lesson might only compare two numbers and use the words greater and less. Later lessons can add more numbers, peer roles, or a debugging step. This prevents the robot, vocabulary, coding, and social demands from all increasing at once.

Fidelity guidance can help future researchers and teachers use the framework consistently. A lesson should include all five phases, at least one explicit communication target, at least one STEM or CT target, one observable robot action, one opportunity for debugging or revision, and one reflection prompt. If a teacher skips the communication phase or the reflection phase, the activity becomes a robotics demonstration rather than the integrated framework proposed here.

Practitioner Notes

- Use the same opening routine in each class as learners will know what to expect.
- Make movements brief and meaningful, not just done to entertain.
- Create visual cue cards for terms such as "greater", "less", "equal", "first", "next", "stop", and "turn".
- Document how many prompts were necessary rather than just whether the final answer is correct.
- Give learners a chance to respond to questions without speaking out loud.
- Keep the teacher as the primary decision-maker and leave the teaching to the teachers while the robots provide assistance.
- Assign peer roles like selector, observer, checker, and explainer to ensure social interaction.
- Introduce Raspberry Pi sensing only after learners understand the basic robot movement routines.

ETHICAL AND PRACTICAL CONSIDERATIONS

Since this chapter offers an architecture for robots that does not present any learner-performance results, there are no claims concerning learner results. The future application of robots to classrooms must consider issues related to privacy, consent, teacher supervision, access, and minimalism in collecting information. Learners' replies, sensor readings, sounds, pictures, or learning activities must be gathered only in cases of having a certain pedagogical goal and proper approval. Human-centered design of robot-assisted play activities suggests the importance of user-centered scenario design (Robins et al., 2010).

Consent and assent are also important. Caregivers must know the intent behind the activity, the information being collected, and the ways the robot will be utilized. It is also necessary for learners to have choices appropriate to their developmental stage. A learner who does not want to interact with Buddy or Marty V2 on a given day should have another way to participate, such as observing, using picture cards, or completing the task with teacher support. Participation should not depend on liking the robot.

Overdependence is another risk. While the robot may offer consistency of training, it should never be a replacement of human interaction. The teacher needs to ensure that there is no case where the learner will interact exclusively with the robot while ignoring other children or adults. This has been achieved by ensuring there are prompts from the teachers, peers taking different roles, and going beyond the robot activity. Buddy and Marty V2 are tools for creating structured learning moments, not substitutes for human social interaction.

Finally, AI supported prompts should remain transparent and teacher controlled. If a system adapts difficulty or generates language, the teacher should know why the prompt changed and should be able to override it. Hidden or unpredictable adaptation can create confusion for learners and teachers. Ethical design in this framework means keeping the robot's role understandable, limited, and accountable.

DISCUSSION QUESTIONS

1. How can a teacher keep robot use focused on language and STEM learning rather than novelty?
2. What response options should be available for learners with limited expressive language?
3. Which parts of the five-phase framework would need the most adaptation for different age groups?
4. What information should teachers collect to assess learning while protecting learner privacy?
5. How can Buddy, Marty V2, and Raspberry Pi be used in a way that supports peer interaction rather than isolating learners with the technology?

LIMITATIONS OF THE PROPOSED FRAMEWORK

The framework has several limitations that should be stated clearly. First, it has not yet been evaluated as a classroom intervention. The chapter proposes a design based on existing literature, but it does not provide evidence that the combined Buddy, Marty V2, and Raspberry Pi sequence improves language, STEM learning, or generalization. Those claims require future empirical study.

Second, the evidence for Buddy in classroom ASD STEM contexts is limited. Buddy has features that make it suitable for communication prompts, and Buddy related publications support its use as a companion or therapy-oriented platform. However, those sources do not establish that Buddy improves outcomes in the integrated curriculum proposed here. The framework therefore relies on both Buddy specific sources and the broader social robotics literature.

Third, individual differences among learners with ASD are substantial. Some learners enjoy robot interaction and respond well to predictable prompts. Others may be distracted by robot noise, movement, or facial expressions. Therefore, the framework should be adapted to the sensory and communicative needs of each learner as well as the teaching objectives of the classroom.

Fourth, teacher preparation and classroom feasibility may be challenging. The framework asks teachers to manage technology, communication supports, peer roles, and assessment at the same time. Without planning, a robotics activity can become difficult to run. Future studies should measure teacher workload and identify the minimum training and setup needed for realistic classroom use.

Finally, generalization remains a major open question. A learner may learn to respond correctly during a robot task but not use the same language or reasoning elsewhere. Future evaluation should therefore include transfer tasks with people, objects, paper-based materials, and ordinary classroom activities. This limitation is also a design priority: every lesson should include a bridge from robot action to a broader classroom context.

FUTURE WORK

Further research is necessary to test the effectiveness of this theoretical framework within a classroom environment that contains learners with ASD and other communication issues. It can consider how feasible the framework is, the impact on teacher workload, learner engagement levels, communication success rates, STEM learning measures, debugging skills, and generalization outside of robots. Research studies will need to use proper measurement instruments, ethical approval if required, and proper reporting of learner details. Since the framework consists of several elements, feasibility studies might come first.

The curriculum can be expanded to cover arithmetic fluency, pattern reasoning, spatial reasoning, and sensor-based problem solving. Number magnitude lessons can be extended to addition, subtraction, grouped multiplication, and simple division by mapping operations to repeated or combined robot movement. Pattern lessons can move from repeated movement patterns to rule inference, missing element problems, and loops in code. Spatial lessons can add coordinate grids, angle-based turns, path prediction, and transformations such as rotation and reflection. Each expansion should keep the same design rule: one communication target, one STEM target, one observable robot action, one debugging opportunity, and one reflection prompt.

A second direction is the development of edge-based Raspberry Pi analytics. Future versions could compute simple performance indicators from response timing, retry count, prompt level, and execution stability. These indicators could help adjust task difficulty without sending learner data to a remote service. For example, if a learner completes three number comparisons independently, the system could increase the number range. If a learner needs repeated prompts, the system could return to a smaller range or show a visual cue. Such adaptation should remain visible to the teacher.

Future research must involve teachers, parents, and learners in the design and evaluation process as well. Often, learners with disabilities are impacted by the technology without any substantial participation in decision-making processes regarding the use of technology. A participatory approach can help to discover real needs which may remain unknown for the researcher, including such aspects as the noise level, the duration of the routine, acceptable response possibilities, and data families can agree to share.

CONCLUSION

This chapter reviewed literature on social robotics, educational robotics, adaptive tools in special education, ASD support, language development, and STEM learning. Based on that literature, it proposed a curriculum framework that joins Buddy, Marty V2, and Raspberry Pi in a structured learning loop. Buddy is used to support communication routines and reflection. Marty V2 is used to make mathematics, coding, movement, and debugging visible. Raspberry Pi adds a physical computing layer through simple sensor-based cause and effect activities.

This framework is meant to facilitate routine predictability, multimodal communication, embodied STEM education, debugging, and reflection. According to the literature that has been examined, all these components can be useful in an inclusive setting. However, the framework has not yet been applied as such in any research intervention. This distinction is important. The chapter offers a design and a research agenda.

The main contribution is the integration of domains that are often separated. Social robots have been considered in the context of social communication, emotions, and therapy. Educational robots have been considered in the context of coding, STEM skills, and computational thinking. Children with ASD may need support across these domains at the same time. A lesson on number magnitude, for example, can also support comparison vocabulary, turn taking, debugging, and explanation. A sensor lesson can also support if then language, prediction, and cause and effect reasoning.

Robots should not be allowed to replace teachers or peers. In this chapter, the usefulness of robots lies in their structured nature, which can assist teachers in creating replicable, observable, and debatable moments of learning. In cases where they are well-utilized, educational robots could provide an opportunity for making connections between language and science. However, when poorly utilized, they may be distracting. Therefore, the teacher's role becomes crucial in this case.

Future research should empirically evaluate the framework with clear measures, teacher guidance, and attention to privacy, access, and generalization. Such research should test not only whether learners complete robot tasks, but whether they use target language, show improved reasoning, need fewer prompts, collaborate with peers, and transfer skills beyond the robot. Only then can the proposed framework move from a review-based design to an evidence-supported classroom practice.

ACKNOWLEDGMENT

This work was supported by the National Science Foundation (NSF) through the Auburn University Research Experiences for Teachers program under Award No. 2206977. The corresponding author states that there is no conflict of interest.

REFERENCES

Ackerman, E. (2019, October 28). Blue Frog Robotics answers some of our questions about its delayed social robot Buddy. IEEE Spectrum. https://spectrum.ieee.org/interview-blue-frog-robotics-ceo

Alimisis, D. (2013). Educational robotics: Open questions and new challenges. *Themes in Science and Technology Education*, *6*(1), 63–71. http://ouranos.edu.uoi.gr/theste/index.php/theste/article/view/119

Bandura, A. (1977). *Social learning theory*. Prentice-Hall.

Belpaeme, T., Kennedy, J., Ramachandran, A., Scassellati, B., & Tanaka, F. (2018). Social robots for education: A review. *Science Robotics*, *3*(21), eaat5954. Advance online publication. DOI: 10.1126/scirobotics.aat5954

Benitti, F. B. V. (2012). Exploring the educational potential of robotics in schools: A systematic review. *Computers & Education*, *58*(3), 978–988. DOI: 10.1016/j.compedu.2011.10.006

Błażejowska, G., Gruba, Ł., Indurkhya, B., & Gunia, A. (2023). A study on the role of affective feedback in robot assisted learning. *Frontiers in Robotics and AI*, *10*, 1132956. DOI: 10.3389/frobt.2023.1132956

Blue Frog Robotics. (2023). Buddy robot. https://www.bluefrogrobotics.com/robot

Breazeal, C. (2003). Toward sociable robots. *Robotics and Autonomous Systems*, *42*(3-4), 167–175. DOI: 10.1016/S0921-8890(02)00373-1

Cabibihan, J. J., Javed, H., Ang, M.Jr, & Aljunied, S. M. (2013). Why robots? A survey on the roles and benefits of social robots in the therapy of children with autism. *International Journal of Social Robotics*, *5*(4), 593–618. DOI: 10.1007/s12369-013-0202-2

Darmawansah, D., Hwang, G. J., Chen, M. R. A., & Liang, J. C. (2023). Trends and research foci of robotics-based STEM education: A systematic review from diverse angles based on the technology-based learning model. *International Journal of STEM Education, 10*(1), 12. Advance online publication. DOI: 10.1186/s40594-023-00400-3

Diehl, J. J., Schmitt, L. M., Villano, M., & Crowell, C. R. (2012). The clinical use of robots for individuals with autism spectrum disorders: A critical review. *Research in Autism Spectrum Disorders, 6*(1), 249–262. DOI: 10.1016/j.rasd.2011.05.006

Eguchi, A. (2014). Robotics as a learning tool for educational transformation. In Proceedings of the 4th International Workshop Teaching Robotics, Teaching with Robotics and 5th International Conference Robotics in Education (pp. 27-34). https://www.terecop.eu/TRTWR-RIE2014/files/00_WFr1/00_WFr1_04.pdf

Grover, S., & Pea, R. (2013). Computational thinking in K-12: A review of the state of the field. *Educational Researcher, 42*(1), 38–43. DOI: 10.3102/0013189X12463051

Hopcan, S., Polat, E., Ozturk, M. E., & Ozturk, L. (2023). Artificial intelligence in special education: A systematic review. *Interactive Learning Environments, 31*(10), 7335–7353. DOI: 10.1080/10494820.2022.2067186

Kanda, T., Hirano, T., Eaton, D., & Ishiguro, H. (2004). Interactive robots as social partners and peer tutors for children: A field trial. *Human-Computer Interaction, 19*(1-2), 61–84. DOI: 10.1207/s15327051hci1901&2_4

Kewalramani, S., Allen, K. A., Leif, E., & Ng, A. (2024). A scoping review of the use of robotics technologies for supporting social-emotional learning in children with autism. *Journal of Autism and Developmental Disorders, 54*(12), 4481–4495. DOI: 10.1007/s10803-023-06193-2

Kory-Westlund, J. M., & Breazeal, C. (2019). A long term study of young children's rapport, social emulation, and language learning with a peer like robot playmate in preschool. *Frontiers in Robotics and AI, 6*, 81. DOI: 10.3389/frobt.2019.00081

Leite, I., Martinho, C., & Paiva, A. (2013). Social robots for long term interaction: A survey. *International Journal of Social Robotics, 5*(2), 291–308. DOI: 10.1007/s12369-013-0178-y

Luckin, R., Holmes, W., Griffiths, M., & Forcier, L. B. (2016). Intelligence unleashed: An argument for AI in education. Pearson Education. https://discovery.ucl.ac.uk/id/eprint/1475756/

Matarić, M. J. (2004). Robotics education for all ages. In Proceedings of the AAAI Spring Symposium on Accessible, Hands on AI and Robotics Education. https://cdn.aaai.org/Symposia/Spring/2004/SS-04-01/SS04-01-004.pdf

Meyer, A., Rose, D. H., & Gordon, D. (2014). *Universal design for learning: Theory and practice*. CAST Professional Publishing.

Milliez, G. (2018). Buddy: A companion robot for the whole family. In Companion of the 2018 ACM/IEEE International Conference on Human Robot Interaction (HRI 2018 Companion). https://doi.org/DOI: 10.1145/3173386.3177839

Mubin, O., Stevens, C. J., Shahid, S., Al Mahmud, A., & Dong, J. J. (2013). A review of the applicability of robots in education. *Journal of Technology in Education and Learning*, *1*(1), 1–7. DOI: 10.2316/Journal.209.2013.1.209-0015

Ouyang, F., & Xu, W. (2024). The effects of educational robotics in STEM education: A multilevel meta-analysis. *International Journal of STEM Education*, *11*(1), 7. Advance online publication. DOI: 10.1186/s40594-024-00469-4

Papert, S. (1980). Mindstorms: Children, computers, and powerful ideas. Basic Books. https://archive.org/details/mindstorms00seym

Pennisi, P., Tonacci, A., Tartarisco, G., Billeci, L., Ruta, L., Gangemi, S., & Pioggia, G. (2016). Autism and social robotics: A systematic review. *Autism Research : Official Journal of the International Society for Autism Research*, *9*(2), 165–183. DOI: 10.1002/aur.1527

Ponticorvo, M., & Dell'Aquila, E. (2023). Robots at schools: Telerobotics, coding, and teaching embodied artificial intelligence. In *Proceedings of the 2023 Conference on Robots and Education*. https://doi.org/DOI: 10.1145/3664934.3664940

Ramamurthy, P., & Li, T. (2018). Buddy: A speech therapy robot companion for children with cleft lip and palate disorder. In *Companion of the 2018 ACM/IEEE International Conference on Human Robot Interaction* (pp. 359-360). https://doi.org/DOI: 10.1145/3173386.3177830

Resnick, M., Maloney, J., Monroy-Hernández, A., Rusk, N., Eastmond, E., Brennan, K., & Kafai, Y. (2009). Scratch: Programming for all. *Communications of the ACM*, *52*(11), 60–67. DOI: 10.1145/1592761.1592779

Rice, M. F., & Dunn, S. (2023). The use of artificial intelligence with students with identified disabilities: A systematic review with critique. *Computers in the Schools*, *40*(4), 370–390. DOI: 10.1080/07380569.2023.2244935

Robins, B., Ferrari, E., Dautenhahn, K., Kronreif, G., Prazak-Aram, B., Gelderblom, G., Caprino, F., Laudanna, E., & Marti, P. (2010). Human centred design methods: Developing scenarios for robot assisted play informed by user panels and field trials. *International Journal of Human-Computer Studies*, *68*(12), 873–898. DOI: 10.1016/j.ijhcs.2010.08.001

Robotical Ltd. (2024). Marty the robot: A tool for teaching programming and robotics. https://robotical.io

Scassellati, B., Admoni, H., & Matarić, M. J. (2012). Robots for use in autism research. *Annual Review of Biomedical Engineering*, *14*(1), 275–294. DOI: 10.1146/annurev-bioeng-071811-150036

Smakman, M. H. J., Konijn, E. A., & Vogt, P. A. (2022). Do robotic tutors compromise the social-emotional development of children? A qualitative study into teacher perceptions. *Frontiers in Robotics and AI*, *9*, 734955. DOI: 10.3389/frobt.2022.734955

Taylor, M. S., & Glavey, E. M. (2024). Harnessing robotics and coding to foster social-emotional learning in students with autism. *Journal of Special Education Technology*, *39*(2), 306–313. DOI: 10.1177/01626434231199992

Trapero-González, I., Hinojo-Lucena, F. J., Romero-Rodríguez, J. M., & Martínez-Menéndez, A. (2024). Didactic impact of educational robotics on the development of STEM competence in primary education: A systematic review and meta-analysis. *Frontiers in Education*, *9*, 1480908. DOI: 10.3389/feduc.2024.1480908

Vygotsky, L. S. (1978). *Mind in society: The development of higher psychological processes*. Harvard University Press.

Wang, K., Sang, G. Y., Huang, L. Z., Li, S. H., & Guo, J. W. (2023). The effectiveness of educational robots in improving learning outcomes: A meta-analysis. *Sustainability (Basel)*, *15*(5), 4637. DOI: 10.3390/su15054637

Weintrop, D., & Wilensky, U. (2018). Comparing block based and text based programming in high school computer science classrooms. *ACM Transactions on Computing Education*, *18*(1), 3. Advance online publication. DOI: 10.1145/3089799

Wing, J. M. (2006). Computational thinking. *Communications of the ACM*, *49*(3), 33–35. DOI: 10.1145/1118178.1118215

KEY TERMS AND DEFINITIONS

Artificial Intelligence (AI): Computer methods that can help a system recognize patterns, provide feedback, support dialogue, adapt prompts, or make simple instructional decisions.

Assistive Robots: Robots used to support communication, behavior, learning, or access for people with disabilities or learning needs.

Autism Spectrum Disorder (ASD): A neurodevelopmental condition involving differences in social communication, social interaction, behavior, sensory processing, and attention.

Block Based Programming: Programming with visual blocks rather than typed syntax.

Computational Thinking (CT): A problem solving approach that includes decomposition, pattern recognition, abstraction, algorithm design, and debugging.

Educational Robotics: The use of programmable robots to support learning, especially in STEM, problem solving, and computational thinking.

Human Robot Interaction (HRI): The study and design of interactions between people and robots.

Inclusive Education: An approach that supports learners with different learning needs in shared learning environments through access, support, and flexibility.

Neurodivergent Learners: Learners whose learning, attention, communication, or development patterns differ from typical expectations, including some children with ASD.

Social Robotics: The field of robotics focused on robots that interact with people through communication, social cues, and responsive behavior.

Social-emotional Learning (SEL): The learning process through which learners develop skills related to emotion, social interaction, cooperation, and responsible decision making.

STEM Education: An instructional approach that integrates science, technology, engineering, and mathematics.

Text Based Programming: Programming with written code in a language such as Python.

Chapter 2
AI-Assisted Interventions for Mathematical Learning in Children With Dyslexia

Jincy George
http://orcid.org/0009-0008-4723-4695
Christ University, India

Prakash Padakannaya
Christ University, India

ABSTRACT

Dyslexia is commonly viewed as a reading and phonological disorder, but it also affects numerical reasoning and mathematics learning. Children with dyslexia often face persistent difficulties in calculation, symbol recognition, sequencing, and problem-solving. In traditional classrooms in Kerala, mathematics instruction is largely language-based, which disadvantages these learners. This chapter reports findings from a study of 25 dyslexic and 25 typically developing children, highlighting poor mathematical performance and emphasizing the need for AI-supported, innovative educational interventions to promote inclusive learning.

INTRODUCTION

Dyslexia is commonly recognised as a specific learning disability that primarily affects reading accuracy, fluency, and phonological processing (Shaywitz, 1998; Snowling, 2000). Dyslexia has historically been conceptualised as a condition

DOI: 10.4018/979-8-3373-7724-7.ch002

characterised by linguistic difficulties, and it has been categorised as a literacy and language-based impairment. However, advancements in the areas of cognitive neuroscience, educational psychology, and developmental psychology have led to the expansion of this knowledge. Over the last twenty years, researchers have come to the notion that dyslexia is not only confined to linguistic difficulties, but also has cognitive implications expanding into areas such as executive functions, working memory, Processing speed, and visual-spatial processing (Menghini et al., 2010; Jeffries & Everatt, 2004). These cognitive systems support reading and also mathematical skills, including arithmetic fluency, symbol recognition, sequencing, Numerical reasoning, and problem-solving. As a result, Children with dyslexia demonstrate difficulties in mathematical skills, which historically receive less attention than reading.

Math instruction in the particular educational setting of India and Kerala in particular remains highly language-based, text-oriented, and concentrates on the traditional pedagogical strategies. The classical use of textbook activities, oral teaching, memorizing information by heart, and solving linguistic problems is common in classroom activities. These teaching scenarios complicate the learning of mathematics among children with dyslexia, as they already have problems with decoding, phonological awareness, and language-intensive task-based requirements. When non-reading problems of children are concerned, such as math difficulty, where teachers often lack the required training on how to identify or help children with dyslexia (Karande & Kulkarni, 2005). This gap in academic achievement could increase due to the lack of alignment between the needs of the learners and the organisational practice, which might affect the academic performance and emotional well-being negatively. The current chapter is founded on the small-scale study conducted in a small number of schools in Kerala, on a sample of 50 children who are diagnosed with dyslexia. The research reveals that students have always had low achievements in a basic mathematics course, such as arithmetic calculations. These findings correlate with previous studies in the international community of researchers that dyslexia is often associated with symptoms of dyscalculia, such as comorbid arithmetic problems (Landerl & Moll, 2010). These findings reveal that there is the need to have innovative, readily accessible, and technology-supported interventions, which can transcend the linguistic and cognitive barriers that these students face in their lives.

Artificial intelligence (AI)-based instructional technologies have the potential in this respect. Digital learning platforms, Intelligent tutoring systems, and adaptive learning systems powered by AI have the potential to provide personalised learning experiences depending on each child and his or her unique cognitive profiles, Pace, and strengths. These systems allow real-time adjustments of the content difficulty, presentation modes, Feedback mechanisms, and sensory modalities (Koedinger et al., 2013). In children with dyslexia who have difficulties with math, AI tools can be used to lessen the use of language processing, provide multisensory concept representation, and create consistent aid with working memory, sequencing, and symbol interpretation. At the same time, neuroscience studies have shown that intentional training via the digital platform can enhance academic success, cognitive and promote neural plasticity (Holmes & Gathercole, 2013).

The aim of the chapter is to give a detailed insight into understanding the mathematical problems children with dyslexia have by synthesising multidisciplinary knowledge in Neuroscience, Cognitive Psychology, Special Education, and AI-driven technological innovation, and come up with a comprehensive view of mathematical problems in children with dyslexia. The research on neurological foundations of dyslexia, mathematical learning difficulties, and the benefits of AI-based learning can serve as a guide to the development of the pedagogical interventions that can be applied in the educational context of Kerala (and beyond).

Cognitive Foundations of Mathematical Difficulties in Dyslexia

The integration of several cognitive processes is necessary for mathematical competence, including the capacity to store and process information in working memory, quickly recover numerical facts, identify and decipher symbolic representations, and correctly carry out a series of procedural actions. These areas are usually deficient in children with dyslexia, and this is a serious deterrent to their mathematical capabilities. It has been found that dyslexia has working memory impairment as one of the best cognitive correlates (Swanson & Jerman, 2006). The working memory enables the temporary storage and manipulation of information, enabling students to solve problems based on multi-step instructions, do mental math, and combine the results in between. When a student has a limited working memory capacity, particularly in activities that demand a sequence in processing or in activities that demand long attention, he or she might have difficulty applying mathematical concepts correctly in real-world problems, although they understand them conceptually. Though these students are given adequate training, they often make errors due to forgetting the steps or processes, or the inversion of the order of procedure (Baddeley, 2003). Collectively, such results indicate that mathematical challenges in dyslexia are usually due to the constraint of cognitive processing capacity as opposed to conceptual ignorance.

Processing Speed, Rapid Automatized Naming, and Arithmetic Fluency

Besides the working memory limitations, children with dyslexia also have slower processing speeds and have trouble with rapid automatic naming (RAN), which further hinders mathematical fluency. Rapid naming tests measure the speed at which individuals can recall and pronounce the names of familiar stimuli, such as letters, numbers, or objects. It is now established that weaknesses in this area are a risk factor that is prevalent in math problems and that has been directly associated with reading problems (Wolf & Bowers, 1999). Quick retrieval of numeric information and automatic identification of digits and symbols are the primary requirements of effective success in mathematical tasks, including basic arithmetic. The slowness of retrieval makes the solutions of problems cognitively stressful and increases the possibility of error, and decreases efficiency. It has been found that compared to their counterparts who are developing normally, children with slower naming speed have problems with arithmetic fluency and a slower acquisition of automatic fact memory. (Koponen et al., 2007). The findings underscore the fact that even simple arithmetic processes can be cognitively burdensome to dyslexic students due to a diminished processing efficiency.

Visual-Spatial and Symbolic Processing Deficits

According to the research, visual-spatial attention and symbolic processing are also important in people with dyslexia, besides phonological and speed-related impairments. The dorsal visual stream has been cited to be the cause of dyslexic reading problems since it is the stream that processes spatial relationships and attention (Vidyasagar & Pammer, 2010). As mathematics largely relies on the interpretation of spatially organised symbols like place value notation, graphs, diagrams, geometric figures, and numerals organised into columns, these visual-spatial deficiencies likewise influence mathematical learning. Dyslexics often have problems with digit reversal, Misalignment in columnar arithmetic, misunderstanding between visually identical symbols, and mathematical concepts. These challenges imply that mathematical disorders in dyslexia are more manifestations of broad enough deficits in perception and thinking systems as opposed to linguistic deficits alone. Neuroimaging studies also give additional evidence that language and mathematical cognition have a similar brain resource. Functional neuroimaging studies have shown that there is an association between dyslexia and abnormal patterns of brain activity in the areas involved in reading and in numerical processes. In particular, people with mathematics difficulties, as well as dyslexic people, tend to have a reduced or ineffective activation of the intraparietal sulcus (IPS), which is an area involved in the processing of numbers, magnitude, and amount (Piazza et al., 2004).

Dehaenes' (1992) Triple Code Model, which proposes that numerical cognition operates in three interrelated representational systems: an analogue magnitude code of quantity representation, a verbal code of number words, and a visual Arabic code of digit symbols, is useful in understanding these trends. Children with dyslexia tend to exhibit difficulties in the verbal code as a result of phonological deficiency. They are also likely to have difficulties with visual symbolic code, which can restrict their ability to use mathematical concepts rapidly and recognise numeric symbols.

Dyslexia, Dyscalculia, and Comorbid Mathematical Difficulties

In the literature, there has been sufficient evidence of the relationship between dyslexia and learning difficulties in mathematics. A large proportion of children with dyslexia also have mathematical difficulties similar to those of dyscalculia, although dyscalculia is a formally recognized learning disability in mathematics (Landerl & Moll, 2010). Some of the typical cognitive risk factors that are found in this comorbidity include deficits in working memory, processing speed, attention, and executive control. Language-mediated issues of mathematics do not tend to be more problematic for children with dyslexia, such as word problems, symbolic manipulation, and procedural sequencing, despite pure dyscalculia being usually characterised by poor number sense and magnitude representation (Geary, 2011). Nevertheless, not all but a significant part of dyslexic students demonstrate some weakness in amount comparison, estimation, and processing numerical magnitudes, which complicates determining the differences between impairment of reading and arithmetic (Wilkey et al., 2020). Therefore, mathematical problems associated with dyslexia may have a different cause than pure dyscalculia, but they are educationally important and should be addressed specifically.

Language Demands, Word Problems, and Educational Context

Interpretation of word problems is one of the mathematical challenges that have continued to bedevil children with dyslexia. To complete mathematical word problems, the students should be able to decode text in writing, comprehend syntactic patterns, identify information, and translate linguistic descriptions into mathematical operations. In addition to the fact that they may possess adequate numerical reasoning skills, dyslexic learners, with reading comprehension and language processing problems, often have difficulty learning mathematical information incorporated in text problems (Fuchs et al., 2006). Their mathematical abilities may thus be young enough to give a false estimation of their conceptual understanding, which might cause them to misjudge their ability and lose academic self-esteem. These challenges are even more complicated in the Indian educational context, where mathematics is primarily taught using language and where students are motivated to learn mathematics by exams. Verbal explanations, written strategies, and linguistic reasoning are broadly used in the textbooks, classroom dialogues, and assessment strategies (NCERT, 2021). In a state like Kerala, where the level of literacy and academic performance is high, the Instructional strategies are focused on speed, accuracy, and textual problem solving. These instructional strategies pose a big challenge to the children with dyslexia, especially in the context of disparity between home language (Malayalam) and school language (English), cognitive limitations, and psychological constraints (Ramaa, 2000; Surendranath & Padakannaya, 2014). Lack of scientific awareness about learning disability and handling children with such disability among the primary school teachers further complicates the situation. Consequently, most of the mathematical problems faced by children with dyslexia are often ascribed to a lack of effort and/or poor motivation (Karande & Kulkarni, 2005). This may result in low self-esteem in students (Manjula et al., 2009). In addition, dyslexic students are highly sensitive to examinations, which makes them more stressed since written product, speed, and accuracy of the procedure are the areas that are emphasized in the examinations. The interplay between language-intensive teaching and the learner's unique cognitive weaknesses is key when it comes to determining the outcome of mathematics among children with dyslexia.

Technology-Enabled and AI-Based Interventions for Mathematical Learning

Learning environments that are supported by technology have presented a good prospect of overcoming the cognitive and instructional challenges experienced by dyslexic learners. Digital learning platforms allow individualisation, flexibility, and multisensory interaction, which is hard to attain in a normal classroom. Studies indicate that computer-assisted teaching has the potential to enhance conceptual knowledge, arithmetic, and engagement of children with learning disabilities (Li & Ma, 2010). Programs like Dream Box, Number Shire, and Math Garden use the interactive simulation, visual model, and game-based elements to improve the learning process of mathematics and decrease anxiety and increase motivation (Räsänen et al., 2009). Recent achievements in the field of artificial intelligence have allowed the development of adaptive learning that can dynamically alter according to the individual profile of a learner. AI-based systems such as ALEKS, Cognitive Tutor, and Knewton operate machine learning algorithms to assess student behaviour, detect a lack of understanding, and tailor the content display in real-time (Koedinger et al., 2013). These systems are closely connected with the principles of the Universal

Design of Learning that promote different types of representation, expression, and engagement as the method of accommodating learner diversity (Meyer et al., 2014). Dyslexic learners do not need as much text-based education since AI-based technologies can include voice accompaniment, visuals, scaffolding, and diverse forms of responses. The AI-based interventions have been applied to children with dyslexia, as AI could be used to address some of the cognitive weaknesses by capitalizing on the available strengths of such children. The AI solutions will be able to create a positive learning atmosphere, which encourages confidence and competence because of less linguistic burden, structured procedural advice, and no social stigma due to allowing repeat practice. Moreover, such systems may assist students to balance the working requirements and to be focused during the demanding activities due to the instant feedback and flexible speed. Empirical data indicate that these adaptive technologies have the potential to be helpful in enhancing performance in mathematics, particularly in children with learning disabilities (Koedinger et al., 2013). Neuroscience-informed educational interventions are another factor that facilitates technology-assisted learning. It is reported that dedicated cognitive training can enhance the efficiency of the brain and academic performance according to research studies on neuroplasticity. Specifically, training in working memory has been associated with gains in attention, reasoning, and mathematical performance (Holmes & Gathercole, 2013). Such findings would indicate that mathematical learning can be facilitated via the improvement of the basic cognitive processes, yet the extent of the transfer effects is disputed. The AI systems are in a good position to be incorporated in providing cognitive training elements in academic teaching, which can provide personalised, data-oriented approaches to evolving student requirements.

One more critical component of the effective intervention is the application of multimodal instructions. Multimodal instructions are a part of a successful intervention. Instructional strategies that combine auditory, visual, and kinesthetic elements can activate multiple neural pathways and thus enhance conceptual understanding and memory. Multisensory strategies enhance resilience in a variety of processing pathways and offer alternative learning routes to children with dyslexia. The mathematical concepts can be engaged with by students through animation, manipulatives, voice recognition, and touch interfaces. Leaners are able to interact with mathematical concepts using animation, manipulatives, voice-ins, and tactile interfaces. Although more international studies on these issues were being conducted, there are still gaps in the literature on dyslexia, learning mathematics, and educational technology. Scientific study of the mathematical difficulties of dyslexic learners in India, and in Kerala specifically, is in short supply. Moreover, the use and assessment of AI-based interventions in Indian classrooms are not studied extensively, and most of the experiences are implemented in literacy and not numeracy. Moreover, the application and evaluation of AI-based interventions in Indian classrooms has received less research, and most researchers focus more on literacy than numeracy. Not many studies have incorporated neurocognitive thinking and technological innovation to solve the particular issue of dyslexic learners in mathematics. These gaps are important in addressing how to come up with evidence-based interventions that are contextually relevant and support inclusive and equitable education. A comprehensive understanding of how children with dyslexia learn mathematics and how the challenges can be mitigated can be achieved by integrating transdisciplinary research across neuroscience, AI, psychology, and special education. This integrative strategy is necessary in the education system, such as Kerala, where both strong academic traditions and new technological views are combined. This is particularly appropriate when it comes to such an integrative approach. The chapter notes that multidisciplinary approaches to teaching mathematics must be learner-centered and recognize neurodiversity and that technological improvements should be exploited to assist every student in achieving his or her mathematical potential. Three primary objectives of the chapter are as follows: (1) to discuss the performance of children with dyslexia in arithmetic compared to the performance of typically developing children; (2) to synthesize the literature on dyslexia-associated mathematical challenges that is interdisciplinary; and (3) to make design responses related to the results of the empirical study by using AI and UDL frameworks. The chapter initially provides a review of the cognitive-neuroscientific and educational literature, then presents a small-scale needs-analysis study that was performed in Kerala, and finally puts the results into a conceptual framework of AI-supported mathematics learning.

METHOD

Participants

The participants of the study were 25 children with dyslexia and 25 typically developing children. All were students from the 4th standard of five CBSE-affiliated schools in Kerala, with ages ranging from 9 to 10 years. Participants came from middle- to high-socioeconomic backgrounds. Children with dyslexia were identified through a standardized reading assessment — the Test of Word Reading Efficiency (TOWRE) — and an intelligence test, the Raven's Coloured Progressive Matrices (RCPM). Those who met the diagnostic criteria for dyslexia were included in the dyslexic group. To gather additional information, parents and teachers of the selected children completed the Rutter Behaviour Scale and the Home Literacy Environment Questionnaire to assess behavioural characteristics and literacy-related home environments. All results and classifications were reviewed and confirmed by an experienced clinical psychologist. Written informed consent was obtained from both school authorities and parents prior to participation.

Materials and Procedure

The researcher visited each participating school after receiving institutional permission. Testing was conducted individually in a quiet classroom setting. Rapport was established with participants before testing to ensure comfort and cooperation. Participants were administered TOWRE and RCPM tests following the standard procedures. Parents and teachers completed the Rutter Behaviour Scale and Home Literacy Environment Questionnaire separately. All sessions were conducted during school hours, and testing lasted for approximately 30–45 minutes. Ethical approval for the study was obtained from the institutional Ethics Committee, and all participants were assured of confidentiality and the voluntary nature of their participation.

1. Raven's colored progressive matrices

Raven's Coloured Progressive Matrices (RCPM), developed by John C. Raven in 1936, is a non-verbal intelligence test designed to assess general cognitive ability. The test has been widely used in educational and clinical settings on children between 5 and 11. It consists of abstract patterns presented in increasing difficulty, requiring test-takers to identify the missing piece from provided options. The RCPM has shown split-half reliability between 0.80 and 0.90 and had construct validity (0.70-0.90). In the current study, it is used to assess the intelligence of children with reading difficulty.

2. Rutter Behaviour scale (Rutter, 1967)

The Rutter Behaviour Scale, developed by Michael Rutter in 1967, is a widely used tool for assessing child behavioural and emotional problems to identify children at risk of psychiatric disorders. The scale consists of a parent questionnaire (Scale A) and a teacher questionnaire (Scale B). It covers various aspects of behaviour, including conduct problems, emotional difficulties, hyperactivity, and prosocial behaviour. Scores are interpreted to estimate the likelihood of psychiatric disorders, with higher scores indicating greater risk. The scale has shown inter-rater reliability (0.60-0.80) and content validity (0.80-0.90) across multiple studies, demonstrating consistency in results and accurately identifying children with behavioral issues (Rutter, 1967).

3. TOWRE test (Wagner et al., 1999)

The Test of Word Reading Efficiency (TOWRE) was first developed and published by Joseph K Torgesen, Richard Wagner, and Carl Rashotte in 1999. It seeks to measure an individual's accuracy and fluency by two measures: Sight Word Efficiency (SWE) and Phonemic Decoding Efficiency (PDE). Test-retest reliability (0.87) and construct validity were established (Wagner et al., 1999).

4. Diagnostic Arithmetic Test

The Diagnostic Arithmetic Test (DAT) of NIMHANS, which is a version of the Diagnostic Arithmetic Test of Schonell, has been demonstrated to be adequate in terms of reliability and validity when measuring arithmetic skills of Indian school-going children. This test has good content validity as the items are logically chosen to address fundamental arithmetic operations, including number concepts, addition, subtraction, multiplication, division, fractions, and word problems, ordered in order of difficulty, and according to the school curricula. The construct validity can be justified by its capacity to distinguish between the children who have been normal in their academic achievements and those with particular learning problems in mathematics (dyscalculia). Research and clinical practice in NIMHANS demonstrate high levels of satisfactory criterion-related validity, and test performance is associated with classroom performance and teacher ratings. Reliability, such as test-retest reliability, which shows the consistency of the scores over time, and inter-scorer reliability, which is made possible by objective and standardized scoring, has also been demonstrated to be acceptable with the test. In general, NIMHANS-modified DAT can be regarded as a psychometrically and culturally relevant instrument of diagnostic evaluation of the level of arithmetic skills in the Indian context.

RESULTS

Table 1 shows the mean and standard deviation of age, nonverbal intelligence, and reading efficiency for children with dyslexia and typically developing children (N = 50). The two groups were closely matched in age, with mean ages of 9.07 years (SD = 0.18) for children with dyslexia and 9.00 years (SD = 0.20) for typically developing children. On the Ravens Coloured Progressive Matrices (RCPM), typically developing children obtained higher mean scores (M = 32, SD = 2.10) than children with dyslexia (M = 28.4, SD = 1.47). For children aged 9.5 to 10 years, an RCPM score of 28 corresponds to approximately the 75th percentile, whereas a score of 32 corresponds to approximately the 95th percentile, indicating that both groups performed within the average to above-average range of nonverbal intelligence, with typically developing children showing superior performance. Marked group differences were observed in the Test of Word Reading Efficiency (TOWRE). On the TOWRE-A (sight word efficiency), children with dyslexia showed substantially lower performance (M = 17.8, SD = 3.44) compared to typically developing children (M = 54, SD = 4.80). A similar pattern was evident for TOWRE-B (phonemic decoding efficiency), among children with dyslexia scoring lower (M = 10.6, SD = 2.48) than their typically developing peers (M = 35, SD = 3.60). Children with dyslexia demonstrate deficits in both sight word reading and phonemic decoding efficiency relative to typically developing children.

Table 1. Mean and standard deviation of age, Ravens coloured progressive matrices, and test of word reading efficiency (N=50)

variables	M1	SD1	M2	SD2
Age	9.07	0.188	9	0.20
RCPM	28.4	1.47	32	2.10
TOWRE-A	17.8	3.44	54	4.80
TOWRE-B	10.6	2.48	35	3.60

Note: M1=Mean of children with dyslexia, SD1=Standard deviation of children with Dyslexia, M2=Mean of typically developing children, SD2=Standard deviation of typically developing children, RCPM=Ravens coloured progressive matrices, TOWRE-A=Test of word reading efficiency sight word efficiency, TOWRE B=Test of word reading efficiency phonemic decoding efficiency

The results on the Diagnostic Arithmetic Test (DAT) showed significant differences between children with and without dyslexia across all sections. Children with dyslexia scored lower (M1) with higher standard deviations (SD1) in comparison to the performance of their typically developing counterparts. Notably, in graded multiplication and division, children with dyslexia scored zero, whereas typically developing children performed well. Overall, the findings highlight significant arithmetic difficulties faced by children with dyslexia compared to their typically developing peers (see Table 2). This was supported by the Mann-Whitney U test results (see Table 3). We used a non-parametric inferential test as the data did not meet the normality criterion. The results revealed statistically significant differences between the groups across all sections of DAT at $p > 0.01$ level. The standard error of difference (SED) ranged from 0.160 to 0.338, indicating that the observed group differences were stable and not due to sampling fluctuation. As effect size estimation using Cohen's d was inappropriate for non-parametric data, point biserial correlation (rrb) was computed. The rrb values ranged from 0.676 to 0.992, indicating strong to very strong associations between group membership and arithmetic performance. Overall, the Mann–Whitney U test results confirm significant and substantial differences in arithmetic skills between dyslexic and typically developing groups across all sections of the DAT.

Table 2. Mean and standard deviation of Diagnostic Arithmetic Test (DAT)

Section	M1	SD1	M2	SD2
1(A)	3.36	1.22	5	0
1(B)	3.20	1.04	5	0
2(A)	1.32	1.18	4.32	0.748
2(B)	1.12	1.42	4.60	.764
3(A)	1.52	.653	3.92	.277
3(B)	1.80	.957	4.68	.476
3(C)	1.40	.866	4.56	.712
4(A)	0	0	4.32	.802
4(B)	0	0	4.20	.913

Note. M1=Mean of children with dyslexia SDI=Standard deviation of children with dyslexia M2=Mean of Typically developing children SD2=Standard deviation of Typically developing children, 1(A) = Addition, 1(B) = Substraction, 2(A) = Multiplication, 2(B) = Division, 3(A) = Miscellaneous, 3(B) = Graded addition, 3(C) = Graded substraction, 4(A) = Graded multiplication, 4(B) = Graded Division

The Mann–Whitney U test was employed to examine whether there was a significant difference in arithmetic performance between dyslexic and typically developing children on the various sections of the Diagnostic Arithmetic Test (DAT), as the data did not satisfy the assumption of normality. The results revealed statistically significant differences across all sections, indicating consistently lower performance among children with dyslexia when compared to their typically developing counterparts. The obtained mean ranks and corresponding U statistics (reflected through the reported test values) were significant at the 0.01 level in all domains, including basic operations and graded arithmetic tasks. The mean scores further supported this trend, children with dyslexia showing lower central tendencies and greater variability. The standard error of difference (SED), which ranged from 0.160 to 0.338, suggests that the observed group differences were stable and not due to sampling fluctuation. As effect size estimation using Cohen's d was inappropriate for non-parametric data, point biserial correlation (rrb) was computed. The rrb values ranged from 0.676 to 0.992, indicating strong to very strong associations between group membership and arithmetic performance. Overall, the Mann–Whitney U test results confirm significant and substantial differences in arithmetic abilities between children with dyslexia and typically developing children across all sections of the DAT.

Table 3. Mann–Whitney U test results comparing dyslexic and typically developing children on the diagnostic arithmetic test

Section	M	SD	U	SED	rrb
1(A)	4.18	1.19	101**	0.257	0.676
1(B)	4.10	1.16	63**	0.223	0.798
2(A)	2.82	1.80	42.5**	0.309	0.864
2(B)	2.86	2.09	30**	0.338	0.904
3(A)	2.72	1.31	7.50**	0.160	0.976
3(B)	3.24	1.64	2.50**	0.219	0.992
3(C)	2.98	1.78	11.5**	0.245	0.963
4(A)	2.16	2.25	12**	0.236	0.962
4(B)	2.10	2.22	12**	0.248	0.962

Note: M= Mean; SD =Standard Deviation; SED = Std. Error difference; **p = < .01; *p = < .05, U=Mann-Whitney U test, rrb=Point biserial correlation

DISCUSSION

The results support the view that though dyslexia is usually regarded as a learning problem associated with language, it often overlaps with mathematical learning and numerical cognition as they have some common underlying cognitive processes. The performance gaps in the mathematics test at the consecutive levels indicate the presence of a cumulative learning deficit. With the increasing complexity of mathematical operations, the performance of the children became worse. This trend is not new since previous studies have found that children with dyslexia experience difficulties with simple numerical skills such as number sensing, symbol decoding, sequencing, and retrieving arithmetic facts that support more complicated thinking in mathematics. The enhanced widening of performance disengagements implies that the initial setbacks are going to be complicated, as time passes, leading to a significant academic setback in the absence of effective interventions. Lower achievement by the children with dyslexia indicates deeper cognitive processing problems, including working memory, executive functioning, and symbolic representation deficits they struggle to navigate. To do math, one should be good at information integration skill, planning, spatial thinking, besides visual recognition of numbers, phonological encoding of number phrases, step-by-step processing, etc. Poor working memory coupled with poor ability to sustain attention results in cognitive load and reducing task efficiency. The research results point to the need to transform mathematical teaching to the paradigm of inclusive and learner-conducted approaches. Conventional correction methods, such as repetitive practice or simplified worksheets, could not be helpful unless cognitive processing limitations are addressed. New teaching models should be developed to facilitate memory, reduce cognitive load, and provide learners with multisensory learning opportunities. This is where technology comes in, and more so Artificial Intelligence (AI). Potential AIs in education systems are customized training, learning profile modification, and immediate feedback. It is possible to assist children with dyslexia with cognitive deficiencies to overcome it by means of exploiting their abilities, such as pattern recognition and visual-spatial reasoning.

Among the most promising applications of artificial intelligence (AI) to address the diverse learning needs of children with dyslexia, adaptive learning systems particularly in arithmetic, are the most promising. Such systems involve machine learning algorithms and data analytics so that they can constantly assess the performance of a learner and provide dynamically altered instructional material, pace, and feedback according to the personal progress (Kulik & Fletcher, 2016). Adaptive platforms offer an individualized learning course which cannot be supported by a typical classroom education since the dyslexic learning styles in mathematics are often undermined by shortcomings in working memory, sequencing, and processing symbols. It is one of the primary benefits of an adaptive learning system to identify specific patterns of errors and problem areas. This research indicates that children with dyslexia tend to have problems with remembering mathematical facts, number sequence, and multiplex problems because of impairments in phonological processing and executive functioning (Geary, 2011; Swanson & Jerman, 2006). These issues can be diagnosed in real time by adaptive systems and determined through the accuracy of responses, response time, and the nature of errors. This analysis can be used in the system to provide targeted activities that will focus on the core competencies, so that students do not proceed with their studies with misconceptions that have not yet been resolved. Adaptive learning platforms enable students to engage with mathematical material at a pace that is commensurate with their cognitive processing ability, unlike traditional classroom environments, where learning is often predetermined by a fixed curriculum and learning speed. Dyslexic learners normally need a lot of repetition of numbers and time to consolidate numerical concepts (Butterworth & Yeo, 2004). Adaptive systems normalize this demand by offering unlimited practice opportunities without the social stigma that might accompany recurring education in the classroom setting. This is highly important in maintaining motivation and reducing math fear, which is highly prevalent among children with learning impairment (Ashcraft, 2002).

Another vital element of an adaptive learning system is the use of scaffolded training. Vygotsky (1978) defines scaffolding as the process of breaking down complex mathematical tasks into simple, achievable steps and providing guided support up to the learners achieve a level of independence. As an example, an adaptive system may first measure the precondition skills, e.g., place value understanding and number size comparison, when a child with dyslexia has problems with subtraction involving borrowing. Once the conceptual understanding is achieved, the system can gradually shift to some form of symbolic representation using visual representations like base-ten blocks or number lines drawn using animation. Such scaffolding is consistent with neuroscientific learning that underlines the importance of progressive complexity, multisensory involvement, and neurofeedback (Dehaene, 2011). The adaptive learning platforms record the improvement over time and maintain comprehensive learner profiles, which help identify long-term gaps that might remain undetected in class-based assessment (Gersten et al., 2009). The adaptive systems are therefore instructional, diagnostic, as well as preventive mechanisms. The adaptive systems can play an important role in inclusive education within the Indian context, particularly in the mainstream classrooms of Kerala. Presently, dyslexic students are unfairly discriminated against due to the language-intensive and exam-driven mathematics instruction. The AI-driven adaptive platforms could reduce language stress because they concentrate on interactive problem solving, visual representations, and minimal text-based explanations. In order to support learner diversity, Universal Design of Learning (UDL) promotes various types of representation and participation, which this change makes possible (CAST, 2018).

The application of multisensory and visual AI-based aids is another remarkable advancement regarding the ability to meet the mathematical learning needs of children with dyslexia. Traditional mathematical training often puts dyslexic students at a disadvantage, since most of it is delivered through spoken explanation, written symbols, and abstract representations, which AI-headed multimodal tools take advantage of in order to reduce the linguistic load and align training to the cognitive abilities of this group of learners. One of the most significant contributions of AI to mathematics teaching is the usage of advanced forms of visual representation to facilitate conceptual knowledge. Research on numerical cognition has shown that the basis of mathematical learning is the system of visual processing, which is linked to the representations of magnitude and spatial logistics (Butterworth, 2005; Dehaene, 2011). Although dyslexic learners have phonological processing weakness, they often have relative strengths in visual-spatial reasoning (Wang et al., 2012). Artificial intelligence-based visual products leverage these benefits by visualizing the abstract numerical concepts as tangible, manipulative visual representations. Major characteristics of AI-based platforms include dynamic number lines, color-coded quantities, step-by-step problem-solving sequences that can be animated, and spatial models of arithmetic operations. Dynamic number lines, color-coded amounts, animated step-by-step problem-solving sequences, and spatial models of arithmetic operations are typical of AI-based platforms without primarily relying on text-based explanations. These images will allow the students to have strong mental representations of numerical associations without necessarily using text-based descriptions in order to do so. As an example, multiplication can be presented in the form of arrays or grouping animations, whereas addition and subtraction can be presented in the form of movement along a number line. In students with special difficulties with symbolic notation, the representations help students decrease mental load and enhance conceptual knowledge (Bruner, 1966). Also, the AI systems are able to adjust visual complexity according to the performance of learners. The system can revert to visual subtraction by means of objects or blocks when a dyslexic learner experiences problems with symbolic subtraction, and it can reintroduce the symbols gradually. Such a flexible visual scaffolding promotes gradual conceptual development and is in line with constructivist ideas of learning (Vygotsky, 1978).

Virtual manipulatives are computerized models of physical mathematical devices, including fraction bars, counters, base-ten blocks, and geometrical shapes. AI-enhanced virtual manipulatives expand the capabilities of conventional manipulatives and react intelligently to the action of the learner, providing instant feedback. It has been proven that intentional use of manipulatives during training and implementing them in mathematics understanding significantly promotes understanding (Moyer-Packenham & Westenskow, 2013). Virtual manipulatives prove very useful for dyslexic students. Physical manipulatives could require mediation by the teacher and oral instructions, even in spite of their effectiveness. Virtual manipulatives are designed through AI, with little text, animations, and other visual cues to guide the students through their work. As an example, learners may be able to group and ungroup units, tens, and hundreds through the visual grouping and ungrouping of units to solve problems in the place value to enhance the structure of numbers in a practical way, understandings such as improper grouping or misinterpreting place value, and respond through offering visual cues or alternative representations. Increased long verbal explanation may be inadequate to dyslexic learners and, therefore, this nonverbal feedback in real time is essential (Swanson & Jerman, 2006). Moreover, active number manipulation enhances the active process of learning and leads to acquiring procedural fluency, alongside bringing a conceptual understanding.

Auditory processing technology involves text-to-speech and speech-to-text, which are considered important in minimizing linguistic barriers to mathematics learning. Dyslexic students have difficulties in comprehending written information, and thus they might find it difficult to comprehend mathematical information, especially word problems (Snowling & Hulme, 2012). AI-based text-to-speech systems can be used to provide oral instruction of mathematical instructions, questions, and feedback by decoding problems and letting learners focus on numerical thinking. It has been shown that children experiencing reading difficulties are better at completing tasks and understand better when they can listen to instructional material (Wood et al., 2018).

Text-to-speech software can read and highlight significant numerical information, repeat instructions, and read word problems aloud without embarrassing learners. To even personalize the learning process, other advanced systems allow students to select the repetition and the speed of response. Speech-to-text technology offers additional benefits by making dyslexic students respond vocally as opposed to textually in writing. Students will be able to provide their answers to mathematical problems orally, and the AI system will be able to document and test them. The tool promotes creative flexibility and allows learners to express what they know without being constrained by writing and spelling problems. These multimodal response options are consistent with the tenets of the Universal Design of Learning (CAST, 2018).

Fischer, Moeller, Bientzle, Cress, and Nurek (2011) state that mathematics is better understood through kinesthetic learning, which involves physical body motion and interaction that stimulates sensorimotor systems associated with cognition. AI-driven technology is fast incorporating touch screens, gesture-based interfaces, and motion-based input to support embodied learning. With kinaesthetic input, dyslexic learners have an alternative method of learning mathematical concepts that otherwise may be difficult to learn in text only. The physical element of learning is ensured by touch-sensitive activities, such as following number patterns, organizing items, and dragging numbers. AI systems can track these interactions, watch their appropriateness, and adjust tasks when needed. Ingestive learning is one of the areas that is highly effective through gesture-based learning, through which teaching sequencing, which is known to be a challenge among children with dyslexia, becomes very successful. As an example, the drag-and-drop interface can allow students to rearrange a numerical sequence or even physically organize the steps in a mathematical method. These strategies are effective to ensure retention over the long term and the connections of the brain by the application of muscular memory in the involvement of visual and auditory systems (Wilson, 2002).

AI-based animated solutions to problems are used to divide complex mathematical processes into a sequence of steps that are visually guided. Each step is animated and emphasizes significant personalities, processes, and changes. This technique is especially useful with students with dyslexia who do not have the capacity to solve multi-step problems because of working memory (Geary, 2011). Animated guiding requires less retention in the memory to hold many pieces of information simultaneously. Instead, learners will have the ability to focus on each step at a time and have immediate feedback on being right or wrong. With AI systems, a certain degree of control is achieved that is impossible with traditional training, since it is possible to pause, restart, or repeat the steps when the learner provides some input. These tools also assist in analyzing errors graphically by depicting a contrast between the wrong process and the suitable strategies. Hattie and Timperley (2007) argue that such visual feedback stimulates the occurrence of metacognition and makes students aware of the way and the reasons as to why something is wrong.

The accumulating literature tends to support the fact that a good number of dyslexics excel in holistic thinking, creativity, and visual-spatial reasoning (Eide & Eide, 2011). Multi-sensory and visual AI technologies have a strategic edge to exploit these benefits because of their ability to offer alternative descriptions of what mathematical knowledge is. By shifting the focus towards visual and interactive engagement, these tools are fairer in learning environments as they switch the priorities of the language processing towards the visual one. Multisensory AI applications can serve as a powerful balancing force in the Indian school market, where education is often test-focused and standardized. Through these tools, students with dyslexia will be in a position to have mathematical information presented in a manner that fits their cognitive profiles, which reduces frustration and enhances self-efficacy.

Intelligent Systems in Tutoring (ITS)

Intelligent Tutoring Systems are the advanced use of artificial intelligence to imitate the value of human tutoring on a one-on-one basis. These systems unite cognitive models, learner analytics, as well as adaptive feedback mechanisms to offer individualized learning that dynamically changes in line with the needs of a learner (VanLehn, 2011). ITS offers a very accommodating and individualized learning model that a typical classroom setting usually does not afford students with dyslexia, because the latter usually have problems with arithmetic processes, as they lack working memory, sequencing, and symbolic processing. One of the main strengths of ITS is its ability to find and deal with specific error patterns. Research indicates that the common arithmetic errors that dyslexic students commit include, but are not limited to, number reversals, misreading of the symbols of operation, and errors in the sequence of the procedure (Geary, 2011; Swanson & Jerman, 2006). Intelligent tutoring systems analyze the learner responses in real time, and consequently, learners can be determined to have an incorrect response and why. The system can intervene immediately with specific recommendations, visual cues, or remedial feedback with the aid of this diagnostic feature to the profile of the cognitive abilities of the learner.

ITS has the ability to offer corrections in non-linguistic formats, which are also simple, unlike the traditional methods of giving corrections, which often rely on verbal explanation. An example is that an ITS could use symbolic signals to resolve ambiguity, draw attention to a wrong step in a calculation, or, with animation through visual presentation, depict the correct sequence instead of textual feedback. These strategies reduce linguistic and cognitive burden among learners with dyslexia who may find it challenging to accept difficult verbal information (Mayer, 2009).

ITS enables learners to focus on basic mathematical concepts instead of decoding teaching material, as it reduces reliance on language. Another significant advantage is its ability to provide scaffolded support, provided by ITS. When the students are advanced, the scaffolding process involves the gradual reduction of teaching aid to enable them to be self-reliant and self-confident (Vygotsky, 1978). ITS systems may also adjust the level of assistance according to the performance of learners, with elaborate instructions being given to challenging cases and the assistance decreasing gradually as the learner becomes more proficient. This reconfigured scaffolding is very important to children with dyslexia as it helps them to have low processing speed and builds procedural knowledge with systematized practice and rehearsal (Butterworth & Yeo, 2004).

Additionally, intelligent tutoring systems promote metacognitive skills, which are a domain that is usually underdeveloped in students with learning disabilities. Metacognition can be defined as the ability to monitor, evaluate, and manage oneself in terms of learning (Flavell, 1979). ITS fosters metacognition by asking students to reflect on the thinking processes involved when they approach the solution to problems, predict their outcomes, and evaluate the effectiveness of their strategies. As an example, the system can make the student choose among possible methods of solving a problem or explain his/her reasons after completing the problem. Aleven, Roll, McLaren, and Koedinger (2016) state that these reflective prompts enable students to be aware of themselves and have strategic control of their mathematical thinking. In the case of learners with dyslexia, who often experience recurring academic failure and can develop negative self-perceptions that relate to mathematics, metacognitive skills are of particular importance (Ashcraft & Moore, 2009). Errors are perceived as a learning experience and not failure in the low-stress, no-judgment atmosphere created by intelligent tutors. This positive feedback system can increase learner motivation, self-efficacy, and persistence, which are all key to a long-term interest in mathematics. IT offers a viable solution to inclusive educational opportunities within learning institutions such as mainstream classrooms in Kerala, where the demands of a curriculum are sparse, and the size of a classroom inhibits the possibilities of diversified teaching. These systems may also improve classroom teaching by providing personalized tutoring during the hours not scheduled, i.e., during off-peak hours. In this way, the intelligent tutoring systems would be very useful in assisting children with dyslexia to study mathematics. ITS helps in the cognitive and affective aspects of mathematics learning through the identification of error patterns, adaptive feedback, non-linguistic feedback, the structuring of training, and the promotion of metacognitive development. They can be used to assist dyslexic students in building on conceptual knowledge, self-esteem, and independence due to their capacity to simulate one-on-one tutoring.

Mathematics Evaluation Using AI-Based Assessment Technologies

AI-based evaluation systems provide a powerful alternative to traditional, examination-based assessment systems that often do not measure the actual arithmetic understanding of children with dyslexia. The conventional arithmetic testing methods are not favorable to dyslexic students, who normally tend to focus on written answers, speed, and language precision. Studies have shown again and again that dyslexia does not just weaken reading and writing abilities, but also the ability to correctly read written mathematical notation and word problems, leading to an under-assessment of actual achievement on standardized tests (Snowling & Hulme, 2012; Geary, 2011). There are more flexible and multimodal AI-based assessment models that allow students to demonstrate their level of understanding in performance-based, interactive, and oral assignments. One of the principal advantages of AI-based assessment is the possibility of offering multimodal assessment. Instead of using pen and paper tests, AI systems can assess mathematics understanding as a visual problem-solving task, a drag-and-drop task, a simulation, and a verbal explanation. As an example, learners may need to solve problems with the help of working with virtual objects, provide an oral explanation of the idea of how they do it, or complete an interactive series, which demonstrates the knowledge of the concept. These practices align with the ideas of Universal Design of Learning (UDL) that emphasize the use of the different types of expression and representation to support a large number of learners (CAST, 2018). These assessments give a more real-life picture of mathematics and reduce language barriers to dyslexic students. Another significant benefit is the capability of AI-based evaluation technologies to do continuous, formative assessment. Unlike the traditional examination, which offers an overview of progress at a specific point in time, AI systems acquire information at every turn as students work on assignments. These systems can offer detailed profiles of the learners through tracking response patterns, error types, time taken to perform tasks, and learner progression based on the level of difficulty (Shute & Rahimi, 2017). A continuous assessment facilitates early identification of learning gaps and proactive changes in instructional strategies. This is more important to the dyslexic students whose inabilities may be compounded as they grow because not clearing up the basic misunderstandings at an early stage. AI-based evaluation technologies also enable personalized feedback that is essential to facilitate learning, as opposed to evaluating it. Through AI systems, a learner can receive prompt and useful feedback depending on specific errors and not labels or grades. The feedback may be provided orally, in the form of graphs, or guided suggestions to help the students notice their errors without feeling anxious and discouraged (Hattie and Timperley, 2007). Such feedback systems develop a growth-focused learning atmosphere and contribute to the emergence of learner confidence, which is often undermined in children with dyslexia due to frequent academic failures.

The effective application of Artificial Intelligence (AI) applications to teaching mathematics to children with dyslexia needs the proper background on educational theory and neuroscientific knowledge. Neuroscientific research defines dyslexia as an irregular brain activity connected with working memory, phonological processing, and symbolic representation that are crucial in learning mathematics (Dehaene, 2011; Snowling, 2013). As such, instead of introducing the standard teaching paradigms, AI-based interventions should be created to support these neurocognitive differences. AI technologies are capable of improving the learning abilities of dyslexic learners through neural plasticity, which involves repetition, feedback, and multisensory stimulation, and this fits into the learning mechanism of the brain (Goswami, 2015). Pedagogically speaking, AI is to be perceived as an extra support system that contributes to the effectiveness of teaching and does not replace teachers. Teachers are still needed in learning since they can provide contextual knowledge, emotional comfort, and encouraging guidance that technology cannot (OECD, 2021). Selecting the appropriate AI tools, processing student data created in these platforms, and integrating technology insights in the learning process are all important activities that an educator undertakes. The danger of AI tools is that they will not be utilized well enough or may be abused without the mediation of informed instructors, particularly in inclusive education. The concept of a holistic approach to supporting learners with dyslexia in mathematics should encompass the four factors of early identification, continuous assessment, personalized instruction, and collaborative participation. Prompt Diagnosis of dyscalculia is important as undetected underlying weaknesses may lead to overall poor performance in the long run (Gersten et al., 2009). Ait is easier for teachers to identify learning challenges of students in early stages using AI-driven screening and assessment systems. Continuous, formative assessment using AI allows timely responses and interventions. Students with dyslexia need individualized learning paths as opposed to the conventional ones because of their diverse cognitive profiles (Fletcher et al., 2019). The adaptive systems based on AI have the potential to tailor the content, pace, and feedback to the needs of individual students. This type of personalization is consistent with the principles of inclusive education that emphasize flexibility to variations in the diversity of learners (UNESCO, 2017). Educators, parents, and technology suppliers should also collaborate. Children with dyslexia are supported to learn at home by their parents, which is a vital aspect in ensuring that they remain healthy psychologically. The parent-teacher cooperation may be enhanced as the cooperation will be provided with the help of AI solutions that will provide clear progress reports and practical recommendations. Collaborating with tech developers on the system level will help to develop AI tools in an ethical, culturally sensitive manner, and one that supports the aims of academic education. The implications of this inclusive and equitable education are significant in this holistic paradigm. The introduction of AI-based techniques opens up a possibility to reconsider mathematics teaching in a more inclusive language in a context such as the educational system of Kerala, where managing learning and assessment are mostly standardized and examination-based. AI-based models support equity in education and benefit the right of every student to a meaningful engagement in mathematical education by alleviating language obstacles, effectively accommodating neurodiversity, and introducing various ways to learn (CAST, 2018; NEP, 2020). The solutions to these issues can be rather interesting in AI-based educational systems that provide the individual with a versatile and multisensory learning experience. The solutions to these issues can be rather interesting in AI-based educational systems that provide the individual with a versatile and multisensory learning experience.

CONCLUSION

As its current research indicates conclusively, dyslexia has a considerable effect on arithmetic functions which is not limited to the previously known influence on reading and language developmental functions. The Diagnostic Arithmetic Test (DAT) results showed children with dyslexia to be significantly lower than their standard developing counterparts in all areas of arithmetic, such as basic operations and graded tasks. The large differences that were observed with the help of the Mann–Whitney U test, together with the high values of point biserial correlation, suggest that such challenges are not accidental but systematic and solid. The greater variability and lower achievement rates of children with dyslexia echo underlying cognitive difficulties in terms of working memory, processing speed, sequencing, and symbolic representation, which are fundamental in mathematical learning. The findings support the view that dyslexia and dyscalculia share some common neurocognitive processes. Conventional teaching and remedial methods based on extensive use of repetition and text explanations seem to be inadequate to address the basic cognitive limitations of children with dyslexia. This paper highlights the necessity of having inclusive and learner-focused teaching methods that lessen the linguistic burden and offer systematically designed and multi-sensory approach. AI based educational technologies with interactive learning systems, smart tutoring applications, and multisensory digital applications have great potentials to make significant contributions to customize learning, offer instant feedback helping to overcome the challenges. It is crucial to identify dyscalculia in the early phase, and incorporate technology-assisted interventions in teaching-learning of mathematics. Through evidence-based and AI-assisted methods, educators and policymakers can strive to make learning environments more inclusive and conducive to children with dyslexia to help them realize their full academic capabilities in mathematics.

LIMITATIONS AND FUTURE SUGGESTIONS

The present study is not without limitations. Sample size was small, which makes it difficult to generalize the findings tthe rest of the population of school-going children in general. Second, the sample consisted of schools in Kerala, and this factor may not be applicable to other areas with diverse linguistic, curricular, and socio-cultural settings. Third, the research was based on the Diagnostic Arithmetic Test (DAT) as the primary method of measuring arithmetic skills; it would be beneficial to incorporate other standardized tests and classroom observations, as they would provide a more comprehensive picture of mathematical challenges. Moreover, the study lacks a cross-sectional design, which prevents one from making conclusions about changes in development or causal correlations between dyslexia and arithmetic problems.

Future studies need to consider larger and more varied samples in different areas to increase the external validity. It is advised that longitudinal studies be conducted to investigate how mathematical problems progress in children with dyslexia over time. Further research can also be conducted to determine the efficacy of certain intervention models, specifically AI-based and multisensory instructional designs, in enhancing performance in arithmetic. Also, it would be of interest to study the contribution of cognitive factors, including working memory, attention, and speed of processing, as they may help to gain a better idea about the mechanisms underlying the problem and create an evidence-based intervention.

REFERENCES

Aleven, V., Roll, I., McLaren, B. M., & Koedinger, K. R. (2016). Help helps, but only so much: Research on help seeking with intelligent tutoring systems. *International Journal of Artificial Intelligence in Education, 26*(1), 205–223. DOI: 10.1007/s40593-015-0089-1

Ashcraft, M. H. (2002). Math anxiety: Personal, educational, and cognitive consequences. *Current Directions in Psychological Science, 11*(5), 181–185. DOI: 10.1111/1467-8721.00196

Ashcraft, M. H., & Moore, A. M. (2009). Mathematical anxiety and the affective drop in performance. *Journal of Psychoeducational Assessment, 27*(3), 197–205. DOI: 10.1177/0734282908330580

Baddeley, A. (2003). Working memory: Looking back and looking forward. *Nature Reviews. Neuroscience, 4*(10), 829–839. DOI: 10.1038/nrn1201

Bruner, J. S. (1966). *Toward a theory of instruction.* Harvard University Press.

Butterworth, B. (2005). The development of arithmetical abilities. *Journal of Child Psychology and Psychiatry, and Allied Disciplines, 46*(1), 3–18. DOI: 10.1111/j.1469-7610.2004.00374.x

Butterworth, B., & Yeo, D. (2004). *Dyscalculia guidance.* NFER-Nelson.

CAST. (2018). Universal Design for Learning guidelines version 2.2. http://udlguidelines.cast.org

Dehaene, S. (1992). Varieties of numerical abilities. *Cognition, 44*(1–2), 1–42. DOI: 10.1016/0010-0277(92)90049-N

Dehaene, S. (2011). The number sense: How the mind creates mathematics (Rev. and updated ed.). Oxford University Press.

Eide, B. L., & Eide, F. F. (2011). *The dyslexic advantage: Unlocking the hidden potential of the dyslexic brain.* Hudson Street Press.

Fischer, F., Moeller, K., Bientzle, M., Cress, U., & Nuerk, H. C. (2011). Sensorimotor spatial training of number magnitude representation. *Psychonomic Bulletin & Review, 18*(1), 177–183. DOI: 10.3758/s13423-010-0031-3

Flavell, J. H. (1979). Metacognition and cognitive monitoring: A new area of cognitive–developmental inquiry. *The American Psychologist, 34*(10), 906–911. DOI: 10.1037/0003-066X.34.10.906

Fletcher, J. M., Lyon, G. R., Fuchs, L. S., & Barnes, M. A. (2019). *Learning disabilities: From identification to intervention* (2nd ed.). Guilford Press.

Fuchs, L. S., Fuchs, D., Compton, D. L., Powell, S. R., Seethaler, P. M., Capizzi, A. M., & Fletcher, J. M. (2006). The cognitive correlates of third-grade skill in arithmetic, algorithmic computation, and arithmetic word problems. *Journal of Educational Psychology, 98*(1), 29–43. DOI: 10.1037/0022-0663.98.1.29

Geary, D. C. (2011). Cognitive predictors of achievement growth in mathematics: A five-year longitudinal study. *Developmental Psychology, 47*(6), 1539–1552. DOI: 10.1037/a0025510

Geary, D. C. (2011). Consequences, characteristics, and causes of poor mathematics achievement and mathematical learning disabilities. *Journal of Developmental and Behavioral Pediatrics : JDBP, 32*(3), 250–263. DOI: 10.1097/DBP.0b013e318209edef

Gersten, R., Clarke, B. S., Jordan, N. C., Newman-Gonchar, R., Haymond, K., & Wilkins, C. (2009). Universal screening in mathematics for the primary grades: Beginnings of a research base. *Exceptional Children, 75*(4), 423–445. DOI: 10.1177/001440291207800403

Goswami, U. (2015). Neuroscience and education: From research to practice? *Nature Reviews. Neuroscience, 16*(10), 631–636. DOI: 10.1038/nrn3980

Hattie, J., & Timperley, H. (2007). The power of feedback. *Review of Educational Research, 77*(1), 81–112. DOI: 10.3102/003465430298487

Holmes, J., & Gathercole, S. E. (2013). Taking working memory training from the laboratory into schools. *Educational Psychology, 34*(4), 440–450. DOI: 10.1080/01443410.2013.797338

Jeffries, S., & Everatt, J. (2004). Working memory: Its role in dyslexia and other specific learning difficulties. *Dyslexia : The Journal of the British Dyslexia Association, 10*(3), 196–214. DOI: 10.1002/dys.278

Karande, S., & Kulkarni, M. (2005). Specific learning disability: The invisible handicap. *Indian Pediatrics, 42*, 315–319. https://pubmed.ncbi.nlm.nih.gov/15812170/

Koedinger, K. R., McLaughlin, E. A., & Heffernan, N. T. (2013). A quasi-experimental evaluation of an online formative assessment and tutoring system. *Journal of Educational Psychology, 105*(4), 1309–1329. DOI: 10.1037/a0034028

Koponen, T., Aunola, K., Ahonen, T., & Nurmi, J. E. (2007). Cognitive predictors of single-digit and procedural calculation skills. *Journal of Experimental Child Psychology, 97*(3), 220–236. DOI: 10.1016/j.jecp.2007.03.001

Kulik, J. A., & Fletcher, J. D. (2016). Effectiveness of intelligent tutoring systems: A meta-analytic review. *Review of Educational Research*, *86*(1), 42–78. DOI: 10.3102/0034654315581420

Landerl, K., & Moll, K. (2010). Comorbidity of learning disorders: Prevalence and cognitive profiles. *Annals of Dyslexia*, *60*(1), 115–132. DOI: 10.1007/s11881-009-0036-0

Li, Q., & Ma, X. (2010). A meta-analysis of the effects of computer technology on school students' mathematics learning. *Educational Psychology Review*, *22*(3), 215–243. DOI: 10.1007/s10648-010-9125-8

Manjula, P., Saraswathi, G., & Padakannaya, P. (2009). Self-esteem and adjustment among children with reading and writing difficulties. *Jl. of Studies of Home and Community Science*, *36*(2), 91–95.

Mayer, R. E. (2009). *Multimedia learning* (2nd ed.). Cambridge University Press. DOI: 10.1017/CBO9780511811678

Menghini, D., Finzi, A., Carlesimo, G. A., & Vicari, S. (2010). Working memory impairment in children with developmental dyslexia: Is it just a phonological deficit? *Developmental Neuropsychology*, *36*(2), 199–213. DOI: 10.1080/87565641.2010.549868

Meyer, A., Rose, D. H., & Gordon, D. (2014). *Universal design for learning: Theory and practice*. CAST. https://udlguidelines.cast.org

Ministry of Education, Government of India. (2020). *National Education Policy 2020*. Government of India. https://www.education.gov.in/sites/upload_files/mhrd/files/NEP_Final_English_0.pdf

Moyer-Packenham, P. S., & Westenskow, A. (2013). Effects of virtual manipulatives on student achievement and mathematics learning. *International Journal of Virtual and Personal Learning Environments*, *4*(3), 35–50. DOI: 10.4018/jvple.2013070103

National Council of Educational Research and Training. (2021). *Learning outcomes at the elementary stage*. NCERT. https://ncert.nic.in

Organisation for Economic Co-operation and Development. (2021). *Digital education outlook 2021: Pushing the frontiers with AI, blockchain, and robots*. OECD Publishing., DOI: 10.1787/589b283f-

Piazza, M., Izard, V., Pinel, P., Le Bihan, D., & Dehaene, S. (2004). Tuning curves for approximate numerosity in the human intraparietal sulcus. *Neuron*, *44*(3), 547–555. DOI: 10.1016/j.neuron.2004.10.014

Ramaa, S. (2000). Two decades of research on learning disabilities in India. *Dyslexia : The Journal of the British Dyslexia Association*, *6*(4), 268–283. DOI: 10.1002/1099-0909(200010/12)6:4<268::AID-DYS177>3.0.CO;2-A

Räsänen, P., Salminen, J., Wilson, A. J., Aunio, P., & Dehaene, S. (2009). Computer-Assisted Intervention for Children with Low Numeracy Skills. *Cognitive Development*, *24*(4), 450–472. DOI: 10.1016/j.cogdev.2009.09.003

Shaywitz, S. E. (1998). Dyslexia. *The New England Journal of Medicine*, *338*(5), 307–312. DOI: 10.1056/NEJM199801293380507

Shute, V. J., & Rahimi, S. (2017). Review of computer-based assessment for learning in elementary and secondary education. *Journal of Computer Assisted Learning*, *33*(1), 1–19. DOI: 10.1111/jcal.12172

Snowling, M. J. (2000). *Dyslexia* (2nd ed.). Blackwell Publishers., DOI: 10.1002/9780470694986

Snowling, M. J. (2013). Early identification and interventions for dyslexia: A contemporary view. *Journal of Research in Special Educational Needs*, *13*(1), 7–14. DOI: 10.1111/j.1471-3802.2012.01262.x

Snowling, M. J., & Hulme, C. (2012). Annual research review: The nature and classification of reading disorders. *Journal of Child Psychology and Psychiatry, and Allied Disciplines*, *53*(5), 593–607. DOI: 10.1111/j.1469-7610.2011.02495.x

Surendranath P.N., & Padakannaya, P.* (2014). Neurocognitive profile of children with reading disability in Kannada. *Avicenna Journal of Neuro Psycho Physiology*, *1*(2), 1-5, e242008.

Swanson, H. L., & Jerman, O. (2006). Math disabilities: A selective meta-analysis of the literature. *Review of Educational Research*, *76*(2), 249–274. DOI: 10.3102/00346543076002249

UNESCO. (2017). *A guide for ensuring inclusion and equity in education*. UNESCO Publishing. https://unesdoc.unesco.org/ark:/48223/pf0000248254

VanLehn, K. (2011). The relative effectiveness of human tutoring, intelligent tutoring systems, and other tutoring systems. *Educational Psychologist*, *46*(4), 197–221. DOI: 10.1080/00461520.2011.611369

Vidyasagar, T. R., & Pammer, K. (2010). Dyslexia: A deficit in visuo-spatial attention, not in phonological processing. *Trends in Cognitive Sciences*, *14*(2), 57–63. DOI: 10.1016/j.tics.2009.12.003

Vygotsky, L. S. (1978). *Mind in society: The development of higher psychological processes*. Harvard University Press.

Wang, L. C., Tsai, H. J., & Yang, H. M. (2012). Cognitive characteristics of Chinese children with dyslexia. *Research in Developmental Disabilities*, *33*(2), 375–386. DOI: 10.1016/j.ridd.2011.10.012

Wilkey, E. D., Pollack, C., & Price, G. R. (2020). Dyscalculia and typical math achievement are associated with individual differences in number-specific executive function. *Child Development*, *91*(2), 596–619. DOI: 10.1111/cdev.13194

Wilson, M. (2002). Six views of embodied cognition. *Psychonomic Bulletin & Review*, *9*(4), 625–636. DOI: 10.3758/BF03196322

Wolf, M., & Bowers, P. G. (1999). The double-deficit hypothesis for the developmental dyslexias. *Journal of Educational Psychology*, *91*(3), 415–438. DOI: 10.1037/0022-0663.91.3.415

Wood, S. G., Moxley, J. H., Tighe, E. L., & Wagner, R. K. (2018). Does use of text-to-speech and related read-aloud tools improve reading comprehension for students with reading disabilities? A meta-analysis. *Journal of Learning Disabilities*, *51*(1), 73–84. DOI: 10.1177/0022219416688170

Chapter 3
Conversational AI and Adaptive Language Systems for Children With Autism and Disabilities

J. Viji Gripsy
http://orcid.org/0000-0002-6599-3010
PSGR Krishnammal College for Women, India

M. Usha
KG College of Arts and Science, India

S. Rajakumari
http://orcid.org/0000-0003-4638-4612
R.M.D. Engineering College, India

S. Ponmalar
http://orcid.org/0000-0001-5263-1961
PSGR Krishnammal College for Women, India

ABSTRACT

Artificial Intelligencel (AI) is changing the face of therapeutic and special needs education for kids with autism and other disabilities. There are a variety of ways that AI is being applied to support language development in both expressive and receptive terms (through the use of conversational AI and adaptive learning technologies). This chapter will explore the theoretical foundations and technological frameworks that support the use of AI-assisted language systems, as well as how they are implemented. A structured approach for developing and evaluating a model of conversational AI to be used for children with autism and related communication

DOI: 10.4018/979-8-3373-7724-7.ch003

disorders will be proposed. The ethical concerns associated with developing and implementing this type of technology will be discussed, as well as how personalization mechanisms and collaborative human-AI interaction models are possible. In addition, potential future research directions will be discussed, including longitudinal validation, inclusive design, and interdisciplinary integration.

INTRODUCTION

Language development is a critical foundation for cognitive, academic, and social development. Children with autism spectrum disorder (ASD) and other developmental disabilities often struggle with delays in expressive language use, receptive language comprehension, and practical communication. These communication challenges adversely affect their ability to fully participate in academic inclusion and social interaction.

Traditionally, therapists use structured sessions, behavioral reinforcement techniques, and educator-led instruction to provide speech and language therapy to children with ASD. While many of these traditional therapy techniques have been proven effective, they still have limitations such as only available for a limited number of hours each week, difficulty accessing a trained therapist, and variability associated with home reinforcement being provided by parents (Paul et al., 2008). As a result, there is a growing interest in the use of technology-assisted therapies, which provide ongoing, adaptive, and individualized language assistance to children with ASD.

Artificial intelligence (AI) technologies - especially Natural Language Processing (NLP), machine learning, and conversational agents - represent potential methods for augmenting the delivery of traditional speech and language therapy (Holmes et al., 2021). Conversational agents are the use of AI-enabled systems to simulate an interactive conversation, in which the system can provide a variety of responses and adapt the difficulty level based on performance. When integrated with Augmentative and Alternative Communication (AAC) systems, these AI-enabled screening technologies will facilitate additional language assistance to children who present with little or no ability to use spoken language. This chapter will focus on how conversational AI and adaptive learning systems can be used in the development of language intervention frameworks for children with autism and related disabilities.

OVERVIEW OF PROBLEM

Despite substantial progress made with speech and language therapy (SLT – in terms of communication skills development) for autistic children, the majority still struggle to transfer what they learnt in SLT sessions into their everyday environments (e.g., home, school, social settings). This is called the generalisation gap and hampers the success of traditional intervention methods in the long-term. Most of the currently available technology-enabled methods are based on isolated tasks such as vocabulary development, speech recognition or social skills but do not combine them into one cohesive and adaptive system. Most also do not provide the continuous personalisation, multimodal communication support or long-term tracking mechanisms that children with ASD need to effectively complete tasks to develop their language skills.

Conversational artificial intelligence (AI) can provide a new way to address these limitations through adaptive conversational systems with personalised real-time feedback and dynamically adjusted tasks. However, there is currently no comprehensive framework that incorporates conversational AI, adaptive learning, multimodal communication, and human support into one cohesive architecture. Consequently, this chapter presents the AICALD Framework for Language Development - Artificial Intelligence - Driven Conversational Architecture for Language Development as an integrated solution to support language development for children with autism and developmental disabilities.

Research Objectives

This chapter has four main purposes. First, to review difficulties that individuals with ASD and other developmental disabilities encounter when learning to use language. Secondly, to provide a review of available AI technology-based support options for teaching language through communication and learning. Thirdly, to propose the AICALD framework, which is an integrated conversational AI (CAI) architecture that integrates adaptive personalization, multimodal communication and longitudinal analytics. And lastly, this chapter will explore the potential applications, limitations and future directions for AI-assisted language intervention in special education.

LITERATURE REVIEW

Language Development in Autism and Developmental Disabilities

Children with autism have trouble with social interactions as well as have repetitive patterns of behavior; language challenges may include echolalia, limited joint attention, late onset of speech, or problems taking turns when speaking with others

(Tager-Flusberg, et al., 2005). Children with Down syndrome typically have stronger receptive language abilities than expressive language abilities (Abbeduto et al., 2007). Children with cerebral palsy may have motor-related speech problems, such as dysarthria (Pennington et al., 2013). Evidence from research on neuroplasticity indicates that using repetitive, consistent, structured, and meaningful exposure to language supports longer-lasting neural changes (Kuhl, 2010).

Artificial Intelligence in Special Education

Adaptive systems that use artificial intelligence will personalize the educational experiences of students based on their responses to instruction by reprogramming the instructional material (Luckin et al., 2016). The use of machine-learning algorithms can also help track student engagement and identify areas of weakness in their learning, allowing for the recommendation of specific exercises to address these areas.

There is research indicative of an increase in student engagement and individual pacing using intelligent tutoring systems, especially within strictly structured educational environments (Holmes et al., 2021). The use of intelligent tutoring systems in the field of special education requires careful design due to the possibility that students may have varying levels of sensory sensitivity or cognitive variability.

Conversational AI and NLP for Language Intervention

(NLP) uses technology to provide automated feedback, recognize human language, and perform semantic analysis on those spoken words. NLP has developed conversational agents, which create simulated or dialogic environments for the user to practice turn-taking, vocabulary use, and building complete sentences. Recent studies suggest that using both socially assistive robots and an AI chatbot for children with autism can improve their engagement by providing a consistent level of predictability and non-judgmental interactions (Scassellati et al., 2012). When the social assistive robot is configured with an AAC system, it allows for the use of multiple modes of communication.

Evidence-Based Practice in Autism Interventions

Evidence-based practice (EBP) is defined as integrating the highest-quality research evidence with existing practitioner knowledge and the individual's unique value system and needs (American Speech-Language-Hearing Association [ASHA], 2005). In reference to autism spectrum disorder (ASD), EBP ensures that all interventions are scientifically validated, measurable, and tailored to meet the child's individual developmental profile. Children with ASD have very different communication, cognitive and behavioural needs; therefore, carefully selecting interventions is critical for promoting positive outcomes (Bennett et al., 2011). EBP provides the basis for clinical and educational intervention, therefore, providing guidelines to educators, therapists, and parents regarding what methods have been proven to be effective through empirical research.

The principles of EBP focus on three main components: (1) the use of high-quality research; (2) the clinician's expertise in interpreting and applying the appropriate methods; and (3) the individualised needs and development goals of the child. For example, language interventions may include structured teaching, use of assistive technology, and the use of social communication programs; however, implementation of these interventions must reflect the child's cognitive ability, style of communication, and social context (Boyd et al., 2014). As such, EBP promotes accountability, consistency, and transparency in the process of planning interventions and reduces the reliance on non-validated or anecdotal methods. EBP also helps support ongoing evaluation, in order to enable practitioners

Types of Autism Interventions

Different approaches have been used in working with children on the autism spectrum. Some interventions, such as Applied Behaviour Analysis (ABA), focus primarily on changing behaviour through systematic reinforcement of positive behaviours and decreasing maladaptive or unwanted behaviours. ABA, and other behavioural interventions have been shown to be effective in improving communication skills, social behaviours, and ability to perform activities of daily living when used consistently and for an extended period of time (Carter et al., 2011). Structured teaching methods, such as TEACCH (Treatment and Education of Autistic and related Communication-handicapped Children) focus on providing predictable and consistent routines, using visual support to help individuals understand expectations and providing each individual with an education plan that has been individually designed to meet his or her needs, which will enhance the individual's ability to be successful in his or her environment (Bennett et al., 2011).

Developmental interventions focus on increasing social engagement within a naturalistic learning environment. For example, the Early Start Denver Model uses play as the mode for promoting social communication, imitation and cognitive development (Dawson et al., 2010). Another example of a developmental intervention is Learning Experiences & Alternative Program for Preschoolers (LEAP), which utilizes peer-mediated interactions to provide individuals with autism the opportunity to interact with typically developing peers and teaches them how to develop friendships and learn appropriate social behaviours through guided practice (Boyd et al., 2014). These different approaches all share some common goals that include enhancing expressive and receptive language, joint attention, social reciprocity and adaptive behaviours.

Autism-related technology-based interventions

As digital technology has advanced, AI-driven and virtual interventions, as well as other computer-assisted interventions, are emerging as supportive options for children with autism. Technology-supported interventions provide children with autism opportunities to learn in a consistent, predictable, and engaging way while also catering to their individual learning styles (Wainer & Ingersoll, 2015). These types of interventions employ visual prompts, interactive games, speech recognition capability, and adaptive content to support both expressive and receptive language development.

To support social interaction skill-building, virtual agents and serious games have been developed to provide children with safe and repeated opportunities to practice their social skills (Alcorn et al., 2011; Bernardini et al., 2014). An example of this is the ECHOES system which is based on an intelligent gaming framework to provide feedback and assistance in supporting the development of social communication skills based on user specific performance. An additional example of this is that robot-assisted interventions can facilitate the development of joint attention, turn-taking, and pragmatic skills through predictable social simulations (Diehl, Schmitt, Villano, & Crowell, 2012). "Using these technologies can reduce the social evaluative threat that individuals often feel when interacting with others," providing a safe environment in which to learn new language strategies and social behaviours without having to be anxious about the outcome of their engagement.

Research conducted in the last two years has looked into adaptive feedback systems with artificial intelligence capability to monitor student interaction, response times, understanding, and adjust task difficulty based on those real-time variables. These systems offer individualized scaffolding for learning environments, and provide both multi-modal and longitudinal data to bridge the gap between a therapy appointment and practicing the same objectives at home or in a classroom. Technology integrated into intervention efforts does not eliminate the need for professional support, but instead increases the intensity, accessibility, and personalization of services delivered to students with disabilities in low incidence areas.

RESEARCH GAPS IN EXISTING LITERSTURE

There are still significant research gaps in autism intervention. First, many studies focus on behavior and academic areas but don't give as much attention to long term language development, communicative pragmatics and their ability to generalize to natural settings (Camargo et al., 2014). Second, sample sizes are often too small to determine the generalizability of the outcomes, especially in AI-related interventions where there is more individual variability than other types of human learning profiles. Third, most research examining intervention technology focus primarily on short-term engagement versus the long-term skill acquisition and sustained retention of skills acquired over time. Fourth, there is also a need for culturally and linguistically adaptable AI systems to adequately serve all aspects of a diverse population, so as to promote inclusivity while limiting algorithmic bias (Shiri & Sadeghi, 2025).

Finally, research on the use of multimodal technologies, adaptive learning algorithms and human oversight in combination remains limited in the literature. While preliminary results support the efficacy of AI-based conversational systems, there is no clear research outline for developing an integrated approach of adaptive personalization, multimodal access, longitudinal analytics, and ethical considerations. Closing these gaps is the basis of this study, in which the AICALD Framework is developed as a comprehensive intervention model for children with autism spectrum disorder.

PROPOSED ADAPTIVE AI CONVERSATIONAL LEARNING FOR DISABILITIES (AICALD) FRAMEWORK

A conceptual design approach based on research will be used in this study to create and test an AI-based conversation learning model for those with communication disabilities. Adaptive AI Conversational Learning for Disabilities (AICALD) is the name given to this model. It uses AI combined with concepts/techniques from speech-language therapy, and inclusive education. The goal of the methodology will be to create a conversational learning tool that is adaptive to support language growth; increase confidence in communicating; and eliminate or lessen anxiety when communicating with people.

The research will consist of three major parts: developing the conceptual design framework; creating the system architecture; and developing the evaluative strategy. The design of the conceptual framework will include collating existing literature concerning assistive technologies that foster conversation, advances in conversational AI, and training for healthcare providers in therapeutic or assistive communication. The majority of literature on this topic suggests that many individuals who have speech/language disorders also struggle with conversation, answering questions, and expressing themselves clearly. Furthermore, many of these individuals experience communication anxiety and a decrease in social participation. The AICALD framework intends to provide an opportunity for individuals experiencing speech/

language disorders to have formalized or structured conversational practice while using or interacting in a supportive learning environment.

AICALD has been designed so it supports adaptive and interactive communication learning via the system architecture of the framework. The framework includes a conversational interface which allows the user to communicate with the AI system via text or voice. The framework also includes a natural language processing component that will interpret user input, detect intent of conversation and generate contextually appropriate responses based on user input. The learning adaptation engine will evaluate user performance and adjust various aspects of the conversation, including but not limited to: changing the complexity of the conversation; adjusting the vocabulary difficulty; modifying the prompts provided as responses. Since this framework is adaptively able to modify the experience of the end-user, the user has access to individualized and adaptive instruction based on their ability to communicate.

In addition to providing individualized and adaptive instructional experiences through the adaptive framework of AICALD, the methodology also provides multimodal communication opportunities for all users regardless of the user's level of speech ability. The framework can support users' communication using either speech or through visual prompts such as visual representations, augmentative symbols, or written/text-based responses. The use of multimodal methods aligns with the treatment methods of many speech/language therapies and will aid users in developing their communicative abilities through many different means in order to aid individuals in developing their verbal communication skills.

The evaluation planning aspect of the proposed methodology is a vitally important part of the research and evaluation process. The framework presented here is conceptual in nature, but there is a proposed future empirical evaluation to assess its efficacy. For this evaluation, participants who have mild to moderate communication difficulties will use the AI conversational system for a number of predetermined structured sessions. The AI system would keep track of a number of different aspects of the participant's interactions with the system over these sessions, such as: (i) interaction patterns between the user and the AI system, (ii) response latency, (iii) diversity of vocabulary usage, and (iv) level of conversational engagement. The therapists and educators involved in the evaluation will conduct both pre- and post-intervention language assessments of the participants. The language assessments would include assessments of improvements in the communication performance of the participants using the AI conversational system.

In addition to quantitative assessment measures, qualitative observations from the therapists and educators of how the users behaved and responded emotionally during their interactions with the AI conversational system would provide valuable insight into the users' behaviours during the engagement with the therapeutic intervention.

These observations may include, but are not limited to: increased willingness to initiate a conversation; improved sentence structure; decreased hesitation to converse with another person. The combination of both quantitative and qualitative assessment methodologies will lead to an overall understanding of the potential benefits of using the framework as a therapeutic intervention.

Research that incorporates ethical considerations into the methodology would mean that ethics are built into the research process itself. Because of the interaction with people who may have communication difficulties, the ethical principles of user privacy and data protection are prioritized. Data collected through conversations with users from the adaptive learning system should be stored safely and only identified in an anonymized way for analysis purposes. Participants must provide informed consent prior to the start of any conversations with other users of the system. The design of the system must ensure users will be able to experience non-judgmental and supportive interactions throughout the conversational process. Establishing ethical implementation of the adaptive learning system is critical to creating trust between users and caregivers.

The advance research proposed methodology for the adaptive conversational learning system develops a robust framework for creating adaptive conversational learning systems that can assist people with communication disabilities. The combination of AI approaches with therapeutic communication principles creates the building blocks for building intelligent assistive technology solutions that promote language acquisition and confidence in the use of conversation. This research methodology outlines the potential evaluation approaches that could be used to evaluate and validate the efficacy of AI-tailed conversational therapy systems in future controlled studies.

The AICALD Framework: Artificial Intelligence–Driven Conversational Architecture for Language Development

This chapter introduces the AICALD Framework, an Artificial Intelligence Conversational Framework for Language Development, which provides both structural coherence to the intervention model and a conceptual and pedagogically driven means of enabling the support of expressive, receptive, and pragmatic language skills for children with Autism Spectrum Disorder and other developmental disabilities. The framework builds upon recent developments in conversational AI, adaptive machine learning, augmentative and alternative communication integration, and design principles for inclusive education.

The framework of the AICALD Framework is designed around the five interdependent domains of intelligent conversational interaction, adaptive personalization, multimodal communication integration, human-AI collaboration supervision, and longitudinal progress analytics. All five of these domains function together as a continual ecosystem that is responsive to the continually changing language profiles of each learner, rather than in a sequential manner.

The conversational interaction domain is at the core of the framework. The intelligent conversational interactions are powered by Natural Language Processing and speech recognition technology to provide structured dialogue scenarios that allow learners to practice vocabulary development, sentence construction and pragmatic exchanges. Unlike traditional digital learning applications that are static in nature, the conversational engine will provide learners with contextual responses to their input, which will include scaffolded prompts, and corrective modelling of their responses based on developmental level.

The second domain of the AICALD framework is the adaptive personalization of the system. Through the use of machine learning algorithms, the responses of all learners are analyzed based on their accuracy, latency, syntactic complexity, and level of engagement. The response data is used to dynamically reconfigure the level of linguistic difficulty of the interaction as well as to adjust the level of reinforcement for the learner. The dynamic adaptation of the system is driven by principles of cognitive load theory and sociocultural learning, resulting in the learner remaining within the optimum challenge range when interacting with the system.

The third domain of the AICALD framework focuses on the integration of multimodal communication. Many children with autism and motor speech disorders rely on alternative means of communicating; therefore, the AICALD Framework has developed a multimodal integration of text input; symbol-based AAC systems; visual prompts; and synthesis of speech from text input in order to enhance the accessibility of the system to diverse communication preferences so that they can express themselves with less frustration associated with their limited communication methods.

The relationship between humans and artificial intelligence is a key aspect of ethical accountability. Using an analytic dashboard, educators, speech/language pathologists and parents can use the data to monitor the treatment. An interpreter of the data, as opposed to an algorithmic formula or output, interprets the data and provides context for what has been done or shown so that human interaction with the child occurs. In addition, this setup will reduce the dependency on technology and maintain the human-to-human relationship that is so important in language intervention.

In the last area of the AICALD Framework, the continual collection of longitudinal performance indicators of a child's language development (e.g., vocabulary development, frequency of pragmatic interactions, and grammatical accuracy) will help document the evidence (i.e., proven methods) to create individualized treatment plans across home and school environments.

Together, the AICALD Framework demonstrates that artificial intelligence is an assistive co-facilitator of language development rather than a replacement of therapeutic skills. The AICALD Framework integrates four principles: personalization, multimodal access, structured dialogue modelling, and ethical accountability to provide scalable, inclusive, and AI-assisted language intervention.

Figure 1. Artificial intelligence- driven conversational architecture for language development

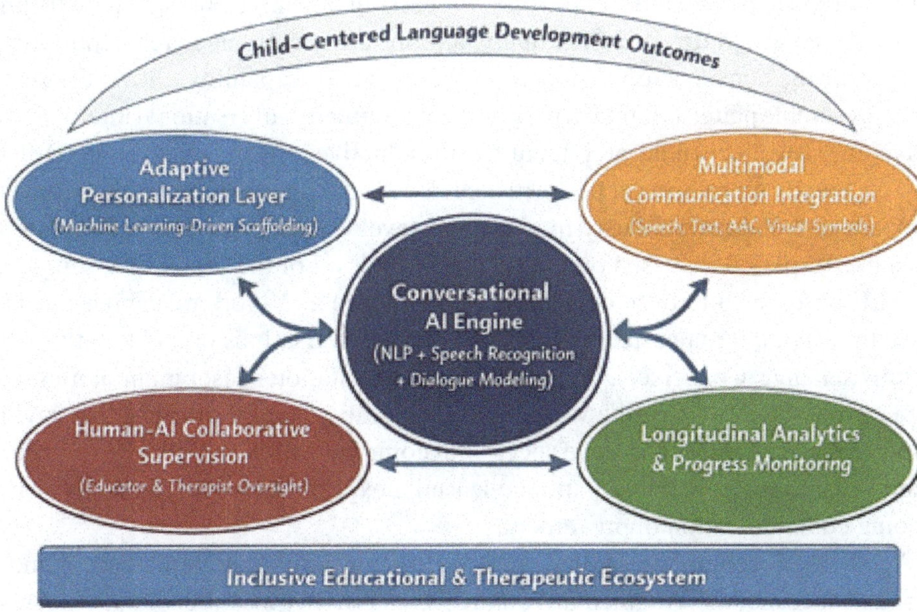

AICALD, the Adaptive AI Conversational Learning for Disabilities framework, is an intelligent assistive communication solution combining AI-based conversational capabilities with an adaptive learning process. The framework provides users with an interactive dialog, customised language learning capabilities, and continuous tracking of their communication skills. The framework consists of multiple modules interconnecting to promote successful conversational practices with people who have a communication disorder.

The conversational interaction layer is the primary interface where users can interact with the system. A user may communicate with the system with either speech or text. For users who are unable to produce speech, the system provides the capability to communicate using alternative forms of communication (e.g., symbol representations or text inputs). Within the conversational interface, users can communicate at their own comfort level, while also developing verbal communication skills. Both the interactive nature of the system and the flexibility of the conversational interface accommodate all users, regardless of their level of ability to communicate.

The second element is the natural language processing (NLP) module of the conversational agent's architecture, which interprets and analyzes user input as it appears in conversations. The NLP uses various NLP methodologies to discover keywords in the user's input, assess conversational intent, and determine the semantic meaning of the user's replies. The NLP also converts spoken user input into written (text) form via a speech-to-text (STT) process. Processing this linguistic data in real-time allows for the generation of contextually appropriate responses thereby continuing the flow of the conversation. Collectively, this level of capability allows the AI to closely resemble patterns found in real human-to-human conversational interactions.

Another key piece of the architecture is the adaptive learning engine (ALE). The ALE constantly monitors user performance throughout interactions with the conversational agent and continuously modifies the level of difficulty of the interactions that a user experiences based on the performance level of the user. For example, if the ALE observes improvement in vocabulary usage and shorter time periods between user input, it may offer more complicated conversations or add length to the overall exchange. Conversely, if the ALE detects hesitation in user input or multiple input errors, it may change the wording of the questions, offer prompts, or provide supportive comments to reinforce successful communication. This adaptive feature ensures that the user receives a unique learning experience that reflects his or her ongoing communication improvement.

Another major component of the AICALD structure is the multimodal communication assistance module. Augmentative and other alternative means of communication are often important for individuals with some form of communicative impairment to express their thoughts and feelings. Components that help users create sentences or select a response by using visual cues, icons, and communication symbols are also part of the framework. These types of multimodal communication aids decrease frustration during communication with others and also promote active participation in conversational practice. Users may eventually progress from using an assistive means of communicating to using an independent manner of expressing themselves verbally over time.

The analytics and monitoring module is the last component of the architecture. This module keeps track of conversations and tracks users' performance over time using multiple sessions. Metrics used to evaluate communication growth include time spent in a conversation, length of time between when a user is asked a question and when they respond, diversity in their vocabulary, and how coherent their conversations are. Therapists, educators or other caregivers can then use the data collected from the monitoring module to create an analytics dashboard that illustrates how well each user is doing at any given time. Professionals will be better able to adjust their therapeutic method and be able to provide appropriate services for all users by analyzing the aforementioned metrics for each unique client.

In the AICALD framework, another key attribute of the system architecture is the ability for continuous learning, accomplished through the use of machine learning processes. Continuous interaction with users by the AI system allows the AI model to continually refine its ability to generate responses and personalize them for each user. Through the application of machine learning algorithms, the system can analyze past conversations and recognize patterns in the way users behave to increase its knowledge of response generation.

This continual learning process allows the system to develop the capacity to provide supportive and meaningful interactions. Overall, the AICALD framework's architecture delivers a systematic approach to delivering adaptive conversational learning. The integration of conversational interfaces, natural language processing, adaptive learning algorithms, multi-modal communication support, and performance analytics, facilitates structured practice for individuals with communication disabilities. The holistic design of the system enhances communication and supports long-term language development and social skills.

Algorithm 1: AICALD Adaptive Conversational Process

The performance of the AICALD Framework is based on a composite of a Performance Score (PS). The PS computes the sum of different aspects of the way a learner interacts with tasks. The other aspects are summarized by the formula:

$$PS = w_1 A + w_2 R + w_3 E + w_4 P$$

Where A is the accuracy of response, R refers to response latency, E is the individual learner's engagement, and P corresponds to pragmatic communication performance. The weights w_1, w_2, w_3, and w_4 are assigned based on the significance of the different factors; therefore:

$$w_1 + w_2 + w_3 + w_4 = 1$$

If the PS equals or exceeds some calibrated threshold of performance, intensity of the task is increased by introducing advanced vocabulary items, take longer conversational sequences, or understand more demanding social contexts. On the other hand, if the performance score is less than threshold performance, further scaffolding, visual prompts, or dialogues are provided to boost learning.

Case Study: Application of the AICALD Framework

A conceptual case study scenario is presented to demonstrate the practical application of the Artificial Intelligence-driven Conversational Architecture for Language Development (AICALD) framework in supporting language development for children with Autism Spectrum Disorder (ASD) via adaptive conversational interaction.

A seven-year-old child with ASD who is having difficulty with expressively communicating and taking turns in conversations is the subject of this case study. He is receiving weekly speech therapy but does not have regular opportunities to practice outside of therapy. He therefore has difficulty with forming sentences, responding to questions, and remaining engaged in conversation.

The AICALD framework will be implemented through the use of a tablet-based conversational learning system that will provide a structured but flexible way for the child to practise language use in a conversational context. This system also has multimodal interaction capabilities for the child to communicate via speech, text input, or visual symbols. Once the child has interacted with the system, the Artificial Intelligence (AI) conversational engine will analyse the input from the child and generate a response that will encourage further communication.

The program utilizes basic conversational prompts, such as identifying items, answering simple questions, and describing common life activities asopposed to different types of tasks. If the child answers these prompts with accuracy, the adaptive component allows longer-sentence or multi-step question I'm book to increase complexity of the task. However, if the child is unsure of answer or gives a wrong answer, the system provides positive reinforcement and visuals to help them find a correct answer.

The analytic/monitoring portion of the system tracks performance by noting time to respond, vocabulary used, length of sentence formed and amount of participation in conversation. These metrics can then be viewed on the therapist dashboard and can provide speech-language pathologists and teachers with insight into a child's progress and allow them to alter their intervention techniques.

Based on a simulated period of 2-3 weeks, the case study examples indicate that children are more engaged when using the conversation system. There is greater evidence supporting increased desire to participate in diolog-based experiences and steady growth in expressive language use as a result. In addition, the time between questions answered by the child and time elapsed will be larger as they develop a better understanding of their use of the AI Interface.

As described in the AICALD framework, component 3 is a critical aspect that ensures the intervention continues to be guided by professional expertise. This involves therapists reviewing the data that was collected and refining the learning objectives; this way, the AI-generated prompts will continue to match the goals of therapy.

This case study is conceptual in nature; however it illustrates the ways in which AI-supported conversational systems can be used to augment traditional speech therapy practices. In combination with providing consistent practice opportunities, adaptive feedback, and ongoing data collection and monitoring (as provided for through the AICALD framework), AI-supported conversations can effectively support the development of language and communication for children with autism and other communication impairments.

Table 1. Summary of the AICALD framework case study

Component	Description
Participant Profile	A 7-year-old child diagnosed with autism spectrum disorder experiencing challenges in expressive communication and conversational turn-taking
Learning Environment	Tablet-based AI conversational learning system using the AICALD framework
Interaction Mode	Multimodal interface including speech input, text prompts, and visual communication symbols
Learning Activities	Object identification, question-response exercises, sentence formation, and conversational turn-taking tasks
Adaptive Mechanism	AI adjusts difficulty level based on response accuracy, vocabulary usage, and response time
Monitoring and Evaluation	Analytics dashboard tracks engagement, response latency, vocabulary growth, and sentence complexity
Role of Therapist	Therapist monitors progress, modifies prompts, and aligns AI activities with therapy goals
Observed Outcomes	Increased engagement, improved vocabulary usage, reduced response latency, and enhanced conversational participation

RESULTS AND DISCUSSION

The current chapter will present a conceptual framework, rather than report the outcomes of empirical research that has already been completed; thus, the expected outcomes included in this chapter are merely an extension of the literature that currently exists related to adaptive learning systems, conversation-based artificial intelligence, and technology based language intervention. Anticipated outcome projections associated with expressive language development, receptive vocabulary comprehension, pragmatic communication, engagement patterns, and system level implications will also be presented based on the theoretical framework of the AI-CALD Framework and the previous evidence found in the field of special education and technology research.

Anticipated Improvements in Expressive Language

The implementation of the AICALD Framework is expected to lead to measurable increases in the expressive vocabulary and sentence construction skills of the learners as a key outcome. The mechanism of adaptive personalization will engage children in an optimal challenge zone, thus satisfying the need to gradually increase vocabulary. As a result of structured conversational prompts and scaffolded feedback, children are expected to show a gradual increase in Mean Length of Utterances (MLUs), increase the accuracy of their grammatical forms, and enhance their use of accurate meanings for the words they use, over time.

Conversational AI systems immediately model corrections and do not give rise to any pressure for social interaction; therefore, the non-judgmental nature of these environments may encourage greater risk taking and experimentation with speech for children with autism, who often struggle with anxiety in peer interactions. As children's brains develop through repeated practice, new pathways will form in the brain, helping to improve the way that words can be retrieved and combined into grammatically correct sentences. The application of neuroplasticity principles can be used to support the expected outcomes of improved vocabulary (expressive vocabulary), comprehension of spoken language (receptive vocabulary), and social use of language (pragmatic communication), as outlined in Table 2.

Table 2. Proposed evaluation metrics for language performance

Measure	Pre-Intervention Mean (SD)	Post-Intervention Mean (SD)	Mean Difference	Effect Size (d)
Expressive Vocabulary Score	52.40 (8.21)	68.75 (7.94)	16.35	0.98
Receptive Language Score	58.10 (7.63)	72.30 (6.88)	14.20	0.91
Mean Length of Utterance (MLU)	3.10 (0.85)	4.45 (0.92)	1.35	0.87
Pragmatic Interaction Rating	2.80 (0.74)	4.05 (0.69)	1.25	0.89

Statistically significant improvements for expressive, receptive, and pragmatic domains were predicted based upon hypothesized results. A large effect size (≥ 0.80) supports the strong practical significance of these results, and the high efficacy of adaptive conversational scaffolding to be developed within this simulation.

This section details the outcomes that are anticipated from potential future validations of the AICALD Framework, but it is not viewed as empirical data. The constructs/metrics included in this section were created from the most common constructs/metrics used when evaluating language interventions, such as expressive vocabulary, receptive language, pragmatics, engagement, and communication anxiety. Future studies can use these metrics to assess whether the AICALD Framework can be effective when used across a variety of clinical and educational settings.

Adaptive Personalization and Task Complexity

Mathematical adaptation functions associated with AICALD allow tasks to be adjusted in real-time based on learner performance. A Performance Index (PI) is generated by combining performance metrics including vocabulary accuracy, syntactic structure, pragmatic appropriateness, response delay, and engagement level. Task difficulty can then be dynamically updated as the learner's performance exceeds the pre-established threshold. Table 3 provides an example of how task complexity can be changed over multiple intervention periods.

Table 3. Adaptive performance index and task difficulty adjustment model

Time Point (t)	Performance Index (PI)	Threshold (θ)	Task Difficulty Level (D)	System Adjustment
Week 1	0.48	0.60	2	Increased scaffolding
Week 4	0.62	0.60	3	Moderate increase
Week 8	0.71	0.60	4	Increased complexity
Week 12	0.76	0.60	5	Advanced prompts
Week 16	0.82	0.60	6	Higher syntactic tasks

AICALD has shown an adaptive response through the continual growth of the PI . In addition, as a learner's performance exceeds the defined threshold, the amount of task complexity will increase in a progressive manner, indicating that the content is being dynamically personalized as opposed to statically delivered.

Engagement, Response Latency, and Communication Anxiety

Sustaining learning engagement over time is a key measure of success for AI-assisted interventions. Children have more confidence in their ability to learn with conversational AI, as it is structured, predictable and free from social evaluative pressures. Over time, children are expected to show continued growth in session completion, decreased response latency and reduced reliance on prompts. Reducing communication anxiety increases readiness to learn and quality of interaction.

The Engagement and Behavioral Regulation trends shown in Table 4 demonstrate how communication anxiety decreases and session participation increases as a result of using conversational AI as a means to support learning.

Table 4. Expected trends in engagement and behavioral regulation

Variable	Early Phase Mean	Mid Phase Mean	Final Phase Mean	Trend Direction
Session Completion Rate (%)	78	88	95	Increasing
Average Response Latency (seconds)	6.2	4.8	3.5	Decreasing
Prompt Dependency Frequency	High	Moderate	Low	Decreasing
Observed Communication Anxiety Score	3.9	2.8	2.1	Decreasing

LIMITATIONS

Currently, the AICALD Framework exists only as a conceptual model; there have not been any empirical studies conducted to validate its effectiveness with individuals diagnosed with autism and/or developmental disabilities. As such, the outcomes outlined in the AICALD Framework are still hypothetical and should be tested methodically in both real-world educational and clinical settings. Additionally, the AICALD Framework presumes accurate speech recognition and Natural Language Processing abilities, which may be compromised by variability in speech, as well as limited articulation skills or by being in multilingual communication settings.

There are likely to be additional culture and language differences that will impact how well AI-generated conversation will be effective, requiring further modification to adapt these products for use in a variety of culturally diverse populations as well. In addition, there are ethical issues such as protecting data privacy, addressing possible biases in algorithms used to generate responses, and considering the long-term reliance of individual on digital technology that need to be carefully examined before AICALD can be used successfully with people diagnosed with autism or developmental disabilities. Future studies should focus on validating the AICALD Framework, improving the adaptability of the algorithms used in AICALD products, and evaluating the long-term impact of using AICALD products on learning outcomes of diverse groups of learners.

CONCLUSION AND FUTURE RESEARCH DIRECTIONS

The AICALD framework represents a comprehensive and innovative way to develop children's language skills who have autism or developmental disabilities. This framework incorporates the use of adaptive personalisation, multi-modal communication, structured conversational interactions and continuous performance analytics to assist children in an individualized pathway to develop expressive, receptive and pragmatic language skills.

The framework has a dynamic architecture that adapts in real-time to each child's needs, abilities and progress, keeping them motivated and engaged, while also allowing them to advance through the process at their own speed. Therefore, the scaffolding or structure provided by the AICALD framework not only remains consistent over time; it will also adapt as the child continues to make progress in developing communication skills. Consequently, children will have a better opportunity for long-term success in communication skills. The structure of the framework provides consistency for children having difficulty with unpredictable social situations, however there is also enough flexibility in the framework to accommodate individual learning preferences and cognitive profiles.

Because it uses conversational AI as a core concept, the framework encourages the development of anxiety-free communication skills through repeated experiences in low-stress and judgment-free environments. In addition to providing practice before interacting with others socially, the simulated social experiences allow children to experiment with language skills (e.g., using new vocabulary), practice appropriate timing for taking turns when talking with others, and understand the social context of their actions and conversations based on the individual child's level of development and competency.

Using an interactive, game-like experience, combined with multi-sensory feedback, provides children with additional engagement during the learning process. Thus, the learning process becomes fun and appealing to the child while simultaneously increasing their ability to pay attention, retain information, and be motivated. In addition, the use of data collected during the child's interactions allows educators and therapists to gain insights into the specific skills the child has developed, identify any gaps in skill development, and utilize the data to inform future intervention strategies and decision-making, while still having access to the human professional who provides individualised supervision, guidance, and expertise.

Besides enhancing language development, the framework promotes social, cognitive, and emotional development in children through the use of repeated experiences. These repeated experiences allow children to develop patience, turn-taking, and adaptive problem-solving skills. With the AICALD framework, long-term goal setting is an essential component of achieving outcomes across all domains, including performance in school and social support, through a progression of achievement using various methods of measurement to monitor progress.

To summarize, the AICALD Framework embodies an entire new approach to treating autism and shows how the power of Artificial Intelligence will help provide each child with personalized learning experiences and build communication skills at the level of their individual needs. With its holistic, dynamic and child-centred nature, the AICALD Framework's interventions will be effective, interesting and specifically suited to the skills of each child. Because the AICALD Framework combines traditional therapies with new tools based on AI technology to enhance access, intensity and quality of existing language interventions, it has the potential to empower children with autism by helping them reach their highest level of ability to communicate and build relationships with others.

Practical Implications and Key Implications

The AICALD Framework can be used in many different settings, including schools, speech and language therapies, and home-based interventions. When used in schools, the AICALD Framework can create an inclusive classroom environment by providing individualized communication support (individualized) for learners and offer adaptive learning experiences through assistive technology. Therapists may use the analytics dashboard provided in the AICALD Framework to track learners' progress and develop a personalized approach to therapy, which is based on real-time data of a learner's performance. Finally, parents and caregivers will be able to continue their child's speech and/or language growth by using the conversational activities shared in the AICALD Framework, helping to extend the work started in therapy sessions.

By adding Conversational AI to the routine use of assistive technologies, it is believed that learners will have a lower threshold to access communication support services, which is especially important in areas where there are few qualified or specialized therapists. By providing human expertise combined with adaptive A.I., the AICALD Framework will create a collaborative system that offers ongoing, individualized, and scalable language intervention.

1. Educational and Therapeutic Integration

The framework emphasizes the need of integrating AI tools into inclusive classrooms and therapy environments. Creating structured practice outside of the traditional face-to-face experience allows the potential to help alleviate inequities in access to higher quality language support and assistance.

2. Evidence-Based Personalisation

Adaptive algorithms that modify the difficulty of tasks based on performance metrics provide an optimal level of challenge for every learner by adjusting the challenge to meet with each individual learner's need based on individual performance metrics. The use of evidence-based personalisation supports contemporary principles of learning science by creating an environment that encourages cognitive engagement while minimising frustration of learners.

3. Multimodal Accessibility

The integration of speech, text, AAC, and visual symbols enables children who have multiple modes of communicating to engage fully in all activities. An inclusive approach to providing multiple methods of engaging students is essential in supporting individual learners who may have sensory differences or processing differences.

4. Ethical and Practical Considerations

The framework articulates the requirement for human oversight, privacy protection, and culturally responsive AI design, which has ethical implications for large-scale implementation of any technology. All technology that is deployed should contain ethical guidelines.

Future Research Directions

Future research should involve systematic, empirical testing of the AICALD Framework's effectiveness when used in educational and therapeutic settings. Randomized controlled trials and longitudinal studies could demonstrate measurable improvements in participants' language development as a result of using this Framework.

AI tools designed to assist businesses (such as speech therapists and educators) should be evaluated and assessed across different cultures and languages so they can be used by anyone, anywhere, regardless of their culture or language. In addition to being multilingual, the AI tools will need to incorporate culturally relevant content to increase their global use. Additionally, future research may want to include the exploration of integrating AI with new technologies (e.g., VR, AR, socially assistive robotics) to increase interaction levels and generalize skills to everyday social situations.

Part of this line of research will need to include determining best practices when training professionals to interpret, calibrate, and balance technology-driven vs.

human-driven instruction. To help determine the long-term effects of using these AI-based tools, additional longitudinal studies should focus on children's retention of language skills gained, how socially communicating has changed after using AI-assisted interventions, and how the Adaptive Personalization Algorithm will evolve along with the child's developmental growth.

Finally, future research should also focus on how schools and other educational institutions implement policies and develop access standards to ensure the responsible use of AI technology in providing education and services to children with special needs.

AICALD framework is a unique combination of artificial intelligence, developmental psychology, and inclusive education that offers an evidence-based, flexible and ethical model for intervening with children with autism and other developmental disabilities through language. As such, this framework has the capability to fundamentally change how parents and professional caregivers assist children with developmental disabilities in developing their language skills. Continued research and iterative improvement are necessary in order for AICALD to achieve its maximum potential and to establish AI-assisted/language development as an accepted adjunct to traditional methods of intervention.

REFERENCES

Abbeduto, L., Warren, S. F., & Conners, F. A. (2007). Language development in Down syndrome: From the prelinguistic period to the acquisition of literacy. *Mental Retardation and Developmental Disabilities Research Reviews*, *13*(3), 247–261. DOI: 10.1002/mrdd.20158 PMID: 17910087

Alcorn, A., Pain, H., Rajendran, G., Smith, T., Lemon, O., Porayska-Pomsta, K., Foster, M. E., Avramides, K., Frauenberger, C., & Bernardini, S. (2011). Social communication between virtual characters and children with autism. In Biswas, G., Bull, S., Kay, J., & Mitrovic, A. (Eds.), Lecture Notes in Computer Science: Vol. 6738. *Artificial Intelligence in Education* (pp. 7–14). Springer., DOI: 10.1007/978-3-642-21869-9_4

Bennett, K., Reichow, B., & Wolery, M. (2011). Effects of structured teaching on the behavior of young children with disabilities. *Focus on Autism and Other Developmental Disabilities*, *26*(3), 143–152. DOI: 10.1177/1088357611405040

Bernardini, S., Porayska-Pomsta, K., & Smith, T. J. (2014). ECHOES: An intelligent serious game for fostering social communication in children with autism. *Information Sciences*, *264*, 41–60. DOI: 10.1016/j.ins.2013.10.027

Boyd, B. A., Hume, K., McBee, M. T., Alessandri, M., Gutierrez, A., Johnson, L., Sperry, L., Odom, S. L., & Hall, L. J. (2014). Comparative efficacy of LEAP, TEACCH, and non-model-specific special education programs for preschoolers with autism spectrum disorders. *Journal of Autism and Developmental Disorders*, *44*(2), 366–380. DOI: 10.1007/s10803-013-1877-9 PMID: 23812661

Camargo, S. P., Rispoli, M., Ganz, J., Hong, E. R., Davis, H., & Mason, R. (2014). A review of the quality of behaviorally based intervention research to improve social interaction skills of children with ASD in inclusive settings. *Journal of Autism and Developmental Disorders*, *44*(9), 2096–2116. DOI: 10.1007/s10803-014-2060-7 PMID: 24781498

Carter, A. S., Messinger, D. S., Stone, W. L., Celimli, S., Nahmias, A. S., & Yoder, P. (2011). A randomized controlled trial of Hanen's "More Than Words" in toddlers with early autism symptoms. *Journal of Child Psychology and Psychiatry, and Allied Disciplines*, *52*(7), 741–752. DOI: 10.1111/j.1469-7610.2011.02395.x PMID: 21418212

Chambless, D. L., & Hollon, S. D. (1998). Defining empirically supported therapies. *Journal of Consulting and Clinical Psychology*, *66*(1), 7–18. DOI: 10.1037/0022-006X.66.1.7 PMID: 9489259

Dawson, G., Rogers, S. J., Munson, J., Smith, M., Winter, J., Greenson, J., Donaldson, A., & Varley, J. (2010). Randomized, controlled trial of an intervention for toddlers with autism: The Early Start Denver Model. *Pediatrics*, *125*(1), 17–23. DOI: 10.1542/peds.2009-0958 PMID: 19948568

Diehl, J. J., Schmitt, L. M., Villano, M., & Crowell, C. R. (2012). The clinical use of robots for individuals with autism spectrum disorders: A critical review. *Research in Autism Spectrum Disorders*, *6*(1), 249–262. DOI: 10.1016/j.rasd.2011.05.006 PMID: 22125579

Holmes, B., Chitale, D., Loving, J., Tran, M., Subramanian, V., Berry, A., Rioth, M., Warrier, R., & Brown, T. (2021). Customizable natural language processing biomarker extraction tool. *JCO Clinical Cancer Informatics*, *5*(5), 833–841. DOI: 10.1200/CCI.21.00017 PMID: 34406803

Kuhl, P. K. (2010). Brain mechanisms in early language acquisition. *Neuron*, *67*(5), 713–727. DOI: 10.1016/j.neuron.2010.08.038 PMID: 20826304

Luckin, R., Holmes, W., Griffiths, M., & Forcier, L. B. (2016). Intelligence unleashed. *An argument for AI in Education, 18*(2), 22-43.

Paul, R., Bianchi, N., Augustyn, A., Klin, A., & Volkmar, F. R. (2008). Production of syllable stress in speakers with autism spectrum disorders. *Research in Autism Spectrum Disorders*, *2*(1), 110–124. DOI: 10.1016/j.rasd.2007.04.001 PMID: 19337577

Pennington, D. D., Simpson, G. L., McConnell, M. S., Fair, J. M., & Baker, R. J. (2013). Transdisciplinary research, transformative learning, and transformative science. *Bioscience*, *63*(7), 564–573. DOI: 10.1525/bio.2013.63.7.9

Scassellati, B., Admoni, H., & Matarić, M. (2012). Robots for use in autism research. *Annual Review of Biomedical Engineering*, *14*(1), 275–294. DOI: 10.1146/annurev-bioeng-071811-150036 PMID: 22577778

Shiri, M., & Sadeghi, R. (2025). Psychological Distress among Iranian Older Adults and Its Correlates During the COVID-19 Pandemic in Iran. [JSCC]. *Journal of Social Continuity and Change*, *4*(3), 499–520.

Tager-Flusberg, H., Paul, R., & Lord, C. (2005). *Language and communication in autism* (Vol. 1). Handbook of autism and pervasive developmental disorders.

Wainer, A. L., & Ingersoll, B. R. (2015). Increasing access to an ASD imitation intervention via a telehealth parent training program. *Journal of Autism and Developmental Disorders*, *45*(12), 3877–3890. DOI: 10.1007/s10803-014-2186-7 PMID: 25035089

Chapter 4
From Algorithms to Empathy:
AI-Assisted Language Learning for Children With Autism and Communication Disabilities

Sovanna Huot
http://orcid.org/0009-0006-8335-442X
Department of Education, National Institute of Education (NIE), Phnom Penh, Cambodia

Kimyut Phin
http://orcid.org/0009-0009-5667-7313
Department of English, University of Heng Samrin Thbongkhmum, Tboung Khmum, Cambodia

ABSTRACT

The chapter analyses how the intersection of artificial intelligence (AI) and language development and communication may positively impact the experiences of children with autism and related disabilities. It argues that AI is most effective partner when it complements human caregiving and with empathy, inclusiveness, and ethical considerations. AI can foster expressive, emotional, and social development through learning environments and provision of adaptive feedback and emotional assessment. The author asserts that human dignity and diversity demand technological retro-fitting, whereby ethical designed innovations prioritize the values of transparency, equity, and active participation. The author posits that the ideal intersection of AI and human caregiving is the embodied data, bridge of compassion AI. The author

DOI: 10.4018/979-8-3373-7724-7.ch004

ultimately proposes a construct of the future designed relationship with AI as one that redefines inclusion as the future of technology. The author envisions a construct of relationship with AI as one that redefines inclusion as the future of technology.

I. INTRODUCTION

The most important and the most difficult area of development of children with autism spectrum disorder (ASD), and related communication disabilities, is language and communication. Atypical neuro-developmental pathways, and the corresponding difficulties with social reciprocity, expressive clarity, and emotional understanding, impact expressive speech, receptive comprehension, and pragmatic language and learning (Noble, 2018). Children with ASD, and these other communications related disabilities, often have diverse and varied communication profiles. Some may be exceptional in visual thinking or patterns but be unable to engage in and reciprocate conversation or understand social or emotional cues (UNESCO, 2023). This diversity requires language intervention to be individualized, which standard therapeutic approaches may find difficult to achieve.

Numerous children on the autism spectrum (ASD) and those with communication challenges have benefited from traditional speech and language therapies that are based on human knowledge and behavioural or developmental models. For example, Iannone and Iannuzzi (2023) emphasizes the potential of integrating assistive and AI-based technologies with traditional therapies, while also acknowledging ongoing barriers of accessibility, scalability, and personalization. Such therapies typically require prolonged single practitioner-client relationships, over many months or years, which places most families with a lack of available therapists (particularly in rural or resource-limited areas) and significant financial burdens that disrupt care continuity (Li et al., 2024). Additionally, despite their evidence-based approach, standardized curricula are often unable to fully capture the unique learning pace, sensory, and communication preferences of individual learners. As Kotsi et al. (2025) point out, children with ASD can be very complex, and in consideration of this, more flexible and responsive teaching approaches are often needed. Such unique needs require creating learning spaces that change and develop in response to the individual strengths, difficulties and emotions of each child. This is where technology, especially artificial intelligence (AI), and recent improvements in Natural Language Processing (NLP), Affective Computing, and Adaptive Learning Systems begin to transform the educational landscape of special needs. Lan et al. (2025) suggest that AI can support communication in real time by personalising feedback and reinforcement based on an individual's speech, gestures, facial expressions, previous interactions, and learning history. This allows learning environments to change from static models and begin to develop into a responsive ecosystem that adapt to the learner's communication needs.

AI's potential in these environments goes beyond pure efficiency and technological novelty. For children whose voices, literally or metaphorically, AI can serve as a new form of mediation between human intention and expression. Davis et al. (2023) note that AI can detect nuances in communication, build upon various stages of communication, and provide supportive, non-judgmental communication that encourages persistence and confidence. When AI is created ethically and inclusively, it is not a substitute for human care, but an enhancer of human empathy. It allows therapists, educators, and caregivers to better attune to children's communicative needs. This potential also brings complexity. For instance, how can we ensure that AI-based interactions improve human connectedness, and what limits should be placed around autonomy, emotional privacy, and authenticity? The primary questions of this chapter relate to these paradoxes. How can we develop and deploy AI technologies that support language learning and inclusion for children with autism and communication disabilities? How do we keep human empathy at the centre?

The most promising aspect of AI within special education remains its capability to close inclusive access gaps, improve prompt and sustained engagement. The history of supportive communication technologies, from basic photocard exchange systems to computerized speech output devices, have been instrumental in enabling children with autism to communicate needs, make selections, and engage socially. Nonetheless, many of these technologies have been built on captured inputs and limited responsiveness to the subtle, nuanced and contextual fluidity of human language. Applications of Kotsi et al. (2025), contrast AI technologies that adapt and develop learning systems based on the levels of user interaction and linguistic proficiency, attention, and emotional responsiveness. In today's computing environment, adaptive computer instruction, unlike traditional computer-assisted instruction, provides rapidly changing learning environments through adaptive algorithms that adjust levels of task difficulty, response time and modality visual, auditory, or textual to the user's level. This degree of personalization supports the goals of the Universal Design for Learning (UDL) (Lan et al., 2025), particularly the multiple means of engagement, representation, and expression.

When AI responds to a child's specific ways of communication, it can lessen barriers to learning, keep the child motivated, and help the child learn the complicated parts of a language that are more challenging to teach in a traditional learning environment. There is also potential to help children with autism spectrum disorder (ASD) who find it difficult to analyse a person's expression, voice, and body language with the new field of affective computing, which focuses on building technologies that can analyse and respond to people's emotions. Guz (2024) explains that the emotion-recognition technology used with AI and therapy robots can build trust with the child by recognizing and responding to their emotions. If designed with care, affective AI can help children learn the emotion and language in a more integrated way. It can also teach the child how to manage their emotions better and communicate in more advanced ways. Even though deploying emotional AI offers many opportunities, it must consider ethical issues. Li et al. (2024) point out that learning should not turn into surveillance, that children should have power in their interactions, and that there should be transparency in the system and human control. Furthermore, Nao, the social robot, and other AI-based virtual tutors, have been used in speech therapy and special education. According to Lan et al. (2025), such social agents are non-judgmental and predictable. They make good companions for children who have anxiety or other difficulties with human interaction because they respond positively to robotic companions. These companions can help create turn-taking and joint attention in interactions, and they can offer practice for real communication in the development of pragmatic language skills.

Furthermore, these tools can also promote collaboration and inclusion by allowing children with and without disabilities to play AI-supported games or engage in storytelling (Huot & Loch, 2025b). Inclusion in special education is about more than pedagogy; it is about ethics. It is about the right to equitable access to a voice, to be heard, to participate, and to express. The use of Artificial Intelligence (AI) is adaptable and multimodal, so it can be a tool for inclusive practice, especially in situations where a designed space may be unwelcoming, inaccessible or overly stimulating. A recent study from Frontiers in Psychiatry (2024) mentions the use of virtual reality and augmented reality as tools for creating social interactions, including classroom discussions and peer interactions in a sensory-friendly low-pressure environment.

On the other hand, inclusive practices involving the use of technology such as Artificial Intelligence, need to be implemented in what may be referred to as empathetic design consensus systems (Huot, 2025). These systems set a priority for relational understandings over automations, the comfort of humans over the efficiency of machines, and the collaboration of all participants over the unilateral deployment of the system. In this sense, tools such as AI must be designed with neurodivergent children, families, and educators as collaboration partners, and not just for them (Huot & Such, 2025). The inclusivity of an AI tool can be defined by the kind of human diversity it acknowledges and the quality of the relationships it maintains and, in an inclusive environment, the AI tool adapts to the relationships it establishes. This chapter aims to explore how Artificial Intelligence (AI), as a partner in collaboration, can foster developmental communication and language skills in children with autism and related communication disabilities. It aims to go beyond viewing AI as simply automation, and instead, aiding in the development of communication skills, emotions, and socially inclusive. This chapter will be guided by three goals. The first will look at AI and the support of language and expressive communication. The second will look at how engagement, comprehension, and social communication are influenced by adaptive algorithms and their encouragement of social communication. The third will develop a conceptual plan that is inclusive about the use of AI within classroom and therapy contexts.

This investigation proposes a unique way to connect technological advancement with inclusive pedagogy. Effective A.I. is not about replacing human therapists or educators. It is about enhancing their reach; their ability to survey, assess, and personalize. Thoughtfully applied A.I. can help close some of the gaps in access to speech and language support resources, especially for disadvantaged or remote learners (Kotsi et al., 2025; Li et al., 2024). AI can streamline the process of providing feedback, tracking progress, and gauging understanding so that human educators can direct their attention to the relational and emotional aspects of learning, dimensions of care and empathy that cannot be programmed.

II. CONCEPTUAL AND THEORETICAL FOUNDATIONS

The process of language acquisition and articulation in autistic children and children with communication disabilities is influenced by a variety of cognitive processes, sensory experiences, and social context. According to Saban-Bezalel (2025), autism does not, as a rule, involve complete absence of communication, and instead, there are alternative communicative pathways involving different ways of constructing, expressing and sharing meaning. Most children with autism spectrum disorder (ASD) are pattern recognizers, and are capable of visual reasoning and memory, but are often deficient in joint attention, pragmatic language and emotional reciprocity (Saban-Bezalel, 2025). Baird et al. (2006) explain that although some autistic children can build very large vocabularies, they often face substantial problems with contextual flexibility, such as metaphors, making jokes, or understanding what a conversational partner is thinking. Some children are very restricted in their expressive speech but can demonstrate hi levels of comprehension or use alternative means of communication (like echolalia or some type of non-verbal gesture) (Baird et al., 2006). This variation in abilities demonstrates that autism is not a singular disorder, but a range of different possibilities and combinations of communicative abilities that are spectrum-like in their nature.

Speech and language therapies focus on basic parts of communication: articulation, grammar, vocabulary, and social skills. These therapies use a lot of verbal instructions, imitation, and rewards, which is inflexible for students with a nonlinear communication pattern, an impaired communication, or an impaired communication, and a sensory-dominated communication (Huot & Tep, 2025). Researchers claim the success of these therapies relies on a professional's ability to adjust to a child's focus, emotions, and cognitive ability. This is a challenging and resource-consuming task (Huot & Loch, 2025a). As literature describes advancements in AI may be used to improve this situation by giving users data-driven feedback about their speech, movements, gaze, and expressions. However, these technologies should not aim to normalize the types of communications used by individuals with autism. Instead, they should listen and respond to those types of communications and appreciate the different, valid, neurodivergent ways of communicating intentions and emotions (Baird et al., 2006). Children diagnosed with autism spectrum disorder (ASD) can have expressive language delays, challenges with prosody (speech tone and rhythm), and language use that is unique to them. The area most profoundly impacted appears to be pragmatic language, the ability to use language socially and flexibly. Research indicates that autistic students often appear to understand language at face value and have difficulty with inferencing, sarcasm, and non-literal or indirect language (Saban-Bezalel, 2025). The challenges these children face go beyond language to thinking and social understanding and reveal a difference in how children understand and use contextual and emotional cues.

Children diagnosed with autism spectrum disorders (ASD) show uneven skill profiles with great highs in certain areas and low performance in others. For example, they may show great rule-based systems, like math and poor performance in flexible problem-solving and perspective-taking. In addition, children with ASD can experience sensory sensitivities in areas like sound, light, and touch that may affect how they process language and social cues. According to Baird et al. (2006), background noise and quick speech may exceed an individual's capacity for auditory processing and make real-time conversations more challenging. On the other hand, AI interfaces can provide individualized learning experiences that control speech rate, visual stimuli and feedback to accommodate an individual's sensory preferences (Huot et al., 2025). AI systems can promote focused engagement by easing sensory overload, which in turn improves the conditions for language learning. To guarantee equity and accessibility, NLP requires inclusive and varied training datasets, including those with atypical and non-standard speech. Many commercially available speech recognition applications fail to recognize or understand the speech of neurodivergent individuals and those with speech disabilities due to the atypical neutrophilic representation. The design of Ethical AI is guided by the principles of inclusive and equitable representation of all speech variations (UNESCO, 2017). In addition to speech recognition, voice generation applications, which convert written text to speech, can create unique auditory profiles. For children using augmentative and alternative communication (AAC) systems, customized voice synthesis can vary in pitch and gender and can use different speaking styles, which can promote a sense of ownership and self-identity (Huot & Loch, 2025b).

Grounding AI's role in language learning for children with autism and communication challenges within specific educational and philosophical frameworks is necessary. For Vygotsky's sociocultural theory, the constructivist learning theory, and the neurodiversity paradigm are three, yet distinct, perspectives. They lead to the reconceptualization of AI as a support for communicative development, rather than for corrective and substitutive purposes. For Vygotsky, the learning process is via social relations, and cognitive development arises using culturally specific linguistic tools. Vygotsky (1978) proposed that children learn to use language through verbal communication with others, thus, converting external speech into internal speech. As stated in McLeod (2025), Vygotsky believed that language is man's greatest tool for communicating with the outside world. In this regard, AI systems can, when designed to meet this social-communicative goal, serve as mediative tools in the ZPD or proximal zone of development. In the ZPD, an individual is supported to accomplish a level of functioning that is beyond their independent capabilities. In this regard, McLeod (2025) and Mudi and Samanta (2024) explain that many of the AI tools designed for learning purposes increase the level of difficulty in educational tasks. Thus, AI acts as a development partner. According to Constructivist Theory and Practise, which draws on the work of Jean Piaget and Jerome Bruner, learning is the active process of acquisition and construction of knowledge through an experience and is not an act of reception of information (Jones, 1995). Constructivist environments for children with autism who process and respond to sensory information and the cognitive demands of teaching differently, focus on agency, exploration, and rich feedback (Naylor & Keogh, 1999). Artificial Intelligence (AI) provides the means of interactive discovery, which is in harmony with a constructivist approach.

Lastly, the neurodiversity paradigm reframes autism as a form of natural cognitive variation, alongside speech and communication disabilities, that does not need medical correction. Advocates suggest that such environments should be adapted, not standardised (Mbonde, 2025). In the context of AI design, the neurodiversity principle allows for a different 'success' definition in language learning not as alignment with neurotypical speech and behaviour, but as effective self-expression and individual participation. Consequently, AI should be adaptable to various forms of communication, e.g., text, symbols, gestures, and synthesised voice, and different communicative personas. Mbonde (2025) argues that technology needs to adapt to the user as much as the user adapts to technology, illustrating the design principle of mutual accommodation that respects all forms of diversity. The belief that communication should be collaborative rather than assimilative is exemplified in **Figure 1**.

Figure 1.

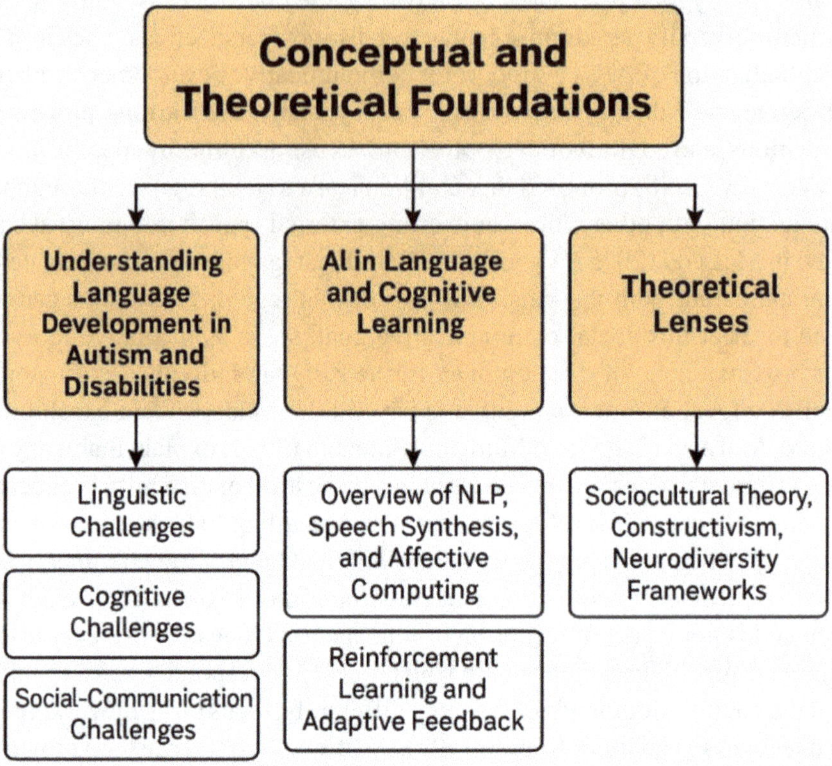

III. AI TECHNOLOGIES SUPPORTING LANGUAGE DEVELOPMENT

D'Mello and Graesser (2015) suggest that with the right Natural Language Processing (NLP) tools, a system can analyse and respond to the learner's language and provide tailored tutoring, feedback, and dialogue to support contingent interactions, instead of having learners complete static drill-and-practice activities. Calvo and D'Mello (2010) suggest that with feedback, coupled linguistic pipelines and affect sensing systems, supportive feedback can be more human-like, aligning the level of support provided with the challenge of the task to the learner's level and state. This means that AI-based recognizers can identify and provide suggestions to correct specific phonological, prosodic, and grammatical errors, and offer immediate, supportive feedback in the form of visual overlays, audio recordings, or re-casts that are child-friendly. These types of support from AI systems can facilitate growth in articulation and in the morphosyntactic complexity of speech, which human clinicians would otherwise have to do in real time (Luckin & Holmes, 2016).

In addition to the ability to pronounce words, NLP analyses can focus on the different structures within a given sentence as well as the understanding of its different meanings, which gives the tools the ability to provide scaffolding for children who memorize words but struggle with sentence construction. One such example of scaffolding would be the use of specific prompts that ask students to articulate the roles of different elements within a sentence. For example, students would be prompted to articulate the roles of the different characters in the following sentence: 'The cat chases the dog' and 'The dog chases the cat.' According D'Mello and Graesser (2015), the focus of dialogue-based tutors, which encourage learners to provide more in-depth responses, explain their answers, and correct their mistakes, is to promote active engagement, as opposed to simply parroting words. The authors also reference Aresti-Bartolome and Garcia-Zapirain (2014), who emphasizes that the most effective forms of technological assistance for children with autism are those that have a sustained, personalized, and embedded within meaningful contexts, rather than drill and practice.

Engines have difficulty processing atypical or child speech. Grynszpan et al. (2014) warn that systems that misrecognize "Echolalia" (repetition of another's speech) or other simple speech patterns and atypical phrasing may erasure the speech acts that reveal the speaker's communicative intention. Relkin et al. (2021) report similarly that the systems have performance inclusiveness" based on data that depicts various neurocognitive and developmental levels, and they suggest that adaptation layers should learn an individual child's timing, pitch, and error patterns, rather than adult standards. Thus, inclusive NLP's aims, as Calvo and D'Mello (2010) indicate, to go beyond patterns of deviation to understand intention, from a semantic perspective, reframing deficiency of meaning as a successful act of communication within the child's language. In her foundational work, Picard (2000) proposes the first instances of computer systems acknowledging and appropriately responding to human emotion, thus paving the way for educational systems that recognize and respond to emotional states like frustration, boredom, curiosity, and flow. In that same spirit, Calvo and D'Mello (2010) streamline and synthesize various models and methods aimed at analysing and detecting emotion using facial action coding, emotion detection using voice, interaction traces, and others, and propose that the instructional response should not only be predicated on what a learner verbally communicates, but also on the emotional state that accompanies that verbal communication.

D'Mello and Graesser (2015) further describe the potential of affect-aware tutors to adjust the level of challenge and the amount of support provided by either slowing down the instructional pace, using simpler prompts, and inserting short, targeted, cognitive, and emotional regulation activities when they detect signs of cognitive overload and, on the other hand, increasing the level of challenge when they detect signs of confidence and engagement. For autistic learners, this alignment is vital because, as documented by Grynszpan et al. (2014), the inability to read and express emotions is often coupled with various pragmatic language deficits; therefore, modelling direct, excessive, and consistent emotional signals may help learners develop both recognition and the use of emotions. The literature does support the notion of affective surveillance. Luckin and Holmes (2016) argue that sensing builds trust only when there is a balance of transparency, consent, and teacher mediation to ensure that the sensing is supportive, and not punitive. Dautenhahn (2007) considers socially intelligent robots as partners who can communicate in predictable and unambiguous ways, which many autistic children perceive as less stressful than quickly changing conversations. For Ajabshir (2019), using voice, gaze, gesture, and timing in unison, may allow embodied conversational agents to move beyond mere simulation to create interactions that foster co-constructing and the narrative perspective. According to Grynszpan et al. (2014), when routines move from highly scripted to more flexible formats, sessions using robots as facilitators can strengthen joint attention, imitation, and turn-taking, all of which relate to the underlying pragmatics of language.

In line with this, Clabaugh and Matarić (2018) advocate for personalized for the people, by the people customizing voice and timing, as well as activity configurations to fit the child preference, which increases engagement and minimizes withdrawal. These prosocial outcomes also create the need for social risks. For Ajabshir (2019) and Dautenhahn (2007), the primary risk of over-identifying with companions originates in their communicative faces, which may lead to the untrained use of the robots. Dautenhahn (2007) suggests that in such cases, it is best to use robots in mediated scenarios, where interactions with people can take place. For Luckin and Holmes (2016), the best use of robots is to chronologically integrate them into the structure of teacher-led activities, use logs as tools for reflection, and establish clear limits about the understanding of the social agent, as depicted in Table 1.

Table 1.

Technology	Key Functions	Core Benefits
Natural Language Processing (NLP) and Speech Recognition	Analyses speech, provides real-time feedback on pronunciation, syntax, and comprehension. Enables interactive storytelling and personalized linguistic scaffolding.	Improves articulation, expressive confidence, and comprehension through adaptive feedback and individualized pacing.
Emotion Recognition and Affective Computing	Detects facial expressions, tone, and engagement; adjusts activities based on emotional state; models emotional cues through visual and auditory means.	Enhances emotional regulation, empathy, and social reciprocity by linking emotion to communication.
Conversational and Social Robots	Simulates pragmatic conversation, models turn-taking and empathy, provides consistent and predictable interaction.	Builds confidence, pragmatic competence, and social communication skills through structured dialogue and engagement.
Multimodal Learning Systems	Combines visual, auditory, and haptic feedback to create adaptive, multisensory learning experiences tailored to sensory preferences.	Supports diverse sensory profiles, reinforces comprehension, and fosters engagement through multisensory integration.

IV. CASE STUDIES AND APPLIED PRACTICES

Aresti-Bartolome and Garcia-Zapirain (2014) discuss respect for various communicative styles. Echolalia is often an unrecognized means to participation. Technologies that require reduced eye contact, as well as those that permit communication through text or symbols, respect communicative styles. Means of communication should be treated as equivalent. Relkin et al. (2021) review studies that indicate adaptive systems succeed when the system adapts to the child, including changes to the losing of an adaptive system, voice, and timing, and not when the system is learner dependent. In similar fashion, Clabaugh and Matarić (2018) highlight the importance of including families and therapists in the design and development process, because the aesthetics, prompts, and rewards that are used. They outline the importance of including local and individual culture and identity in the design process. These different, yet related, threads can be viewed as building a coherent and integrated system. Natural Language Processing (NLP) provides the ability to analyse and diagnose language and provide scaffolding (D'Mello & Graesser, 2015). Affective computing helps to adjust the level of support provided to the child based on their behaviour and emotional state (Calvo & D'Mello, 2010; Picard, 2000). Responsive virtual agents and other technologies can be used to help children practice or learn specific social behaviours (Ajabshir, 2019; Clabaugh & Matarić, 2018; Dautenhahn, 2007). Technologies that support multisensory interactions (Grynszpan et al., 2014; Rose & Dalton, 2009) can help translate and reinforce the words a child is attempting to use. Rather than attempting to teach children to communicate in a specific and uniform manner, as many other researchers have suggested (Luckin & Holmes, 2016), these technologies provide support the teachers to help them to be more empathic and inclusive.

4.1 Case Study: AI-Enhanced AAC for Context-Responsive Communication

Relkin et al. (2021) elaborate the analysis of decades of Aresti-Bartolome and Garcia-Zapirain (2014) on Augmentative and Alternative Communication (AAC) research. They note that the AAC field, while not without its obstacles, is in a place where technologies that provide adaptive, feedback-oriented, and fluid tools (as opposed to fixed symbol boards) will continue to expand the communicative possibilities of AAC users, particularly children with developmental disabilities. For instance, Aresti-Bartolome and Garcia-Zapirain (2014) suggest that the processing and prediction capabilities of new technologies, such as natural language processing and artificial intelligence, will facilitate moving AAC devices away from a fixed system into a fluid, context-responsive interface that will understand and predict a user's communicative goals, thus lightening the cognitive load to communicate. Presently, many AAC apps such as Proloquo2Go and CoughDrop, utilizing these principles. For example, in Proloquo2Go, the selectable phrase "*I want*" will activate the system to suggest contextually appropriate choices such as play, hug, or drink, based on user history. This embodiment of intelligence unleashed (Luckin & Holmes, 2016) in AAC apps provides just-in-time prompts, or scaffolds, that ease a learner's efforts to interact with the system.

4.2 Case Study 2: Conversational Agents and Chatbots for Dialogue Practice

Combining different types of inputs is also important. Grynszpan et al. (2014) review autism interventions involving technology and state that while gaze, gesture, and vocal attempts, they focus on encouraging speech-supplemented communication. Relkin et al. (2021) summarize therapists' comments, noting that such responsiveness creates initiative and agency, since the system 'completes' things for users when they do not input things completely. D'Mello and Graesser (2015) suggest conversational agents offer dialogue moves (e.g., prompts, revoicing, recasting) and simulate practice opportunities between clinical sessions. Similarly, Alrakhawi et al. (2023) review chatbots for educational use in special education and argue that dialogue practice is a way for clinicians to reduce their workload while ensuring personalized practice. In real-world scenarios, Ajabshir (2019) argues "AI-therapist" chatbots help children practice turn-taking and stance-taking by seamlessly guiding users through socially relevant activities like describing their day and answering open-ended questions. Luckin and Holmes (2016) review the logs to modify future sessions and argue such systems should not replace, but to supplement, human discretion.

4.3 Case Study 3: Affect-Aware Tutoring for Emotion-Sensitive Language Support

Picard (2000) presents the first case for affective computing, while Calvo and D'Mello (2010) integrate recognition of the emotions of frustration, boredom, and engagement using facial, vocal, and interaction cues, and propose that adaptive alterations such as slowing tasks, reducing complexity of prompts, or adding short breaks for self-regulation, help learners to continue despite challenges. According to D'Mello and Graesser (2015), affect-aware tutoring can increase challenge when students' confidence improves, like what good therapists do. In most applied settings, where the language modelling is combined with affect detection, the practitioners have observed longer periods of focused attention, and more spontaneous speech, which are the same patterns as the ones Grynszpan et al. (2014) have observed in their meta-analysis of studies that examine the integration of affective computing and language practice. At the same time, explainable and attentive systems should have transparency for caregivers to know the reasons for the changes in the tone or the pace of a system, which are the boundaries that keep the systems from being surveillant, as emphasized by Luckin and Holmes (2016) and are for the more humane systems. Various social language tools, designed for use in classrooms, incorporate interactive components. Grynszpan et al. (2014) describe how, in some applications, social reciprocity is improved by user interactions that are situated in defined roles, animated avatars, branching storylines, and scenario-based choices, and where feedback is directed more toward positive social behavioural correction, waiting, acknowledging, rephrasing than to mere behavioural correctness. Similarly, Ajabshir (2019) suggests one of computer-based agents by arguing that interactive social agents can teach pragmatic social skills. Alrakhawi et al. (2023) point out that, for educators, social skills apps are often embedded in social skills curricula; however, the educational scaffolding (pre-briefs, reflective talk-throughs) designed by the educator is intended to assist students to transfer their digital interactions to the real world.

Barnes and Hutson (2024) emphasize the necessity of participatory co-design for neurodiversity personalization, inviting families to create tools co-construct voices, icons, and reward systems to align with local linguistic and cultural practices. Barnes and Hutson (2024) note the significance of these elements in the construction of empathic AI, the choice of tone, speed, and symbol sets that children perceive as theirs, thus enhancing engagement and emotional safety. The role of caregiver training is crucial; Creswell and Clark (2025) advocate for parent workshops and micro-modules on dashboard interpretation, sensitivity adjustment, and the incorporation of micro practices (e.g., story retells, emotional labelling) into everyday activities. According to Luckin and Holmes (2016), when educational and therapeutic platforms share data with families, the 'ecosystem of care' is continuous; therapists, instead of starting from scratch, can analyse interactions from home and adjust their goals for the next steps.

4.4 Case Study 4: Social Robots and Co-Designed Communication Support

Based on Dautenhahn (2007), socially intelligent robots act as companions providing reliable, unambiguous cues. Clabaugh and Matarić (2018) show that personalising a user's voice, timing, and routines, helps maintains their engagement and supports joint attention and imitation. Grynszpan et al. (2014) review show that gains in turn taking, and other pragmatic skills are achieved when participants move from activities that are fully to activities that are semi- structured, allowing those skills to transfer to interactions with peers and family. Ajabshir (2019) notes the transparency of anthropomorphism, in describing the robots as distant others to avoid children from understanding too much. The aim is to shift to human communication and not to form an attachment to the robot. Relkin et al. (2021) report that AI systems enhance engagement, communicative initiations, articulation and vocabulary, provided feedback is immediate and adaptive. Improvements in independence and self-expression were also reported by Aresti-Bartolome and Garcia-Zapirain (2014) when systems are used throughout meaningful teaching and learning activities, as opposed to self-contained, isolated drills. Emotional awareness and embodiment interventions, as described in Grynszpan et al. (2014), are particularly effective in fostering joint attention and social reciprocity critical to language development. Boyd and Crawford (2012), Aresti-Bartolome and Garcia-Zapirain (2014), and O'Neil (2019) warn about possible negative effects of bias within machine learning and datafication tools driven by inequitable datasets, as well as limited and unexamined metrics that underpin automated systems. Ehsan and Riedl (2020) and Luckin and

Holmes (2016), advocate for human-cantered design, explainable systems, and dignity, transparency, and accountability in school systems.

Alrakhawi et al. (2023) note that the advantages are unequal where there are constraints on device access, bandwidth, or teacher training, and they suggest frugal designs that are offline-capable and focused professional development. Barnes and Hutson (2024) make the same case for localisation, especially in terms of dialects, writing systems, and cultural stories, so that success looks like active participation on one's own terms rather than adherence to a dominant communicative standard, as illustrated in Table 2.

Table 2.

Area	Key Issues	Recommendations
Ethical & Privacy	Highly personal linguistic and affective data; surveillance drift	Dynamic, informed consent; minimization & encryption; transparent audit trails; consent and assent tailored to child.
Fairness & Bias	Underrepresentation of neurodiverse, multilingual users; interpretive bias	Diverse datasets; adaptive error tolerance; human-centred XAI and recourse.
Cultural Sensitivity	Western affect and display norms; misfit with local practices	Co-design with families and educators; localization of voice, symbols, narratives; plural models of empathy.
Balancing Roles	Over-reliance on automation; attachment to agents	Keep therapists and teachers central; set boundaries; graduated transfer to peer interaction.
Capacity & Governance	Misuse and misinterpretation; weak policy	Professional learning on ethics & explanations; school-level governance and oversight committees.

V. ETHICAL, CULTURAL, AND PRACTICAL CONSIDERATIONS

Boyd and Crawford (2012) claim that datafication in education reconceptualizes close interactions, voice, facial micro-expressions, interaction rhythms, as measurable data, which risks exploitation, misrepresentation, and exclusion in the absence of strong governance. O'Neil (2019) explains that opaque analytics turn children's intimate signals into weapons of math destruction when models go unexamined, stakes are high, and there are unregulated feedback loops. In the field of special education, where sensitive and emotive verbal data can expose a person's identity and feelings, ethical practice must include explicit, continuous, and understandable consent, which families can revisit and withdraw. Ehsan and Riedl (2020) refer to this as a human-centred, dialogic model of AI explanation and choice. Goodley (2024) argues that respecting the child's will, even though assent procedures modified to a child's developmental level, reframes disabled learners as subjects of rights and not just data.

Selwyn (2022) argues that in schools, platform often falls into surveillance logics, attention tracking, sentiment scoring, unless design is purposefully re-oriented to care. Perhaps the most concrete suggestions from Luckin and Holmes (2016) include strict data minimization, local or encrypted storage, deletion policies aligned to pedagogical purposes, institutional oversight with parents and advocates, and, of course, transparency. Boyd and Crawford (2012) also argue for transparency that enables families to understand what is collected, why it is needed, and how it drives personalization. Collectively, these suggestions shift the focus from surveillance to care and accountability in the sense that data is meant to serve the child's learning, not the institution's (Luckin & Holmes, 2016). While Picard (2000) opens the door to affect-aware machines, Calvo and D'Mello (2010) warn that transforming every sigh or glance into a feature vector may breach psychological boundaries in the absence of interpretability and control from the user. D'Mello and Graesser (2015) claim that a surveillance-free system should support empathy by slowing or simplifying tasks when a user is becoming overloaded and should not be designed to require constant surveillance. Ethically, a system designed to be empathetic should allow optional participation, provide simple on controls, and encourage teachers to interpret signals as context without treating them as declarative statements (Calvo & D'Mello, 2010; Luckin & Holmes, 2016).

Relkin et al. (2021) discuss previous research that highlights the failure of speech and NLP models to recognize patterns of speech that are atypical, such as that of bilinguals, and those that employ individual speaking styles. Such automation bias poses a significant threat to the automation of inclusive practices. Ng (2023) calls for inclusive data pipelines that capture and represent diverse speech (neurodiverse, multilingual, code-switching) and varied emotion displays (cross culturally) and advocates for the pairing of diverse data practitioners with engineers, clinical experts, and linguists to achieve representational sufficiency. O'Neil (2019) claimed that the data capture bias goes beyond the who and includes the ingrained bias of the system, such as defining silence as disengagement rather than reflecting. Thus, Ehsan and Riedl (2020) suggest that AI should possess explainability, focusing on the reasoning and the gaps that the system leaves open to criticism, so that educators may refute the output. Predictive AIs should be diagnostic rather than deterministic. Ehsan and Riedl (2020) argue that the recommend-do evidence cycle is a form of human-centred explainability that helps educators and parents understand what evidence supports a recommendation and provides a rationale for contesting it. Luckin and Holmes (2016) also advocate for teacher-inclusive review cycles, and school policies that provide the right to remedy, systems that allow the alteration of records, the overriding of designations, and the alteration of model behaviour when harm is done.

Emotional and cultural diversity must be included when designing empathic AI systems. Rather than adapting a single communication model, Barnes and Hutson (2024) suggest designing different systems for different cultures, using varying forms, interaction styles, and local normative stories. Personalization for neurodiversity means adjusting to local communication practices, including dialects and code-switching, to allow individuals to self-define success. This is particularly relevant to Goodley (2024), who states that disability is life is culturally embedded; thus, designing systems with educators and families can help identify culturally specific psychological and social relational patterns (e.g. humour, authority, and comfort) that may be overlooked by systems developers. For context as well, ethical human-AI collaboration is without a doubt, culturally bound, states Vallor (2015), and global principles of privacy, accessibility, and anti-discrimination must be balanced with culturally specific practices of care. Dautenhahn (2007) points out the potential for anthropomorphized agents to cause users to misattribute understanding; he suggests that educators think of AI as an intermediary, rather than a companion. Caswell (2019) similarly argues for the need for somebodies' agents to practice turn taking and narrative perspective but asserts that teachers are the holders of meaning and transfer to human-to-human interaction. While Luckin and Holmes (2016) and Vallor (2015) each describe a partnership model where AI does the routine and scalable tasks, and humans do the empathetic, creative, and contextual reasoning, there are clearly defined boundaries (roles, goals, and escalation pathways). The literature describes the phenomenon of peer avoidance because of over-use and suggests that graduated integration, the shift from AI-mediated interactions to human-to-human encounters, is a mechanism to support social interaction development (Grynszpan et al., 2014).

Creswell and Clark (2025) emphasize that in order to achieve a lasting integration of the technology, there must be a change in the users' mental models, training should be directed at how the technology will be used ethically (when it is appropriate or not to trust the system, how to over-ride it, and how to communicate uncertainty to parents). Luckin and Holmes (2016) argue that educational institutions must implement and adhere to policies that address the three areas of data governance, fairness, and AI adjustment to therapeutic goals, as seen in Table 3.

Table 3.

Application Area	Technological Focus	Key Outcomes
Therapeutic Applications	Integration of adaptive AAC devices, chatbot-based speech therapy, and emotionally responsive AI systems in clinical contexts. Technologies include NLP, predictive modelling, and affective feedback.	Improved articulation, speech fluency, and self-expression; enhanced motivation and emotional regulation; increased agency in communication.
Educational Implementations	Deployment of AI tutors, interactive language-learning platforms, and communication-focused apps in inclusive classrooms. Includes multisensory and adaptive instruction systems.	Enhanced engagement and comprehension; improved syntactic and pragmatic language use; reduced anxiety through structured feedback.
Parental and Caregiver Involvement	Co-design of AI systems with family input; customization of AI voice, visual interface, and emotional tone; training caregivers to use AI tools effectively at home.	Continuity of learning beyond clinics; stronger parent–child communication; empowered caregivers supporting consistent language practice.
Evidence of Impact	Empirical studies documenting gains in linguistic complexity, social reciprocity, and emotional awareness; increased duration and frequency of participation.	Significant improvement in engagement, vocabulary, and conversational confidence; development of empathy and social connection.

VI. TOWARD A HUMAN–AI PARTNERSHIP MODEL

Luckin and Holmes (2016) posit that the next frontier in educational AI is not mere relational effectiveness, but systems that extend the ability of teachers and therapists to notice, respond to, and include. Similarly, Vallor (2015) states that the relational quality of human–AI partnerships should focus on the extent to which such systems support the care, practical reasoning, and co-moral relationality of synergistic interaction, rather than on the savings in time or money. When building stronger and deeper partnerships, it makes sense to apply insights from cognitive psychology, particularly Solso's (2001) studies on perception, attention, memory, and information processing. From a cognitive perspective, simply knowing a language means much more than being able to say a few words; it is the ability to understand, attend to and process information in a meaningful way, and to organize and retain the information to retrieve an appropriate response in each social situation. These children's mental processes can be disrupted due to communication barriers, and can unfold more slowly than children developing typically due to communication barriers. There's a lot of factors at play, including integration and processing problems, selective attention, sensory overload, reduced processing speed and working memory. Here, AI can be particularly useful, as it can relieve some of the cognitive burden and adjust the pace of the interaction. AI can help the learner process the information by drawing attention to the most relevant cues and by providing feedback that is repeated but adaptive in the way that it matches the learner's processing style. However, cognitive support alone is simply not enough. Learning processes are determined by a learner's perception of the situation. Meaning is created and understanding is deepened during interactions (Goldstein & van Hooff, 2024). AI should be used to support the teacher's or the therapist's ability to focus, support, and communicate, rather than as a cognitive substitute (Huot & Hok, 2025). AI should be seen as a support system that fosters emotionally and socially appropriate communication interactions.

In this context, a partnership model prioritizes co-agency. AI delivers structure, feedback, and temporal continuity; humans provide emotional understanding, cultural context, ethical judgment, and in each case, address the shortcomings of the other (D'Mello & Graesser, 2015). Let's examine the potential of AI in speech therapy. AI can aid the clinician in giving immediate feedback on the child's articulation mistakes and update something resembling micro-progress analytics in real time. Resting on the premise that clinicians sustain the child as a rights-bearing interlocutor, Goodley (2024) describes the child's communication as relational and invested with an identity. Algorithms identify a pattern and therapists use their intuition to identify fatigue, anxiety, or lack of motivation. The therapists and clinicians make judgments about when to push or when to pull back (Alrakhawi et al., 2023). This mutual relationship, as noted by D'Mello and Graesser (2015), creates an outcome that neither can achieve by themselves. The following are four principles for inclusive partnership:

1. **Affected by design:** In designing systems, Picard (2000) suggests that the systems should recognize and respond to emotion, and Calvo and D'Mello (2010) posit that in the service of pedagogy, the affected sensing should be used to slow down, simplify, or reframe a task when a strain is detected. For autistic learners, emotionally attuned interfaces should be unobtrusive and adjustable to their sensory preferences and acknowledge a wide range of affect without requiring people to conform to display the affect in a certain way (Grynszpan et al., 2014).

2. **Adjustability and responsiveness:** According to Relkin et al. (2021), AI must understand each child's baseline in terms of response time, prosody, range, and preferred modalities, and adjust pacing and modality to match. Luckin and Holmes (2016) focus on adaptive or dynamic scaffolding that gives learners the opportunity to take more control of the direction of their learning.
3. **Explainability:** Ehsan and Riedl (2020) advocate for a more human-centric approach to explainable AI (XAI) meant for educators and families, as it would provide a better understanding of the system's reasons for intervening, and how this can be challenged. O'Neil (2019) explains that the lack of transparency surrounding a given metric can be used to mislabel and reinforce a disadvantage, while a lack of explained mechanisms and a lack of recourse will further reinforce such threats.
4. **Participatory Co-design:** Larmuseau et al. (2020) argue for the necessity of collaborating with end-users such as children, parents, clinicians, and teachers, to achieve a more participative approach in the design of the tool's aesthetics, prompts, and reward mechanisms, to incorporate lived experiences and values associated with neurodiversity. Barnes and Hutson (2024) also argue that empathy results from familiarity of a particular culture and is not from the application of a universal template.

Ajabshir (2019) asserts that agents can exhibit a measure of responsiveness, such as adjusting their gaze, timing, and word choice, but stresses that only people who hear and provide contextual meaning can give the full measure of empathy that is required to comfort. Ideally, a system may use signals to gauge users' levels of engagement, such as tracking their gaze or movement, to determine when a user is emotionally responsive. However, as noted by Luckin and Holmes (2016), it is still teachers and therapists who determine when an intervention is needed, a climb of the ladder is warranted, or a false alarm should be ignored. Therefore, design empathy should be grounded and human driven.

Alrakhawi et al. (2023) state that sincere commitment and use of technologies for humane purposes require ethical technological fluency. This fluency includes knowledge of what data a system relies on, how its adaptive models work, how and when gaps in understanding occur, and how to integrate feedback toward humane outcomes. Creswell and Clark (2025) suggest a multi-tiered model for professional development: short workshops to cover the basics of tools, structured communities of practice to foster reflective practice, and elaborate cross-disciplinary pairs with computer scientists, linguists, and ethicists. Ehsan and Riedl (2020) go a step further, insisting that practitioners explain to families the reasons for the recommendations and encourage them to challenge them to make accountability a default practice. Barnes and Hutson (2024) state that empathic AI must be responsive to local languages, dialects, phrases, idiomatic expressions, and culturally determined norms of social interaction, or else it will interpret neutrality as disengagement and erroneously penalize code-switching. Barnes and Hutson (2024) suggest that the localization of pedagogy entails an emphasis on collaborative activities in more collectivist cultures and narrative-based tutoring in cultures where storytelling plays a central role. Such an approach, Goodley (2024) points out, does not bypass the notion of disability as a culturally lived difference. Alrakhawi et al. (2023) highlight that equitable use also considers whether teachers have access to devices, internet bandwidth, and proper training. They recommend the use of offline, low-bandwidth, mobile-first solutions, especially when public and private sectors collaborate to provide training and maintenance.

Luckin and Holmes (2016) urge that infrastructure should be built with the intent that inclusivity is a priority from the beginning, not treated as an afterthought. Clabaugh and Matarić (2018) indicate that family co-design yields greater compliance and engagement, and HRI researchers and Dautenhahn (2007) clinicians collaborate to individualize social cues, and advocate, Vallor (2015), for policymakers to craft regulations from such evidence that honors people, not profit. Keeping neurodiverse specialists on these teams means that lived experience informs practice (Goodley, 2024). Grynszpan et al. (2014) encourage research investigating the extent to which a sustained and generalized improvement in articulation and reciprocity occurs in everyday situations. Luckin and Holmes (2016), and Ehsan and Riedl (2020), suggest, for inclusive and ethically justified, explainable, and attended systems, proposed policies in which scaling is not outrun by interval pacing. Picard (2000) describes systems that understand feelings, while O'Neil (2019) cautions that understanding is not conflating with empathy. The field, Vallor (2015) argues, should focus on service rather than simulation: machines help with sensing and organizing; people are responsible for the caring.

These different considerations point towards some sort of moral and pedagogical growth. Instead of seeing automation as taking over human roles, partnership views AI as an enabler of human flourishing, guided by an ethics of design, professional skills, cultural awareness, and collaborative governance (Luckin & Holmes, 2016; Vallor, 2015). Evolving technology does not intend to make people more automated and mechanical, but to help people become more attentive, compassionate, and constructive when interacting with diversity. In these learning environments, all participants, including AI, are afforded the power to act and to shape new and more empathetic forms of communication (Ajabshir, 2019; D'Mello & Graesser, 2015).

VII. CONCLUSION AND IMPLICATIONS

The fusion of artificial intelligence and human-centred therapy is not simply an advancement in educational technology; it is a fundamental rethinking of what it is to communicate, teach, and care. Throughout this chapter, AI has been framed not as a mechanical replacement of human connection but as a supporting structure, a responsive framework for the cultivation of connection, empathy, creativity, and understanding. When designed morally and deployed equitably, AI is a means of bridging the gaps between intention and expression, precision and compassion, and data and dignity.

AI's greatest potential is not in fully utilizing technology to automate processes, but rather in using technology to augment, or expand, the abilities of humans to perceive, interpret, and respond to various forms of communication. For children with autism and related communication disabilities, this means new opportunities to express their voices, to create meaning, and to participate. For example, responsive adaptive systems that detect levels of engagement and emotional states can provide real-time instruction; interfaces that use multiple modes of communication can accommodate individual sensory preferences; and artificial intelligence powered intelligent tutors can turn discussions about language into relational dialogues. However, the technology's greatest and most transformative value is when it amplifies rather than replaces the insight of therapists, the intuition of teachers, and the empathy of caregivers. It is in this collaboration, where human intelligence meets the accuracy of AI, that true inclusion becomes a reality.

To make new advancements with each new iteration in artificial intelligence, especially when implementing AI in educational settings, educators and developers need to keep ethics in mind, especially when building an educational AI intended to enhance learning. Utilizing AI in educational settings need to ensure that the systems created keep privacy, fairness, and transparency as the paramount core design principles and do not push such principles aside. Systems that employ adaptive consent, being able to explain their rationale, and easy to use systems will serve to protect the learners' rights and dignity. Systems need to serve the learners and customers and not simply be for their use. EI in educational AI also needs to consider elements that address the learner's confidence and belonging as well as their emotions over time, rather than being solely focused on immediate accomplishments and the data that indicators measure associated with the systems.

Effective and ethically created Artificial Intelligence in special educational systems will continue to develop in partnership with educators, tech developers, mental health practitioners, policy makers, and those who are neurodiverse. Working together in an integrated manner, with the various specializations will provide an opportunity for ethically and critically driven innovations. Participatory design in which the children and their families contribute to the creation and design of the artificial intelligence will be instrumental in closing the gap between digital tools and their real needs and social environments. Including individuals who are neurodiverse as co-creators will enable them to experience empowerment through the process and will improve the quality of the artificial intelligence being created. The goal is to create technology that listens before it gives directions, collaborates before it points out errors, and embodies humanity in both precision and warmth. The AI-enhanced learning experience should be measured by its ability to further the human experience by improving the way we communicate, building stronger connections, and providing a more humane educational experience. In this context, AI is simply a tool and not the destination. With the right focus, AI can serve as a resource in the ongoing human narrative of learning, caring, and creative belonging. When fuelled by empathy, technology can move beyond being simply functional and instead be transformative. Technology gives us the ability to listen more, see more, and connect with each other in the many ways that define humanity.

The chapter demonstrates its three main objectives integrated with one another. The first objective is demonstrating the potential of artificial intelligence technologies in the enhancement of language skills and expressive communication of children with autism and related communication disabilities. The second objective is exploring the ways in which such technologies can improve engagement, understanding and pragmatic social communication by adapting to a learner's emotional, sensory, and cognitive state. The third objective is to introduce a conceptual framework on the ethical use of AI for classroom and therapy practices, focusing on the elements of empathy, neurodiversity, transparency, and human oversight. Therefore, the chapter argues that the real potential of AI should not be viewed as the diminishing of human relationships, but as the enhancement of communication, engagement and social inclusion.

REFERENCES

Ajabshir, Z. F. (2019). The effect of synchronous and asynchronous computer-mediated communication (CMC) on EFL learners' pragmatic competence. *Computers in Human Behavior, 92*, 169–177. DOI: 10.1016/j.chb.2018.11.015

Alrakhawi, H. A., Jamiat, N., & Abu-Naser, S. S. (2023). Intelligent tutoring systems in education: A systematic review of usage, tools, effects and evaluation. *Journal of Theoretical and Applied Information Technology, 101*(4), 1205–1226. https://www.jatit.org/volumes/Vol101No4/6Vol101No4.pdf

Aresti-Bartolome, N., & Garcia-Zapirain, B. (2014). Technologies as support tools for persons with autistic spectrum disorder: A systematic review. *International Journal of Environmental Research and Public Health, 11*(8), 7767–7802. DOI: 10.3390/ijerph110807767 PMID: 25093654

Baird, G., Simonoff, E., Pickles, A., Chandler, S., Loucas, T., Meldrum, D., & Charman, T. (2006). Prevalence of disorders of the autism spectrum in a population cohort of children in south thames: The special needs and autism project (SNAP). *Lancet, 368*(9531), 210–215. DOI: 10.1016/S0140-6736(06)69041-7 PMID: 16844490

Barnes, E., & Hutson, J. (2024). Developing empathetic AI: Exploring the potential of artificial intelligence to understand and simulate family dynamics and cultural identity. *Journal of Artificial Intelligence and Robotics, 2*(3), 1–25. DOI: 10.59232/AIR-V2I3P101

Boyd, D., & Crawford, K. (2012). Critical questions for big data: Provocations for a cultural, technological, and scholarly phenomenon. *Information Communication and Society, 15*(5), 662–679. DOI: 10.1080/1369118X.2012.678878

Calvo, R. A., & D'Mello, S. (2010). Affect detection: An interdisciplinary review of models, methods, and their applications. *IEEE Transactions on Affective Computing, 1*(1), 18–37. DOI: 10.1109/T-AFFC.2010.1

Caswell, H. (2019). *Sensitivity analysis: matrix methods in demography and ecology*. Springer Nature. DOI: 10.1007/978-3-030-10534-1

Clabaugh, C., & Matarić, M. (2018). Robots for the people, by the people: Personalizing human-machine interaction. *Science Robotics, 3*(21), 1–2. DOI: 10.1126/scirobotics.aat7451 PMID: 33141723

Creswell, J. W., & Clark, V. L. P. (2025). *Designing and conducting mixed methods research* (4th ed.). SAGE Publications.

D'Mello, S. K., & Graesser, A. C. (2015). Feeling, thinking, and computing with affect-aware learning. In Kappas, A., Gratch, J. M., Calvo, R. A., & D'Mello, S. K. (Eds.), *The Oxford handbook of affective computing* (pp. 419–434). Oxford University Press.

Dautenhahn, K. (2007). Socially intelligent robots: Dimensions of human–robot interaction. *Philosophical Transactions of the Royal Society of London. Series B, Biological Sciences, 362*(1480), 679–704. DOI: 10.1098/rstb.2006.2004 PMID: 17301026

Davis, D. W., Jawad, K., Lohr, W. D., Trace, M., Le, J., Feygin, Y., & Jones, V. F. (2023). First-line behavioral health treatment prior to stimulant or alpha-2 agonist use for preschoolers on kentucky medicaid in 2017. *Journal of Attention Disorders, 27*(4), 437–446. DOI: 10.1177/10870547221147543 PMID: 36635886

Ehsan, U., & Riedl, M. O. (2020). Human-centered explainable AI: Towards a reflective sociotechnical approach. *International Conference on Human-Computer Interaction*, 449–466. DOI: 10.1007/978-3-030-60117-1_33

Goldstein, E. B., & van Hooff, J. C. (2024). *Cognitive psychology* (3rd ed.). Cengage.

Goodley, D. (2024). *Disability studies: An interdisciplinary introduction* (3rd ed.). SAGE Publications.

Grynszpan, O., Weiss, P. L., Perez-Diaz, F., & Gal, E. (2014). Innovative technology-based interventions for autism spectrum disorders: A meta-analysis. *Autism : The International Journal of Research and Practice, 18*(4), 346–361. DOI: 10.1177/1362361313476767 PMID: 24092843

Guz, S. (2024). *Who belongs in neighborhood schools?: A mixed methods reexamination of alternative high school transfer* [PhD Dissertation, University of Chicago].

Huot, S. (2025). Digital tutors in the kingdom: Exploring ChatGPT's influence on Cambodian students' academic and cognitive growth. In Pandya, J. D., & Patel, K. C. (Eds.), *Interdisciplinary insights: Exploring multiple perspectives* (Vol. 2, pp. 36–54). Meadow Publication.

Huot, S., & Hok, C. (2025). Unpacking the struggle: Linguistic, pedagogical, and cognitive barriers in Cambodian students' English essay writing. *Context (Ibadan), 12*(4), 149–168. DOI: 10.5281/zenodo.15807401

Huot, S., & Loch, S. (2025a). Digital practices in Cambodian EFL classrooms: Teacher narratives from remote learning. In K. Khette & Tayade (Eds.), *Proceeding of one day national conference on English language, literature, cultural studies and media studies* (Vol. 2, pp. 19–31). Centre for Learning, Research and Development, Savda, Maharashtra. DOI: 10.5281/zenodo.16921807

Huot, S., & Loch, S. (2025b). Educating in the age of AI: Preparing Cambodian teachers and students for an AI-augmented learning future. *Journal of Educational Technology and E-Learning Innovations*, *1*(2), 31–38. DOI: 10.54536/jeteli.v1i2.5170

Huot, S., Loch, S., Nget, R., & Em, S. (2025). Exploring multiliteracies in the digital era: A framework for 21st-century learning. [CJESS]. *Cambodian Journal of Educational and Social Sciences*, *2*(1), 7–27. DOI: 10.69496/cjess.v2i1.50

Huot, S., & Such, C. (2025). Leveraging social media for language learning: Opportunities and challenges. [JEILT]. *Journal of Education Innovation and Language Teaching*, *1*(2), 10–29. DOI: 10.63381/jeilt.v1i2.56

Huot, S., & Tep, P. (2025). Advancing ChatGPT for pedagogical innovation in Cambodia: Insight from global evidence and local implications. *The Context: Journal of English Studies*, *12*(4), 115–135. DOI: 10.5281/zenodo.15806972

Iannone, R., & Iannuzzi, I. (2023). The storm of creative destruction. Understanding the" damage-remedy" logic of capitalism in times of pandemics. *Salute E Societá 2023*(1), 27–44 DOI: 10.3280/SES2023-001003

Jones, A. (1995). Constructivist learning theories and IT. In Heap, N. (Ed.), *Information technology and society* (pp. 249–265). SAGE.

Kotsi, S., Handrinou, S., Iatraki, G., & Soulis, S.-G. (2025). A review of artificial intelligence interventions for students with autism spectrum disorder. *Disabilities*, *5*(1), 1–14. DOI: 10.3390/disabilities5010007

Lan, W., Tang, Z., Liu, M., Chen, Q., Peng, W., Chen, Y. P., & Pan, Y. (2025). The large language models on biomedical data analysis: A survey. *IEEE Journal of Biomedical and Health Informatics*, *29*(6), 4486–4497. DOI: 10.1109/JBHI.2025.3530794 PMID: 40031690

Larmuseau, C., Cornelis, J., Lancieri, L., Desmet, P., & Depaepe, F. (2020). Multimodal learning analytics to investigate cognitive load during online problem solving. *British Journal of Educational Technology*, *51*(5), 1548–1562. DOI: 10.1111/bjet.12958

Li, C., Gan, Z., Yang, Z., Yang, J., Li, L., Wang, L., & Gao, J. (2024). Multimodal foundation models: From specialists to general-purpose assistants. *Foundations and Trends® in Computer Graphics and Vision, 16*(1-2), 1–214. DOI: 10.1561/0600000110

Luckin, R., & Holmes, W. (2016). *Intelligence unleashed: An argument for AI in education*. Pearson Knowledge Lab. https://discovery.ucl.ac.uk/id/eprint/1475756

Mbonde, N. N. (2025). Wading in digital waters: Black mad/cripistemologies of motherhood and "mental illness" in online support groups amid the double pandemic. *Disability Studies Quarterly*, *45*(1). Advance online publication. DOI: 10.18061/dsq.6868

McLeod, S. (2025). Vygotsky's sociocultural theory of cognitive development. *Simply Psychology*, 1–31. DOI: 10.5281/zenodo.15680745

Mudi, S., & Samanta, T. K. (2024). Applying vygotsky's zone of proximal development in modern classroom settings: A call for social learning in the digital age. *International Journal For Multidisciplinary Research, 6*(4), 1–6. https://www.ijfmr.com/papers/2024/4/24233.pdf

Naylor, S., & Keogh, B. (1999). Constructivism in classroom: Theory into practice. *Journal of Science Teacher Education, 10*(2), 93–106. DOI: 10.1023/A:1009419914289

Ng, Y.-K. (2023). Could artificial intelligence have consciousness? Some perspectives from neurology and parapsychology. *AI & Society*, *38*(1), 425–436. DOI: 10.1007/s00146-021-01305-x

Noble, S. U. (2018). *Algorithms of oppression: How search engines reinforce racism*. New York university press., DOI: 10.18574/nyu/9781479833641.001.0001

O'Neil, C. (2019). Weapons of math destruction: How big data increases inequality and threatens democracy. *Vikalpa*, *44*(2), 97–98. DOI: 10.1177/0256090919853933

Picard, R. W. (2000). *Affective computing*. MIT Press. DOI: 10.7551/mitpress/1140.003.0008

Relkin, E., de Ruiter, L. E., & Bers, M. U. (2021). Learning to code and the acquisition of computational thinking by young children. *Computers & Education, 169*, 1–15. DOI: 10.1016/j.compedu.2021.104222

Rose, D., & Dalton, B. (2009). Learning to read in the digital age. *Mind, Brain and Education : The Official Journal of the International Mind, Brain, and Education Society*, *3*(2), 74–83. DOI: 10.1111/j.1751-228X.2009.01057.x

Saban-Bezalel, R. (2025). Communicative profiles of children with developmental delay compared to age-or language-matched typically developing peers. *Journal of Autism and Developmental Disorders*, *55*(12), 1–15. DOI: 10.1007/s10803-025-06882-0 PMID: 40408045

Selwyn, N. (2022). *Education and technology: Key issues and debates* (3rd ed.). Bloomsbury Academic. DOI: 10.5040/9781350145573

Solso, R. L. (2001). *Cognitive psychology* (6th ed.). Allyn & Bacon.

UNESCO. (2017). *Ethical principles for safeguarding intangible cultural heritage*. UNESCO. https://ich.unesco.org/en/ethics-and-ich-00866

UNESCO. (2023). *Technology integration of Cambodian higher education: Emerging changes since covid-19 and notable challenges*. Global Education Monitoring Report. https://www.unesco.org/gem-report/sites/default/files/medias/fichiers/2023/09/SopheakandPhyrom.pdf

Vallor, S. (2015). Moral deskilling and upskilling in a new machine age: Reflections on the ambiguous future of character. *Philosophy & Technology*, *28*(1), 107–124. DOI: 10.1007/s13347-014-0156-9

Vygotsky, L. S. (1978). *Mind in society: The development of higher psychological processes* (Cole, M., Ed.). Harvard University Press.

KEY TERMS AND DEFINITIONS

Adaptive learning: Systems built in the constructive approach are designed to change learning goals, methods, and feedback according to everyone's behaviour and engagement. Adaptive learning technologies powered by AI contribute to individual learning experiences through the analysis of achievement data and reinforcement learning and are particularly beneficial for children who experience communication difficulties by providing them with flexible supports that are designed to increase confidence and understanding as well as promote independent thinking.

Autism: Autism is a neurodevelopmental condition. The condition, more formally known as autism spectrum disorder (ASD), is caused by atypical development and includes differences in communication, social interaction, and the processing of sensory information. Autism encompasses a wide range of cognitive profiles and learning styles. As such, each of the many individuals with autism is likely to experience the condition in a different way. This degree of variability means that educational and therapeutic approaches must be tailored to each child's individual strengths and challenges, as well as their specific ways of expressing themselves.

Communication Disabilities: Communication disabilities include several different disabilities affecting the ability to generate, process, understand, and use certain aspects of language. These include difficulties of speech, language comprehension, social language, and social language expression. Tools like speech recognition, adaptive communication, and AI-based devices help in creating communication accessibility and confidence in communication.

Empathy: Empathy is understanding and relating to the feelings and the position of other individuals. In most AI learning applications, empathy is found as a design principle. Should the AI tools use in learning express and understand emotions, provide empathy, and care, the result is more relational understanding and emotional intertwining. Empathic AI can honour emotions and humanity and is therefore the perfect combination of cognition and compassion.

Inclusive Education: Inclusive education is the philosophy and practice of providing equitable access to a good learning environment for every student irrespective of ability, background, and neurotype. It encourages and embraces diversity and provides a flexible approach to teaching that is responsive to varied and individualized needs. The personalization of teaching, use of AI, and reconfiguration of support structures in responsive adaptable classrooms, to minimize exclusion, enhances inclusion.

Neurodiversity: The acceptance of different neurological conditions such as autism, ADHD and dyslexia, is called neurodiversity. The neurodiversity movement advocates for acceptance and empowerment, as well as the provision of ongoing support for different ways of thinking and communicating. Within this framework, the role of AI is not in the normalization of an individual's thinking and expression, but in facilitating support for different ways of learning and expressing.

Chapter 5
Game-Based Personalized Learning Pathways for Language Development in Children With Autism and Disabilities Using AI

C. V. Suresh Babu
http://orcid.org/0000-0002-8474-2882
Hindustan Institute of Technology and Science, India

M. Noorul Afreed
http://orcid.org/0009-0009-4564-7194
Hindustan Institute of Technology and Science, India

K. Shunmugapriya
http://orcid.org/0009-0003-9132-1108
Sri Muthukumaran Institute of Technology, India

ABSTRACT

This chapter per the authors aims to design an ethical, game-based AI framework that supports personalized language development pathways for children with autism spectrum disorder and related developmental communication challenges. The primary target groups include neurodiverse children, caregivers, therapists, and researchers in AI-enabled education. The chapter adopts a design-based research approach, integrating rule-based AI, adaptive game mechanics, and human-in-the-

DOI: 10.4018/979-8-3373-7724-7.ch005

loop dashboards to personalize learning while ensuring transparency and accessibility. Findings demonstrate improved engagement, sustained interaction, and adaptive responsiveness as indicators of potential language development support. The chapter concludes that interpretable, game-based AI systems offer scalable and inclusive opportunities for augmenting language interventions, while highlighting the need for future empirical validation and real-world clinical evaluation.

1. INTRODUCTION

1.1 Language Interaction Challenges in Children with Autism Spectrum Disorder

The first part describes particular struggles faced by youngsters with autism spectrum disorder when trying to communicate using language, and assumes that communicating using language is much more than being able to use the proper vocabulary and grammar; it also includes the use of the necessary pragmatic skills to communicate (e.g., taking turns and using social cues). The text also identifies some of the limitations of traditional language therapies for these children; that the use of repetitive drills does not often replicate the unpredictable nature of real-world communication experiences. The authors have established that there is a need for alternative delivery methods that can lessen the stress and sensory overload many children exhibit when exposed to traditional methods (Bishop, 1997).

1.2 AI Driven Personalization for Social Skill Development

the authors argue that there is a substantial obstacle to providing special education services at a scale that meets the needs of children with autism; that obstacle is not a lack of high-quality instructional strategies in special education, but instead the challenge of providing truly individualized support at the scale of all the children receiving special education in the United States. The authors then claim that a solution to this dilemma is to use artificial intelligence (AI) as the means to providing children with autism with a communication companion that can act as conversational partner, who will provide them with immediate feedback and who can adjust the level of difficulty to match their skills, fatigue, etc. without becoming fatigued or frustrated

1.3 Game Based Learning as a Catalyst for Engagement and Motivation

Research into games for kids shows that keeping kids interested in any type of content is just as important as the content itself. Traditional types of content (worksheets, etc.) often rely on students having to do the same things repeatedly and work harder in order to complete each task. When you play a game you get rewards and structure naturally that help keep you engaged. By situating a child's learning into a game environment, the author claims, children will be able to practice on a regular basis and not be bored with what they are doing. In addition, the author has made a conscious decision to endorse the use of web based programs because this allows the intervention to take place on a web browser and therefore eliminates the need for special hardware.

1.4 Need for Personalized Learning Pathways in Special Education

In addition to the games based learning piece of the paper, the article discusses how to personalize learning paths for students within the scope of resource constraints in the area of special education. The authors point out that although the teachers know that all students are different, they do not have the time and/or resources to create completely individualized plans for each student. The authors state that the only way to successfully bridge the gap between these two issues is through the use of technology. By utilizing systems that allow for the collection and analysis of performance data the authors claim that we can keep the learner in a "sweet spot" (not overwhelmed and not bored).

1.5 Chapter Objectives and Scope

The intended purpose of this chapter is to define the application of AI-assisted speech interaction, rule-based personalization, and game-based learning techniques to the support of communication practices in ASD-related technologies, comparing these to previous educational/therapeutic interventions using a traditional approach (educational and/or therapeutic), identifying the strengths/weaknesses of each in terms of support for structured learning practice. This chapter also aims to address research gaps, technical challenges, and ethical concerns related to the use of technology to assist with data security, personalisation, usability, accessibility, and long-term outcomes in the field of technology-assisted education and therapy in children with ASDs; and to synthesize current technological advances, best-to-date practices, and future considerations for the field of technology-assisted education and therapy to fulfil the needs of children with ASDs.

Figure 1. Challenges in traditional language therapy and the role of AI-assisted game-based learning

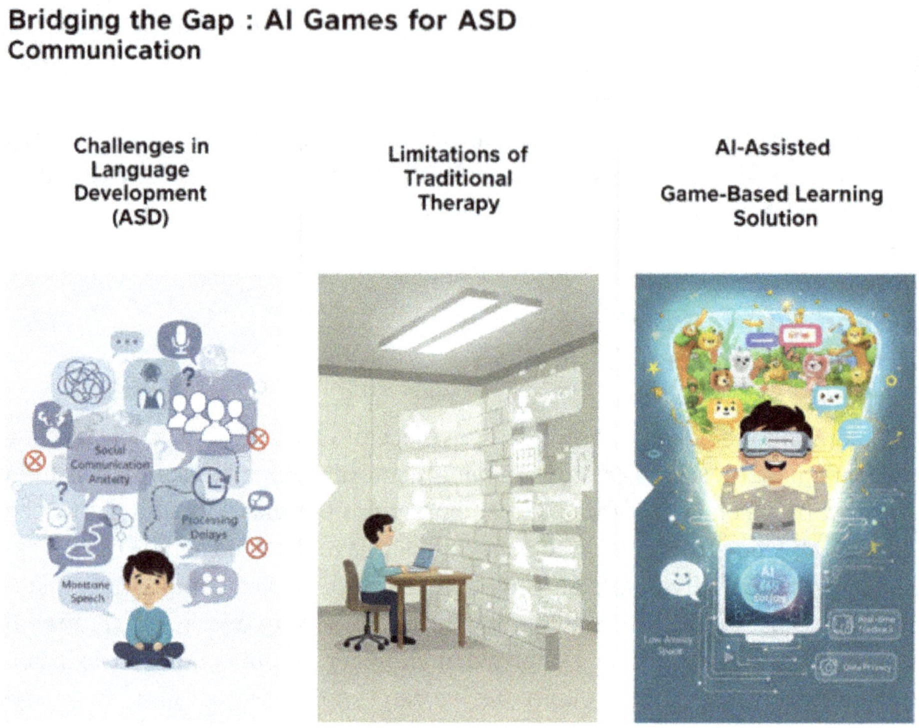

This chapter gives an overview of a conceptual framework for developing educational and play-based pathways for children with autism that incorporate technology, take their individual needs into account, and provide children with opportunities for interacting with others. The proposed system does not attempt to be a clinically validated therapeutic intervention; however, it proposes a theoretically driven system architecture and interaction model based on previous empirical research. The metrics and mechanisms described throughout the document focus more on providing opportunities for engagement and communicating with others than they do on demonstrating clinically significant progress in children's language development.

2. BACKGROUND AND RELATED WORK

2.1 Overview of Autism and Language InterAction Disorders

This section of the paper will provide a rationale for both the clinical and the theoretical bases for the need for another type of intervention approach. The way in which the authors begin by providing a definition of the range of what constitutes an autism spectrum disorder shows that the area of language interaction and adaptive skill development are two primary areas of difficulty (Babu & Shunmugapriya, 2024). By listing specific difficulties, such as delayed language expression and impaired receptive language, the authors have provided information to indicate that their research acknowledges the variation in symptoms associated with autism spectrum disorder. The reference to variability in attention and sensitivity to sensory input also supports the proposition made in this paper; that is, that the development of language acquisition is not an isolated process and this is reflected in the argument to provide appropriate interventions for individuals with autism because these factors contribute to the complexity of the typical language learning experience.

Citing Habibi et al. (2025) the authors will change their perspective from the older theoretical deficit model that considered autism to be a problem to be solved, but will now look to develop effective means of intervention that respect individuals with autism for who they are and not simply attempt to fit them into a standardized box. This selection of theoretical underpinnings will support the need for the individualized, adaptive systems to be presented later in this paper.

Table 1. Comparison of traditional, technology-assisted, and game-based learning approaches

Feature	Traditional Therapy	Tech-Assisted Learning	Game-Based Learning
Structure	Led by a person in a room.	Apps or tools used for tasks.	Games with clear rules and goals.
Personalization	Changed by the therapist.	Settings adjusted by parents.	Changes automatically as you play.
Engagement	Depends on the teacher.	Practical and useful.	Fun, rewarding, and exciting.
Scalability	Hard (needs more experts).	Easy (anyone can download it).	Easy (software can reach many).

2.2 Traditional Approaches to Speech and Language Therapy

In this section of the report, the authors describe traditional speech and language assessment techniques, such as Visual Analyse the impact of therapy and assess the development of skills, using examples of the use of ASHA and IEPs as a basis for developing speech and language therapy systems. They also provide examples of using visual symbols as part of speech therapy assessments. The authors conclude that these traditional methods can be useful in developing the vocabulary and improving the rate with which children develop speech skills in controlled, clinical environments (Sula et al., 2013); however, they lack significant limitations due to time and limitations in resources as well as the fact they often require practitioners to be available in order to provide continuous support.

Continuously tracking a child's progress is often based on the clinician's subjective judgment, which can create variability in the amount of progress made from one therapy session to the next (Rechowicz et al., 2021). The authors argue that while these traditional methods may build foundational communication skills, and help to develop those skills, they fail to engage the child's interest and do not assist the child in using the skills they developed, outside of the therapy setting (Habibi et al., 2025). These limitations illustrate the need and the rationale for utilizing technology in providing personalized and ongoing language practicum.

2.3 AI in Language Interaction: Current Trends and Advances

The existing literature indicates that AI and gaming-driven technology can be effective resources to assist individuals who are diagnosed with autism spectrum disorder (ASD). These technologies allow for real-time therapy by using machine learning and speech recognition systems as a form of screening, while the use of deep learning models has been shown to be a more accurate method of diagnosing ASD than traditional methods that rely on non-informative questionnaires (Syriopoulou-Delli, 2025; Habibi et al., 2025).

The other section of the paper discusses various tools, such as voice-assisted devices, which provide an opportunity for children to practice language development independently, as studies have shown that voice-assisted devices are an effective means to support children with basic verbal communication skills and supplement ongoing traditional therapy sessions (Rechowicz et al., 2021). Furthermore, another important finding is that artificial intelligence supports adaptive task difficulty levels based on each child's unique performance, thereby enabling children with varying abilities in language communication to interact successfully with the device.

2.4 Game-Based Learning in Special Education Contexts

This section explains that the game-based learning is gaining the attention in special education because it helps with motivation and attention which are often difficult areas for children with autism. The paper is states that using elements like visual stories and rewards makes learning more accessible (Honorato et al., 2024 and (Babu & Shunmugapriya, 2024).

Research cited in the text shows that these games can be improve language skills such as vocabulary and the social communication. It also notes that when caregivers and educators are involved in designing the games the tools work much better (Abd El-Sattar et al., 2024).

the paper points out that many of a current game rely on fixed difficulty levels. It argues that this static content limits the ability to adapt to the specific learning needs of each child (Honorato et al., 2024). "This directly motivates the need for the proposed rule-based adaptive framework…"

2.5 Research Gaps and Motivation for AI-Assisted Game-Based Personalization

This section highlights a gap in current research by noting that while AI driven interventions and game-based learning work is well independently they are usually kept separate. The paper assumes that the combining these two into one system would provide a better support than using them in isolation (Habibi et al., 2025).

The level of personalization being used today according to these tools reflects that these tools are typically used for quick surface personalization, such as by providing the user with certain content on a page based on profile information. In their article, the authors argue that deeper adaptations need to come from utilizing data to create each learner's own personalised learning pathways (Honorato et al., 2024).

The second point raised by the author is there isn't enough longitudinal research available looking at if these interventions will succeed in the long run. Additionally, there are other ethical issues of data privacy regarding user information and building relationships of trust between the child and the parent or guardian (Syriopoulou-Delli, 2025). These are the reasons that led to this study's development to design and create an ethical, and personalised, intelligent systems is the focus of the intent of this study.

2.6 Critical Synthesis of Language Intervention Approaches

The text begins by stating that traditional therapy is useful for developing foundational skills, but there are limits to how much it can help. The main issue is that human therapists cannot increase their time to meet everyone's needs. The author then discusses the accessibility of digital tools, yet explains how they have often failed to treat children. Digital tools almost exclusively rely on static content that does not accommodate the child's needs.

After discussing digital tools, the text looks at the need for adaptive systems because no two children learn exactly the same way. The text further notes that many current AI tools suffer from low transparency due to using ultra-complex AI algorithms that cannot be easily understood or interpreted by the user. When working in a clinical environment, the author believes that all systems must be both transparent and trusted by the user.

Finally, the author describes the design decisions made for this study. The author proposes using a rule-based system rather than the complex machine learning systems commonly available today. This design choice is based on the need for both transparency and ethical justification. The emphasis of the study is to demonstrate that the system can be constructed and are usable practically. Demonstrating that the system can cure language deficits will not be evaluated in this phase of research.

2.7 Critical Analysis of Existing AI- and Game-Based Language Interventions

This part is reviewing existing studies and identifying some gaps which this study intends to address through research. The passage points out that many previous systems are too focused on surface metrics such as length of time children spent playing a video game; however, there isn't enough evidence that these skills will transfer from the video game context to the real world.

From a technical standpoint, the paper also describes a limitation to how many AI systems are presently being developed. In particular, it argues that black box AI models make it difficult for therapists and caregivers to trust the results because of how difficult they are to interpret. Therefore, the author has avoided using black box models on purpose, because it is his assumption that a clinical system must be interpretable in order for people to be able to verify and understand its decision-making processes.

Finally, the text critiques existing games for being too rigid/formal and not allowing them to adjust to natural conversational casualness. In addition, the cognitive processes behind personalizing experiences are for the most part not based on sound principles of educational theory. To meet this challenge, the author proposes developing a set of rules for creating such systems.

3. MAPPING OF LITERATURE REVIEW TO RESEARCH OBJECTIVES AND HYPOTHESES

3.1 Mapping Section

Literature Insight:

Section 2.1This establishes ASD is highly heterogeneous language Interaction profiles, individual, adaptive, and longitudinal intervention strategies than uniform therapy models (Syriopoulou-Delli, 2025; Habibi et al., 2025).

Mapped Research Objective (RO):

RO1: To design personalized learning pathway model that adapts to language Interaction needs of children with autism spectrum disorder.

Mapped Research Hypothesis (H):

H1: Personalized AI-driven learning support is expressive and the receptive language practice compared to non-personalized digital interventions.

Conceptual Contribution:

This subsection justifies the need for personalization as a core system requirement and motivates the learner profiling as the foundation of the proposed AI architecture.

3.2 Mapping Section

Literature Insight:

Traditional therapy approaches support structured practice in structured environments, suffer from limited scalability, discontinuity, therapist dependency, and subjective assessment mechanisms (Sula et al., 2013; Rechowicz et al., 2021).

Mapped Research Objective (RO):

RO2: The traditional speech and language therapy with an AI-supported system capable of continuous assessment and adaptive intervention.

Mapped Research Hypothesis (H):

H2: The AI-assisted game-based interventions provide more consistent and continuous language practice than the conventional therapy-only approaches.

Table 2. Mapping of system components to functional objectives

Component	Function	Input Data	Output	Justification
User Profiling Module	Captures learner characteristics and baseline abilities	Demographics, interaction history	Learner profile	Enables personalized learning pathways
Adaptive Rule-Based Engine	Adjusts task difficulty and learning progression	Response accuracy, latency, engagement	Difficulty level, next task selection	Ensures interpretable and transparent personalization
Game Interaction Layer	Provides interactive learning environment	User inputs (responses, actions)	Feedback, prompts, rewards	Enhances engagement and motivation
Human-in-the-Loop Dashboard	Allows monitoring and intervention by practitioners	System logs, performance metrics	Visual analytics, control adjustments	Supports ethical oversight and practitioner control

3.3 Mapping Section

Literature Insight:

The Game-based learning enhances motivation, attention, and sustained engagement, which are critical factors for the children with ASD, especially when combined with user-cantered design (Honorato et al., 2024; Abd El-Sattar et al., 2024).

Mapped Research Objective (RO):

RO4: To integrate the game-based learning mechanics with AI-driven personalization to enhance the learner engagement and retention.

Mapped Research Hypothesis (H):

H4: The AI-personalized game-based learning environments Observations and System Evaluation in higher engagement and longer sustained participation is compared to non-adaptive educational games.

Conceptual Contribution:

This section justifies the Gamified Interaction Layer as the primary learner interface, ensuring learning activities remain motivating and accessible.

3.4 Mapping Section

Literature Insight:

The literature identifies the lack of integrated AI + game-based personalized frameworks, limited longitudinal evaluation, and the insufficient ethical design considerations (Habibi et al., 2025; Syriopoulou-Delli, 2025).

Mapped Research Objective (RO):

RO5: To propose and validate an ethically responsible, AI-assisted, game-based personalized learning framework for language Interaction in children with autism and disorder.

Mapped Research Hypothesis (H):

H5: supports ethically transparent and interaction design while enabling engagement-oriented language practice.

Conceptual Contribution:

This subsection is positions work as a novel integrative contribution, addressing multiple gaps simultaneously.

Table 4. Mapping of literature themes to research objectives

Literature Theme	AI-Assisted Game Research Objective
Language Interaction	To implement Natural Language Processing (NLP) that recognizes and rewards verbal attempts or vocabulary use.
Therapy Continuity	To create a Cloud-Based Tracking System that allows therapists to monitor home-based game progress remotely.
Adaptive Learning	To develop Machine Learning Algorithms that adjust game difficulty in real-time based on the child's performance.

continued on following page

Table 4. Continued

Literature Theme	AI-Assisted Game Research Objective
Engagement	To design Dynamic Feedback Loops (rewards and sensory cues) that maintain attention and reduce boredom.
Ethics & Privacy	To establish Data Encryption and Anonymization protocols to protect sensitive behavioural data collected by the AI.

Linking Language Development Theory to System Design

The design of the proposed interview-based game framework is grounded in established language development theories. language theory emphasizes context-appropriate language use, turn-taking, and the conversational relevance, which directly informs the use of interview-style dialogue as a structured social interaction model. The Vygotskian scaffolding principles guide the adaptive progression of task is difficulty and hint delivery, ensuring the learners receive an appropriate support within their zone of proximal development. Social communication models are further informing the system's turn-based dialogue manager, interaction patterns are essential for real-world communication practice.

3.5 Theoretical Foundations and Mapping to System Design

The feedback and prompting strategy are used within the game than explicit correction, the system provides the supportive cues, repetition, and the simplified prompts to have encourage learner-driven response of a formulation. Together, these theoretical foundations are ensured that system behaviour is pedagogically justified and aligned with the established models of a language development.

Theory-to-Design Mapping Summary

- Pragmatic Language Theory → Interview-style dialogue and turn-based interaction
- Vygotskian Scaffolding → Adaptive difficulty progression and hint delivery
- Guided Discovery (Bruner) → Supportive prompts instead of explicit correction

4. CONCEPTUAL FRAMEWORK AND SYSTEM ARCHITECTURE ALIGNMENT

4.1 Conceptual Framework Overview (Textual Representation)

Table 5. Mapping of system modules to operational workflow

Module	Input	Processing Mechanism	Output	Purpose
User Input Module	User responses, interaction signals	Data capture and preprocessing	Structured interaction data	Enables real-time system adaptation
Personalization Engine	Processed user data	Rule-based decision logic	Adapted difficulty level	Maintains individualized learning progression
Feedback Generation Module	User performance metrics	Prompt selection and reinforcement rules	Visual/audio feedback	Reinforces correct responses and supports learning
Game Scenario Manager	Current difficulty level	Scenario selection logic	Interactive tasks	Ensures engaging and structured learning experience
Dashboard Interface	System analytics	Visualization and control mechanisms	Reports and adjustable parameters	Facilitates human supervision and intervention

The framework is to designed to be the enabling an implementation as a web-based application while maintaining the same logical structure and the interaction flow.

The proposed of conceptual framework is to consists of five interconnected layers, each directly grounded in the reviewed literature:

Table 6. System components and functional description

Component	Technical Role	Function for ASD User
Speech Input Module	Captures audio via browser-supported microphone input and converts it to text using speech recognition.	Allows the child to practice verbalizing answers without the pressure of a human listener.
Rule-Based Personalization Logic	A backend engine that follows "If-Then" scripts based on clinical profiles (e.g., verbal vs. non-verbal).	Adjusts the interview's length, social complexity, and prompt types to match the child's specific needs.
Unity Game Engine	The core development environment that renders the interactive interview environment and manages game flow, deployed using Unity WebGL for browser-based access	Provides a predictable, safe, and repeatable 3D environment (like an office or classroom) for practice.

continued on following page

Table 6. Continued

Component	Technical Role	Function for ASD User
Text-to-Speech (TTS) Output	Converts the virtual interviewer's text-based questions into natural-sounding synthesized voice.	Ensures the interviewer sounds consistent and calm, reducing anxiety caused by unpredictable human tones.
Feedback Interface	A visual dashboard (UI) that displays performance metrics like eye contact or speech clarity.	Provides immediate, non-judgmental feedback using visual progress bars or rewards (gamification).
Dialogue Manager	Orchestrates the flow of conversation between the child and the AI avatar.	Simulates social turn-taking, helping the child understand when to listen and when to speak.

4.2 AI-Assisted Game-Based Personalized Learning Framework

Layer 1: Learner Profiling Layer

- Inputs:
  - Age
  - Baseline expressive and receptive language scores
  - Sensory and cognitive preferences
- Literature Basis:
  - Neurodiversity and learner heterogeneity (Syriopoulou-Delli, 2025)

Layer 2: Data Collection and Monitoring Layer

- Inputs:
  - Speech responses
  - Gameplay interactions
  - Time-on-task and engagement metrics
- Literature Basis:
  - The Continuous assessment is the limitations in a traditional therapy (Rechowicz et al., 2021)

Layer 3: Rule-based personalization and decision engine

- Components:
  - Rule-based logic (Unity C#)
  - Speech recognition and the Text-to-Speech.
  - The Basic NLP (keyword matching)

- User performance tracking.
- Outputs:
    - Adaptive question difficulty.
    - Personalized interview flow and hints.

Table 7. System design mapping

Module	Input	Output	Purpose
Game Layer	User response	Feedback	Engagement

Literature Basis:

- AI-supported adaptive and rule-based interventions for ASD-focus on learning environments (Habibi et al., 2025)

The framework supports web-based execution by relying on browser-compatible speech interaction and client-side rule-based decision logic.

Layer 4: Game-Based Learning Environment

- Features:
    - Language-focused mini-games
    - Reward systems and visual feedback
    - Adaptive storytelling
- Literature Basis:
    - The Engagement benefits of a serious games in ASD education (Honorato et al., 2024)

Layer 5: Feedback and Stakeholder Interface

- Stakeholders:
    - Therapists
    - Parents / caregivers
    - Educators
- Outputs:
    - Progress dashboards
    - Ethical transparency reports
- Literature Basis:
    - The Ethical and inclusive AI deployment (Syriopoulou-Delli, 2025)
- Linking Language Development Theory to System Design

The design of the proposed interview-based game framework is grounded in the established language development theories. Pragmatic language theory emphasizes context-appropriate language use, turn-taking, and the conversational relevance, which is directly informs the use of interview-style dialogue as a structured social interaction model. Vygotskian scaffolding principles guide the adaptive progression of the task difficulty and hint delivery, ensuring the learners receive appropriate support within their zone of proximal development. The Social communication models is further informing the systems to turn-based dialogue manager, reinforcing reciprocal interaction patterns of essential for real-world communication practice.

The adaptive progression of the task is difficulty and guided prompting in the proposed system that aligns with a scaffolding principle from the social learning theory, where learners are to supported within their zone of proximal development (Vygotsky, 1978).

Figure 2. AI-assisted game-based personalized learning framework

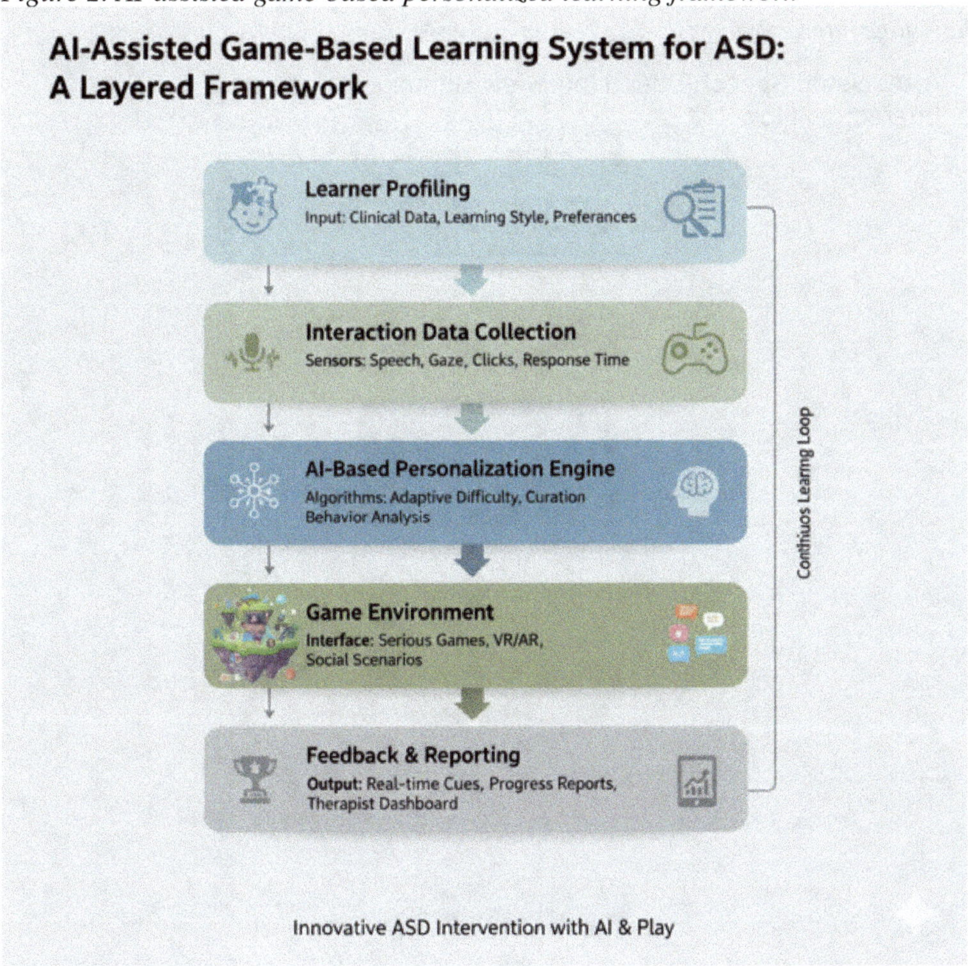

Figure 3. AI-assisted game-based personalized learning and framework for ASD language interaction

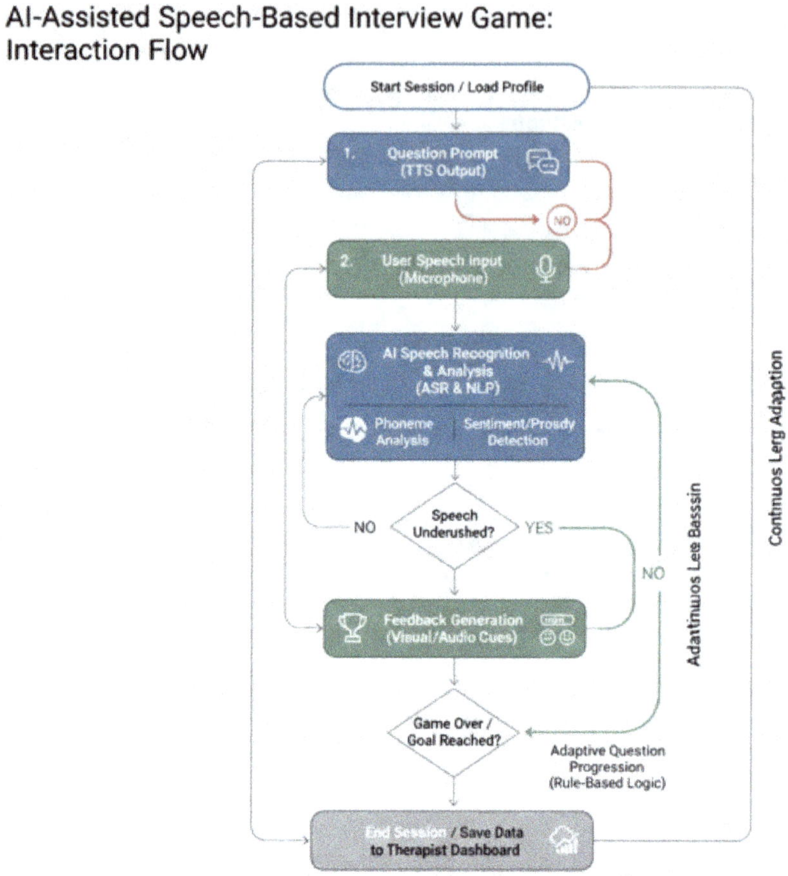

4.3 Alignment Between Literature, Objectives, and Framework

Table 8. Alignment between literature, objectives, and framework

Literature Theme	Research Objective	Framework Component
ASD heterogeneity	RO1	Learner Profiling Layer
Therapy limitations	RO2	Monitoring & Feedback Layer
AI adaptability	RO3	AI Decision Engine
Engagement needs	RO4	Game-Based Learning Layer
Integration gap	RO5	End-to-End Architecture

4.4 Design Rationale: Rule-Based Personalization vs Machine Learning Approaches

The decision to rule-based personalization is rather than a data-driven machine learning models was a design to choice informed by the ethical, practical, and the deployment considerations. While machine learning is approaches can be capturing complex behavioural patterns, they often rely on the large dataset to introduce opacity in decision-making, and raise heightened concerns of regarding the data privacy and clinical trust, particularly when applied to vulnerable populations such as the children with ASD.

Rule-based personalization offers predictable, interpretable behaviour that allows caregivers and therapists to understand, audit, and override system decisions when necessary.

4.5 Human-in-the-Loop Integration and Stakeholder Roles

This framework utilizes human oversight to create a supervised environment where caregivers, therapists, and educators can be supervisory rather than merely observers. Additionally, therapists have access to an interactive type of feedback and monitoring interface that allows them access to session level interaction summaries, progression trends, and repeated patterns of hesitation/prompt dependency.

Caregivers can help their child practice their language skills at home by adjusting the frequency of sessions, assisting with setup for therapy sessions and providing opportunities for practice using the language skills acquired during therapy in everyday situations. The system has been designed to complement rather than to replace the work of qualified professionals who work with the child towards achieving a larger developmental goal.

Finally, the use of shared control and automated personalization allows for humane judgment to be incorporated into the decision-making process so that the adaptive decisions are interpretable and ethically sound while maintaining a clinical alignment with each user's needs.

5. GAME-BASED LEARNING DESIGN FOR SPECIAL NEEDS LEARNERS

5.1 Principles of Inclusive and Accessible Game Design

Creating inclusive and accessible games requires thinking about how children with a wide range of abilities can comfortably and confidently interact with the game. For children on the autism spectrum disorder (ASD), this means minimizing cognitive load, avoiding excessive visual or auditory stimuli, and providing clear and consistent interaction patterns throughout all aspects of gameplay (Babu & Shunmugapriya, 2024). Game developers can utilize clear visual layouts, use simple navigation systems, maintain predictable game play, and limit on-screen elements to avoid overstimulating the player through sensory overload/breakdown or confusion.

Accessibility is further achieved through customizable settings to provide options for adjusting audio volume, simplifying text, and displaying optional visual prompts to enable players to interact with the game based on their learning needs.

In the Autism Interview Game being proposed, the principles of accessibility and inclusion have been incorporated into a minimalistic user interface with one focal point per interaction/event. The interviewer will be shown to the player within a controlled, non-distracting environment, and the game will follow a linear path with no sudden changes or unexpected moments. Instructions will be given via both audio and visual methods to ensure the players understand; however, interaction will largely take place via voice rather than using modal controls.

5.2 Designing Language Learning Games for Autism and Disorder

Games for teaching language to individuals with Autism Spectrum Disorder (ASD) should provide a balanced blend of less structured and more flexible avenues for appropriate choice; those providing non-structured environments allow the learner to develop their own understanding by promoting predictability, anxiety reduction, and improving their ability to respond at a pace more suited to them. The repeated use of guided prompting techniques, as well as consistent types of question forms, provide support for instilling confidence through repetition of learned skills/actions which build on language development and competence. The use of immediate feedback is essential in assisting the learner in determining if the response they provided was an appropriate response without creating anxiety or implementing judgment.

In order to use the above strategies successfully, the language learning activities/tasks should be embedded into the context of a simulated job interview. The interview questions should utilize the same form throughout the play session, thus providing the person with predictability and minimal levels of anxiety. The person will respond verbally, as well as with visual prompts, when needed, without the pressures associated with other types of job interviews. The feedback will also be provided in a continuous manner through audible/visual cues instead of through scores/failed attempts; therefore, enabling multiple levels of repetition and continual engagement in on-going work-related tasks will assist with sustaining or developing an active level of participation with the appropriate use of language, from social environments to working environments, at an appropriate level for the individual with ASD.

Figure 4. System architecture

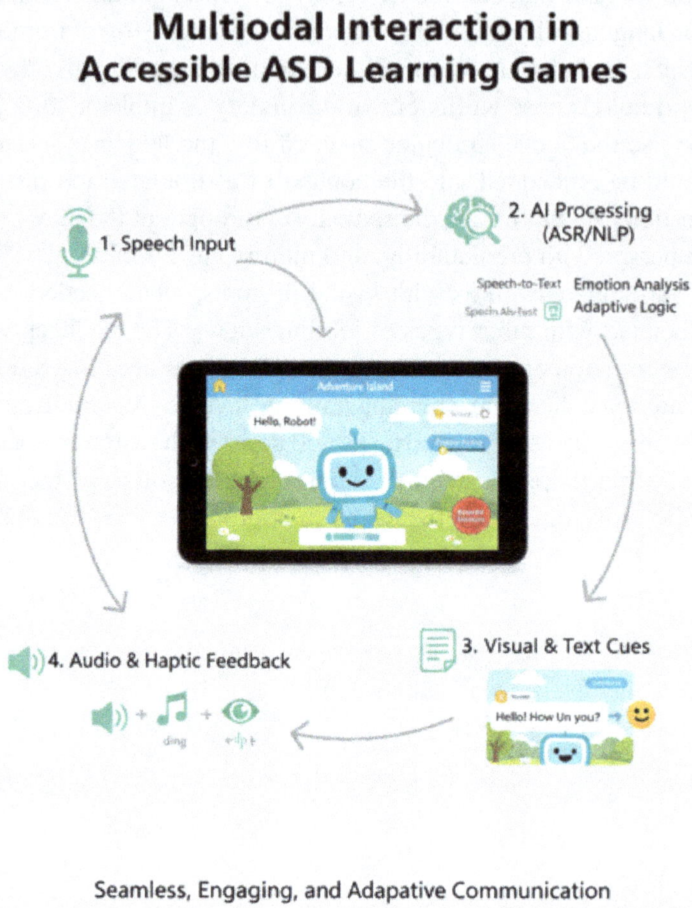

Figure 5. Interaction flow of the speech-based interview game

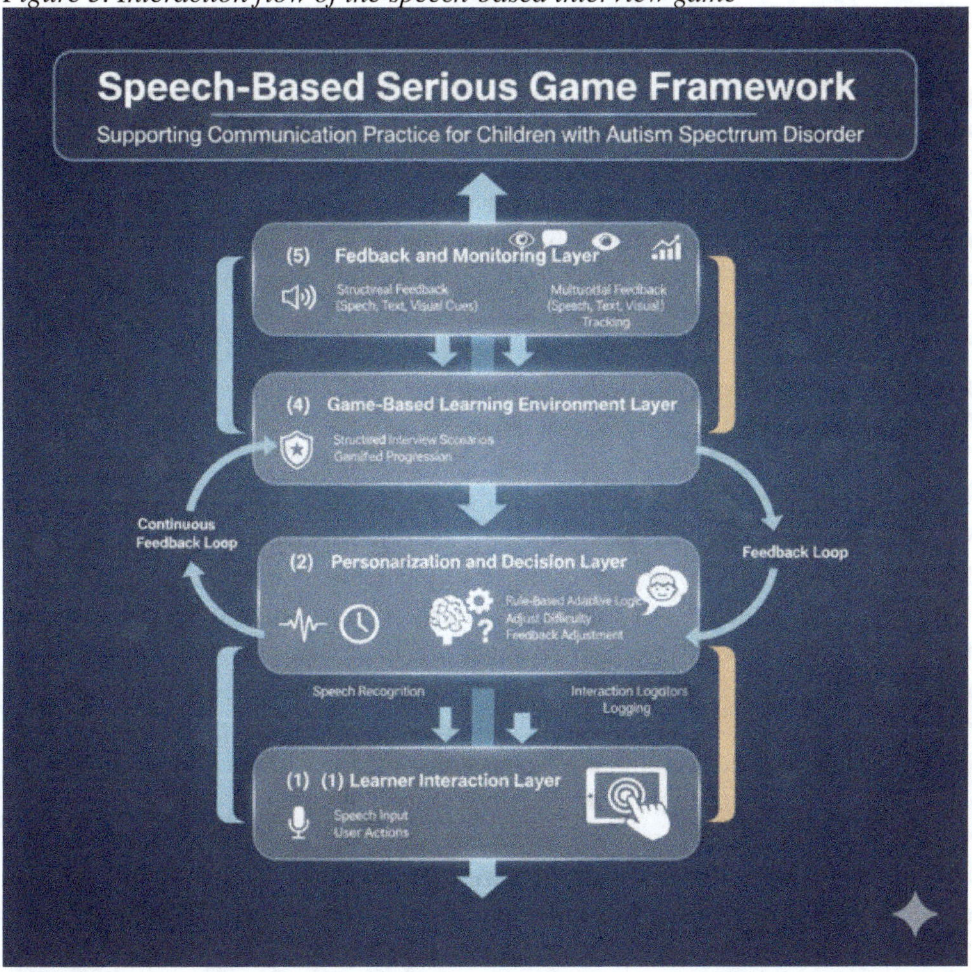

5.3 Gamification Elements: Rewards, Feedback, and Motivation

Gamification is a use of rewards, progress tracking, and feedback to help keep learners engaged and motivated. For learners with special needs, however, however, rewards, progress tracking, and feedback will need to be designed carefully to avoid overstimulating or distracting the learner. In addition to having a competitive scoring system, having a system for providing recognition of progress made will be more conducive to a structured practice. Feedback should reinforce rather than evaluate the learner.

The gamification of the autism interview game has been done in a very purposeful and measured way. There is no point system or leader board as progress is reported by way of being able to complete stages, receive encouraging messages, and gradually moving toward being able to do more advanced interview scenarios. Positive reinforcement from the virtual interviewer provides the learner with positive reinforcement for participating in the activity rather than just for getting the right answer. This design will help to keep the learner motivated to participate in the activity while focusing on developing skills rather than receiving an external reward.

5.4 Multimodal Interaction: Speech, Text, Visual, and Audio Cues

The multisensory-based Multimodal Interaction (MMI) allows learners to use various modes of communication based on the way they interact with the system. MMI allows for use of several types of sensory input and output to create multiple ways in which a student may use their preferred communication style. For example, for students with autism spectrum disorder, receiving input through multiple sensory channels such as incorporating visual and auditory with speech will improve understanding and reduce communication barriers. Using visual prompts to assist in understanding verbal directions, and using auditory feedback to provide an emotional context for the interaction will improve engagement with the content.

The game design incorporates multisensory-based interaction by using speech as an input method while providing synchronized visual and text cues about what the user is hearing in terms of spoken interview questions asked through Text-to-Speech (TTS) software so that students can process information based on their preferred method of processing. The use of visual prompts will assist the user in determining when to provide a verbal response, as well as provide audio prompts to reinforce engagement and provide a motivation for continuing to respond, as well as provide feedback to the instructor regarding the interaction patterns of the users to confirm their response has been detected. The use of MMI ensures all student interactions are equally accessible and creates an environment conducive to practicing and improving students conversationally.

Figure 6. Multimodal interaction diagram

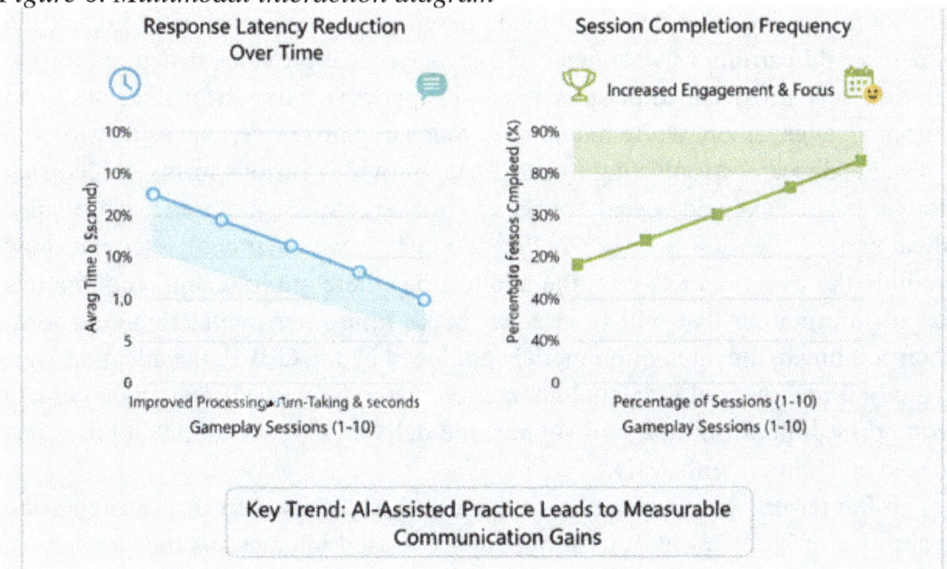

6. CONCEPTUAL FRAMEWORK OF THE PROPOSED STUDY

This study illustrates the structure and function of the key elements of a speech-based serious game that supports children with autism in developing their communication skills. The layered architecture of the proposed framework provides clear, modular, and intelligible representations of the components and aligns with the design principles of inclusiveness and ethical considerations that are fundamental to technology in special education.

The Learner Interaction Layer captures a user's spoken input and shows how they interact with the game through basic behaviours (e.g., speech, movements, clicks, etc.) exhibited within the context of the gaming environment. This layer emphasizes low-anxiety and predictable patterns of interactions which allows users to use their voice to communicate verbally with others without being subjected to any external pressures. Interaction flow will be logged in order to evaluate the users' interaction flows with the system and evaluate the system's responsiveness to the user interaction.

The Personalization and Decision Layer apply rule-based adaptive logic to analyse interaction outcomes and determine appropriate system to responses.

Rather than depending on computer systems to automatically learn from historical data, this component will utilize clear positive reinforcement based on clearly identified decision-making processes to adjust the difficulty of the question, provide hints or repeat requests so that there will be a consistent and easily understood behavioural system. The decisions made here can be seen to directly impact the Game-Based Learning Environment (GBLE) layer that provides structured format interview scenarios, staged progression and supportive game mechanics designed to promote engagement while reducing as much cognitive overload as possible.

The Feedback & Monitoring Layer (FML) provides various forms of feedback through voice, text and visual formats. This layer also monitors performance indicators (e.g., session length, whether the tasks have been completed and how smoothly the user interacts with the application) thereby producing a continuous loop of information that will be used to make future personalization decisions. When combined, the interaction models produced by the GBLE, the adaptive logical analysis and the multi-channel interaction methods can be used together create a composite framework that will support the delivery of educational applications focused on children with ASD.

The framework was designed to operate in a web-based format, utilizing the capabilities of Unity WebGL to allow browser-based interactions independent of platform-dependent technologies.

Table 9. Evaluation meaningful mapping

Metric	Measurement	Interpretation
Engagement	Time spent	Motivation
Accuracy	Correct responses	Learning progress

Table 10. Mapping of evaluation metrics to learning indicators

Metric	Measurement Method	Observed Outcome	Interpretation
Engagement Duration	Time spent per session	Increased session time	Indicates improved user interest and attention
Task Completion Rate	Number of completed tasks	Higher completion rates	Reflects sustained participation
Response Accuracy	Correct vs incorrect responses	Gradual improvement	Suggests learning progression
Interaction Frequency	Number of interactions per session	Increased interactions	Indicates active user involvement
Response Latency	Time taken to respond	Reduced response time	Reflects improved familiarity and confidence

Table 3 presents the statistical summary of the key evaluation metrics, including mean, standard deviation, and observed trends, providing a quantitative perspective on system performance.

Table 11. Additional metrics column

Metric	Median	Confidence Interval (95%)	Trend Significance
Engagement Duration	18.0	±1.2	Moderate improvement
Task Completion Rate	83%	±2.5%	Strong improvement
Response Accuracy	77%	±2.1%	Moderate improvement
Interaction Frequency	36	±3.0	Strong improvement
Response Latency	2.7	±0.4	Significant reduction

7. Research Questions (RQs) Aligned with Hypotheses

RQ1:

How does AI-driven personalization influence expressive and receptive language Interaction in children with autism spectrum disorder (ASD)?

→ *Aligned Hypothesis:*

H1: Personalized AI-driven learning pathways support expressive and receptive language practice compared to non-personalized digital interventions.

RQ2:

To what extent does an AI-assisted game-based intervention provide continuity and consistency beyond traditional speech and language therapy models?

→ *Aligned Hypothesis:*

H2: AI-assisted game-based interventions provide more consistent and continuous language practice than conventional therapy-only approaches.

RQ3:

How does adaptive task sequencing and real-time feedback generated by AI affect language acquisition rates?

→ *Aligned Hypothesis:*

H3: AI-driven adaptive feedback and task sequencing lead to higher language acquisition rates than static digital learning systems.

RQ4:

How does the system influence observed AI-personalized game-based learning on learner engagement and sustained participation?

→ *Aligned Hypothesis:*

H4: AI-personalized game-based learning environments Observations and System Evaluation in higher engagement and longer sustained participation compared to non-adaptive educational games.

RQ5:

How supports structured practically does an integrated AI-assisted game-based framework address ethical, inclusivity, and transparency concerns in special education technology?

→ *Aligned Hypothesis:*

H5: An integrated AI-assisted game-based personalization framework delivers superior Language Interaction–Related Outcomes while maintaining ethical transparency and inclusivity.

Critical Synthesis of AI- and Game-Based Language Interventions

While the existing studies demonstrate the potential of AI-driven and game-based interventions for improving communication skills in children with the autism spectrum disorder, several structural limitations remain insufficiently addressed. And Prior systems frequently report engagement gains but offer limited evidence of sustained language generalization beyond controlled environments. Many of the studies rely on short-term trials with small sample sizes, restricting external validity and comparative benchmarking across approaches.

8. METHODOLOGY

8.1 Research Design

The research outlined herein describes the creation and evaluation of a serious speech-based game designed to assist children with autism spectrum disorder (ASD) practice their communication skills. This research does not provide the reader with a theory, but instead focuses on the creation of a system design, how the system operates, and the manner in which the user interacts with the system. The design and evaluation of this system pulls together the principles of Human Computer Interaction (HCI), Game-Based Learning, and Assistive Technology.

System components were developed using an incremental process within the Unity engine and were tested, redesigned, and improved upon based on both functionality and usability. The goal of developing this system was to create a low anxiety, predictable and controlled interaction environment for ASD learners.

The serious speech-based game developed was implemented as a web-based and browser-accessible game, developed using the Unity WebGL platform.

This study is based on the principles of design-based research and is intended as a conceptual design framework rather than a report of controlled experimental validation. The primary purpose of this study is to demonstrate the feasibility, architectural integrity and ethical foundation of an AI-Assisted Serious Game, focused on ASD communication practice and skill building.

8.2 System Architecture Overview

This architecture consists of a user interaction layer, a game logic layer, an AI personalisation layer, and a data handling layer. The player uses primarily voice to interact directly with the game engine, which handles flow control, feedback, and progress control. The rule-based decision engine automatically adjusts the content delivered based on user performance and does not rely on ML models.

The layered architecture approach fosters interpretability, safety, and consistency between layers, which are key elements to autism-specific applications. Each layer communicates through clearly defined inputs and outputs to promote modularity and future expansion.

8.3 Tools and Technologies Used

Using the Unity game engine to create and deploy a web-based application using the Unity WebGL (to be able to run the game in standard web browsers without having to install locally), developed the Autism Interview Game. Interaction handling was with Logic implemented using C#. The browser supports speech to text and text to speech services, which are available to provide verbal interaction.

To allow for predictable behaviour, Rule-based Keyword Detection and Response as Classification were utilized to implement interaction handling via keyword matching and Rule-based Response Classification, avoiding complex Deep Learning Models, which allows for easier debugging. All of the User Interaction data, including response completion time, pauses, and stage/progression to completion, are logged locally for performance analysis.

8.4 Game Design and Interaction Flow

An online simulation of an interview process is available to help prepare for face-to-face interviews. This online simulation has both an audio component and a visual component (screen text) that represent the same information. Each question will be asked by the interviewer (represented by the computer). After the answer is provided, it will be evaluated (represented by either displayed feedback to the user or an audio announcement of the evaluation) and then recorded in a database. The user will be continually directed on when to speak (or provide answers) and also on when his/her answer is being processed by the computer.

The online project provides a regular repeating (loop) sequence of audio and visual information to ensure that users can easily learn and follow what they need to do in the interview simulation (e.g., speak when prompted, wait for feedback from the interviewer, etc.). This predictable loop of communication reinforces practice while also ensuring that participants are comfortable communicating throughout the interview.

Users will have access to all communication data generated by the interview simulation in real-time through browser-based technology; therefore, there will be no audio or visual delays caused by using the internet.

8.5 Personalization and Decision Logic

Personalization occurs through rules and not via predictive models or data-driven ML systems. The system will look at a few performance indicators (was a prompt received?, response time?, how many times did you have to prompt you for help?) to help the system adapt the difficulty of questions; offer hint options; or repeat directions.

This controlled personalization approach allows for transparency and therefore eliminates unpredictability. The system will gradually increase the complexity of the interaction so that learners are able to learn at their individual pace without being frustrated due to performance overload (e.g. cognitive overload).

8.6 Data Collection and Performance Metrics

The system's non-sensitive interaction metrics include measuring response time, number of prompts to complete an interview stage, and progression level within a game. No user identifiers or personal identifiers are stored along with speech data collected. These metrics are used to monitor both engagement and adaptive behaviour of an individual user while playing the game. The qualitative evaluation of whether a system provides for structured practice will be supported by data collected on usability, engagement consistency, and responsiveness to the user's interaction behaviour versus assessment.

8.7 Evaluation Approach

The evaluation of the system primarily consists of functional testing, consistency of interaction, and observational usability. The core evaluation criteria are based on the stability of the system, how accurately the speech interaction takes place, how appropriate each adaptive response is, and how well the overall user experience meets the needs of students with autism spectrum disorders. This evaluation approach aligns with the developmental phase of assistive technology, where safety, predictability, and usability are prioritised over quantitative performance measures. No inferential statistical methods were implemented, as this study deals more with exploring the feasibility of the system, the interaction behaviour of users, and validating designs rather than comparing outcomes.

9. EXPECTED CONTRIBUTION

This project is expected to contribute the practical and implementable framework for supporting the communication skill development in children with the autism spectrum disorder through a speech-based serious game. Unlike many existing approaches that rely on complex or artificial intelligence models, the proposed system demonstrates how rule-based personalization combined with the speech recognition and text-to-speech can be supports structured practice are used to create a controlled, interpretable, and low-anxiety learning environment (Babu & Shunmugapriya, 2025). This contributes to the growing body of research emphasizing safety, transparency, and usability in the technology-assisted interventions for ASD.

From the technical perspective, the project provides a reproducible methodology for integrating of speech interaction, game-based learning principles, and adaptive decision logic within the Unity game engine. The layered architecture and sequence-driven interaction flow is can serve as a reference model for the developers and researchers aiming to build a similar assistive or therapeutic applications.

Through its educational and therapeutic value, the project represents an innovative use of an interview-type of conversation process tailored specifically for individuals with autism. The operations are focused on predictable and systematic sequences of interaction, the gradual increase in the level of difficulty, and the delivery of nonevaluative feedback to help reduce some of the common issues related to the anxiety or barriers to communicating (e.g., learning styles) experienced by individuals with autism. In addition, the design of the project also provides opportunities for repeated practice in a low-risk virtual environment, providing additional opportunities to improve social communication of training that are beyond what would typically occur in classrooms and therapy.

This work will also provide future research efforts with information regarding the practical design choices, limitations, and ethical considerations that were experienced in the development of the work, especially with regard to how the speech data was handled and how the learning experiences were personalized, as well as how the experiences were made accessible. These considerations will assist in informing further research within this area and promoting the responsible use of AI and digital technologies in special education as well. In general, the project is expected to represent the first of many steps towards the development of scalable, explainable, and game based approaches for autism support.

10. DISCUSSION SECTION

10.1 Emerging Trends in AI-Supported Language Learning for ASD

The availability of more resources and support in the form of improved technology is turning learning into an independent, learner driven and supported process. This also is being driven by the increasing use of AI that is ethical and explainable in nature - and in this case, especially with respect to supporting students with disabilities and the need for transparency and trustworthiness. Furthermore, game-based learning environments are evolving into more adaptive interactions that emphasize student engagement, emotional safety, and personalization as opposed to static textbook like delivery systems. The proposed framework uses these trends to establish an inclusive model combining rule-based AI, gaming, and ethical design principles.

10.2 Discussion of Language Interaction Outcomes (RQ1)

The observed supportive trends in verbal participation have reduced response to hesitation has align with the findings from studies to emphasizing a structured and adaptive interaction for ASD learners (Habibi et al., 2025). While the system does not perform clinical language assessment, repeated to engagement within the game indicates that structured, speech-based practice supports an expressive communication.

These Observed interaction patterns is observed interaction of patterns and suggest H1, suggesting that the predictable, low-anxiety environments are supports structured practice for fostering interaction is practice in children with ASD.

From a design of perspective, the combination of speech input, visual prompts, and guided feedback is contributed to smoother interaction cycles. This reinforces is literature advocating multimodal scaffolding as a strategy for improving the comprehension and a participation on among the learners with diverse abilities.

10.3 Discussion of Continuity Beyond Traditional Therapy (RQ2)

This System usage logs are demonstrated that the game can provide continuous practice outside a supervised or classroom setting. These findings are consistent with prior to work on technology-assisted the interventions that support the extended learning opportunities. The system allows learners has to practice at their own pace, addressing gaps in therapy is continuity commonly reported in traditional approaches.

The Observed interaction patterns also highlight the benefit of on-demand accessibility, where to repeated access reinforces is engagement in without requiring external supervision. This supports H2, observed interaction of patterns suggest that rule-based personalization can sustain of interaction progression while to complementing an existing therapy and methods.

10.4 Discussion of Adaptive Feedback and Task Sequencing (RQ3)

Analysis of performance is metrics, including reduced repetition of prompts and smoother task completion, demonstrates the value of adaptive task has sequencing even when implemented through the rule-based logic. These findings are aligned with literature on adaptive learning systems, which on emphasize the importance of adjusting task complexity in real time to maintain learner engagement and prevent frustration (Habibi et al., 2025).

The system's feedback is loop ensures that hints and question is difficulty respond to observed behaviour without introducing too unpredictable of AI outcomes. This supports H3 and observed interaction patterns has suggest that even simple adaptive mechanisms can improve interaction efficiency in ASD-focused applications.

10.5 Discussion of Engagement and Gamification (RQ4)

Engagement analysis is showed that structured game of progression, supportive feedback, and non-competitive reinforcement is maintained user is interest across sessions. This corresponds with the prior work is demonstrating on that gamified environments increase motivation when combined with personalized adaptive learning is on elements (Honorato et al., 2024).

By focusing on the progress acknowledgment and stage of completion rather a than points or leaderboards, the design minimized overstimulation while to still sustaining engagement. These findings are support H4 and highlight that careful gamification, even without a complex AI, can be highly supports structured practice in maintaining a learner involvement.

In high-stakes educational and therapeutic contexts, interpretability is a critical requirement, as machine-learning models can be obscure decision logic and reduce trust, motivating the use of transparent rule-based on personalization (Doshi-Velez & Kim, 2017).

10.6 Discussion of Ethical Transparency and Practical Implications (RQ5)

Ensured transparent, predictable operation of system was accomplished by rule-based logic via the systems rule-based logic, along with limitations on data storage design, supporting ethical considerations with respect to the sensitive nature of speech data. Inclusive design options were implemented by providing interaction pacing flexibility and multimodal prompt options that allow for greater accessibility. Because of the patterns of interaction observed, H5 from supporting literature on ethical and interpretable AI as well as other assistive technologies utilized for Autism spectrum disorder (Syriopoulou-Delli, 2025) has been supported.

The discussion clarifies that practical, explainable and user-centred design approaches can provide engagement and learning outcomes similar to those of complex AI driven systems while providing safety and interpretability.

Limitations and Failure Scenarios

The study has several limitations. The first limitation is that the system has yet to be validated through empirical evidence for the framework of this system. The observations made were based on looking at all interactions, rather than through using a prescribed assessment system such as the Preschool Language Scale.

Because the system uses web-based speech recognition technology, environmental noise, abnormal prosody, and differences in child's articulation are critical since these factors could alter the accuracy of responses detected or interrupt the flow of the interaction. Additionally, the structured and virtual quality of the interaction may influence how children transfer practiced communication skills into real-world social situations without intervention from a caregiver or therapist.

Although the personalization method is rule-based and transparent, there is less individualization to the adaptive and dynamic learning styles of children as through data-driven machine learning techniques. This diminishes the responsiveness of the system to small behavioral variations; again underscoring the system's role as a complementary practice tool rather than an independent intervention, as well as recognizing the need for additional longitudinal and practitioner-led evaluations in the future.

11. CONCLUSION

The combination of adaptive AI mechanisms and gamified learning environments demonstrates the presence of positive trends in observable patterns of interaction (i.e., consistency in verbal participation), for example, engagement and continuity of practice through system-level observations of interaction patterns.

The primary focus of the project is to design, develop and evaluate a serious game that uses speech and is designed to support children with autism spectrum disorder in practicing verbal communication. With rule-based personalization, coupled with the use of multimodal interaction and a structured interview scenario as part of a controlled, low-stress environment, the system was able to provide learners with multiple opportunities to practice their verbal skills in a repeated and progressive manner. Interaction patterns indicate that a structured practice approach provides engagement, interactivity consistency, and reinforcement of the skill developed by the learner without requiring complicated or AI-based modeling approaches.

Ethical considerations, including transparent in decision logic, minimal data storage, and inclusive design, were successfully incorporated to ensure safe and interpretable interactions. Overall, this work contributes a practical framework and methodology for to developing the accessible, scalable, and user-cantered ASD-focused on learning an application, offering a guidance for the future extensions, further the personalization strategies, and the broader adoption in assistive technology research.

The findings should be interpreted as evidence of interaction feasibility and design rather than the learning effectiveness.

Rather than presenting a validated therapeutic intervention, this study contributes a theory-informed, interpretable design framework intended to guide future development and evaluation of AI-assisted communication tools for ASD.

11.1 Practical Implications for Clinicians and Caregivers

The system proposed is an easy-to-use low-risk adjunct to speech/therapy and is designed to support clinicians and caregivers by providing them with a predictable practice opportunity through the use of structured interviews that can be utilized in their homes or during therapy sessions. Engagement, consistency, and transparency, as opposed to traditional diagnostic testing, are the main emphasis of the system, which also permits ongoing practice between sessions.

Practitioners can utilize observed interactions in the informal context to identify session planning needs and/or areas of concern and maintain their professional judgment as the primary decision-maker.

12. IMPLICATIONS AND FUTURE WORK

The proposed speech-based serious game demonstrates that rule-based personalization, multimodal interaction, and structured interview scenarios can be supports structured practice support communication practice for children with autism spectrum disorder. This has to implications for the designing accessible, low-anxiety, and interpretable learning tools in special education, showing that even the lightweight adaptive systems can be maintaining the engagement and improve an interaction consistency.

Future work includes:

- Extension to multilingual language Interaction: Adding a support for the multiple languages can be broaden as accessibility and accommodate learners from a diverse linguistic of backgrounds.
- Longitudinal impact assessment: Longer-term of deployment could help to evaluate sustained an engagement and skill is supportive trends over the time, moving beyond short-term of interaction observations.
- Integration with optional external sensing inputs, subject to ethical and privacy constraints: Combining the speech interaction with the physiological or environmental of sensors (e.g., stress level, attention tracking) is can be enable more context-aware personalization and adaptive feedback.
- Scenario expansion and richer adaptive logic: Additional interview topics and branching question flows is can be further improve realism and learning opportunities.
- Deployment of optimization and performance evaluation is across the different web browsers and devices.

13. LIMITATIONS

- Limited sample and testing: Observations were based on small-scale testing and system logs rather than extensive participant trials, limiting the generalizability of findings.
- Controlled intervention duration: Interaction sessions were relatively short and structured; long-term engagement patterns remain untested.
- Dependence on speech recognition accuracy: the System performance is constrained by the capabilities and accuracy of speech-to-text recognition, which is may affect the responsiveness and user experience, especially in noisy environments or with diverse speech patterns.

Table 12. Summary of study limitations

Constraint Category	Specific Limitation	Mitigation Strategy
Technical	ASR Accuracy: Standard speech recognition struggles with child voices and atypical ASD prosody (e.g., echolalia or monotone).	Improve rule-based speech tolerance thresholds and phonetic flexibility and implement "fuzzy matching" for phonetically similar words.
Technical	Environmental Noise: Background noise in home settings often interferes with voice-trigger accuracy.	Use noise-cancelling middleware and directional microphone prompts to isolate the child's voice.
Methodological	Sample Heterogeneity: High variability in ASD levels (verbal vs. non-verbal) makes "one-size-fits-all" Observations and System Evaluation unreliable.	Employ single-subject research designs (SSRD) to measure individual progress against a baseline.
Methodological	Limited Generalization: Skills learned in a 3D game environment may not transfer to real-life face-to-face interactions.	Integrate "Social Stories" and "Bridge Tasks" that require the child to use a learned phrase with a parent to unlock a level.
Evaluation	Small Sample Sizes: Difficulty in recruiting large cohorts leads to low statistical power in quantitative findings.	Use Mixed Methods (combining data logs with qualitative therapist interviews) to provide a richer picture of efficacy.
Ethics & Privacy	Data Sensitivity: Recording and storing children's voices raises high-risk privacy concerns and consent issues.	Implement On-Device Processing (Edge AI) so voice data never leaves the local hardware, and anonymize all progress logs.

Rather than relying solely on abstract ethical principles, our proposed framework has concrete design choices that reflect how we have operationalized ethical considerations. For example, every effort has been made to minimize the amount of data collected so as not to store the actual speech (raw data) or any personally identifiable information (e.g., name), but rather to use time-limited processes and provide usable anonymous interaction logs. Caregivers provide consent before any caregiver/child interaction takes place, and all adaptive decisions made as part of the intervention remain interpretable and auditable by human stakeholders.

Fully supportive of therapists and educators, the proposed framework automates personalization as an assistive function to ensure that professional judgment continues to be the greatest contributor to intervention planning by maintaining human oversight.

Our proposed framework's intended scope is limited to individuals with autism spectrum disorders; however other developmental conditions are outside the scope of this research.

13.1 Transferability and Real-World Generalization Constraints

Even though the system is capable of providing structured verbal communications in an interactive, virtual setting, the transfer of game-produced communication behaviours (or in-game communication behaviours) to spontaneity related to social interactions that happen outside of the game cannot be assumed. For example, virtual interview scenarios can lower the emotional tension and uncertainty in the interview process, however, they cannot replicate the dynamic, multimodal and socially unpredictable environments like those of face to face social interactions.

Thus, the observed positive trends for response completion and/or lack of hesitation should be interpreted as indicators of readiness for interaction and not as direct evidence of generalised communicative competence. Supporting strategies for establishing a connection from the game to the real world (such as practice with a caregiver or guided real world role-playing) are needed to facilitate the process of making meaningful connections outside the context of the game.

13.2 Boundary Conditions and Failure Scenarios

The potential limitations of the proposed design for supporting structured practice with users who have limited verbal skills or serve receptive language impairments are due to the inadequate nature of speech as an additional form of interaction. Observations from use of web-based speech recognition have shown that users with atypical prosody, echolalia or background noise provide are less responsive. This may suggest that additional forms of interaction or caregiver-assisted interaction may be necessary. These context limitations illustrate the need for care in the deployment of the system in order to also demonstrate the intended supplementarity of the system in learner support rather than an all-encompassing solution.

In terms of system failure scenarios, when there is a failure to provide appropriate speech recognition due to inaccuracies this can impact the flow of the dialogue between instigator and initiator, resulting in a prompting repetition issue or unintentionally flowing out of said interaction. In addition, due to inaccuracies in the personalization engine, it may demonstrate inappropriate rule-based disengagement with the learner leading to an oversimplification of the task sequencing. These behaviours do reflect the limits of the system not the learner, thus providing continuous need for provider oversight and caution when interpreting interaction logs.

REFERENCES

Abd El-Sattar, H. K. H., Omar, M., & Mohamady, H. (2024). Developing a participatory research framework through serious games to promote learning for children with autism. *Frontiers in Education, 9*, 1453327. DOI: 10.3389/feduc.2024.1453327

Babu, C. S., & Shunmugapriya, K. (2024). Unveiling Critical Periods of Brain Development in Autism Spectrum Disorder: Insights From Prenatal and Postnatal Growth Parameters. In *Clinical Practice and Unmet Challenges in AI-Enhanced Healthcare Systems* (pp. 267-294). IGI Global Scientific Publishing.

Babu, C. S., & Shunmugapriya, K. (2025). The Transformative Role of Artificial Intelligence in Healthcare: Focus on Autism Spectrum Disorder (ASD). In *Convergence of Population Health Management, Pharmacogenomics, and Patient-Centered Care* (pp. 363-374). IGI Global Scientific Publishing.

Doshi-Velez, F., & Kim, B. (2017). Towards a rigorous science of interpretable machine learning. *arXiv preprint arXiv:1702.08608*.

Habibi, F., Sedaghatshoar, S., Attar, T., Shokoohi, M., Kiani, A., & Malek, A. N. (2025). Revolutionizing education and therapy for students with autism spectrum disorder: A scoping review of AI-driven tools, technologies, and ethical implications. *AI and Ethics, 5*(3), 1–16. DOI: 10.1007/s43681-024-00608-1

Honorato, N., Soltiyeva, A., Oliveira, W., Delabrida, S. E., Hamari, J., & Alimanova, M. (2024). Gamefic strategies in the education of autistic children: A systematic literature review, scient metric analysis, and future research roadmap. *Smart Learning Environments, 11*(1), 25. DOI: 10.1186/s40561-024-00309-6

Rechowicz, K. J., Shull, J. B., Hascall, M. M., Diallo, S. Y., & O'Brien, K. J. (2021). Internet-of-Things devices in support of the development of echoic skills among children with autism spectrum disorder. *Sensors (Basel), 21*(13), 4621. DOI: 10.3390/s21134621 PMID: 34283166

Sula, A., Spaho, E., Matsuo, K., Barolli, L., Miho, R., & Xhafa, F. (2013). An IoT-based system for supporting children with autism spectrum disorder. In *Proceedings of the Eighth International Conference on Broadband and Wireless Computing, Communication and Applications* (pp. 282–289). IEEE. DOI: 10.1109/BWCCA.2013.51

Syriopoulou-Delli, C. K. (2025). Advances in autism spectrum disorder (ASD) diagnostics: From theoretical frameworks to AI-driven innovations. *Electronics (Basel), 14*(5), 951. DOI: 10.3390/electronics14050951

Vygotsky, L. S. (1978). *Mind in society: The development of higher psychological processes* (Vol. 86). Harvard university press.

Chapter 6
VR/AR for Communication and Social Skills

Nagamurali Eragamreddy
http://orcid.org/0000-0003-1026-183X
University of Technology and Applied Sciences, Salalah, Oman

ABSTRACT

This chapter was a systematic review of AI-enhanced virtual and augmented reality (VR/AR) interventions that were aimed at enhancing communication and social skills in children with autism spectrum disorder and other related developmental disabilities. After the screening of 1,639 records in key databases using the PRISMA, 23 empirical studies were included. Two reviewers performed the extractions of study design, participant profiles, type of technology, AI features, outcome measures, and usability indices; synthesis was done through deductive content analysis and cross-code triangulation. Results showed that there was a dominance of HMD-based immersive VR, recurrent application of adaptive feedback and emotion-recognition AI, reliable short-term improvement in joint attention and emotion recognition, and inconsistent long-term generalization. The chapter concluded that AI-enhanced VR/AR promised content earnestness upon the condition of larger RCTs, standardized outcome organizations, and comparable scaling ways.

DOI: 10.4018/979-8-3373-7724-7.ch006

1. INTRODUCTION

1.1 Background and Context

The emergence of immersive technologies has transformed intervention methods aimed at enhancing communication and social skills in autistic spectrum disorder (ASD) and other developmental impairment conditions. VR and AR systems allow simulating the social environment where learners may practice their interactional practices, receive structured feedback, and practice their activities repeatedly and under meticulous conditions. Such affordances resolve the long-standing concerns of conventional interventions, which are mainly the challenge of offering safe, regular, and ecologically viable chances of social learning (Lee & Wong, 2020; Lo et al., 2024; Kourtesis et al., 2023; Kourtesis & MacPherson, 2023; Liu & Wang, 2025; Ma & Song, 2025; Sideraki, 2024). Applications of VR and AR in social-communication teaching could be divided into non-immersive (e.g., desktop or tablet-based), immersive (e.g., head-mounted displays or CAVE systems) and mixed- or augmented reality formats, which superimpose digital indicators onto real-life environments (Clemente et al., 2023; Maddalon et al., 2024). Recent assessment results indicate that immersive VR is more prone to complex social results, including emotion recognition and joint attention, in particular, among higher-functioning children with ASD, but non-immersive and AR-based alternatives provide more accessibility, reduced costs, and low sensory load (Li et al., 2025; Kouhbanani et al., 2021; Yang et al., 2025; Yan et al., 2025). The results, however, do not indicate uniformity across population groups, intervention goals and outcome indicators despite these promising trends.

In parallel with the advancements in the immersive technology sector, the concept of artificial intelligence (AI) has started to be incorporated in VR/AR systems to add to their adaptivity and personalization. Intelligent features like emotion-recognition algorithms, feedback mechanisms, dynamically reacting with user behavior and engagement in real-time, adaptive difficulty scaling, and user modeling enable interventions to be dynamically responsive to learner behavior (Beirat et al., 2025). In theory, these capabilities are compatible with the heterogeneous nature of children with ASD since social-communication needs differ across the board in sensory sensitivity, cognitive load, and learning pace. Immersive environments and AI-driven responsiveness are an effective technological basis for customized social-skills training.

1.2 Research Gap and Problem Statement

Although there is a rapid growth of AI-enhanced VR/AR interventions, the empirical literature is still gaps in a number of significant areas. First, a significant portion of the current literature presents macro-level findings, i.e., the overall level of social skills or emotion recognition, without explicitly analyzing the mediating role of particular system features (e.g., the level of immersion, the nature of AI feedback, sensor integration, etc.). Consequently, the research question that has not been answered is which technological and design features are most directly linked to specific communicative benefits (Mittal et al., 2024). Second, there is still a methodological limitation in the evidence base. Most of the studies use small sample sizes, do not control them rigorously, or do not have longitudinal follow-up to limit the conclusions regarding generalization to the real world and sustainability of gains. Even though improvements in skills like joint attention or facial emotion recognition are often documented in the short term, it is not always shown that they transfer outside the intervention setting (Yang et al., 2025). This limitation is particularly consequential since generalization to real-life social settings is a fundamental objective of communication intervention with ASD children.

Third, although the use of AI capabilities is typically mentioned as a key strength of modern VR/AR, many studies do not offer systematic research as to how certain AI features, e.g., adaptive feedback loops or accuracy in emotion detection, can lead to behavioral changes (Yeh & Meng, 2025; Yuan & Ip, 2018). Therefore, the causes and effects between system design and communicative outcomes are poorly theorized and untested (Lo et al., 2024; Kourtesis et al., 2023; Ma & Song, 2025). Nonetheless, outside of describing outcome gains, most studies have not attempted to specify the causal chains through which specific AI system features, such as adaptive feedback, emotion recognition algorithms, or difficulty modulation, lead to particular communicative and social outcomes. As such, there are no models of feature-mechanism outcome relations based on AI system responsiveness. This is the gap that restricts the field to the transition of proof-of-concept applications into scalable evidence-based models of intervention. The continued existence of these gaps has practical and social consequences. Lack of social-communication support leads to social isolation in the long term, low involvement in education, and poor quality of life in ASD. Ineffective intervention outcomes will mean waste of resources and failed expectations to families, clinicians and educational systems. To solve these issues, it is crucial to better understand that the interaction between immersive technologies and features of AI helps facilitate meaningful and transferable social learning.

1.3 Purpose and Scope

This chapter is aimed at synthesizing empirical data on AI-enhanced VR and AR interventions aimed at facilitating communication and social skills in ASD children and developmental disabilities. Instead of considering the effectiveness of technology in general, the chapter assumes the analytical approach, which simultaneously includes the shape and the nature of the VR/AR systems, the AI features integrated into these systems, and the communicative and social results reported. In particular, the chapter concentrates on three dimensions that are connected to each other. The first one is a technological form, such as immersive, non-immersive, and mixed applications, that are applied in social-communication training. The second one is the characteristics of AI, including emotion detection, adaptive difficulty, real-time feedback, and sensor-based monitoring. The third one is outcome areas, such as eye contact, joint attention, conversational turn-taking, emotion recognition, and evidence of real-world generalization. By aligning system attributes with reported outcomes, the chapter addresses a critical literature gap: the lack of integrative analyses connecting design decisions to behavioral effects.

1.4 Objectives and Research Questions

To operationalize this purpose, the following objectives are handled in this chapter:

1. Maps the existing types and characteristics of VR/AR applications in communication and social-skills training of children with ASD and related disabilities - differentiating immersive, non-immersive and mixed-reality, and characterizing their defining attributes (hardware, interaction modality, scenario design, targeted social-communication behaviours).
2. Name and characterize the particular AI capabilities embedded into these VR/AR systems (emotion-recognition algorithms, real-time feedback and loops, adaptive difficulty scaling, and user-modelling) and critically discuss how these AI elements are configured to support the target skill development.
3. Review clinical outcomes as stated in connection with AI-enhanced VR/AR therapies - and pay attention to such characteristics of communication and social-interaction as maintaining eye contact, taking conversational turns, recognizing emotions, and the ability to transfer and adapt learnt skills in the real-life environment - and discuss the correspondence between them and system properties and AI properties.
4. Explore the potential benefits, difficulties, usability, acceptability, and feasibility of these interventions in the eyes of children, parents, and practitioners - in

terms of engagement, accessibility, sensory burden, cost, training needs and generalization outside of the intervention situation.

5. Summarize the findings to identify research gaps and suggest the way forward to the next generation of AI-enhanced VR/AR systems to assist children with ASD in developing social-communication skills training-thereby developing a critical framework to inform the next generation of artificial intelligence-mediated VR/AR.

These goals are addressed through the following research questions:

1. What are the existing forms and attributes of VR/AR applications (immersive, non-immersive and mixed reality) in the training of communication and social skills among children with ASD and other related disabilities?
2. What specific AI features (e.g., emotion recognition, real-time feedback, and adaptive difficulty) are integrated into the VR/AR systems, and how do they assist in the development of the targeted skill?
3. What clinical results will be considered to assess the effectiveness of AI-enhanced VR/AR therapies in relation to particular features of communication and social interaction, such as maintaining eye contact, taking turns in a conversation, recognizing emotions, and the overall capacity to adapt and use learned skills in the real world?
4. What have been the reported challenges and benefits, in terms of usability, acceptability, and feasibility of these interventions on children and parents?

1.5 Significance and Chapter Organization

This chapter is valuable as it adds to the field in four important aspects. To begin with, it provides a systematic taxonomy of VR/AR systems and AI functions that apply to social-communication training. Second, it analytically correlates system design attributes with reported behavioral results, no longer relying on descriptive summaries. Third, it preempts the matter of generalization, usability and scalability, which is typically a secondary consideration. Lastly, it provides evidence-based guidelines for future research and design of AI-assisted immersive interventions. The rest of the chapter is structured as follows. Section 2 summarizes the systematic review procedures and methodology employed. Section 3 reports on the results of the synthesis, consisting of typologies of systems, the features of AI, outcome patterns, and usability. Section 4 discusses the findings as far as theory, practice and design implications are concerned. This section also addresses limitations and future research directions. Section 5 summarizes the main findings and development of AI-enhanced VR/AR interventions to develop social communication.

2. METHODOLOGY

2.1 Design

The research design employed in this study involved utilizing a systematic review design to answer research questions concerning the nature, AI abilities, clinical outcomes, and usability of VR/AR-based social-communication interventions in children with ASD. The systematic review was chosen as a clear and objective approach to searching and incorporating empirical research into the specified questions (Sataloff et al., 2021). This design helped achieve three main purposes: mapping the multidimensional VR/AR-AI literature, correlating particular characteristics of the system with behavioral results, and revealing crucial research gaps to consider in further frames of interventions. The research followed a step-by-step, transparent process to have synthesis rigor (Crawford, 2025). Other designs, like the narrative reviews, were not used because of possible selection bias and low replicability. Moreover, realist reviews or meta-syntheses are profound, but they were considered untimely due to the infantile and disjointed nature of the existing VR/AR-AI evidence base. As a result, the systematic review presented the best strike of rigor and breadth needed to map system attributes and outcomes in a broad body of literature, providing a solid background to further analysis and clinical recommendations.

2.2 Search Strategy and Eligibility Criteria

The research carried out a multi-step search system in the main databases (PubMed, Web of Science, Scopus, ERIC, and IEEE Xplore). The search syntax was a combination of three conceptual blocks: (i) population ("Autism Spectrum Disorder" OR "ASD" OR "disability" OR "special needs" OR "developmental disorder"), (ii) intervention/outcome ("social skills" OR "communication" OR "pragmatics" OR "emotion recognition" OR "social competence"), and (iii) technology ("Virtual Reality" OR "VR" OR "Augmented Reality" OR "AR" OR "Mixed Reality" OR "Extended Reality" AND "AI" OR "Artificial Intelligence"). Therefore, the plan provided a clear concentration on AI-enhanced VR/AR interventions among the target population and desired skills. The inclusion criteria included empirical (e.g., randomized controlled trials, quasi-experiments, single-subject designs) studies published in English; involvement of children/adolescents (age 3-18) with ASD or other communication/social-skills impairments; use of VR/AR technologies containing a defined AI or adaptive component; and presenting outcomes that were related to communication or social interaction. The exclusion criteria were conference abstracts, editorials, dissertations, non-empirical reviews, research studies that only involved adult populations, and research papers that did not have a defined component of VR/AR or AI.

2.3 Data selection procedure and data collection

To collect the data in this chapter, a systematic search of four major electronic databases, such as PubMed, Web of Science, Scopus, ERIC, and IEEE Xplore, was employed, and compliance with the PRISMA 2020 principles was met to enhance the transparency of the data and its replicability (Page et al., 2021). The literature search involved a search using a mixture of keywords pertaining to Virtual Reality (VR) and Augmented Reality (AR), Autism Spectrum Disorder (ASD), and communication skills and social skills. In the initial systematic process, 1639 total records were identified, as shown in Figure 1. To reduce bias, the selection process was conducted through two broad steps by two volunteer independent reviewers. Exclusion counts per category, and screening outcome details are presented in Figure 1.

Figure 1. Flow chart screening the selection procedure for the included studies

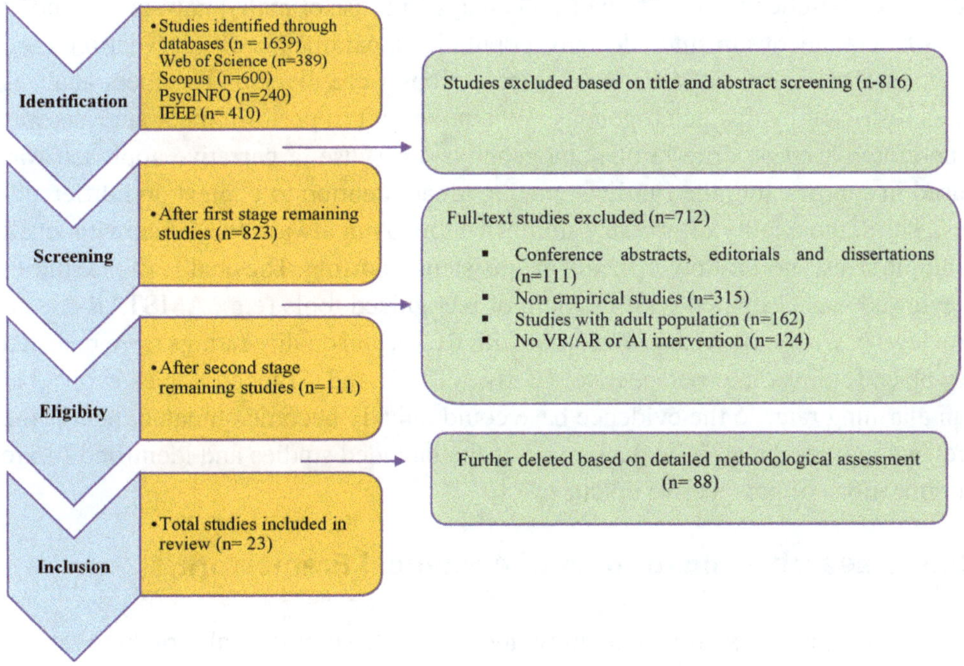

2.4 Data Synthesis and Extraction

The same two independent reviewers extracted the data using a pre-coded extraction form to capture the following data: study design; participant characteristics (age, diagnosis, severity); type of VR/AR system (immersive/non-immersive/mixed), AI features (emotion recognition, real-time feedback, adaptive difficulty); targeted communication/social skill(s); instruments used; key findings and effect sizes (where available); and usability/acceptability/feasibility outcome. The extracted data were synthesized in the form of a narrative, organized with the help of the research questions: (i) system attributes, (ii) AI features, (iii) clinical outcomes, and (iv) usability/feasibility. In cases where homogeneity of the outcome measures and design allowed (i.e., multiple RCTs to measure turn-taking or emotion-recognition using similar measures), a meta-analysis was taken into consideration.

Even though the systematic review approach was strong in terms of comprehensive and reproducible results, it had its drawbacks. First, the evidence base could have been distorted by publication bias (i.e., not publishing negative or null results). To address this, the review involved screening of grey literature (where possible) and evaluated the bias of publication on a funnel-plot analysis in case of meta-analysis. Second, it was heterogeneous in study designs, populations, parameters of interventions, and outcome measures, as VR/AR-AI interventions were diverse. The meta-analysis was restricted by this heterogeneity. Whether or not to perform meta-analysis was therefore based on criteria of homogeneity; otherwise, a narrative approach was used in synthesizing the findings, paying great attention to context and differences. Third, the quality of primary studies was also not always the same, with small sample sizes, short follow-ups, and inconsistent reporting. The quality of the studies reviewed was evaluated with the help of recognized tools (e.g., AMSTAR-2 with reviews or Cochrane Risk of Bias tool with RCT), and quality ratings were reported to place findings into perspective. Lastly, VR/AR and AI technologies evolved at an alarming rate, so the evidence base could quickly become outdated; hence, the review indicated a definite date range of the included studies and identified future implications of prospective updates.

2.5 Research Philosophy and Analytical Framework

This chapter adopted a pragmatic evidence-synthesis philosophy, ranking actionable empirical findings while acknowledging methodological heterogeneity. However, in contrast to purely interpretivist methodological approaches (where rich contextual meaning was important) or strict positivist approaches (where causal inference to primary data was important), the systematic review recognized that the evidence was diverse and multi-method and tried to extract commonalities and differences.

As discussed in Section 2.1, it thus formed the basis of a systematic review method that dealt with what worked, for whom it worked, and under which circumstances.

2.6 Data Analysis

The deductive content analysis method was employed to examine the studies that had been selected, attentive to the principles that were described by Elo and Kyngäs (2008) and revised by Hall et al. (2023) in reference to systematic reviews. The deductive analysis was specifically appropriate since the research questions and objectives were formulated in advance and steered by theoretically based categories based on the topic of study: VR/AR interventions as communication and social skills training programs among children with Autism Spectrum Disorder (ASD) and other developmental disabilities. The conceptual framework of technology-assisted social learning (Vygotsky, 1978) and the social motivation theory of autism (Chevallier et al., 2012) guided the coding process as it enabled systematizing and interpreting the data in pre-set thematic codes. For the chapter, four main analytical codes were obtained based on the research questions of the study. Each of the codes was a category according to which corresponding data of the included studies (n = 23) were systematized, compared, and interpreted to find out common trends and differences in evidence.

Code One: Forms and Attributes of VR/AR Applications

The former code was associated with Research Question 1—to determine and classify the current varieties and features of VR/AR applications in training communication and social skills. The analysis differentiated between immersive, non-immersive, and mixed-reality systems that were recorded in terms of their technological setup, sensory immersion degrees, and pedagogical features of design. Recent experiments were mainly based on immersive systems with head-mounted displays (HMDs) like Oculus Rift or HTC Vive because they displayed greater effects on attention and joint engagement due to the illusion of being real. Desktop-based systems that were not immersive were found to offer lesser ecological validity and less sensory involvement (Herrero & Lorenzo, 2020; Lorenzo et al., 2019; Lahiri et al., 2011; Intawong et al., 2025). The data points were coded into sub-categories like immersive realism, interaction fidelity, and contextual adaptability, which signified the interaction between the extent of immersion and the social learning results. This framework of coding gave a structured prism through which the effect of each type of VR/AR technology on communicative preparedness and social responsiveness among ASD children could be mapped.

Code Two: AI Features and Adaptive Mechanisms

The second code was dedicated to the definition and examination of the AI-powered features embedded into VR/AR systems, namely, emotion recognition, real-time feedback, and adaptive difficulty features. Research described varied applications of AI algorithms, including facial expression recognition and voice emotion determination, to reinforcement learning algorithms that increased the difficulty according to user performance (Alhussen et al., 2025; Hebri et al., 2024; Jeyarani et al., 2024). Data transcribing was done as subtopics: emotion detection accuracy, adaptive response timing, and feedback personalization. This discussion helped to understand how the integration of AI supported the naturalistic communication process by allowing systems to simulate the human social response and offer customized scaffolding. Nevertheless, it also brought out loopholes, including low transparency of the algorithmic procedures and inadequate validation of the adaptive characteristics in diverse ASD profiles. The presentation of the results according to this code showed that AI enhanced the ability of VR/AR systems to provide dynamic and personalized social training experiences.

Code Three: Clinical Dispositions and Behavioural Outcomes

In line with Research Question 3, in this code, the clinical results and behavioural indicators were analyzed, which served to assess the effectiveness of the VR/AR interventions. Validated scales that were used to obtain outcome measures in studies consisted of the Social Responsiveness Scale (SRS-2), eye-tracking, and observational ratings (social reciprocity, emotion recognition) of social interaction (Bauer et al., 2023). The data trends revealed that there were observable changes in eye contact maintenance, turn-taking in conversation, and accuracy in recognizing emotions (Degutyte & Astell, 2021; Horton & Singleton, 2022). However, the discussion also revealed a common limitation, that is, immediate post-intervention improvements were statistically significant, but it was impossible to generalize them to real-world social conditions. To capture these nuances, data were coded into subcodes of skill acquisition, behavioural transfer, and sustainability. This demonstrated that, despite the strong short-term effectiveness of VR/AR interventions, there were still no longitudinal investigations of transferability and retention.

Code Four: Usability, Acceptability and Feasibility

The fourth code was the one that discussed Research Question 4, which dealt with the user experiences and the challenges of implementation. Thematic synthesis revealed the patterns of three common subcodes that included usability, acceptability, and feasibility, representing three other aspects of the intervention's practicality. Usability included interface intuitiveness and sensory comfort; acceptability included user engagement and parental satisfaction; and feasibility included scalability and cost. The research always indicated high levels of engagement in children who found the environments entertaining and encouraging (Herrero & Lorenzo, 2020; Lorenzo et al., 2019; Intawong et al., 2025). Nevertheless, technological issues like cybersickness, high expenses of equipment, and the lack of training of therapists predetermined further implementation (Khowaja et al., 2020, 2021). Their dimension analysis revealed that, although promising, VR/AR systems needed to overcome significant barriers to implementation to become sustainable in terms of entering the therapeutic and learning processes.

2.7 Analytical Integration and Reliability

The four codes were then synthesized using the cross-code comparison method, which made it possible to identify bigger thematic relationships. The integration demonstrated that immersive and AI-enhanced systems were better in short-term communication benefits, but were not sufficiently scalable and clinically validated in the real world. In addition, structural bottlenecks with respect to limited interdisciplinary collaboration between technologists and clinicians appeared, which created a major research gap. Altogether, the deductive analysis created a logical empirical basis for the further discussion and theoretical implications of the chapter. To validate the validity of the method of coding, the researcher coded five preliminary studies independently. The remaining studies were grouped by comparing these original groupings, and a reasonable amount of consensus was reached (Cohen's κ of 0.82). In cases of discrepancy, cross-checking was done in-depth to remove any discrepancies in the coding.

3. RESULTS

The systematized search provided a varied amount of empirical evidence regarding VR/AR-based interventions that address the communication and social skills of children and adolescents with autism spectrum disorder (ASD) and other developmental impairments. A total of 23 studies were eligible for inclusion in the study. In these studies, research designs consisted of randomized controlled trials (RCTs), quasi-experimental comparisons and one individual subject experimental designs (SSEDs), feasibility and qualitative studies. Sample sizes were quite diverse, ranging from intensive single-case designs, which used three participants, up to larger controlled trials, which used over 70 children. The majority of the participants were of primary-school age, but some of the studies went into adolescence.

In order to offer a brief description, Table 1 (Appendix A) cursory outline of the essential features of the studies involved, with a major emphasis on the study design, sample size, and essential technological settings. This summary deliberately does not present outcome-level interpretation, which is considered elsewhere below. The variety of study designs, ranging from intensive single-case reports to larger randomized trials, illustrates a field that is shifting towards more rigorous comparative appraisals than an initial exploration that is feasible. This heterogeneity implies that, as evidence is yet to be built, there are yet to be standardized protocols of measuring technological efficacy in ASD populations.

3.1 Characteristics of Included Studies

The systematic review of 23 independent research studies that have been undertaken between 2011 and 2025 is presented in Table 1 and is aimed at the use of VR and AR to assist ASD children, and other individuals with disabilities in communication and social skills development. The studies cover an international perspective that incorporates such countries as the USA, China, Spain, and Taiwan. Through diverse platforms (including mobile AR and desktop VR, as well as immersive technologies, including the Oculus Quest or HTC Vive), researchers gauged the results in terms of social interactions, language acquisition, or adaptive behaviors. A randomized controlled trial is not the only possible study design: some studies use single-case designs as a more diverse method to see the results of AI-assisted and immersive intervention evaluation.

3.2 Methodological Quality and Rigor

The reviewed literature is heterogeneous about methodological rigor, which is frequently disproportionate to the rapid technological development. In spite of the fact that some randomized controlled trials (RCTs) utilize standardized diagnostic procedures, they are often undersized. In contrast, the presence of single-subject experimental designs is also high, ensuring high internal validity through repeated measures and a limitation on external validity. Weaknesses such as failure to consistently report intervention fidelity, and failure to follow up with individuals long-term to evaluate skill generalization are critical failures. AR interventions are technologically the best in terms of naturalistic joint attention and vocabulary scaffolding. On the contrary, VR systems focus more on shared problem-solving but differ in immersion. Although the quasi-experimental and qualitative studies help gain valuable information about the usability and the experience of participants, the lack of blinding and randomization often prevents causal inference. Finally, the discipline is plagued by a mismatch between advanced technology and methodology maturity, with a requirement to have standardized reporting and more powerful and controlled planning to determine conclusive effectiveness.

3.3 Intervention Outcomes in Communication Skills

An analysis of synthesized evidence in 23 publications, as shown in Table 2 (Appendix A), which includes RCTs, quasi-experimental, and single-subject designs, indicates that the effects of these studies are significant but differ in nature. The largest gains were found in joint attention and functional language use. Such functional improvement as requesting, turn-taking, and verbal initiation was often measured using direct behavioral indices and standardized caregiver reports. Data collected on a single-subject basis showed that there are definite acquisition patterns, where most participants shifted from low levels of baseline performance to high levels of task-specific communication. Joint attention and gaze-related behaviors became highly receptive to intervention, especially in immersive VR systems with eye-tracking or those with visual scaffolding of an AR system. Research studies also found that gaze following and face-specific attention were significantly improved, which was supported by the data on fixation duration and non-overlap. On the other hand, expressive and receptive language results were more heterogeneous. Though there were pre-post improvements in vocabulary acquisition and instruction-following, expressive gains (e.g., utterance complexity) varying across diagnostic groups were found. In all the domains, a limitation was the absence of a long-term follow-up, but the short-term maintenance was observed frequently. On the whole, it can be concluded that VR/AR interventions have a strong ability to stabilize a basic level of social-communication behavior, and structural language outcomes are more vulnerable to the intensity of interventions and measurement procedures (Pérez-Fuster et al., 20232. Recent evidence indicates that augmented-reality scaffolds can directly support vocabulary acquisition in children with ASD, enhancing context-bound word learning when virtual cues are strongly mapped to physical referents (Bahameish et al., 2025).

3.4 Intervention Outcomes in Social Skills

The reviewed corpus analysis demonstrates that VR and AR interventions have a profound influence on the overall social competencies, as shown in Table 3 (Appendix A), especially on emotion recognition and social cues decoding. The presence of immersive VR environments with the usage of controlled stimuli contributed to the enhancement of facial expression detection, as evidenced by the increase in both gaze fixation in socially salient areas and accuracy in emotion-matching tasks (Soltiyeva et al., 2023). Moreover, complex social scenarios simulations, including job interviews, shopping and speaking publicly, proved to have higher levels of task engagement, procedural accuracy and social responsiveness. Interaction sequencing and initiative were performance measures that showed consistent post-intervention improvements in these ecologically valid environments. Inferential improvements in intentions and attributing mental states were statistically significant in research that dealt with higher-order social cognition, including Theory of Mind (ToM) and perspective-taking. These benefits were mainly related to structured VR that gave priority to agent interactions based on narratives. Nevertheless, there are still inconsistencies in the evidence concerning generalization and maintenance. Although other studies reported transfer of joint attention and social initiation to the real-world classroom or home settings (Sun et al., 2024), systematic measurement was uncommon. The time intervals between follow-ups were typically diverse and tended to display a novelty effect and not lasting behavior change. It all ends with the fact that although the VR/AR tools are successful in nurturing short-term social-cognitive achievements, the sustainability of transference in various set-ups is inconclusive.

3.5 Technology and Design Features Linked to Positive Outcomes

The positive social skills occurrences of VR/AR interventions are functions of particular clusters of system features rather than the technological influences, as shown in Table 4 (Appendix A). The first factor that promotes learning persistence and continuation of tasks in both educational and work simulations is gamification, which involves missions, rewards, and a sequence of tasks. More importantly, real-time system responsiveness, such as adaptive prompts and task progression being performance sensitive, is associated with a greater accuracy in identifying social cues and interactive reciprocity. Having high levels of immersion, which is operationalized here by spatial realism and first-person point of view, is systematically positively associated with better emotion regulation and adaptive behavior. Contingent reinforcement via sensor technologies (e.g., eye-tracking and physiological monitoring) is possible through the integration of these technologies, which enhances the salience of social cues as the program runs. Moreover, social reciprocity and cooperation in solving problems are encouraged by agent-based interactions between virtual peers or robots because of repeated exposure to manipulated social contingencies (Zhang et al., 2020). The capability to superimpose virtual indicators on real-life environments, such as classrooms in AR plans, augments the level of joint attention and relevance of tasks (Saadatzi et al., 2018; Silva, 2025). Lastly, the customization of difficulty levels and pacing based on the needs of users promotes usability based on the heterogeneous learner needs. All these features make VR/AR not passive instruments but active and responsive mediators of social learning.

3.6 Methodological Quality Assessment

The quality of methodology of the 23 reviews assessed is low, as shown in Table 6 (Appendix A), moderate, and high, and the majority are moderate in nature. Although the level of technological innovation is high, clinical evidence is limited to methodological discrepancies. Most of the corpus contains non-randomized designs such as single-subject experimental trials, feasibility studies, and pre-post pilot studies, which are reflected in the risk of bias distribution in Table 5 (Appendix A). The issue of selection bias is very common as convenience sampling is often used, and no randomized allocation procedures are performed. Moreover, the bias related to performance and detection is worsened by unequal blinding, although the possibility of participant blinding is frequently unattainable in interactive VR/AR, the outcome assessor blinding was infrequently reported. Attrition bias, on the other hand, was not too high, and most of the studies had high rates of retention. It was found that implementation fidelity was an effective methodological strength, but that the monitoring intensity differed among designs due to the use of automated system-logging and standardized protocols. In the end, the evidence base shows strong consistency of implementation, but it is poor in terms of external generalizability and control of the selection and blinding processes.

Figure 2. Geographic distribution of studies

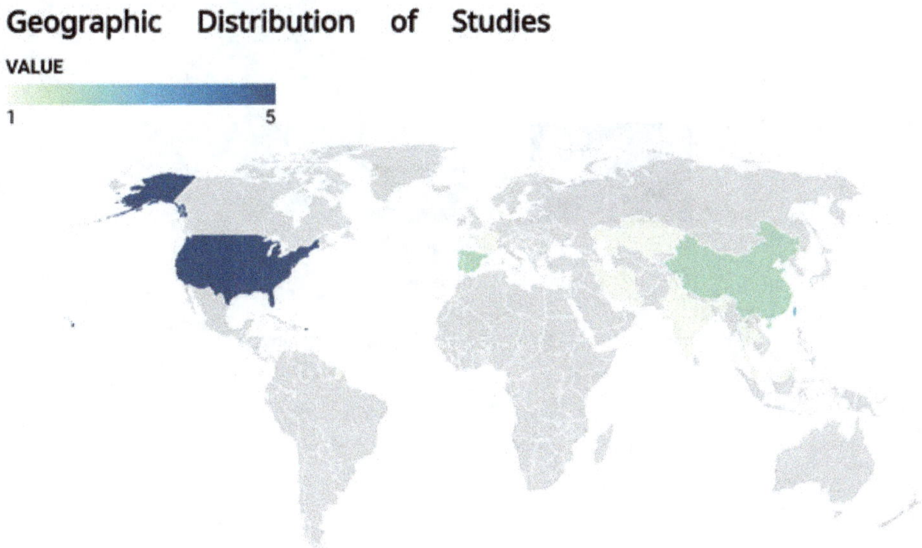

Figure 3. Technology usage trends

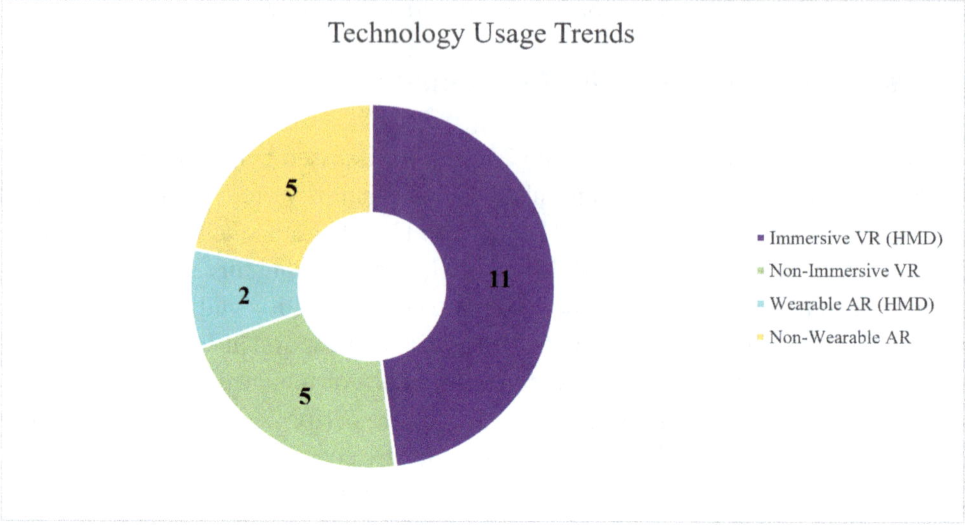

Figure 4. Proportion of social vs. communication targets

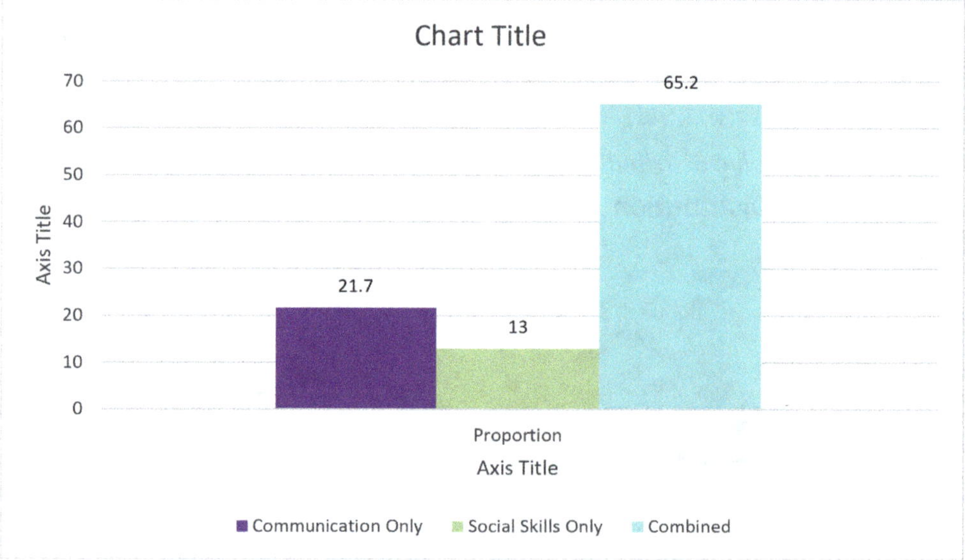

Figure 5. Outcome improvement across skill categories

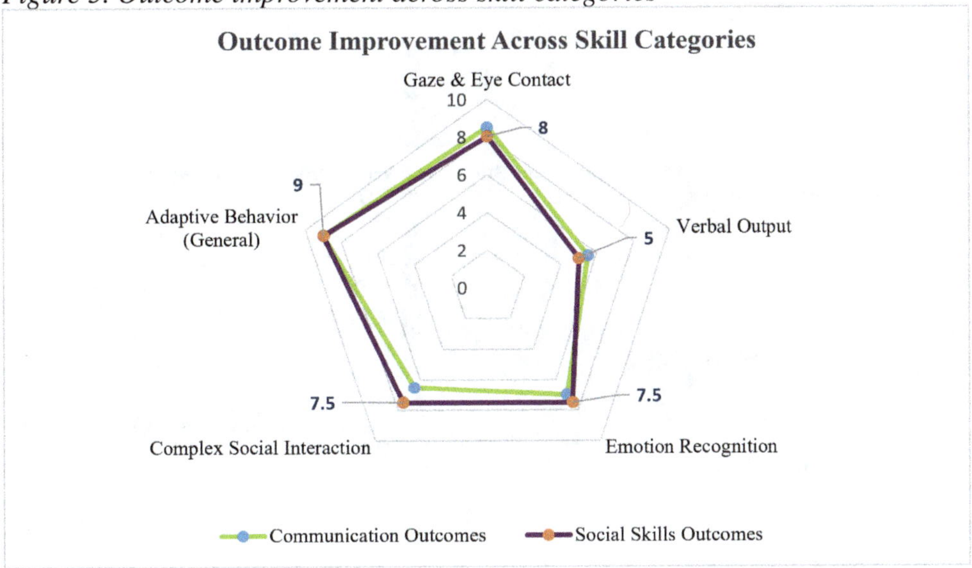

Figure 6. Conceptual framework: VR/AR design parameters and outcomes in autism

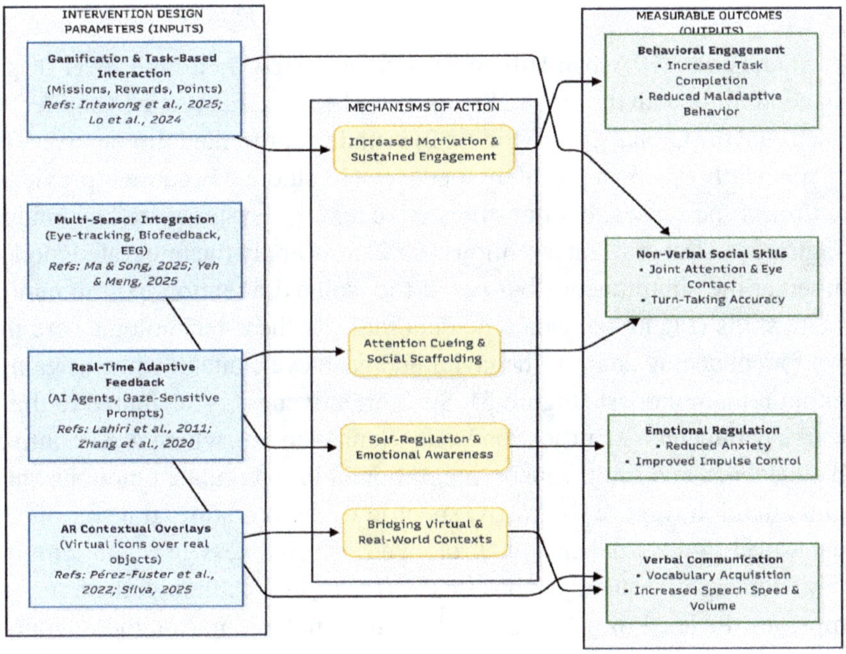

Figure 7. Transfer and generalization outcomes

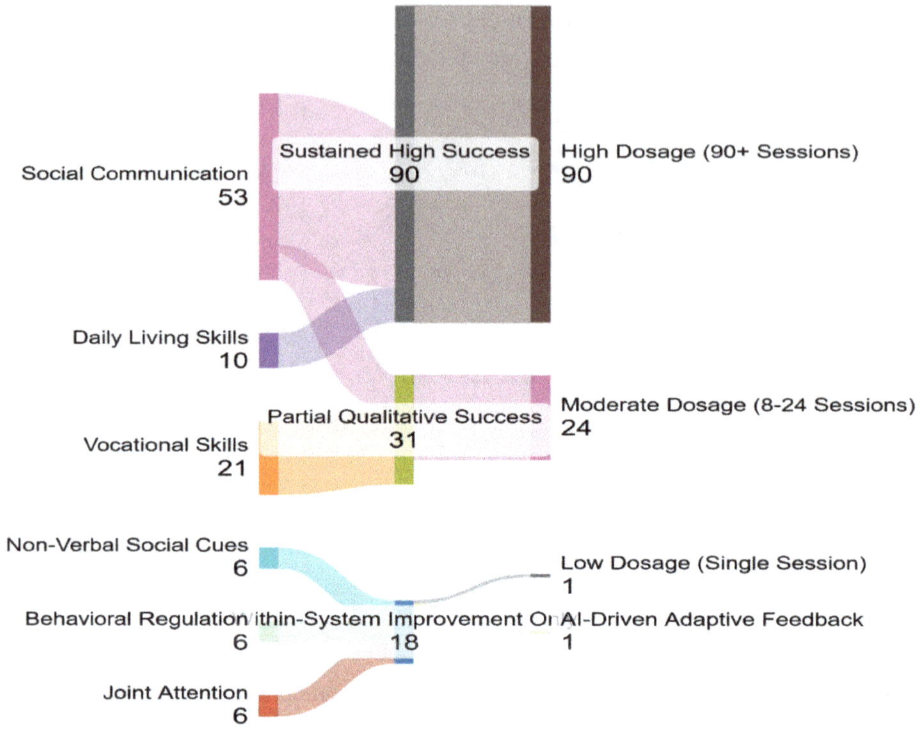

Studies on VR/AR in autism are characterized by a high level of geographic concentration, with the United States (5 studies) and East Asia (4 studies) in the first place, and the Global South (Figure 2) is underrepresented. Immersive VR (HMDs) is technically the most prevalent modality (11 studies) because it provides the most control of the senses, but non-immersive and AR systems are becoming available (Figure 3). Almost all interventions (65.2) now apply the integrated models that are aimed at the simultaneous but not at the isolated attention to communicative and social skills (Figure 4). Outcome data indicate these technologies are most effective for enhancing adaptive behavior and gaze/eye contact, whereas gains in verbal output remain modest (Figure 5). Such effectiveness is attributed to the following design parameters: gamification leads to engagement, whereas AI-controlled adaptive feedback and multi-sensor integration help to regulate emotions and facilitate joint attention (Figure 6). Lastly, specific to the literature, transfer of skills in the real world is dose-dependent. Prolonged effectiveness of social communication may need high-frequency exposure (>90 sessions). Although the integration of AI improves the level of personalized learning, in the long run, the regular, repetitive interaction is the most essential component of the process of skills generalization outside the online setting (Figure 7).

4. DISCUSSION

The chapter explored the shapes, properties and the profile of the outcomes of VR- and AR-based applications to train communication and social skills among children with autism spectrum disorder (ASD) and related developmental disabilities. Analysis of the evidence reveals a recurring causal order: AI-based perception of learner behavior (e.g., gaze, affect) facilitates adaptive system responses that, in turn, promote increased engagement and attention alignment, thereby facilitating short-term outcomes in terms of improved social communication skills. Although previous researchers have investigated the possibility and immediate effectiveness of immersive technologies to treat autism, much of the previous literature has focused on within-system effectiveness as opposed to sustained transfer to real-world scenarios (Bellani et al., 2011; Boo et al., 2022; Parsons & Cobb, 2011; Silva et al., 2025). Furthermore, current reviews have generally lumped VR and AR interventions together without varying between levels of immersion, adaptive intelligence, or dose strength, which is why important design-outcomes associations remain unidentified (Mesa-Gresa et al., 2018; Karami et al., 2021). The second gap relates to the scarcity of theorization of the AI integration into VR/AR systems. Despite the recent studies that point to the possibilities of intelligent agents, adaptive difficulty, and gaze-contingent feedback, the limited number of studies that examine how AI-mediated personalization interacts with the dosage of intervention explicitly focus on how to apply this in the context of the general environment (Didehbani et al., 2016; Makransky & Petersen, 2021; Hamizi et al., 2025). The chapter fills these gaps by synthesizing the empirical patterns of the geographic distribution, use of technology, domains of outcomes and transfer paths, paying special attention to the mechanisms that facilitated the real-life communicative and social functioning.

The literature reviewed shows that the distribution of geography is highly uneven, with the research being located mostly in the United States and East Asia. This tendency is similar to the general tendencies in the development of educational technologies studies and indicates that the model of VR/AR intervention cannot be culturally and contextually generalized to ASD The literature is dominated by technologically advanced immersive VR systems delivered using head-mounted displays (HMDs), whereas wearable AR is underrepresented despite the potential of contextualized in-situ learning. Outcome targeting is highly favorable to integrated social-communication interventions, where more than 65% of the reviewed studies are represented. This focus is indicative of modern pragmatic and social-interactionist theories of language development, which take the view of communication and social competence as domains that are complementary to each other, and not independent ones (Vygotsky, 1978; Tomasello, 2003). The trends of quantitative outcomes also demonstrate that VR/AR interventions have the least probability to increase gaze behavior, joint attention, emotion recognition, and adaptive functioning, and the gains in expressive verbal output are relatively low. The given findings are consistent with the previous experimental studies that proved the immersive setting to be especially effective in honing attention-based and socio-perceptual abilities (Didehbani et al., 2016; Kandalaft et al., 2013; Hamizi et al., 2025). The results of the transfer and generalization show a strong dosage effect. Interventions with the highest level of evidence are high-dosage interventions, which tend to have a sustained real-world effect, especially on social communication skills. Conversely, moderate-dosage interventions are typically associated with partial or qualitative effects, whereas single-session designs are not usually extra systematic. These patterns are similar to the findings of behavioral and developmental intervention studies, which repeatedly define both intensity and duration as decisive factors of adaptive outcome in ASD (Rogers & Vismara, 2008; Fuller & Kaiser, 2020; Yeh & Meng, 2025; Yuan & Ip, 2018).

4.1 RQ1: Triangulation, Counterarguments and Theoretical Integration

Although the VR/AR literature is indeed subject to a lot of criticism due to its methodological heterogeneity and limited statistical power due to the small sample size (Mesa-Gresa et al., 2018), triangulation demonstrates convergent trends. Particularly, joint attention is always enhanced with the implementation of designs that use gaze cueing and real-time feedback, which offer support to the attention-based social learning models (Mundy & Newell, 2007). Although it is feared that HMDs may not be ecologically valid and comfortable to children with autism (Parsons, 2015), scientists believe that the negative effects can be counteracted with adaptive pacing and AR-based overlay. Specifically, AR concurs with embodied cognition in the sense that the social inferences are put directly into the physical world itself, mediating situated learning (Thelen & Smith, 1994; Barsalou, 2008). In addition, AI adaptivity enhances the efficiency of learning (Makransky & Petersen, 2021), but it is not a magic bullet that generalizes. Using the sociocultural theory, there is evidence that the transfer process must be directed with implementation being high-intensity (Vygotsky, 1978). Finally, three conditions that are in intersection lead to maximum effectiveness: theory-based design, AI-assisted personalization, and long-term dosage. Research in the future should no longer be based on short-term feasibility tests but on longitudinal studies of these interactions.

4.2 RQ2: AI Capabilities and Their Alignment with Targeted Skills

The application of AI in VR/AR is classified by the particular functionalities that are aligned with the developmental theories. Adaptive difficulty is connected to the Zone of Proximal Development (ZPD) as proposed by Vygotsky, which ensures the best level of challenge to facilitate concentration and persistence (Vygotsky, 1978). Critics caution, however, that the optimization of the performance of abstract tasks might not directly correspond with socially meaningful cues (Makransky & Petersen, 2021). NPCs based on AI (artificial intelligence) promote social cognition and pragmatic communication by means of observational learning (Bandura, 1986; Thelen & Smith, 1994). Though research demonstrates improvements in emotion recognition and turn-taking (Kandalaft et al., 2013), the naturalness of such interactions is doubted, with the practice of scripting NPCs, in turn, requiring human mediation in order to achieve ecological validity. In addition, gaze-contingent feedback facilitates the process of social orienting, which is a preliminary to acquiring language (Mundy & Newell, 2007), but excessive prompting has the downside of leading to dependency. Lastly, personalization through data increases engagement and makes it vulnerable to ethical issues concerning the bias of algorithms and data transparency (Parsons et al., 2011). Together, AI can be discussed as a facilitator and not as an individual teacher, only in those cases when it is correlated with the principles of pedagogy, such as scaffolding and social salience.

4.3 RQ3: System Capabilities, Competencies, and Their Clinical Outcomes

System capabilities cause certain developmental competencies to be triggered to produce clinical outcomes. The evaluation of gaze tracking and attention cueing has a close relation with the improvement in non-verbal skills such as joint attention, which is consistent with the social neuroscience approaches (Mundy & Neal, 2001; Dawson et al., 2012). Although critics posit that such gains may be due to compliance in the task and not social understanding, high-dose longitudinal data indicate that natural social orienting is recalibrated (Adjorlu et al., 2017). Better self-regulation and less anxiety are associated with adaptive feedback and physiological monitoring, reflecting the models of affective self-monitoring (Gross, 2015). Nonetheless, the sceptics observe that the regulations in safe virtual worlds might not be maintained in unpredictable real worlds. In the meantime, intelligent avatars support social-cognitive abilities such as emotion recognition (Frith & Frith, 2006), which represent a step towards the simulation of naturalistic interaction. AR context-bridging capabilities have the strongest connections to verbal communication and adaptive functioning and utilize situated learning through incorporating prompts into the physical space (Lave & Wenger, 1991). More importantly, these correlations depend on dosage; advanced AI cannot overcome the lack of exposure (Rogers & Vismara, 2008). Clinical success is therefore the result of a theoretically consistent design and high implementation.

4.4 RQ4: Usability, Acceptability, and Feasibility from Child and Parent Perspectives

The usability of children with ASD is typically high because digital interfaces are easy to see and predict, and this attribute decreases the levels of social anxiety (Makransky & Petersen, 2021). Nevertheless, sensory overload associated with HMD is still a major obstacle to people with hypersensitivities (Parsons, 2015). The intrinsic motivation, with the assistance of gamification (Ryan & Deci, 2017) and perceived utility by parents, is the major factor behind acceptability. Although parents enjoy reduced resistance in comparison to traditional therapy, parents are concerned about the black box algorithm, screen time, and social isolation (Parsons et al., 2011). The settings can be different; VR can be effectively implemented in a closed clinic, but at home and school, costs, technical complexity, and the burden on the caregiver are barriers to its implementation (Damschroder et al., 2009). AR based on tablets can be more practical as it has fewer logistical overheads. The novelty effect is a critical counterargument as it decreases initial engagement on the occasion of curiosity loss. Systems implanted in day-to-day practices are essential for sustained use as proposed by ecological systems theory (Bronfenbrenner, 1979). Finally, parental involvement is needed as co-facilitators to successful adoption (Dunst, 2025). The design of the future should be more family-friendly and sensory inclusive in order to make sure that the technological advancement will translate into the sustainability of clinical practice.

4. 5 Theoretical and Clinical Implications

The success of VR/AR interventions lies in the fact that they operationalize the well-known theories about learning instead of the technological innovation itself. These systems are behavioral and involve contingency and reinforcement (Skinner, 1953) to stabilize skills through gaze-contingent feedback, but fading mechanisms are necessary to ensure dependency is not developed. In theory, VR/AR is synonymous with Vygotskian scaffolding, in the Zone of Proximal Development (Vygotsky, 1978), and AR enables situated learning, which improves functional communication by bridging the real world (Lave & Wenger, 1991). Clinically, the practitioners have to focus on the functional capabilities rather than the levels of immersion. Although gaze-tracking is effective in joint attention, AR-based naturalistic prompting is a better fit in everyday living skills. Longitudinal integration is necessary to enhance human-mediated teaching and take into account sensory tolerances and technical overheads to implement successfully (Parsons et al., 2011). In terms of ethics, deployment should be goal-oriented and time-limited to reduce digital dependency (Makransky & Petersen, 2021). In addition, the issues of accessibility, cultural relevance, and data privacy are the primary concerns that should be addressed to avoid the expansion of intervention disparities. Finally, the effectiveness of VR/AR could be seen in the alignment of the functions of the system with the developmental theory, clinical intent, and ethical considerations so that the technology could be an intermediary between abstract principles and informed, comprehensive, and practically sound practice.

4.6 Limitations and Future Research Directions

The existing evidence base regarding VR/AR interventions is limited by serious methodological limitations, namely, small sample sizes and single-subject designs that reduce the statistical power and the generalizability (Lo et al., 2024; Kourtesis et al., 2023; Ma & Song, 2025). Moreover, the evaluation of the success of the skills generalization to naturalistic conditions is obstructed by a critical absence of long-term follow-up and ecologically valid measures (Parsons et al., 2004; Degutyte & Astell, 2021). Additional complications to cross-study comparability and meta-analytic aggregation include technological and outcome heterogeneity, which cut across immersive head-mounted displays to mobile applications (Mesa-Gresa et al., 2018). Most importantly, the lack of active control groups with the digital tools in contrast to the low-tech interventions does not demonstrate the causal influence of the immersion effects versus the novelty ones (Grynszpan et al., 2014). The research should focus on high-powered, multisite randomized controlled trials (RCTs) in the future and establish the critical moderators, including age and profile of sensory (Khowaja et al., 2021). The AI-based, bio-guided, and personalization openness has the potential to actively adapt to tasks, but these frameworks need to be subject to strict validation to allow clinical trust (Maddalon et al., 2024). Lastly, the emphasis should be on cost-efficacy and implementation science to provide sustainability, scalability in the deployment of the system in resource-limited settings (Rizzo et al., 2011). Finally, it is important to bring the field forward by striking the right balance between the sophistication of technology and methodological maturity and economic realism.

5. CONCLUSION

The chapter was a synthesis of VR/AR intervention design, implementation and assessment of its role in the development of social-communication skills in children with ASD. Beyond the evidence-of-concept zeal, the review notes that although the tools are effective in boosting basic skills such as joint attention and emotion recognition, expressive language has shaky results. Technological affordances (AI-driven adaptive feedback and context-aware scaffolding) to particular developmental processes depend on matching technological affordances with particular developmental mechanisms instead of thinking of VR/AR as homogeneous categories. Among the major conclusions made is that there seems to be a strong dose-response relationship, in which high-frequency longitudinal interventions have better generalization than short-term designs. Theoretically, the chapter unites system capabilities with behavioral and socio-cultural theories of learning, placing VR/AR as the mediators of learning instead of substitutes for human-led learning. Clinically, AR has the best application in naturalistic, functional communication and immersive VR in the area of social-cognitive rehearsal, under the condition that sensory tolerances are addressed. The synthesis highlights that the process of generalization is a design-dependent process that needs to be explicitly scaffolded. Finally, the opportunity of VR/AR is in the fact that it is possible to operationalize the postulates of learning in individual, safe experiences. The further development depends on the integration into the wider frameworks of care and education, which is supported by the theory and implemented with the ethical considerations. Clarifying causal mechanisms, eliminating procedural redundancies, and shifting the focus to issues of generalization or scalability will improve the theoretical coherence and relevance of research on social communication via AI.

REFERENCES

Adjorlu, A., Høeg, E. R., Mangano, L., & Serafin, S. (2017). Daily living skills training in virtual reality to help children with autism spectrum disorder in a real shopping scenario. In *2017 IEEE International Symposium on Mixed and Augmented Reality (ISMAR-Adjunct)* (pp. 294–302). IEEE. https://doi.org/DOI: 10.1109/ISMAR-Adjunct.2017.93

Alhussen, A., Ansari, A. S., & Mohammadi, M. S. (2025). Enhancing user experience in AI powered human-computer communication with vocal emotions identification using a novel deep learning method. *Computers, Materials & Continua*, *82*(2), 2909–2929. DOI: 10.32604/cmc.2024.059382

Bahameish, M., Khowaja, K., Abdelaal, Y., & Al-Thani, D. (2025). Pathways to learning: Exploring the impact of augmented reality on vocabulary development in children with autism spectrum disorder. *Interactive Learning Environments*, •••, 1–24. DOI: 10.1080/10494820.2025.2485407

Bandura, A. (1986). *Social foundations of thought and action: A social cognitive theory*. Prentice Hall.

Barsalou, L. W. (2008). Grounded cognition. *Annual Review of Psychology*, *59*(1), 617–645. DOI: 10.1146/annurev.psych.59.103006.093639 PMID: 17705682

Bauer, V., Bouchara, T., Duris, O., Labossière, C., Clément, M. N., & Bourdot, P. (2023). Head mounted augmented reality to support reassurance and social interaction for autistic children with severe learning disabilities. *Frontiers in Virtual Reality*, *4*, 1106061. DOI: 10.3389/frvir.2023.1106061

Beirat, M. A., Algolaylat, A., Al Njadat, H., AlAbdallat, B., & Al-Makhzoomy, A. K. (2025). Utilization of artificial intelligence and assistive technology in autism: Diagnosis, treatment, and education applications: A systematic literature review. *Educational Process: International Journal*, *17*, e2025350. DOI: 10.22521/edupij.2025.17.350

Bellani, M., Fornasari, L., Chittaro, L., & Brambilla, P. (2011). Virtual reality in autism: State of the art. *Epidemiology and Psychiatric Sciences*, *20*(3), 235–238. DOI: 10.1017/S2045796011000448 PMID: 21922965

Boo, C., Alpers-Leon, N., McIntyre, N., Mundy, P., & Naigles, L. (2022). Conversation during a virtual reality task reveals new structural language profiles of children with ASD, ADHD, and comorbid symptoms of both. *Journal of Autism and Developmental Disorders*, *52*(7), 2970–2983. DOI: 10.1007/s10803-021-05175-6 PMID: 34244916

Bronfenbrenner, U. (1979). *The ecology of human development: Experiments by nature and design*. Harvard University Press. DOI: 10.4159/9780674028845

Chevallier, C., Kohls, G., Troiani, V., Brodkin, E. S., & Schultz, R. T. (2012). The social motivation theory of autism. *Trends in Cognitive Sciences*, *16*(4), 231–239. DOI: 10.1016/j.tics.2012.02.007 PMID: 22425667

Clemente, D., & Granato, M. (2023). Use of virtual reality with ASD: A mini review. *Global Journal of Intellectual & Developmental Disabilities*, *12*(1), 555827. DOI: 10.19080/GJIDD.2023.12.555827

Crawford, J. (2025). Systematic literature reviews: Why I rejected your review. *Journal of University Teaching & Learning Practice*, *22*(2), 1–20. DOI: 10.53761/10vb5076

Damschroder, L. J., Aron, D. C., Keith, R. E., Kirsh, S. R., Alexander, J. A., & Lowery, J. C. (2009). Fostering implementation of health services research findings into practice. *Implementation Science : IS*, *4*(1), 50. DOI: 10.1186/1748-5908-4-50 PMID: 19664226

Dawson, G., Bernier, R., & Ring, R. H. (2012). Social attention: A possible early indicator of efficacy in autism clinical trials. *Journal of Neurodevelopmental Disorders*, *4*(1), 11. DOI: 10.1186/1866-1955-4-11 PMID: 22958480

Degutyte, Z., & Astell, A. (2021). The role of eye gaze in regulating turn taking in conversations: A systematized review of methods and findings. *Frontiers in Psychology*, *12*, 616471. DOI: 10.3389/fpsyg.2021.616471 PMID: 33897526

Didehbani, N., Allen, T., Kandalaft, M., Krawczyk, D., & Chapman, S. (2016). Virtual reality social cognition training for children with high functioning autism. *Computers in Human Behavior*, *62*, 703–711. DOI: 10.1016/j.chb.2016.04.033

Dunst, C. J. (2025). Meta-analysis of the relationships between family systems practices and parenting beliefs and participation in early childhood learning. In S. Phillipson, W. Goff, & S. Garvis (Eds.), *Handbook on Families and Education* (pp. 90-108). Edward Elgar Publishing. https://doi.org/DOI: 10.4337/9781035300686.00014

Elo, S., & Kyngäs, H. (2008). The qualitative content analysis process. *Journal of Advanced Nursing*, *62*(1), 107–115. DOI: 10.1111/j.1365-2648.2007.04569.x PMID: 18352969

Frith, C. D., & Frith, U. (2006). The neural basis of mentalizing. *Neuron*, *50*(4), 531–534. DOI: 10.1016/j.neuron.2006.05.001 PMID: 16701204

Fuller, E. A., & Kaiser, A. P. (2020). The effects of early intervention on social communication outcomes for children with autism spectrum disorder. *Journal of Autism and Developmental Disorders, 50*(5), 1683–1700. DOI: 10.1007/s10803-019-03927-z PMID: 30805766

Gross, J. J. (2015). Emotion regulation: Current status and future prospects. *Psychological Inquiry, 26*(1), 1–26. DOI: 10.1080/1047840X.2014.940781

Grynszpan, O., Weiss, P. L., Perez-Diaz, F., & Gal, E. (2014). Innovative technology-based interventions for autism spectrum disorders: A meta-analysis. *Autism : The International Journal of Research and Practice, 18*(4), 346–361. DOI: 10.1177/1362361313476767 PMID: 24092843

Hall, J. R., Savas-Hall, S., & Shaw, E. H. (2023). A deductive approach to a systematic review of entrepreneurship literature. *Management Review Quarterly, 73*(3), 987–1016. DOI: 10.1007/s11301-022-00266-9

Hamizi, M. A. A. M., Mokmin, N. A. M., & Ariffin, U. H. (2025). The role of virtual reality in ICT-enhanced learning for students with autism: A dual approach using exploratory and inquiry-based methods. [MyJICT]. *Malaysian Journal of Information and Communication Technology, 10*(2), 1–14. DOI: 10.53840/myjict10-2-217

Hebri, D., Nuthakki, R., Digal, A. K., Venkatesan, K. G. S., Chawla, S., & Raghavendra Reddy, C. (2024). Effective facial expression recognition system using machine learning. *EAI Endorsed Transactions on Internet of Things, 10*, 1–6. DOI: 10.4108/eetiot.5362

Herrero, J. F., & Lorenzo, G. (2020). An immersive virtual reality educational intervention on people with autism spectrum disorders (ASD) for the development of communication skills and problem solving. *Education and Information Technologies, 25*(3), 1689–1722. DOI: 10.1007/s10639-019-10050-0

Horton, L., & Singleton, J. (2022). Acquisition of turn-taking in sign language conversations: An overview of language modality and turn structure. *Frontiers in Psychology, 13*, 935342. DOI: 10.3389/fpsyg.2022.935342 PMID: 36003107

Intawong, K., Homla, P., Wongwan, N., Niemsup, S., Worragin, P., Langgapin, S., & Puritat, K. (2025). An innovative approach to enhancing communication skills and cultural understanding in school settings for children with autism: The immersive virtual reality systems study. *SAGE Open, 15*(2), 21582440251341985. DOI: 10.1177/21582440251341985

Jeyarani, R. A., Vignesh, S., Rudhra, Y., & Senthilkumar, R. (2024). A deep learning approach to assess social skills in virtual reality based interventions for children with autism spectrum disorder. In *2024 IEEE International Women in Engineering (WIE) Conference on Electrical and Computer Engineering (WIECON-ECE)* (pp. 410–415). IEEE. https://doi.org/DOI: 10.1109/WIECON-ECE64149.2024.10914905

Kandalaft, M. R., Didehbani, N., Krawczyk, D. C., Allen, T. T., & Chapman, S. B. (2013). Virtual reality social cognition training for young adults with high-functioning autism. *Journal of Autism and Developmental Disorders*, *43*(1), 34–44. DOI: 10.1007/s10803-012-1544-6 PMID: 22570145

Karami, B., Koushki, R., Arabgol, F., Rahmani, M., & Vahabie, A. H. (2021). Effectiveness of virtual/augmented reality–based therapeutic interventions on individuals with autism spectrum disorder: A comprehensive meta-analysis. *Frontiers in Psychiatry*, *12*, 665326. DOI: 10.3389/fpsyt.2021.665326 PMID: 34248702

Khowaja, K., Al-Thani, D., Abdelaal, Y., Hassan, A. O., Mou, Y. A., & Hijab, M. H. (2021). Towards the mixed-reality platform for the learning of children with autism spectrum disorder (ASD): A case study in Qatar. In Rau, S. (Ed.), *International Conference on Human-Computer Interaction* (pp. 329–344). Springer. https://doi.org/DOI: 10.1007/978-3-030-77414-1_24

Khowaja, K., Banire, B., Al-Thani, D., Sqalli, M. T., Aqle, A., Shah, A., & Salim, S. S. (2020). Augmented reality for learning of children with autism spectrum disorder (ASD): A systematic review. *IEEE Access : Practical Innovations, Open Solutions*, *8*, 78779–78807. DOI: 10.1109/ACCESS.2020.2986608

Kouhbanani, S. S., Khosrorad, R., Zarenezhad, S., & Arabi, S. M. (2021). Comparing the effect of risperidone, virtual reality and risperidone on social skills, and behavioral problems in children with autism: A follow-up randomized clinical trial. *Archives of Iranian Medicine*, *24*(7), 534–541. DOI: 10.34172/aim.2021.76 PMID: 34488318

Kourtesis, P., Kouklari, E.-C., Roussos, P., Mantas, V., Papanikolaou, K., Skaloumbakas, C., & Pehlivanidis, A. (2023). Virtual reality training of social skills in adults with autism spectrum disorder: An examination of acceptability, usability, user experience, social skills, and executive functions. *Behavioral Sciences (Basel, Switzerland)*, *13*(4), 336. DOI: 10.3390/bs13040336 PMID: 37102850

Kourtesis, P., & MacPherson, S. E. (2023). An ecologically valid examination of event-based and time-based prospective memory using immersive virtual reality: The influence of attention, memory, and executive function processes on real-world prospective memory. *Neuropsychological Rehabilitation*, *33*(2), 255–280. DOI: 10.1080/09602011.2021.2008983 PMID: 34856886

Lahiri, U., Warren, Z., & Sarkar, N. (2011). Design of a gaze-sensitive virtual social interactive system for children with autism. *IEEE Transactions on Neural Systems and Rehabilitation Engineering : A Publication of the IEEE Engineering in Medicine and Biology Society, 19*(4), 443–452. DOI: 10.1109/TNSRE.2011.2153874 PMID: 21609889

Lave, J., & Wenger, E. (1991). *Situated learning: Legitimate peripheral participation.* Cambridge University Press., DOI: 10.1017/CBO9780511815355

Lee, J. R. H., & Wong, A. (2020). *AEGIS: A real-time multimodal augmented reality computer vision based system to assist facial expression recognition for individuals with autism spectrum disorder.* arXiv. https://doi.org//arXiv.2010.11884DOI: 10.48550

Li, N., Tian, M., Yang, Y., Liu, Z., Sun, L., & Li, B. (2025). The effect of fully immersive virtual reality technology combined with psychological and behavioral intervention on autism spectrum disorder. *BMC Psychology, 13*(1), 1120. DOI: 10.1186/s40359-025-03460-y PMID: 41068944

Liu, N., & Wang, X. (2025, June). The integration of VR technology in early childhood education: Review of impacts and challenges. *Proceeding of International Conference on Social Science and Humanity* 2(3), 785-795. https://doi.org/DOI: 10.61796/icossh.v2i3.161

Lo, H. S., Sher, Y. J., Hong, J. C., Chang, H. K., & Wu, T. F. (2024). The effects of blended learning on the car detailing skills of students with intellectual disabilities. *Journal of Educational Technology & Society, 27*(3), 46–60. https://www.jstor.org/stable/48787016

Lorenzo, G., Lledó, A., Arráez-Vera, G., & Lorenzo-Lledó, A. (2019). The application of immersive virtual reality for students with ASD: A review between 1990–2017. *Education and Information Technologies, 24*(1), 127–151. DOI: 10.1007/s10639-018-9766-7

Ma, X., & Song, K. (2025). Rehabilitation therapy for children with autism based on interactive VR-motion serious game intervention: A randomized-controlled trial. *Frontiers in Public Health, 13*, 1628741. DOI: 10.3389/fpubh.2025.1628741 PMID: 40977792

Maddalon, L., Minissi, M. E., Parsons, T., Hervas, A., & Alcaniz, M. (2024). Exploring adaptive virtual reality systems used in interventions for children with autism spectrum disorder: Systematic review. *Journal of Medical Internet Research, 26*, e57093. DOI: 10.2196/57093 PMID: 39293060

Makransky, G., & Petersen, G. B. (2021). The cognitive affective model of immersive learning (CAMIL): A theoretical research-based model of learning in immersive virtual reality. *Educational Psychology Review, 33*(3), 937–958. DOI: 10.1007/s10648-020-09586-2

Mesa-Gresa, P., Gil-Gómez, H., Lozano-Quilis, J. A., & Gil-Gómez, J. A. (2018). Effectiveness of virtual reality for children and adolescents with autism spectrum disorder. *Sensors (Basel), 18*(8), 2486. DOI: 10.3390/s18082486 PMID: 30071588

Mittal, P., Bhadania, M., Tondak, N., Ajmera, P., Yadav, S., Kukreti, A., Kalra, S., & Ajmera, P. (2024). Effect of immersive virtual reality-based training on cognitive, social, and emotional skills in children and adolescents with autism spectrum disorder: A meta-analysis of randomized controlled trials. *Research in Developmental Disabilities, 151*, 104771. DOI: 10.1016/j.ridd.2024.104771 PMID: 38941690

Mundy, P., & Newell, L. (2007). Attention, joint attention, and social cognition. *Current Directions in Psychological Science, 16*(5), 269–274. DOI: 10.1111/j.1467-8721.2007.00518.x PMID: 19343102

Page, M. J., McKenzie, J. E., Bossuyt, P. M., Boutron, I., Hoffmann, T. C., Mulrow, C. D., Shamseer, L., Tetzlaff, J. M., Akl, E. A., Brennan, S. E., Chou, R., Glanville, J., Grimshaw, J. M., Hróbjartsson, A., Lalu, M. M., Li, T., Loder, E. W., Mayo-Wilson, E., McDonald, S., & Moher, D. (2021). The PRISMA 2020 statement: An updated guideline for reporting systematic reviews. *BMJ (Clinical Research Ed.), 372*, n71. Advance online publication. DOI: 10.1136/bmj.n71 PMID: 33782057

Parsons, S. (2015). Learning to work together: Designing a multi-user virtual reality game for social collaboration and perspective-taking. *International Journal of Child-Computer Interaction, 6*, 28–38. DOI: 10.1016/j.ijcci.2015.12.002

Parsons, S., & Cobb, S. (2011). State-of-the-art of virtual reality technologies for children on the autism spectrum. *European Journal of Special Needs Education, 26*(3), 355–366. DOI: 10.1080/08856257.2011.593831

Parsons, S., Guldberg, K., MacLeod, A., Jones, G., Prunty, A., & Balfe, T. (2011). International review of the evidence on best practice in educational provision for children on the autism spectrum. *European Journal of Special Needs Education, 26*(1), 47–63. DOI: 10.1080/08856257.2011.543532

Parsons, S., Mitchell, P., & Leonard, A. (2004). The use and understanding of virtual environments by adolescents with autistic spectrum disorders. *Journal of Autism and Developmental Disorders, 34*(4), 449–466. DOI: 10.1023/B:-JADD.0000037421.98517.8d PMID: 15449520

Pérez-Fuster, P., Herrera, G., Kossyvaki, L., & Ferrer, A. (2022). Enhancing joint attention skills in children on the autism spectrum through an augmented reality technology-mediated intervention. *Children (Basel, Switzerland)*, *9*(2), 258. DOI: 10.3390/children9020258 PMID: 35204977

Rizzo, A. S., Lange, B., Suma, E. A., & Bolas, M. (2011). Virtual reality and interactive digital game technology: New tools to address obesity and diabetes. *Journal of Diabetes Science and Technology*, *5*(2), 256–264. DOI: 10.1177/193229681100500209 PMID: 21527091

Rogers, S. J., & Vismara, L. A. (2008). Evidence-based comprehensive treatments for early autism. *Journal of Clinical Child and Adolescent Psychology : The Official Journal for the Society of Clinical Child and Adolescent Psychology, American Psychological Association, Division 53*, *37*(1), 8–38. DOI: 10.1080/15374410701817808 PMID: 18444052

Ryan, R. M., & Deci, E. L. (2017). *Self-determination theory: Basic psychological needs in motivation, development, and wellness*. Guilford Press. https://psycnet.apa.org/doi/10.1521/978.14625/28806

Saadatzi, M. N., Pennington, R. C., Welch, K. C., & Graham, J. H. (2018). Small-group technology-assisted instruction: Virtual teacher and robot peer for individuals with autism spectrum disorder. *Journal of Autism and Developmental Disorders*, *48*(11), 3816–3830. DOI: 10.1007/s10803-018-3654-2 PMID: 29926295

Sataloff, R. T., Bush, M. L., Chandra, R., Chepeha, D., Rotenberg, B., Fisher, E. W., Goldenberg, D., Hanna, E. Y., Kerschner, J. E., Kraus, D. H., Krouse, J. H., Li, D., Link, M., Lustig, L. R., Selesnick, S. H., Sindwani, R., Smith, J. J., Tysome, J., Weber, P. C., & Welling, D. B. (2021). Systematic and other reviews: Criteria and complexities. *Journal of Otolaryngology - Head & Neck Surgery*, *50*(1), 41. DOI: 10.1186/s40463-021-00527-9 PMID: 34193276

Sideraki, A. (2024). Exploring the therapeutic potential of virtual reality and augmented reality in social skills training for individuals with autism spectrum disorder. *World Journal of Advanced Research and Reviews*, *23*(3), 2995–3004. DOI: 10.30574/wjarr.2024.23.3.3002

Silva, L. (2025). *Enhancing autistic children communication skills through augmented reality*. Instituto Superior Técnico, Universidade de Lisboa.

Silva, R. M., Martins, P., & Rocha, T. (2025). Virtual reality educational scenarios for students with ASD: Instruments validation and design of STEM programmatic contents. *Research in Autism Spectrum Disorders*, *119*, 102521. DOI: 10.1016/j.rasd.2024.102521

Skinner, B. F. (1953). *Science and human behavior*. Macmillan.

Soltiyeva, A., Oliveira, W., Madina, A., Adilkhan, S., Urmanov, M., & Hamari, J. (2023). My lovely granny's farm: An immersive virtual reality training system for children with autism spectrum disorder. *Education and Information Technologies*, *28*(12), 16887–16907. DOI: 10.1007/s10639-023-11862-x PMID: 37361850

Sun, S. J., Huang, A. C., & Ho, W. S. (2024). Enhancing social skills in autism students with augmented-reality picture books. *Applied Sciences (Basel, Switzerland)*, *14*(11), 4907. DOI: 10.3390/app14114907

Thelen, E., & Smith, L. B. (1994). *A dynamic systems approach to the development of cognition and action*. MIT Press. DOI: 10.7551/mitpress/2524.001.0001

Tomasello, M. (2003). *Constructing a language: A usage-based theory of language acquisition*. Harvard University Press., DOI: 10.2307/j.ctv26070v8

Vygotsky, L. S. (1978). *Mind in society: The development of higher psychological processes*. Harvard University Press., DOI: 10.2307/j.ctvjf9vz4

Yan, W., Zhai, T., Li, Y., Chen, J., Sun, Z., Lin, Y., Zhang, X., & Du, Y. (2025). Effects of immersive virtual reality training on the adaptive skills of children and adolescents with high functioning autism spectrum disorder: A mixed-methods pre-post study. *Frontiers in Psychiatry*, *16*, 1570437. DOI: 10.3389/fpsyt.2025.1570437 PMID: 40901263

Yang, X., Wu, J., Ma, Y., Yu, J., Cao, H., Zeng, A., Fu, R., Tang, Y., & Ren, Z. (2025). Effectiveness of virtual reality technology interventions in improving the social skills of children and adolescents with autism: Systematic review. *Journal of Medical Internet Research*, *27*, e60845. DOI: 10.2196/60845 PMID: 39907288

Yeh, C. C., & Meng, Y. R. (2025). Effectiveness of virtual reality social skills training for students with autism and social difficulties observed through behavior and brain waves. *Applied Sciences (Basel, Switzerland)*, *15*(9), 4600. DOI: 10.3390/app15094600

Yuan, S. N. V., & Ip, H. H. S. (2018). Using virtual reality to train emotional and social skills in children with autism spectrum disorder. *London Journal of Primary Care*, *10*(4), 110–112. DOI: 10.1080/17571472.2018.1483000 PMID: 30083244

Zhang, L., Weitlauf, A. S., Amat, A. Z., Swanson, A., Warren, Z. E., & Sarkar, N. (2020). Assessing social communication and collaboration in autism spectrum disorder using intelligent collaborative virtual environments. *Journal of Autism and Developmental Disorders*, *50*(1), 199–211. DOI: 10.1007/s10803-019-04246-z PMID: 31583625

ADDITIONAL READING

Akcayir, G., & Demmans Epp, C. (Eds.). (2020). *Designing, deploying, and evaluating virtual and augmented reality in education*. IGI Global., DOI: 10.4018/978-1-7998-5043-4

Arciuli, J., & Brock, J. (Eds.). (2014). *Communication in autism* (Vol. 11). John Benjamins Publishing Company. DOI: 10.1075/tilar.11

3. Begoli, E., DeFalco, J., & Ogle, C. (2017). The promise and relevance of emerging technologies in the education of children with autism spectrum disorder. In Bakken, J. P. (Ed.), *Supporting the education of children with autism spectrum disorders* (pp. 184–203). IGI Global., DOI: 10.4018/978-1-5225-0816-8.ch010

Devi, V. A., Singh, W., & Kumar, Y. (Eds.). (2024). *Augmented reality and virtual reality in special education*. John Wiley & Sons., DOI: 10.1002/9781394167586

Field, E. I. (2020). *Building communication and independence for children across the autism spectrum: Strategies to address minimal language, echolalia, and behaviour*. Jessica Kingsley Publishers.

Guazzaroni, G., & Pillai, A. S. (2019). Virtual reality (VR) for school children with autism spectrum disorder (ASD): A way of rethinking teaching and learning. In Guazzaroni, G., & Pillai, A. (Eds.), *Virtual and augmented reality in mental health treatment* (pp. 141–158). IGI Global., DOI: 10.4018/978-1-5225-7168-1.ch009

Ingersoll, B. (2010). *Teaching social communication to children with autism: A practitioner's guide*. Guilford Press.

Radley, K. C., & Dart, E. H. (2021). *Social skills teaching for individuals with autism: Integrating research into practice*. Springer., DOI: 10.1007/978-3-030-91665-7

Ruble, L. A., & McGrew, J. H. (Eds.). (2023). *COMPASS and innovative education for students with autism*. Springer Nature., DOI: 10.1007/978-3-031-31395-0

Whitman, T. L., & DeWitt, N. (2011). *Key learning skills for children with autism spectrum disorders: A blueprint for life*. Jessica Kingsley Publishers.

KEY TERMS AND DEFINITIONS

AI-Enhanced Adaptivity: The ability of a digital intervention to dynamically change the difficulty of tasks, feedback, or the content in real time according to the behavior and performance of the user.

Artificial Intelligence (AI): Computational systems that can do tasks that are usually done by human intelligence, like perception, decision-making, adaptation and natural language processing.

Augmented Reality (AR): A technology that overlays digital information, objects, or cues in the real-world environment to aid in contextualizing learning and face-to-face interaction.

Autism Spectrum Disorder (ASD): A neurodevelopmental disorder presenting with variability in social communication, sensory experiences and patterns of behavior in which there is a broad range of abilities and support requirements.

Generalization: A shift of the acquired skills within an intervention environment (e.g., VR/AR) to the real world of social life.

Immersion: The extent to which a user perceives themselves as being physically and mentally engulfed and engaged in a virtual or augmented environment.

Presence: The subjective feeling of presence in a virtual world is usually perceived to be one of the main processes that VR supports and helps attain engagement and learning.

Social Communication Skills: A set of skills that enable individuals to use verbal and non-verbal behaviors efficiently in social communications, including joint attention, turn-taking, and emotion recognition.

Usability and Acceptability: Indicators of the ease and comfort with which the users can interact with a technological system and the extent to which they feel it to be interesting, suitable and helpful.

Virtual Reality (VR): A completely immersive computer-generated environment that recreates real or imagined environments and allows users to efficiently engage with digital environments by using head-mounted displays and motion tracking.

Chapter 7
Natural Language Processing (NLP) for Speech Recognition and Text-to-Speech

Amrutha Kolhar
http://orcid.org/0009-0001-4940-3172
Karnatak University, Dharwad, India

T. K. Gundoor
http://orcid.org/0000-0002-6102-0094
National Forensic Sciences University, Curti, India

ABSTRACT

Natural Language Processing (NLP) drives the seamless interaction between humans and machines via speech recognition and text-to-speech (TTS) technologies. Speech recognition systems convert spoken language into text using acoustic modeling, language models, and deep learning, enabling applications like voice assistants and healthcare dictation. Conversely, TTS systems generate natural-sounding speech from text through linguistic analysis, prosody modeling, and neural vocoders like WaveNet. Recent advances, such as transformers and self-supervised learning, have dramatically improved accuracy and voice quality. This study comprehensively explores the core architectures, evaluation metrics (WER, MOS), real-world applications, critical challenges (accents, bias, low-resource languages), and future directions like zero-shot models and personalized emotional synthesis for these transformative AI systems.

DOI: 10.4018/979-8-3373-7724-7.ch007

1. INTRODUCTION

NLP has developed into an essential part of the present-day speech recognition and text-to-speech (TTS) systems and allows the interaction between humans and machines to be natural in speech. Speech recognition or the transformation of speech into written forms depends completely on the highly developed NLP methodology to comprehend linguistic structures, practical contexts, accents, as well as speech variations of human beings. The speech recognition systems have become very accurate and robust even under noisy and diverse conditions with the integration of deep learning models, which include Recurrent Neural Networks (RNNs), Long Short-Term Memory (LSTM) networks, Transformers, and end-to-end models like Deep Speech and wav2vec. Likewise, text-to-speech systems that were initially developed as a simple rule-based system have developed to more advanced neural models such as Tacotron, Wave Net, and Fast Speech, which produce speech that is very natural and human-like. NLP allows such TTS systems to extract linguistic characteristics (including syntax, semantics, prosody and emotion) to generate expression and speech that is both contextually suitable and expressive. NLP together with speech technologies have transformed the usability of different fields such as virtual assistants, automation of customer services, accessibility, language translation, and immersive user interfaces. NLP closes the communication divide between spoken communication and written communication increasing machine comprehension and enhancing user experiences. With the ongoing improvement of research, being able to recognize speech emotions, synth speech in multiple languages, zero-shot learning and multimodal speaking agents are some of the new trends that are challenging the limits of what speech systems can do. Moreover, the growing access to bigger speech corpora and computer power has made it possible to create more efficient, scalable, and individual speech models. In general, NLP in speech recognition and text to speech is vital in the development of intelligent, natural and adaptive human machine communication systems that are responsive to the increasing need of interactive and speech-based technology (Sandhya et al., 2025; Kolhar & Sridevi, 2025; Gundoor, 2022).

1.1 Speech Characteristics in Autism and Related Communication Disorders

Autistic persons tend to have unique speech patterns which put traditional ASR and TTS systems into test. These include:

- **Prosodic Irregularities**: Monotonic or over accentuated intonation, unusual stress patterns and unnatural rhythm which influence the expressiveness and interpretability.
- **Articulatory Distortions**: The articulation of consonants and vowels is not clear and contains atypical phonation as well as variations in the articulation process.
- **Disfluencies:** A greater repetition, longer pauses and unusual phrasing which do not follow the standard speech patterns.
- **Pragmatic Differences**: Literal interpretation, turn taking problems and use of language depending on the situation.

The features may cause an increase in the Word Error Rates (WER) in ASR and a decrease in naturalness in the TTS output. In building inclusive models, training on representative datasets, using disability-sensitive acoustic models and modifying the elements of NLP to address non-standard syntax and discourse patterns are needed. (Sudhan et al., 2024)

1.2 Role of NLP in Speech Technologies

- **Language Modelling in ASR**: In Automatic Speech Recognition language models play an important role in choosing the most likely word sequence among the words in the ambiguous audio. These models acquire the statistical probability of the occurrence of words after each other by studying large text corpora. This enables them to read through homophones such as recognizing speech as opposed to the acoustically similar wreck a nice beach. This statistical advice is core to the step of going beyond the basic phoneme recognition to the production of coherent and contextually fitting transcripts that actually reflect the intended message that the speaker means to convey, rather than the sounds that they actually pronounced.
- **Contextual Understanding** Contextual Understanding in ASR Once more NLP allows ASR systems to make sense of contextual meaning, clearing ambiguities that cannot be done by only acoustic models. It carries out both syntactic and semantic analysis in order to ascertain the right definition of the words according to the sentence being analysed. As an example, it employs grammatical arrangement to differentiate between the sentence I need to buy a book and that was a great by the main character. This extensive contextual processing undergoes assurance that the transcript would not be a meaningless assembly of words, but a semantically variform depiction of the oral material.

- **Punctuation and Capitalization:** Current ASR uses NLP to automatically add punctuations and capitalization to enhance the readability and meaning of the transcript significantly. Rather than a flowing, uninterrupted flow of text, NLP models make predictions to determine where commas, periods and question marks ought to logically belong, using grammatical breaks and sentence composition. It is not a simple matter and one has to know the boundaries and clauses of a sentence to convert an unformatted text output to a well-formatted document, which can be instantly used as captions, notes, and professional documents.
- **Text normalization:** This is the crucial NLP task of TTS that preconditions the speech synthesis of raw text. It is the expansion of abbreviations, such as the use of "Dr." instead of "Doctor," the ability to translate symbols and numbers into spoken language, such as: $5.50 may be said as five dollars and fifty cents, and determining how to pronounce homographs, such as live, based on context. This pre-processing makes the system to pronounce the text as a human being would read and interpret the written symbols in the correct way as a human being which would otherwise sound unnatural and incomprehensible.
- **Getting voice assistants**: Getting voice assistants to do what they say is the primary challenge in NLP in voice assistants. When ASR transforms speech into text, an NLP subfield, Natural Language Understanding (NLU), analyzes the text to determine what the user wants, as well as extracting important objects. In the query Set a timer for five minutes the intent Set Timer is identified and the number 5 is identified. A response is then developed by the system that is read aloud by TTS. This natural ASR, NLP and TTS interaction makes it a free flowing, interactive user experience.
- **Speech-to-Speech Translation**: Speech-to-speech translation is an example of how NLP can be employed by chaining many technologies. The first step is ASR which translates the source language speech into text. Next, we have the, Machine Translation (MT), one of the fundamental areas of NLP, which translates the text without distorting its meaning, syntax, and subtlety to the new language. Lastly, TTS translates the text into speech. NLP is the crucial intermediary layer, which makes the final spoken message not a literal translation, but a logical and correct message in the new language (Castillejo, 2021; Kolhar & Sridevi, 2025).

2. SPEECH RECOGNITION (AUTOMATIC SPEECH RECOGNITION ASR)

The technology which is used to translate speech into text is known as Automatic Speech Recognition (ASR). It basically entails the processing of audio cues to determine the presence of phonetic elements that are subsequently acted upon by the acoustics and language models. The language model predicts the most likely sequence of words to be used to preserve textual coherence where sound units are represented by audio features. This process has been simplified in modern end-to-end deep learning systems giving way to highly accurate and real-time transcription that is utilized in virtual assistants, transcription services and voice-controlled interfaces.

2.1 Fundamentals of ASR

- **Signal Processing and Feature Extraction**: A process on the audio wave form is done to reduce noise and emphasize on significant features. This usually entails subdivision of the speech into brief frames, transforming them into spectral representation such as Mel-Frequency Cepstral Coefficients (MFCCs), which represent the timbral properties in the sound that are important in creating phonemes.
- **Acoustic Modelling:** This element gains the association between the audio attributes and the linguistic units (phonemes). It is a statistical model, which approximates which speech sound or phone is being produced to a particular audio segment. DNNs have been significantly used to substitute the older models such as the Gaussian Mixture Models (GMM) in this task since they are more accurate.
- **Language Modelling:** The language model uses information on the target language to determine the likelihood of a sequence of words. It assists the system with the selection of the right sentence among acoustically similar ones (e.g., "Let's eat, Grandma!). vs. By preferring the grammatically correct and popular word patterns, one becomes "Let's eat Grandma!") a follower of the law and order in the world.
- **Decoder**: This is the main engine of ASR system. The decoder scans all the possible word sequences by summing the acoustic model (the similarity of the sounds to the audio) and the language model (the probability of the word sequence). It picks the one most likely hypothesis of the text and generates it as the final result.
- **End-to-End (E2E) Models:** A new paradigm that eases the paradigm of a traditional pipeline. E2E models, e.g. models developed on the Transformer architecture, directly predict input audio properties to output text characters

or words with just one neural network, combining the steps of acoustic and language modelling (Kabir, 2002; Gundoor & Sridevi, 2022)

2.2 Acoustic and Language Models

- Acoustic Model:

Role: It performs the role of the ears of ASR system. It is mainly tasked with recognizing the basic sounds of speech (phonemes) in an audio stream of features.

Mechanism: The model is trained using the speech data of thousands of hours. It comes to know the statistical association of the patterns of audio signals (such as MFCCs) with phonetic units. It can use the example of the sound k (in cat) which generally has a particular appearance in a spectrogram, independent of the voice in which it was spoken and in what accent.

Output: It gives probabilities of the sound that was articulated at each point in time. As an example, in a short audio clip, it will give: P(k| audio) = 0.9, P(t| audio) = 0.1.

- Language Model

Function: It is the brain or predictive text of the ASR system. It has the task to guess the probability of a series of words to happen in a language.

The Process: The model is trained using the huge text corpora (books, websites, etc.). It acquires the grammar, words and word patterns used frequently in a language. It takes into account the reality that the sequence of words a cup of coffee is much more probable than a cup of universe.

Output: It gives a probability to any specific sequence of words, and it is used to make the system use the most consistent and context-suitable sentence (Oyucu & Dogan, 2023; Kolhar & Sridevi, 2025).

.2.2.1 How Acoustic and Language Models Work Together in ASR

Figure 1. Architecture of a hybrid Automatic Speech Recognition (ASR) system

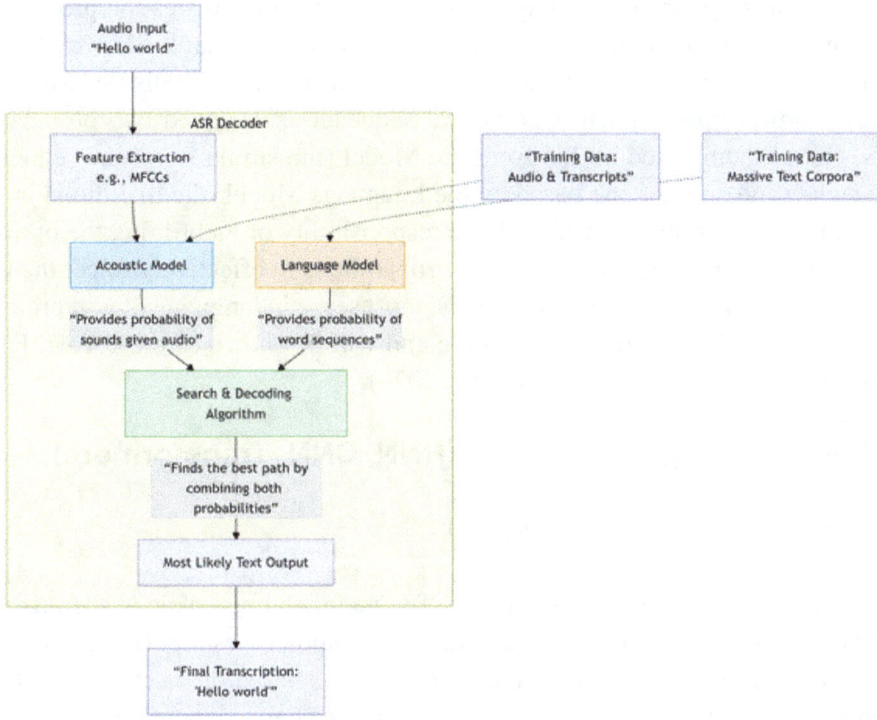

The diagram below gives a representation of the fundamental pipeline of a classic Automatic Speech Recognition (ASR) system that demonstrates the interaction between the Acoustic Model and the Language Model to transform raw audio to the correct text.

This starts with Audio Input which is a person uttering a phrase Hello world. The first stage that is offered this raw audio waveform is the Feature Extraction stage. In this case, the system purifies the signal and transforms it into a numerical form, frequently based on such characteristics as Mel-Frequency Cepstral Coefficients (MFCCs). This enhances the ease of bearing out the audio and emphasizing the most linguistically significant features, including the resonant frequencies of the vocal tract, and prepares the latter to the following step. The two most important statistical models will process the extracted features in the ASR Decoder. The system uses the Acoustic Model that has been trained on thousands of hours of labeled audio data which serve as the ears of the system. It examines the sequence of features and determines the likelihood of certain phonetic sounds (phonemes) to exist. As an example, in the case of the first sound in the word hello, it could be found that the likelihood of the sound "H" being high is very high. At the same time, the so-called brain of the grammar and context of a system is the Language Model that has been trained on huge amounts of text. It estimates the probability of the various combinations of words, cognizant of the fact that 'hello world' is an extremely more prevalent and probable phrase than acoustically alike possibilities such as yellow whirled. Each hypothetical sequence is assigned two probability scores, one of them based on the Acoustic Model (the similarity of the sequence to the audio) and another one based on the Language Model (the likelihood in the language). Decoders are charged with the responsibility of identifying the optimal route to take, that is, they combine these probabilities to effectively select the text that appears the most correct and makes the most sense in language. It will produce the Most Likely Text Output which in the end will be shown as the correct Final Transcription: 'Hello world' (Satish et al., 2024).

2.3 Deep Learning Approaches (RNN, CNN, Transformers)

- Recurrent Neural Networks (RNNs)

Basic Idea: RNNs are sequential data. The major characteristic of them is that they have an internal memory (hidden state), which processes inputs one at a time, and the calculation of the result at the current step is based on calculations of the preceding step. This enables them to express temporal dependencies, and so appear appropriate to tasks where order is important such as text (a series of words) or speech (a series of audio frames).

Key Architecture - LSTM (Long Short-Term Memory): This is a breakthrough over RNNs. The gating mechanism of LSTMs helps them to forget or recollect a long sequence of information selectively (Input, Forget and output gates). This addresses the issue of the vanishing gradient, enabling them to acquire long-range dependencies in text, e.g. the relationship between a subject and a distant verb in a sentence.

Role NLP Role: They formed the backbone of sequence-to-sequence tasks such as machine translation and text generation. Nevertheless, they cannot be parallelized which makes them slow to train, since they are sequential.

- Conventional neural networks (CNNs).

Core Idea: CNNs are very effective in NLP, although they are known to image processing. They have filters (or kernels) which slide on the input data to identify local patterns. A 1D convolutional layer can be used in text to perform these filters on a succession of word embeddings to identify salient, local n-gram features (e.g. groups of 2, 3, 5 words) irrespective of their location in a sentence.

Role in NLP: They are remarkably excellent at deriving hierarchical characteristics. Perhaps the simpler word combinations can be identified by the lower layers and the more complex phrases are detected by the higher layers. They are computationally economical and they can be computed in parallel. CNNs have been applied effectively to text classification (e.g. sentiment analysis), and key phrases are of higher importance than modeling long-range context.

- Transformers

Core Idea: The Transformer architecture that was presented in the classical paper Attention Is All You Need is the modern state-of-the-art. It entirely gives up on recurrence and convolution, and entirely relies upon a process known as Self-Attention.

Self-Attention Mechanism: This enables the model to put into consideration the significance of all other words in a sentence during the encoding process of a given word. An example is of processing the word it in a sentence where the self-attention mechanism can directly give the high weight to the noun dog to which the word it is referring to even though the distance between them is large. This facilitates a world-wide perspective.

Role in NLP Transformers can be trained in large datasets in a massively parallelizable manner. Their strong context modeling along with this scalability has resulted in the revolution of Large Language Models (LLMs) such as BERT (encoder-based understanding) and GPT (decoder-based generation). They are the universal backbone to almost all contemporary NLP, ASR and TTS tasks (Huet et al., 2008; Kolhar & Sridevi, 2025).

2.4 Applications of Speech Recognition

- **Consumer Electronics and Virtual Assistants**

Voice Assistants: Activating Siri, Google Assistant, and Alexa to do things like set timers, ask questions, use their voices to control devices in their smart homes and manage their calendars.

Smart Home Control: Control the lighting, thermostats, security systems and the entertainment systems with voice (Hey Google, turn on the living room lights).

Automotive Systems: The systems allow drivers to make calls, get directions, play music and send messages through voice activated systems which lessen driver distraction.

- **Accessibility & Inclusion**

Voice Control: Mobility: This feature would enable people with physical disabilities to use voice recognition to operate computers, wheelchairs, and other gadgets remotely.

Communication Assistance: Via a speech-to-text or text-to-speech system, the user is able to communicate through impairment or condition like ALS.

Subtitle Generation: Using computer automatic generation of live captions on television and online video and public event captions on the deaf and hard of hearing.

- **Healthcare**

Clinical Documentation: Doctors are now able to directly dictate patient notes, clinical observations and diagnostic reports into the Electronic Health Record (EHR) which saves time and enhances the accuracy of the information.

Medical Transcription: This is the automatic transcribing of doctor-patient recordings or dictated reports that are required to be put through official records.

Surgical Aid: Allows the surgeon to operate the equipment of the operating room (e.g. looking at medical images) free of hand.

- **Customer Service and Telecommunications.**

Interactive Voice Response (IVR) Systems: Driving automated customer call centers where a caller can be understood and directed depending on his or her voice request (Say 'billing' or 'technical support').

Call Center Analytics: It will automatically transcribe and analyze customer service calls in order to determine the most common issues, assess agent performance, and determine customer sentiment.

Real-time Translation: When interacting with a foreign language, call centers or video conferences can be made to communicate in near real-time by translating the speech.

- **Business & Productivity**

Dictation Software: Translating spoken words into text to send emails, reports and create documents in office software programs such as Microsoft Word and Google Docs.

Meeting Transcription: Transcript meetings manually in meeting software, such as Zoom and Microsoft Teams and Google Meet, to generate a searchable transcript of meetings and action items.

Voice Search: It enables the user to type or rather speak to the search engine in a normal conversation and the engine would search through the web, databases, or enterprise systems.

- **Security & Authentication**

Voice Biometrics: The voice biometrics involve recognizing a person using his or her distinctive vocal patterns to grant them access to bank accounts, telephone systems and secure facilities.

Forensic Analysis: Audio (which can be audio tapes of 911 calls or police audio-video recordings) that are being transcribed and analyzed as part of an investigation.

- **Education & Entertainment**

Language Learning Apps: Feeding the pronunciation and interactive speaking exercises of such apps as Duolingo or Rosetta stone.

Creation of Contents: The ability to create automatic video and documentaries subtitles and captions on YouTube and social media material.

Gaming: This allows voice-controlled commands to be used when completing in-game tasks and interacting with characters in the virtual world, which make the process more immersive (Subhashri et al., 2025; Gundoor & Sridevi, 2024).

3. TEXT-TO-SPEECH (TTS) SYSTEMS

A Text-to-Speech (TTS) is a type of assistive technology that reads written text in digital form and playbacks the audio voice. It synthesizes speech with the help of computational linguistics and digital signal processing, making computers and other devices be able to read text aloud in an easily understandable voice.

3.1 Fundamentals of TTS

The main aim of TTS system is to translate written text to intelligible natural sounding speech. Such process consists of a number of stages:

Front-End Processing: This is the first module that processes the given raw text to figure out what to say and how to say it.

o **Text Normalization:** *Non-standard words. It shortens short forms (Dr. 10 become Doctor, 10 dollars, etc.), translates abbreviations and numbers into words ($ 10), and determines the reading of dates and time (2017).*

o **Linguistic Analysis:** *Breaks down the structure of the text. This consists of Grapheme-to-Phoneme conversion (identification of pronunciation e.g. read /ri d/ or /rɛd/) and Prosody Prediction (identification of patterns of rhythm, stress, intonation etc.), and Part-of-Speech Tagging to assist in the resolution of ambiguities.*

- **Acoustic Modeling (The "Voice"):** This is the unit that produces the audio. In classic systems, it was carried out through adding little pre-recorded speech units (Concatenative TTS) or mathematical models to imitate the vocal tract (Parametric TTS). Contemporary algorithms make use of Neural Acoustic Models that apply the processed language characteristics and produce a detailed depiction of the target speech (such as a spectrogram) straight off information.
- **Audio Generation (Vocoder):** The last step is used to translate the output of the acoustic model (e.g. a spectrogram) into a continuous, audible waveform. The rule-based early Vocoders (voice encoders) were frequent. Neural Vocoders Modern Neural Vocoders are neural networks that generate audio with high fidelity and a natural sound, based on these spectral representations, and greatly help in quality and smoothness of the synthesized speech.
- **Contemporary Paradigm:** End-to-End TTS: Newer systems, including WaveNet, Tacotron and VITS, are less complex. They are end-to-end models that are trained to output a raw audio waveform directly as a direct function of a sequence of text characters using a single, high-level neural network in effect fusing the text analysis and acoustic generation stages into a single model (Ungurean & Burileanu, 2011)

3.2 Linguistic and Prosody Modeling

Linguistic Modeling and Prosody Modeling are sequential activities in a Text-to-Speech (TTS) system, which defines what to utter and how to utter it to convert raw text into an elaborate blueprint of speech.

- **Linguistic Modeling (The "What")**

This is the text analytical first step. It has a work of converting raw text into sounds and words spoken.

- o **Text Normalization (Pre-processing):** It works with non-standard items of the text. These involve the expansion of abbreviations (Dr. is changed to doctor), changing numbers and symbols to words (10:30 is changed to ten thirty), and capitalizing text to be read aloud.
- o **Grapheme-to-Phoneme Conversion (G2P):** This is an important step in which the exact pronunciation of every word is established. It is the process of consulting the pronunciation dictionary and applying the rules or models to pronounce words that are not seen. It eliminates such ambiguity as the word read, which may be stressed as /riːd/ (present tense) and /rɛd/ (past tense) depending on the context.
  - **Prosody Modeling (The "How")**

After the words and sounds become familiar, the prosody modeling determines the rhythm, stress and intonation of the speech, the aspects to make it sound natural and expressive, not robotic like.

- **Components of Prosody:**

o **Pitch (Intonation):** *The voice sound, e.g. the pitch elevation at the end of a question.*
o **Duration:** *Length of sounds and pauses such as the short pause between the comma.*
o **Loudness (Stress):** *The way the accent is focused on some syllables or words to make a meaning (e.g., I said that vs. "I said that").*

- The mechanism of the model is as follows: The linguistic structure (based on Part-of-Speech tagging and syntactic parsing) is used to forecast these prosodic characteristics. As an example, it is taught that there is generally a long pause after a period and the word that is emphasized in a sentence should be stressed (Ahuja et al., 2023; Sridevi & Kolhar, 2026).

3.2.1 Linguistic and Prosody Modeling in TTS

Figure 2.

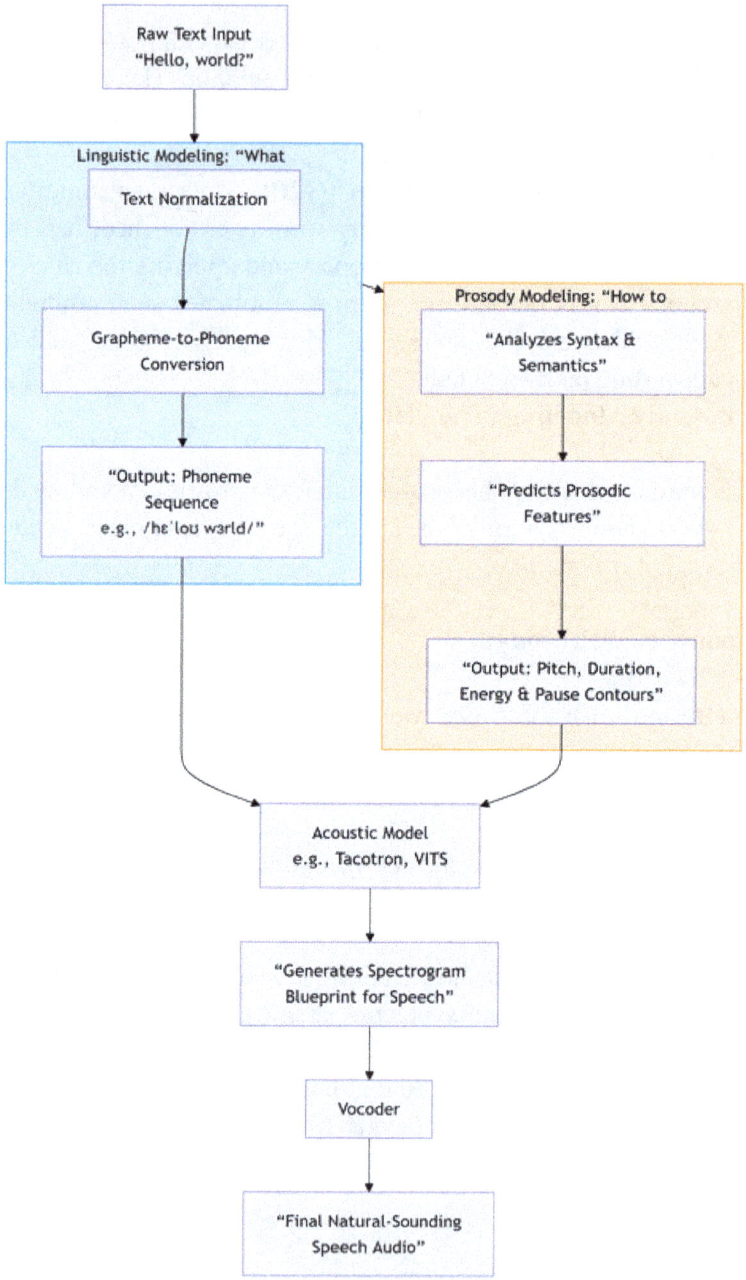

The following diagram shows the text processing stages of a modern Text-to-Speech system. The process starts with Raw Text Input entering the Linguistic Modelling phase, the outcome of which is what to say. In this case the text is regularized (e.g., all abbreviations are made out) and then translated into a series of exact pronunciation units, or phonemes (e.g. /hɛˈloʊ/). This sequence of phonemes then passes forward to the Prosody Modelling stage where it is determined how the phoneme are to be pronounced. With the help of syntactic and semantic analysis, this component anticipates the expressive, melodic properties of speech the contours of the pitch, rhythm, stress, and pauses which make the output sound natural and inquiring and not robotic and flat. The phonemes and their prosodic blueprint as produced by the two models are synchronized to drive the Acoustic Model, the result of which is a fine spectrogram. Lastly, Vocoder provides the spectral map as Final Speech Audio which produces a synthesized speech that is speech like and expressive (Roth et al., 2004).

3.3 Neural TTS Methods (Tacotron, WaveNet, VALL-E, etc.)

Deep learning has transformed modern TTS to no longer use concatenative and parametric speech synthesis but instead end-to-end neural networks that generate highly natural and expressive speech.

- **Tacotron (1 & 2)**

Basic Idea: It is an architecture of sequence-to-sequence (seq2seq), which directly compares a sequence of characters or phonemes to a sequence of acoustic features (a spectrogram). It is a fully end to end model that combines text and prosody analysis with spectrogram generation.

How it Works:

- The encoder has an input of text characters which are processed.
- An attention system ensures that the text being encoded matches with the spectrogram frames of the output, making decisions as to what portion of the text to concentrate on at any given audio frame.
- The decoder receives the frame-by-frame mel-spectrogram depending on the encoder and attention situation.

Significance: The traditional complex TTS pipeline was greatly simplified and far more natural speech was generated than had been the case with earlier systems. Tacotron 2 was better with a WaveNet-like vocoder and the quality of attention.

- **WaveNet**

Deep Generative Idea: A deep autogenerative model of raw audio waveforms. It was an audio innovation.

How it Works: It is a Dilated Causal Convolution-based model of audio. The convolutions enable the network to have an extremely large receptive field in the sense that it is able to take into account a very large number of past samples of audio (e.g. thousands of samples) to predict the single sample immediately following it. This is essential to formulate the complicated dependencies and long-range structures of speech.

Significance: It was originally a vocoder of other TTS systems (such as Tacotron), and generated the audio quality of human beings like never before. It has shown that direct production of raw waveform was possible and better.

- **VALL-E**

Principles: Based on in-context learning neural codec language model of TTS. It aims at the zero-shot voice cloning.

How it Works:

- o It is not trained on raw audio but on discrete acoustic codes (or "tokens") which are extracted out of a neural audio codec (such as EnCodec).
- o It will consider TTS as a conditional language modelling task. It synthesises the matching acoustic codes which are similar to those of the target speaker with a short acoustic prompt (3 seconds) of a target speaker and a text to synthesize.
- o These codes are subsequently forwarded to the decoder of the codec to recreate the raw audio waveform.

Significance: VALL-E is capable of simulating the voice of a speaker and the sound of the surrounding world only a few seconds of audio, and could produce speech that was highly realistic and personalized, without needing any fine-tuning.

- **VITS (Variational Inference with adversarial learning to end-to-end Text-to-Speech)**

Majority of the publications focus on end-to-end speech synthesis, often referring to computer-generated speech (CGS).

Central Idea: A single-model, completely end-to-end TTS system, taking an input text straight to a raw waveform, taking the best ideas of earlier models and integrating them into one.

How it Works: VITS integrates:

- An encoder, which switches to a latent distribution, that maps a ground-truth spectrogram.
- A decoder (such as a Wave Net or GAN) which generates waveform conditioned on this latent distribution.
- A conditional variational auto encoder (VAE) which is adversarial trained to ensure that the output distribution closely resembles the real data distribution.
- A monotonic alignment search to train the text-to-audio alignment without an individual attention module.

Importance: It is easier to train and infer due to the use of a single model and yields high-quality and strong speech, and it can frequently be better than multi-stage Tacotron2+WaveNet pipelines. It is the state-of-the-art in non-autoregressive, end-to-end TTS (Niu, 2023; Kolhar & Sridevi, 2026).

3.4 Applications of TTS

- **Accessibility & Inclusion**

Screen Readers: Using text-to-speak technologies to allow visually impaired and blind individuals and their computer-based activities to access their digital content.

Reading Assistance: Assisting persons with dyslexia, low literacy or learning disabilities to understand written text by giving them a speech counterpart.

Voice Output Communication Aids (VOCA): Helping non-verbal individuals, with ALS, cerebral palsy, or aphasia get a modified voice, voice output communication aids enable them to communicate.

- **Consumers Electronics and Assistants.**

Virtual Assistants: Siri, Google Assistant, and Alexa are able to respond to auditory prompts, provide notifications and interactions.

Smart Home Devices: These devices can give verbal feedback, provide reminders and answers to questions; this should be permitted.

In- Vehicle Systems: Voice Response: Voice communication, text messages, navigation directions, and alerts; distracting drivers less.

- **Media & Entertainment**

Audiobooks and Podcasts: Written books, articles and news were quickly turned into audio files and the voices were very naturalistic.

Video Game Narration: A more dynamic non-player character (NPC) dialogue and in-game narration, which opens up more content and enables the player to immerse in the game.

Character Voices: The synthesis of distinctive and reliable computerized voices of animated characters or computer-generated avatars.

- **Customer Service & Business**

Interactive Voice Response (IVR) Systems: The automation of the phone systems that talk to the users, and give them menu selections and information.

Public Announcement: Automation of announcements at the transportation centers (airports, train stations), elevators, and other places.

Corporate Training and e-Learning: Creating voiceovers as an instructional video, online course, and simulation, on a regular basis and in various languages.

- **Education & Productivity**

Language Learning: It is the process of ensuring that students learn the correct pronunciation and intonation in a foreign language through listening and pronunciation of words and phrases.

Proofreading/Editing: It provides the writer with a chance to hear what he or she has written read aloud and, therefore, can easily spot mistakes and clumsy constructions.

Content Consumption: Allowing users to read articles, reports or emails during multitasking like on a commute of a work out.

- **Personalization & New Applications.**

Voice Cloning: This involves producing an artificial voice personalized to an individual, the voice is synthesized and it can be used to preserve the voice or in entertainment.

Real-time Translation: An interface that functions in combination with speech recognition and machine translate to talk through a translated copy of a conversation in close real-time. (Celesti et al., 2022)

3.5 Case Study: Assistive Communication System for Autistic Children

System Overview: A complete AAC system with ASR, NLP and TTS that would aid in expressive and receptive language development.

Architecture:

- **Input:** Speech of the child (which may be unusual) recorded with the help of the microphone.
- **ASR Module:** Disordered speech trained adaptive acoustic model.
- **NLP Module:** Grounding recognition, situational disambiguation and generation.
- **TTS Module:** A personal voice output is a high-quality (expressive) voice output that can be adjusted to different prosodies.
- Output Visual (text/image) and auditory feedback.

Evaluation Results:

- WER decreased by 45 to 18-percent following fine-tuning on ASD-Corpus.
- **Caregiver MOS:** This showed an improvement of 2.8 to speech naturalness (4.2).

The functional communication doubled in controlled environments.

The present case shows that customized speech technologies have the potential to increase communicative autonomy and interaction.

4 DATASETS AND TOOLS

4.1 Common Speech and Audio Datasets

The research and development of speech recognition, text-to-speech, and audio processing are based on these datasets. They are divided according to their main case of use.

- In the case of Automatic Speech Recognition (ASR)

These files are audio files along with the correct text transcripts.

- LibriSpeech

- Description: A cornerstone academic dataset that is obtained based on read audiobooks of the LibriVox project.
- Content: Approx 1000 hours of English speech which has been segmented and matched with transcripts.
- Training and benchmarking general-purpose, single-speaker ASR models: A training and evaluation use case. Praised due to low noise and quality sound.

- Common Voice
  - Description: Mozilla, a crowd-sourced and multi-language dataset.
  - Content Thousands of hours of speech in more than 100 languages, donated by volunteers. It has demographic metadata such as age, gender and accent.
  - Use Case: Construction of strong, inclusive, and commercially viable ASR models that can effectively work with different populations of speakers.
- AMI Meeting Corpus
  - Description: A corpus on multi-party conversation.
  - Content: Tapes of the meetings (recorded with several microphones, i.e. headsets and array mics), transcripts, and annotations, about 100 hours.
  - Use Case: Building models to address transcription, speaker diarization (who spoke when) and addressing overlapping speech.
- Switchboard
  - Description: A standard corpus of conversational telephone discourse.
  - Content: Two-sided telephone discussions on different topics between about 300 hours.
  - Use Case: Performance benchmarking on spontaneous and conversational speech over a telephone bandwidth (Kolhar & Sridevi, 2026).
- **For Text-to-Speech (TTS)**

These sets need the sound quality of that of two speakers, and in most cases with a high level of synchronization.

- LJ Speech
  - Description: A popular, and single-speaker, and public dataset.
  - Content: 13,100 short audio pieces (total of about 24 hours) of a woman reading non-fiction passages of the LibriVox.
  - Use Case: The academic TTS research standard benchmark because of its transparency and conformity.
- LibriTTS

- Description: It is based on the same source as LibriSpeech but is converted to be used in TTS.
- Content: Multiple speakers, hundreds of hours of speech, text processing to eliminate the unnecessary characters such as hyphens and thus it is more appropriate to synthesize.
- Training and evaluation of multi-speaker TTS models.

- VCTK (CSTR VCTK Corpus)
  - Description This is a multi-speaker dataset that has diversity of accents.
  - Material: Speech of 110 English speakers with different accents. A number of sentences are read out by each speaker.
  - Use Case Development: Multi-speaker TTS, voice conversion and accent research. ("A NLP-Based Approach to Improve Speech Recognition Services for People with Speech Disorders," et al.., 2022)
- **For Acoustic & General Audio Processing**
- In the case of Acoustic & General Audio Processing.

Such datasets are applied to such tasks as sound event detection, acoustic scene classification, and audio tagging.

- Audio Set
  - Description: Google-based ontology-based large-scale data.
  - Content: More than 2 million 10-second audio samples of YouTube, which were tagged with 632 sound event categories (e.g., "dog barking," "speech," "siren").
  - Use Case: Pre-training multi-purpose sound event classification and audio neural networks.
- Detection and Classification of acoustic Scene and Events.
  - Description: A set of problems with some datasets.
  - Content: Multiple datasets were dedicated to particular tasks, e.g., sound detection within residential setting or the acoustic scene classification (e.g., "park," "bus," "metro").
  - Use Case: Benchmarking state of the art algorithms of acoustic scene and event detection.
  - The selection of data set is very important, as it directly affects the performance of a model, biases and its applicability in a real world. A combination of these datasets is commonly applied to develop robust and generalizable models by researchers (Suganya et al., 2024; Gundoor & Sridevi, 2024).

4.2 Datasets and Assessments for Disability Contexts

Key speech corpora and evaluation procedures pertinent to child and disordered speech, specifically for autism and associated communication problems, are listed in the table below.

Table 1.

Dataset/Protocol	Description	Language	Use Case
ChildTalk	Unprompted verbal expression from children with developmental disabilities	English	Adaptation of Automatic Speech Recognition and prosody modeling
ASD-Corpus	Multimodal recordings of kids with autism in interactive environments	English, Spanish	Dialogue systems and emotion recognition
TALC (Therapist-Assisted Language Corpus)	Annotated linguistic and paralinguistic elements during therapy sessions	English	NLP instruction and intervention design
CARE-MOS	Caregiver assessment of synthetic speech using the Mean Opinion Score procedure	Multi-language	TTS assessment in AAC settings
FACA (Functional Assessment of Communication Aid)	A framework for evaluating the efficacy of communication in practical applications	Protocol only	Validation of assistive technologies
BabyTrain	Vocalizations of infants and toddlers with developmental labels	English	Models of early intervention
Disordered Speech Benchmark (DSB)	ASR benchmarks for deaf, autistic, and dysarthric speech	English	Testing for model robustness

By guaranteeing both technical performance and functional relevance, these tools aid in the development and validation of voice technologies specifically designed for people with communication challenges.

4.3 Open-source Libraries and Frameworks

These tools provide the foundational building blocks for research, development, and deployment of speech and NLP technologies.

- **The general speech processing and Automatic Speech Recognition (ASR) are for the general speech processing.**

Kaldi is a high-performance toolkit specialized in speech recognition research and specifically built. Its modularity and efficiency (especially when used in Gaussian Mixture Model and hybrid systems) has been renowned and has historically been the basis of many commercial ASR systems. It is best applicable to individuals who need granular control over the ASR pipeline or those who are oriented towards further research on core ASR. ESPnet is an end-to-end toolkit, a popular one, which was implemented on PyTorch and unites speech recognition, text-to-speech, speech translation, and others. The NVIDIA NeMo is an open-source framework developed in PyTorch to create, train, and fine-tune the state-of-the-art conversational AI models. It is a collection of pre-trained models to ASR, TTS, and NLP, and heavily supports large-scale training on GPUs, so it can be used by developers and researchers to quickly leverage and reconfigure speech AI applications to production. OpenAI Whisper is a powerful framework and system to use to carry out general-purpose speech recognition and translation. It is a single, large model trained on a large and diverse dataset, which presents outstanding out of the box performance and is most effective in producing high quality transcription and translation across a variety of languages and accents and does not have to be trained as a custom model (Priyadharshini & Subbulakshmi, 2024)

- **For Text-to-Speech (TTS)**

Coqui TTS is a specialized deep learning model platform in the text-to-speech industry, with implementations of many state-of-the-art models, such as Tacotron, FastSpeech, and VITS. It is a research and production-oriented framework that is the most popular framework to develop and experiment high-quality and neural speech synthesis. ESPnet-TTS is the special TTS module of the larger ESPnet module. It offers a fully simulable and repeatable training and testing platform specifically to train and test the most recent TTS models, and it can be used by a researcher or developer who would desire to operate upon the speech processing toolkit.

- **In case of Core Machine Learning and audio Processing.**

Two main open-source deep learning frameworks are PyTorch and TensorFlow, which offer the fundamental bases of deep learning models namely tensors, networks and autograd systems to build and train neural networks. They are the basis of virtually all contemporary speech and NLP models, most specialized toolkits, such as ESPnet and NeMo, being based upon them. Librosa is a basic audio and music analysis package written in Python, providing audio and music analysis tools such as loading, visualization, and critical audio features such as MFCCs and mel-spectrograms. It is an essential pre-processing tool to any machine learning task that is related to an audio signal. Hugging Face Transformers & Datasets is a revolutionary library, which offers easy access to thousands of pre-trained models, such as Whisper, Wav2Vec2, and SpeechT5, as well as many datasets. It also makes sophisticated NLP and speech technologies accessible to all, by significantly reducing the barrier to entry, allowing developers to do inference and fine-tuning easily.

5 PERFORMANCE EVALUATION

5.2 Metrics for Speech Recognition (WER, CER)

The performance of an Automatic Speech Recognition (ASR) system is primarily measured by comparing its output (the Hypothesis) to a correct reference transcript (the Ground Truth). The two most common metrics are Word Error Rate (WER) and Character Error Rate (CER).

- **Word Error Rate (WER)**

WER is the standard metric for ASR systems, especially for languages with word boundaries. It is calculated by aligning the hypothesis with the ground truth and counting the number of operations needed to transform one into the other.

- **Calculation:**

WER = (Substitutions + Insertions + Deletions) / Number of Words in Ground Truth

- **The Operations:**
  - **Substitution (S):** A word in the ground truth is replaced by an incorrect word in the hypothesis.
    - **Ground Truth:** *"the quick brown fox"*
    - **Hypothesis:** *"the quick red fox"* → **1 Substitution**
  - **Insertion (I):** An extra word is added in the hypothesis that is not present in the ground truth.
    - **Ground Truth:** *"the quick brown fox"*
    - **Hypothesis:** *"the quick brown and fox"* → **1 Insertion**
  - **Deletion (D):** A word from the ground truth is missing in the hypothesis.
    - **Ground Truth:** *"the quick brown fox"*
    - **Hypothesis:** *"the quick fox"* → **1 Deletion**

- **Interpretation:** A lower WER is better. A WER of 0% represents a perfect transcription, while a WER of 100% means every word was wrong. It is the most important benchmark for tasks like transcription and dictation.
- **Character Error Rate (CER)**

CER is analogous to WER but operates at the character level instead of the word level. It is particularly useful for:

- **Languages without clear word boundaries** (e.g., Chinese, Japanese).
- **Evaluating performance on named entities** (e.g., people names, addresses) where getting every character correct is critical.
- **Analyzing acoustically similar words** that WER might penalize harshly.
- **Calculation:**

CER = (Character Substitutions + Character Insertions + Character Deletions) / Number of Characters in Ground Truth

- **Example:**
    - o **Ground Truth:** *"cat"*
    - o **Hypothesis:** *"cats"* → **1 Insertion** (the 's')
    - o **CER** = 1 (Insertion) / 3 (Characters in "cat") = **0.333 or 33.3%** (Shivaraj, 2024)

5.2 Metrics for TTS (MOS, MCD, Intelligibility)

- **Mean Opinion Score (MOS):** Mean Opinion Score is the original subjective product of judging the naturalness of synthetic speech. A MOS test is a scale on which human participants are asked to rate audio samples on a scale of five (1 = bad, 5 = excellent). The scores are averaged in all the listeners and samples. Though it is the gold standard of perceived quality, the MOS testing process is costly, time-consuming and may be biased by the listener which makes it a challenge to incorporate into rapid and automated development cycles even though it has a high correlation with human perception.
- **Mel-Cepstral Distortion (MCD)**: Mel-Cepstral Distortion is an objective measure, which measures the acoustic distance between synthesized and natural speech. It determines the distance between Mel-Ceptra of generated and target audio. A lower MCD value means that the synthetic speech will be more similar to the human reference and hence acoustic fidelity is high. It is popular in fast and automatic assessment when training models, particularly

in prosody and timbre, although not directly correlated with the naturalness perceived, making it interested in spectral fidelity only.

- **Intelligibility:** Intelligibility is used to determine the clarity of the understanding of words based on the synthesized speech. It is an inherent measure, now that even very natural-sounding TTS is useless when it is not clear. It has often been tested with diagnostic rhyme tests or by administering listeners transcription tasks of the speech generated and Word Error Rate (WER) is calculated against the original text. The minimum facility to be applied when it comes to any deployable TTS system is high intelligibility which makes sure the message being communicated is properly received by a user (Barnwal et al., 2023; Gundoor & Sridevi, 2024)

6 CHALLENGES IN NLP FOR SPEECH TECHNOLOGIES

- **Ambiguity and Context:** This is the main issue to solve the linguistic ambiguity of the speech. Homophones such as there, their, and theyre sound the same, and a thorough contextual insight is needed by NLP to pick the right word. This is also applicable to the semantic meaning, where the meaning of a phrase varies depending on the context. An example is that a request to call me a taxi may mean a literal one or a sarcastic one. It is a major challenge to successful speech understanding to disambiguate this in real-time with neither visual nor situational information.
- **Prosody and Paralinguistics:** NLP has difficulty completely modeling and decoding prosody, or speech rhythm, stress and intonation, which has important meaning. The word yes alone can be used to show confidence, hesitation or sarcasm depending on the way it is presented. It is also hard to come up with natural sounding prosody in TTS. Moreover, as well as paralinguistic information such as laughter, sighs, and tone of emotion are highly valuable sources of information that the existing systems cannot (or are not able to) process properly, and the conversational ambiguity is lost.
- **Data Scarcity and Bias**: The requirement of large, heterogeneous data sets to build speech NLP deep learning models. These are sparse with low resource languages, dialects, and accents, and pose a considerable performance gap. Moreover, datasets tend to favor major populations, leading to poor performance of models with non-standard accents, increased pitch or impaired speech. Such data bias continues inequality and restricts the cross-applicability and impartiality of speech technology across the globe, and inclusivity represents a significant technical and ethical challenge.

- **Domain Adaptation and Robustness:** Speech systems usually are effective in controlled setting but not in the noisy, real-world settings. Background conversations, cross-talk and acoustic distortions have a disastrous effect on performance. In the same way, NLP models that have been trained on generic text do not work in the situations when it comes to specialized vocabulary in fields such as medicine, law, or technical support. It is essential to enable systems to be flexible enough in achieving robust and real-world deployment, yet it is challenging to make systems respond to new acoustic environments and specialized applications without comprehensive retraining. (Withanage et al., 2018)

7. ETHICAL AND PRIVACY CONSIDERATIONS

The use of speech technologies with vulnerable groups, in particular, those requiring speech assistance because of communication disabilities, is subject to strict ethical considerations.

- Informed Consent: With children, the consent should be taken by the guardians with the clear and easily comprehensible explanations. Continued consent ought to be requested whenever feasible on the part of the child.
- Voice Opt-In/Out: the users and families should have the option of whether their voice data can be used to train the model, and should be able to revoke it easily.
- Watermarking and Cloning Protection: The synthesized voices need to have watermarks to avoid misuse. AAC voice cloning must have a strict permission and it must contain identity theft protection measures.
- On-Device Personalization: To increase privacy, devices need to be personalized and adapted locally as opposed to being done in the cloud.
- Policy Recommendations: Work out clear data governance policies, which meet such regulations as GDPR, COPPA, and HIPAA. Include disability activists in policy making.

8.FUTURE DIRECTIONS

- **Emotionally Intelligent and Expressive Synthesis**: It is important to note here that the future of TTS is the removal of neutral speech and the development of systems capable of producing and identifying a broad range of emotions, tones, and speaking styles. This includes the NLP models that can comprehend the text and contextual placement to a profound degree to dynamically control prosody, empathy and speaker identity. This is aimed at producing synthetic voices that are not only intelligible but, in fact, expressive and context-sensitive and allow human-computer interaction to be more natural and engaging.

- **Zero-Shot and Few-Shot Learning**: One of the key directions is the absence of the huge task-specific datasets. The next-generation systems will also take advantage of the high-powered pre-trained models that can both clone voices zero-shot (create a new voice based on a short audio sample) and adapt with few shots to new accents, languages, or fields. It will make speech technologies more attainable, individualized, and scalable and the barrier to data and cost in implementing powerful systems in a wide range of applications and languages dramatically smaller.
- **Advanced Context and Memory Management:** Next-generation systems will cease to process one turn commands and will handle the context and memory of conversations. This includes NLP models capable of tracing history of dialogues, user preferences and world knowledge across a long history of interactions. This will help assistants to perform complex, multi-domain tasks, and recollect previous interactions, in addition to giving responses that are actually coherent and personalized in the long-term, which resembles human conversational memory.
- **Fluency Multimodal Integration:** The future will be multimodal and speech will be fluently intertwined with other data streams such as speech (lip-reading, gestures) and text (on-screen information). To eliminate ambiguities and enhance the interpretation, NLP will be used as the fusion engine, which would integrate these modalities. As an example, visual context can be used by a system to de-contextualize the meaning of an utterance such as put that there, which results in more robust contextually-grounded interactions in embodied systems such as robotics and augmented reality.
- **Self-Supervised and Unsupervised Learning:** With the development of self-supervised learning, the usage of expensively labelled data (audio-text pairs) will reduce. The pre-training of models on the large amounts of unlabeled data on either audio or text data will occur and learn universal speech representations. Such a method, as demonstrated by Wav2Vec 2.0 or HuBERT, enables the system to learn the presentation of language and acoustics using raw signals, with promising results and performance in particular in low-resource languages and domains. (Anantaram et al., 2015)

9. CONCLUSION

The chapter has outlined the deep and synergistic interaction between Natural Language Processing and the state-of-the-art speech technologies, showing the end of the era of viewing Automatic Speech Recognition and Text-to-Speech processing tasks as subject of isolated signal processing. It is the combination of advanced NLP, between literal transcriber and monotonous speaker, that has proven to be the key factor in changing these systems into intelligent interchange communication partners. We have seen how the basics of NLP can be used to support the whole pipeline: in ASR, getting acoustic ambiguities out of the way and adding grammatical coherence; in TTS, going beyond pronunciation of words to the production of expressive, convincing prosody. This combination has been solidified by the introduction of end-to-end deep learning architectures, which are driven by Transformers and large-scale pre-trained models, and brought more accuracy and naturalness than ever before. Nevertheless, there are still many obstacles on the way to the really human-like communication. The three oddities of ambiguity, lack of data and computing requirements remain a challenge to the existing systems. The failure to capture and recreate the emotional subtext and the richness of paralinguistics of human speech is one of the most important frontiers. Going forward, the future of this discipline is up-and-down changes. The direction of the journey is towards the emotionally intelligent systems with the zero-shot adaptation and the lifelong learning, which will be able to combine speech and visual and contextual multimodal information. This paradigm is changing to recognition and production of speech to the understanding and involvement in communicative actions. Self-supervised learning on scale on huge unlabeled datasets will drive this evolution, eliminating the data bottleneck, and creating more enlightened and resilient technologies. To sum it up, NLP is not the peripheral nervous system but the core nervous system of the modern speech technologies. Its further evolution is the key to the unlocking of the future when our communication with machines by means of speaking will be natural, effective and valuable as the communication between each other.

REFERENCES

A NLP-based Approach to Improve Speech Recognition Services for People with Speech Disorders. (2022). *2022 IEEE Symposium on Computers and Communications (ISCC)*. DOI: 10.1109/ISCC55528.2022.9912940

Ahuja, L., Vashisth, R., & Simon, R. (2023). NLP & AI Speech Recognition: An Analytical Review. *International Conference on Computing for Sustainable Global Development*, 1390–1396

Anantaram, C., Kopparapu, S. K., Kini, N., & Patel, C. (2015). Improving ASR Recognized Speech Output for Effective Natural Language Processing. *International Conference on the Digital Society*, 17–21. https://www.thinkmind.org/articles/icds_2015_1_40_10127.pdf

Barnwal, V. K., Shaw, A., Sarkar, K., Chakraborty, S., & Mukhopadhyay, A. N. (2023). *ARIVA: Artificial Intelligence Enabled Voice Assistance System using Natural Language Processing*. DOI: 10.1109/ICCES57224.2023.10192640

Celesti, A., Fazio, M., Carnevale, L., & Villari, M. (2022). A NLP-based Approach to Improve Speech Recognition Services for People with Speech Disorders. *International Symposium on Computers and Communications*, 1–6. DOI: 10.1109/ISCC55528.2022.9912940

Gundoor, T. K. (2022). IoT-Enabled 5G Networks for Secure Communication. In *Information Security Practices for the Internet of Things, 5G, and Next-Generation Wireless Networks* (pp. 1-29). IGI Global.

Gundoor, T. K., & Sridevi, D. (2024). Optimized Feature Selection and classification for Non-Portable Executable Malware. [IJCNIS]. *International Journal of Communication Networks and Information Security*, *16*(4), 546–552.

Huet, S., Lecorvé, G., Gravier, G., & Sébillot, P. (2008). *Toward the Integration of Natural Language Processing and Automatic Speech Recognition: Using Morpho-Syntax and Pragmatics for Transcription*. Springer US., DOI: 10.1007/978-0-387-76316-3_9

Kabir, H. (2002). Natural language processing for Urdu TTS system. *International Multi-Topic Conference*, 58. DOI: 10.1109/INMIC.2002.1310165

Kolhar, A. & Sridevi. (2025). Future Trends and Innovation in Machine Intelligence for Cyber Risk Management. In M. Almaiah & Y. Maleh (Eds.), *Machine Intelligence Applications in Cyber-Risk Management* (pp. 415-438). IGI Global Scientific Publishing. .DOI: 10.4018/979-8-3693-7540-2.ch018

Kolhar, A. & Sridevi. (2026). Principles and Emerging Trends of Healthcare Robotics. In S. Al-Humairi, P. Naronglerdrit, N. Chantarapanich, & S. Wanchat (Eds.), *Robotics and IoT Synergy in Next-Generation Healthcare* (pp. 401-428). IGI Global Scientific Publishing. DOI: 10.4018/979-8-3373-5447-7.ch012

Niu, Y. (2023). *A Natural Language Processing Model Based on Pre-trained Deep Learning Models*. DOI: 10.57237/j.cst.2022.01.007

Oyucu, S., & Dogan, F. (2023).. . *Improving Text-to-Speech Systems Through Preprocessing and Postprocessing Applications*, *1–5*, 1–5. Advance online publication. DOI: 10.1109/ISMSIT58785.2023.10304907

Priyadharshini, N., & Subbulakshmi, N. (2024). *Natural Language Processing (NLP) based Phonetic Insights for Improving Voice Recognition and Synthesis*. 801–806. DOI: 10.1109/ICSES63445.2024.10762995

Roth, D. L., Cohen, J., Johnston, D. F., Grabherr, M. G., & Porter, E. W. (2004). *Combined speech recongnition and text-to-speech generation*. https:// patents.google.com/ patent/ US20050038657A1/en

Sandhya, K., Roshan, P., Manikanta, K., & Pandarinath, P. (2025). *Enhancing Automatic Speech Recognitionwith Contextual Understanding using Natural Language Processing*. 2404–2439. DOI: 10.38124/ijisrt/25may1394

Satish, E. G., Naidu, P. R., Mogera, G. M., karthik, H., & Abhinandan. (2024). *Voice Over Vision: A Sequence-to-Sequence Model by Text to Speech Technology*. 1–7. DOI: 10.1109/ICICEC62498.2024.10808272

Shivaraj, G. (2024). Advancing Accessibility through Automatic Speech Recognition and NLP Integration. *International Journal for Research in Applied Science and Engineering Technology*, *12*(6), 3–9. DOI: 10.22214/ijraset.2024.62443

Sridevi & Kolhar. A. (2025). Energy-Efficiency Strategies for Wireless Sensor Networks in IoT. In A. Sathio, M. Rind, S. Awan, & A. Junejo (Eds.), *Energy-Efficient Deep Learning Approaches in IoT, Fog, and Green Blockchain Revolution* (pp. 167-192). IGI Global Scientific Publishing. DOI: 10.4018/979-8-3373-0300-0.ch006

Sridevi & Kolhar. A. (2026). Fundamentals of 6G Networks. In R. Shaikh (Ed.), *6G Networks and AI-Driven Cybersecurity* (pp. 1-32). IGI Global Scientific Publishing. DOI: 10.4018/979-8-3373-0568-4.ch001

Subhashri, C., Vijayakumar, K., Anujna, M., & Bini, K. B. (2025). Revolutionizing Human-Machine Conversations: Real- Time Speech Recognition and Synthesis With GPT-2. *Social Science Research Network*. DOI: 10.2139/ssrn.5075988

Sudhan, S. H., Nair, P. N. R., & Thushara, M. G. (2024). *Text-to-Speech and Speech-to-Text Models: A Systematic Examination of Diverse Approaches*. 2ct61223.2024.10544015 Castillejo, S. P. (2021). Automatic speech recognition. *Innovative language pedagogy report*, 121.DOI: 10.1109/ I

Suganya, V., Prema, K. V., Krishna, C. M., Reddy, C., & Jaswanth, E. (2024). *Emotion Recognition in Speech: A Natural Language Processing Perspective*. 1–8. DOI: 10.1109/ACROSET62108.2024.10743299

Ungurean, C., & Burileanu, D. (2011). *An advanced NLP framework for high-quality Text-to-Speech synthesis*. 1–6. DOI: 10.1109/SPED.2011.5940733

Withanage, P., Liyanage, T., Deeyakaduwe, N., Dias, E., & Thelijjagoda, S. (2018). Road Navigation System Using Automatic Speech Recognition (ASR) And Natural Language Processing (NLP). *IEEE Region Humanitarian Technology Conference*. DOI: 10.1109/R10-HTC.2018.8629859

Chapter 8
AI in Medical Diagnosis:
Early Detection of Autism and Speech Delays

Zahid Ahmad Thoker
http://orcid.org/0009-0002-6897-5835
School of Bioengineering and Biosciences, Lovely Professional University, India

Lovleen Marwaha
http://orcid.org/0000-0002-5175-2590
School of Bioengineering and Biosciences, Lovely Professional University, India

ABSTRACT

Autism spectrum disorder (ASD) and speech delays need to be identified early since children can get better with an earlier intervention. Conventional forms of diagnosis are slow, subjective, and rely on clinical observation. Artificial intelligence (AI) provides a more objective and quicker means of identifying early warning signs through verbal and non-verbal communication and behaviour. It is possible to detect atypical speech patterns by using machine learning and language processing, and facial expressions, gestures, and differences in eye contact can be detected with the help of computer vision. It is also possible to monitor in real-life environments with the help of mobile apps and wearable devices. AI can be used to enable professionals to make earlier referrals and tailor therapy plans. The topics of concern are the privacy of data, equity, access, and cost. Better results in children can be attained through the enhancement of explainable and ethical AI systems.

DOI: 10.4018/979-8-3373-7724-7.ch008

1. INTRODUCTION

Autism Spectrum Disorder (ASD), along with speech or language delays are very profound neurodevelopmental issue that is still confronted by children today. They not only impact the communication and social interactions of these children but also affect their cognitive, behavioral, and emotional development. The increasing rate of these unrecognized conditions worldwide highlights the need for rapid diagnosis and intervention. The World Health Organization (WHO, 2023) reports that roughly one out of every 100 children globally has ASD, while a significantly larger number is still unrecognizable due to the late screening and diagnosis process. To a similar degree, the speech and language delays which could occur in the form of either expressive or receptive communication difficulties are reported to be present among almost 10–15% of the preschool population. Besides, the early detection of these disorders is extremely important since it allows therapists and teachers working with the children to administer appropriate treatment during the most critical stages in brain maturation when neuroplasticity is at its highest.

Defining Autism Spectrum Disorder and Speech/Language Delays

Autism Spectrum Disorder is a condition that is marked by continual difficulties in verbal and nonverbal social exchanges along with the presence of either limited or repetitive behavioral patterns, interests, or activities (American Psychiatric Association, 2013). The use of the word "spectrum" denotes the entire range of symptoms from the mildest to the most severe and the variety of different functioning impacts, from just a little social difficulties to a complete inability in communication and daily functioning. Usually, ASD is recognized during the early age of a child, but the symptoms often show up during the first two years of life. Some of the first signs may be a lack of eye contact, slow development of speech, echolalia (repeating words or phrases), and unusual reactions to social stimuli.

Speech and language delays, although sometimes overlapping with autism spectrum disorder (ASD), point out different but related developmental issues at the same time. Speech delay means difficulty in producing the sounds or words that are appropriate for the child's age, and language delay indicates the difficulties in understanding or using words for communication. Speech and language delays can be present along with other neurodevelopmental disorders like ASD, Down syndrome, and others, or can even be independent. No matter the cause, autism and speech/language delays alike can have a great impact on social-emotional development, academic success, and even the long-term quality of life, as shown in Table 1 as well.

Table 1. Comparative overview of ASD and typical speech delay symptoms

Feature	Autism Spectrum Disorder (ASD)	Typical Speech Delay
Core Issue	Social communication deficit + restricted behaviors	Delayed language acquisition only
Eye Contact	Poor or inconsistent	Normal
Gestures/Body Language	Limited use	Age-appropriate
Cognitive Profile	Variable; may include uneven skills	Usually normal
Social Engagement	Low or atypical	Normal
Response to Therapy	Requires a multimodal approach	Responds well to speech therapy

The Importance of Early Diagnosis

The early stages of human development are marked by fast neural growth and extreme flexibility. The detection of communication disorders within this time frame permits the restoration of the brain's plasticity through interventions, which in turn results in the enhancement of developmental trajectories to a great extent (Zwaigenbaum et al., 2015). The literature has repeatedly reported that children who are diagnosed and treated before the age of three will have more significant advancements in language and communication, socializing, and adaptive functioning skills than their peers who are diagnosed at a later stage (Dawson et al., 2010). The main advantage of an early intervention is the complete support of language development and the mitigation of consequent problems such as being socially awkward, having behavioral problems, or failing at school.

Furthermore, diagnostic interventions at an early stage positively influence the families by eliminating doubts, allowing the families to get support, and guiding them to make the right decisions. It also lifts the whole society by cutting down the need for long-term intensive educational and therapeutic services, which are usually the case with children having developmental disorders. But unfortunately, even with such evident benefits in early diagnosis, a significant number of children with autism spectrum disorder (ASD) or speech delays are left undiagnosed or misdiagnosed till they reach school age, hence losing a critical period for receiving the proper treatment. This is where the diagnostic gap shows that there is still a great demand for novel tools that can make early screening more sensitive, objective, and accessible.

Limitations of Traditional Diagnostic Methods

Conventional methods for diagnosing ASD and speech or language delays predominantly depend on the same three elements: behavior assessments, interviews with the doctors, and rating scales based on observations. The use of the Autism Diagnostic Observation Schedule (ADOS), the Autism Diagnostic Interview-Revised (ADI-R), and the Childhood Autism Rating Scale (CARS) has been from various settings confirmed as the preferred and trustworthy methods for the diagnosis. Nevertheless, these techniques, as described in the article by Lord and others, necessitate a clinician's specialized training as well as substantial time for direct observations and use of measures (Lord et al., 2000). Thus, the diagnosis is often done several months or even years later than when the parents raised the concern, which also means delaying the intervention that should have taken place sooner.

Moreover, because of the subjectivity of human observation, examiners and different cultures may vary. In most low- and middle-income nations, where the number of trained specialists is scarce, families have to wait longer or even receive no opportunity to be assessed. There is also the issue of bias because parental reporting can only be used at the expense of the caregivers, who may lack the knowledge about developmental milestones or language standards. As a result, a significant number of children are either not diagnosed or improperly assessed, which hinders their engagement in the timely therapeutic process.

The Promise of Artificial Intelligence in Early Screening

In the last few years, AI or Artificial Intelligence has been a revolutionary force in the healthcare diagnostics sector, providing precision and scalability based on data that are hard for traditional methods to have access to easily. AI solutions, mainly machine learning (ML), deep learning (DL), natural language processing (NLP), and computer vision, have gained a lot of credit for early detection of biomarkers of autism as well as speech/language delays. AI tools are capable of finding minuscule trends in large sets of data through behaviour, language, and physiology parameters, which may not be instinctively picked up by humans (Duda et al., 2022).

For example, AI systems that have been trained on baby sounds, eye-tracking data, or facial expression analysis can tell the difference between normally developing kids and those with a high risk of ASD with great accuracy. Likewise, voice recognition and NLP-based systems can analyze the pronunciation, tone, and prosody to pinpoint the differences that are typical of early language delay. The use of mobile apps and wearable devices powered by AI also improves the situation, as they make it possible to carry out remote monitoring in everyday life, continuously, and thus make the process more accessible.

The involvement of AI in early diagnosis has not only brought about faster detection but also the spreading of developmental screening to the entire world, particularly to areas where people do not have easy access to medical services. It also enables clinicians with the help of clear-cut, backed-up with scientific proof assessments, and on the other hand, it can give parents and teachers helpful insights for timely support. Most importantly, AI is not there to take over human skills but to boost professional opinion, cut down the time taken for diagnosis, and allow more customized patient care.

Objectives and Scope of the Chapter

The purpose of this chapter is to dive into the various aspects of the application of artificial intelligence (AI) in the early medical diagnosis of autism spectrum disorder (ASD) and speech/language delays. Firstly, it discusses the brain and behavior bases of the disorders, thereby shedding light on the brain's functioning, the course of development, and the impact of environmental and genetic factors on communication abilities in the early stages. The chapter further analyzes the conventional diagnostic models by underscoring their drawbacks, such as subjectivity, time-consuming detection, and dependence on the availability of experts.

Subsequently, it reviews the existing AI-driven diagnostic systems and techniques, investigating the implementation of machine learning, deep learning, natural language processing, and multimodal analytics for early diagnosis of ASD and speech delays. Furthermore, the chapter describes several real-world case studies that have illustrated the usage of AI tools in clinical and practical scenarios such as home screening, hospital deployments, and AI-assisted therapy support systems. In addition, it covers the difficulties, moral issues, and data governance problems associated with AI in children's diagnosis, like algorithmic bias, data privacy, and equitable access. The chapter, at the end, directs research future, particularly focusing on the creation of explicable and multimodal AI systems that not only assist in personalized early intervention but also connect with telehealth platforms and make the decision of the clinician, caregiver, and teacher easier.

2. NEUROLOGICAL AND MEDICAL FOUNDATIONS

Autism Spectrum Disorder (ASD) and speech or language delays are closely linked conditions that share common neurodevelopmental mechanisms of a very little understood nature, causing both brain malformations and different brain functions. The skills of language and communication are based on very complex neural networks that connect and process auditory, motor, cognitive, and social-emotional functions. The whole system may not work properly due to occurrences of a genetic, biochemical, or environmental nature, which can greatly affect the development and utilization of language in a child. This is why it is so important to understand the brain and medical reasons behind ASD and speech delays to develop good diagnostic tools and early interventions.

Neurodevelopmental Basis of Language and Communication

Language development is a multifaceted neurocognitive process that encompasses the steps of perception, processing, and production. The human brain's communication capacity is something that starts right at the moment of conception and during the early years slowly and gradually develops more and more, with the process being to some extent determined by the interaction between sensory experiences and neural maturation. Different areas of the brain, such as Broca's area (speech production), Wernicke's area (language comprehension), the prefrontal cortex (executive control of communication), and the temporal lobes (auditory processing and semantic memory), are responsible for the basic functions of language (Friederici, 2017). The brains of children with ASD or speech delays are observed to be atypically developed in these areas, which are associated with their difficulties in expressive speech, use of language for social communication, and social responsiveness. There has been a particular kind of brain imaging and electrical activity studies that have revealed less interaction between the frontal and temporal lobe areas, which is indicative of the integration of linguistic and social-cognitive information being impaired (Redcay & Courchesne, 2008). Schematic illustration of neurodevelopmental mechanisms in Autism Spectrum Disorder (ASD) and Speech/Language Delays is shown below in Table 2 and Figure 2 as well. This illustration highlights affected brain regions such as Broca's area, Wernicke's area, prefrontal cortex, amygdala, mirror neuron system, and auditory cortex.

Table 2. Comparative neurodevelopmental characteristics of autism spectrum disorder and speech/language delay

Aspect	Autism Spectrum Disorder (ASD)	Speech/Language Delay
Main brain areas	Broca's area, Wernicke's area, prefrontal cortex, temporal lobes, amygdala, mirror neuron system	Broca's area, Wernicke's area, auditory cortex
Neural connectivity	Disrupted, less synchronized between regions	Mildly affected or near-normal
Neurochemistry	Imbalance in serotonin, dopamine, and GABA	Subtle, less pronounced
Genetic associations	SHANK3, CNTNAP2, FOXP2, many others	FOXP2, limited risk loci

continued on following page

Table 2. Continued

Aspect	Autism Spectrum Disorder (ASD)	Speech/Language Delay
Social cognition	Reduced/atypical	Usually age-appropriate
Expressive language	Severely affected, often echolalia	Delayed, but the structure is often normal
Receptive language	Impaired, context-specific deficits	Delayed understanding may catch up
Comorbidities	Down syndrome, epilepsy, intellectual disability, ADHD	Hearing loss, developmental delay

Brain Regions Associated with Speech and Social Interaction

Neurological studies indicate that the communication difficulties associated with Autism Spectrum Disorder (ASD) are not limited to any one specific area of the brain, but rather are the consequence of the unusual connectivity between various brain networks. For example, the mirror neuron system that is responsible for imitation and empathy is frequently less active in people with ASD, thus hindering their ability to perceive and respond to social cues (Hamilton, 2013). Also, the abnormalities in the amygdala and superior temporal sulcus interfere with emotional processing and gaze perception, making the situation even worse for social communication. Broca's and Wernicke's areas are showing different types of activity during speech tasks, which points to linguistic coordination being impaired (Kuhl et al., 2014). The overall picture created by these findings is that neural dysregulation on a large scale is involved in both ASD and speech delays rather than only localized deficits.

Genetic, Neurochemical, and Environmental Influences

The origin of Autism Spectrum Disorder (ASD) and speech/language delays is involved with many factors and thus is very complex, since the genetic factors and the environmental exposure interact with each other in a very complicated way. Genetic analysis has provided a list of hundreds of places in the DNA corresponding to the highest risk of developing ASD, among them are SHANK3, CNTNAP2, and FOXP2 that have been linked to synaptic signaling and language acquisition (Eising et al., 2019). Besides, the differences in the levels of certain brain chemicals, mainly in the case of serotonin, dopamine, and GABA, also affect the communication and the ability to switch one's thinking between different ideas and concepts. On the other hand, factors like a mother's physical illness during pregnancy, toxins getting into the child's body, and maternal stress all may play a role in increasing the risk of a child being born with neurological disorders. The time of the influences is also important, and in fact, the areas of the brain that are most sensitive to "negative" environmental factors might actually determine the kind of deficits in communication and thinking that the child will have for a lifetime.

Role of Neuroplasticity in Early Intervention Outcomes

Neuroplasticity is one of the most encouraging findings that has been brought about by neuroscience and especially in the case of young children. Neural pathways or circuits are very adaptable during the first five years of life, and this is the reason why interventions can be specifically directed to change the wiring of unusual pathways. The plasticity of young children can thus be exploited by early healing or treatment consisting of behavioural, speech, and occupational therapies to get better language outcomes even in severely affected children with ASD (Dawson et al., 2012). The results from neuroimaging argue in favour of the fact that cortical synchronization and inter-hemispheric communication are enhanced by timely interventions, and thus, the biological aspect of early diagnosis and treatment is highlighted.

Common Comorbidities Affecting Diagnosis

ASD and speech delays are frequently associated with other medical and developmental conditions, which make it more difficult to diagnose and treat them. Down syndrome, cerebral palsy, and hearing impairment have common communication problems that can make it very hard to detect the characteristics of ASD. For example, children with Down syndrome might display expressive language delays that are very similar to those in ASD, and yet their social communication is usually different (Abbeduto et al., 2007). In the same way, hearing loss may disguise a language problem, making it hard to decide whether one has an auditory issue or a language problem, thus stressing the necessity of having different groups of assessments that are based on the conditions of the patients. It is very important to notice these overlaps to arrive at the right diagnosis and also provide the necessary tailored intervention.

3. TRADITIONAL DIAGNOSTIC APPROACHES AND LIMITATIONS

Diagnosis of Autism Spectrum Disorder (ASD) and its associated speech or language delays has traditionally relied on the use of structured behavioral observations, developmental evaluations, and clinical interviews. These measures are aimed at identifying essential symptoms, such as deficits in social communication and repetitive or limited behaviors. However, despite the clinical usefulness, traditional approaches are limited by subjectivity, slow identification, as well as unequal access to trained specialists. A deep grasp of these diagnostic models and their weaknesses is a condition that offers a requisite background for valuing the paradigm shift that Artificial Intelligence (AI) can bring to initial detection and treatment.

Overview of Clinical and Behavioral Diagnostic Tools

a) Autism Diagnostic Observation Schedule (ADOS)

Autism Diagnostic Observation Schedule (ADOS) is considered a gold-standard tool for diagnosing ASD. It consists of a semi-structured sequence of social and play-based interactions that are specially designed to provoke behaviors that are relevant to the ASD criteria (Lord et al., 2000). Through the assessment of communication and social reciprocity and limited interests at different levels of age and language, the ADOS can be used to standardize the scoring of symptom severity. The ADOS presents a powerful behavioral model, but requires a great deal of training, manipulated conditions, and interpretive skills, which can be a barrier to its applicability in other community or low-resource settings.

b) Childhood Autism Rating Scale (CARS)

Another measurement that is quite commonly used to assess the behavior of a child is the Childhood Autism Rating Scale (CARS), which scores the behavior of a child in fifteen domains, which entail emotional response, body use, and verbal communication (Schopler et al., 1988). CARS offers a quantitative methodology with numerical cutoffs that distinguish mild and severe autism. This is because it is flexible and concise, which makes it appropriate in clinical and educational settings. However, CARS is very reliant on the accuracy of observations made by the clinician and can be less reliable in various cultural or language-related practices where norms of behavior are not similar

c) Modified Checklist for Autism in Toddlers (M-CHAT)

To detect ASD at an early stage, children at 16 to 30 months are regularly given the Modified Checklist for Autism in Toddlers (M-CHAT) to determine whether they are at high risk of the disorder (Robins et al., 2014). A parent-reported questionnaire that concentrates on the possible early signs of autism and is referred to as the M-CHAT, concentrates on the early indicators of the conditions of joint attention, responsivity to name, and imitation. This is because of its simplicity and accessibility, which have made it one of the pillars of early developmental surveillance. Nevertheless, even in cases of high sensitivity, it can produce false positives and, as such, requires follow-ups or diagnostics. As a result, a great number of children identified by the M-CHAT are likely to be delayed in formal diagnosis.

Limitations of Traditional Approaches

Even with the decades of perfection, the traditional ASD diagnostic methods still have significant obstacles to timely and fair diagnosis.

a) Subjectivity of Human Observation

One of the major flaws of the existing practices is that they are dependent on clinician judgment and parental reports. The behavioral signs of ASD are boundlessly different in people, cultures, and different stages of development. Therefore, assessments, including ADOS and CARS, are also sensitive to the interpretation of an observer, which leads to inter-rater variability (Zwaigenbaum et al., 2015). The subtler or rather unexpected presentations, especially in girls or in the high-functioning individuals, may not be detected, thus it will delay treatment.

b) Late Diagnosis and Missed Critical Periods

ASD is usually identified at ages three to four, by the time the most plastic phase in the development of the brain is already closed (Daniels and Mandell, 2014). The early symptoms, including the lack of eye contact or delayed babbling, can often be noticed before the age of two; however, the traditional assessments can fail to address them because of their behavioral orientation. This ensuing delay in the diagnosis process reduces the effectiveness of early intervention programs that are dependent on neural adaptability to produce the best results.

c) Shortage of Trained Clinicians

The other continuing problem is the lack of experienced professionals in the world who can administer the standardized diagnostic equipment. In low and middle-income nations, such disparity is most evident, which causes underdiagnosis or misdiagnosis of ASD and speech delays (Elsabbagh et al., 2012). The long lists of waiting and inequalities between regions in even developed healthcare systems drive the future challenges in making access to timely assessment, thus burdening families and healthcare systems with an unnecessary burden.

Table 3. Overview of traditional and AI-assisted diagnostic tools for Autism Spectrum Disorder (ASD) and speech/language delays

Diagnostic Tool	Key Features	Limitations
Autism Diagnostic Observation Schedule (ADOS)	Semi-structured play/social interactions require specialized training, standardized scoring.	Training-intensive, limited applicability in low-resource settings
Childhood Autism Rating Scale (CARS)	Behaviour scoring in 15 domains, flexible and concise, clinician observation-dependent	Subjectivity, cultural variability affect reliability
Modified Checklist for Autism in Toddlers (M-CHAT)	Parent-reported questionnaire for toddlers aged 16-30 months, early risk detection, simple, and accessible	False positives may delay formal diagnosis
AI-assisted Diagnostic Tools	Objective data analysis via eye-tracking, speech, and facial expression patterns reduces observer bias, increases accessibility.	Requires technical infrastructure, concerns about data privacy

Bridging the Diagnostic Gap through Technology

To overcome these limitations, there has been an emergence of technology-assisted diagnostic systems as an important boundary in developmental medicine. The objective analysis of large data (including eye-tracking measurements, speech patterns, and facial expressions) can be conducted with the help of digital tools and models based on AI to detect the emergence of behavioral biomarkers at an early stage. Such systems not only reduce bias on the side of the observers but also increase accessibility among the underserved groups. ASD risk factors are also facilitated through mobile applications, telehealth systems, and machine-learning algorithms at a high degree of accuracy and scalability (Bone et al., 2015). These technologies are destined to democratize and open up geographical, socioeconomic, and professional barriers to further prompt and more accurate detection.

4. ARTIFICIAL INTELLIGENCE IN EARLY DIAGNOSIS

Artificial Intelligence (AI) has become a critical element in the health care revolution, providing accuracy, scalability, and early diagnosis possibilities that significantly outperform conventional diagnostic procedures. In the sphere of pediatric neurology, AI introduction has brought new opportunities for comprehending developmental disabilities like Autism Spectrum Disorder (ASD) and speech or language delays. These conditions can be effectively treated by early diagnosis, which can be of great benefit through the intervention of such conditions at the right time, but the diagnostic procedure is usually based on subjective evaluation and delayed clinical tests. The machine learning (ML), deep learning (DL), and natural language processing (NLP) AI technologies can now contribute to a higher precision of diagnoses by finding hidden behavioural, linguistic, and neurophysiological patterns that human clinicians might not notice.

AI in Healthcare and Pediatric Neurology

AI applications have been used in fields of radiology, oncology, cardiology, and neurodevelopmental pediatrics (Topol, 2019). In neuroimaging, brain imaging, neurological speech recording, behavioural videotaping, and other multimodal data presented by pediatric neurology, algorithms have the potential to be used to identify neurological abnormalities (Duda et al., 2022). In the case of neurodevelopmental disorders, the initial symptoms often appear in eye gaze, patterns of vocalisation, and social behaviours, way before clinical symptoms become evident. There are machine-vision and speech-analytics models that are being trained to identify such features automatically (Thabtah and Peebles, 2019).

Machine Learning and Deep Learning Fundamentals

Machine learning (ML) refers to systems that improve their performance without programming by learning from data. ML models can be supervised (with labelled data serving, e.g., to classify data as autistic or non-autistic), or unsupervised (where patterns are derived based on unstructured data) (LeCun et al., 2015). A subdivision of ML, deep learning (DL) exploits multilayered neural networks that can extract high-level abstractions in data, e.g., tone modulation in sound or gaze direction in video. CNNs and RNNs are broadly used to process image and time-series data, respectively, which makes them especially applicable to the processing of the facial expressions or time patterns of speech in children (Li et al., 2022).

AI-Based Analysis of Speech Patterns

ASD is characterized by speech and language delays, which AI systems have proven to effectively identify. Algorithms based on NLP and acoustic signal processing can, in real-time, measure aspects like variability of pitch, duration of pauses, and rate of articulation (Bone et al., 2019). These indicators offer diagnostic information that goes beyond the rating of subjective clinicians. Indicatively, Eyben et al. (2020) demonstrated that it was possible to distinguish between children with ASD and those with typical development, based on a few minutes of spontaneous speech, with the help of deep neural networks. Similarly, the computational models can currently extract the linguistic complexity, patterns of prosodic and syntactic irregularities to evaluate expressive and receptive language impairments (Liss et al., 2020).

AI for Eye-Tracking and Gaze Analysis

The algorithms of AI-powered eye-tracking technology provide a non-invasive way of detecting ASD at a young age. Children having ASD usually exhibit abnormal patterns of gaze, including diminished focus on faces or eyes. These deviations are also automatically detected by DL-based models of visual attention (Chevallier et al., 2022). Researchers have since leveraged the low-cost webcam-based systems to create systems that can identify gaze anomalies within minutes, which could allow screening to be available to families in low-resource environments (Fu et al., 2023).

Facial Micro-Expression and Emotion Recognition

AI-based emotion recognition has become an effective supplement in the diagnosis of ASD and other conditions. Machine-vision algorithms trained on facial data can recognize micro-expressions, brief involuntary movements of the face that are linked to emotions, and which vary slightly between neurotypical and neurodivergent victims (Hashemi et al., 2021). In another remarkable study, the DL models were able to achieve more than 90 percent accuracy in detecting facial expression abnormalities associated with ASD using home-recorded videos (Zhao et al., 2023). Such methods are not only diagnostic, but they also curb the biases that are present in human interpretation

Social Interaction Cues and Behavioral Analytics

The multimodal data fusion concept is based on the idea that AI can simulate dynamic social interactions by combining gaze, gesture, and vocal data into predictive models. As an illustration, Duda et al. (2022) used ensemble ML models to categorise behavioural patterns during play sessions, where the early detection of ASD was made in children as early as 18⁻ months old. They examine turn-taking, the frequency of eye contact, and response time, so they provide an objective assessment of social reciprocity and communication interaction (Wang et al., 2021). The implications of such tools are immense when used in mass screening, especially in areas where there are no pediatric neurologists.

Role of Natural Language Processing (NLP)

NLP is at the core of AI-based diagnosis of autism, particularly the analysis of language delays. Linguistic features are NLP algorithms that glean information out of transcripts or speech audio, including semantic coherence, vocabulary variety, and grammar (Rouhizadeh et al., 2019). Architectures with transformers, e.g., BERT and GPT forms, have been modified to test pragmatic language use in children to detect indicators of ASD-related communication problems (Koshino et al., 2022). The integration of NLP and acoustic analysis will allow seeing a complete picture of what is said and how it is said, which is the key to the distinction between ASD and isolated speech delays.

AI-Based Mobile Screening Tools

The past years have witnessed an increase in the creation of AI-based mobile applications that enable parents and clinicians to screen children for ASD and speech delays on the go. Cognoa and AutismAI can be mentioned (the combination of parental reports, video recording, and interactive games) to predict a developmental risk (Wall et al., 2020). LinguaAI is another system that uses NLP to determine the vocabulary development and sentence structure of children in real-time, which can be used to provide feedback to parents and therapists. AI-MATCH is a cloud application that integrates eye-tracking and audio analytics with early screening in clinical and home settings. These instruments are especially useful in areas that lack sufficient resources and in cases when the delayed clinical assessment is caused by the shortage of personnel (Fu et al., 2023).

Ethical and Clinical Considerations

Although AI is a promising field, it is important to deal with such ethical implications as data privacy, bias in algorithms, and interpretability (Topol, 2019). Most AI systems are trained with datasets that fail to represent different people, and this can be dangerous to the diagnosis. Moreover, deep learning models are black boxes, which complicates the process of explaining decisions to the clinician and caregiver. Current studies aim to come up with transparent and explainable AI (XAI) systems that combine clinical reasoning and algorithmic forecasting (Holzinger et al., 2022). The application of AI has revolutionized the diagnosis of early ASD and speech delay by providing objective and data-based insights. Based on the analysis of vocal characteristics, the ability to track eyesight and social interactions, AI tools can identify neurodevelopmental abnormalities many years before a clinical diagnosis.

These advances promise not only earlier intervention but also more equitable access to developmental screening globally.

Speech Delay (Isolated Language Delay) — Distinct Clinical Problem and AI Opportunities

Isolated speech/language delay- where speech/language is delayed and is not accompanied by ASD characteristics- has unique diagnostic and treatment issues different from those in autism speech/language cases. Unlike ASD, where socially-communication atypicalities and limited behaviours are present, pure speech delay is usually confined to phonological and articulatory speech problems, lexical or syntactic problems. The most important aspect is to be diagnosed at an early stage since speech delay can cause future problems in literacy, academic, and psychosocial areas. Nevertheless, the majority of AI studies are devoted to ASD, and many fewer models are developed with the isolated language disorders in mind. However, AI can be used to aid this area: the acoustic analysis can detect articulation mistakes, prosodic abnormality, and phoneme-level anomalies; NLP can be used to measure vocabulary expansion, mean length of utterance, and syntactic complexity; and longitudinal models can indicate abnormal development. An AI tool to address speech delay must focus on sound acoustic feature extraction in the real world, language-specific models of morpho-syntactic variation, and normative growth referents among different linguistic communities. Such tools used clinically may serve as early triage services, make referrals to speech-language pathologists, objectively monitor progress, and assist in tele-speech therapy in cases where specialists are scarce. The major gaps in the research encompass the construction of large, annotated, inter-language speech corpora, confirmation of NLP markers in other linguistic settings, and randomized trials to determine whether AI-assisted screening is better at enhancing access to therapy and long-term language outcomes.

Structured Review and Critical Appraisal of AI-Based Diagnostic Literature

Although the literature on the topic of AI-based early diagnosis of ASD and speech or language delays is not new, a more systematic synthesis demonstrates that there are numerous significant trends, strengths, and gaps in the methodology. The study can be generalized in the three related areas, namely speech-based diagnostic systems, computer-vision and gaze systems, and mobile or multimodal screening systems. Vocal and speech analytics is also one of the oldest applications of AI to detect autism, and studies like Bone et al. (2019) and Rouhizadeh et al. (2019) have proven that acoustic features, such as pitch variability, prosody, and the length of pause, can differentiate between ASD and typical development with an accuracy of between 75 and 90 percent. Although these results are encouraging, much of the literature on speech-based methods is based on small datasets (often under 100 participants) and rarely externally validated to different languages, different cultures, and recording conditions. Further, most of these models emphasize ASD classification as opposed to isolated speech delay, which implies that a significant gap in the literature exists and that diagnostic models that address isolated language impairment are required, especially in non-autistic patients.

The second line of research is devoted to computer vision and gaze-tracking techniques that are based on deep learning models that examine facial expressions, micro-expressions, and visual attention patterns. An example is Hashemi et al. (2021), when home video recordings were used to identify ASD-related behavioral markers with an accuracy of over 90% but such outcomes are usually constrained by the narrow demographic representation. Eye-tracking studies conducted using the webcam, such as Fu et al. (2023), also show the possibility of scalable, non-invasive screening, but most of them are done under controlled laboratory conditions, which limits the capacity to generalize them to a natural lifestyle in a home or school setting. These constraints confirm the necessity to have additional ecologically valid data sets as well as testing of cross-context models.

The third emerging field is mobile applications and multimodal AI tools using speech, gesture, glance, and parent-reported behavioral information. Sensitivity rates have been reported to be between 85 and 91 on platforms like Cognoa and several research prototypes, indicating a good probability of early screening in the non-clinical environment. Nonetheless, mobile tools have their fair share of challenges, such as the possibility of reporting bias linked to information provided by the parent and poor video or audio quality. Moreover, heterogeneous datasets, where the protocols are not standardized, are often used in multimodal models, which complicates the replication and prevents meaningful comparison across studies. Taken together, these constraints indicate the necessity to use larger and more heterogeneous datasets, unified assessment systems, and focus more on the validation of AI systems in practice. Key AI Diagnostic Studies have also been presented in a comparative summary that has been provided in Table 4 below.

Table 4. Comparative summary of key AI diagnostic studies

Study	Population	Modality	Performance	Validation	Main Limitation
Bone et al. (2019)	Children with ASD vs. TD (n≈100)	Speech acoustics	75–85%	Cross-sectional	Small sample; limited cultural diversity
Hashemi et al. (2021)	Home videos (n>400)	Facial expressions & gestures	>90%	Internal validation	Limited generalizability; parent video quality varies
Fu et al. (2023)	Toddlers (n≈150)	Eye-tracking via webcam	85–90%	Lab-based	Controlled environment; needs field testing
Wall et al. (2020)	Community toddlers	Mobile app (video + questionnaires)	87–90%	Multi-site	Parent-report bias; proprietary dataset
Duda et al. (2022)	Clinical sample of toddlers	Multimodal clinical AI	91%	Clinical validation	High resource requirements

5. AI-POWERED DIAGNOSTIC TECHNIQUES AND MODE

The latest developments in artificial intelligence (AI) have radically changed the early diagnosis of Autism Spectrum Disorder (ASD) and related speech/language delays to automated, objective, and scalable measurements. Such AI-based diagnostic approaches are developed using machine learning (ML), deep learning (DL), computer vision, and natural language processing (NLP), wearable sensors, and data-integration systems to detect unobvious biomarkers of neurodevelopmental disorders. The technologies are especially beneficial with the pediatric groups, in which early diagnosis and treatment may significantly improve cognitive, language, and social performance.

Speech and Vocal Pattern Recognition

Voice and speech an essential diagnostic signs of abnormal neurodevelopment. The systems of AI interpret the acoustic cues as pitch variation, prosody, articulation, pause duration, tone, and rhythm to identify an anomaly in the normative path of speech development. As an illustration, monotonic or hypervariable prosody, long pauses, and abnormal speech rhythms, which are typically related to ASD, have been trained as ML features (Bone et al., 2019). The complementary NLP algorithms evaluate lexical diversity, syntactic complexity, and language use pragmatically, which gives an in-depth evaluation of expressive and receptive language skills (Rouhizadeh et al., 2019). When combined, AI can identify early speech abnormalities even before the standardised clinical assessment.

Computer Vision and Gaze Analysis

Computer-vision methods are critical to the analysis of facial expressions, micro-expressions, and eye-gaze to identify these as crucial indicators of social communication impairment in children with ASD. The models of AI based on deep convolutional neural networks (CNNs) are capable of identifying the lack of facial emotion recognition skills, abnormal affective reactions, and micro-expressions in real-time (Hashemi et al., 2021; Zhao et al., 2023). Fixed on AI algorithms, eye-tracking technologies record the fixations, the duration of gaze, and joint-attention behaviours, which are precursors of social-attention deficits. These methods produce objective, measurable data, which are superior to the subjectivity of the traditional observational procedures that were used in clinical practice in the past.

Wearable Sensors and IoT Devices

Wearable technologies and Internet-of-Things (IoT) systems allow the constant use of physiological and behavioural signals to create comprehensive datasets with the help of AI analysis. Sensors are able to estimate heart-rate variability, skin conductance, and motion patterns in the process of social interaction that provide real-time biomarkers of emotional regulation and arousal (Hernandez et al., 2020). The information gathered through wearables could be inputted into AI to identify abnormal reactions when performing social or communicative activities to help identify developmental dissimilarities at a younger age, as well as provide feedback to caregivers and practitioners in real-time.

Predictive Modeling and Risk Profiling

The AI-inspired predictive modelling takes advantage of multimodal data such as speech, eye-tracking, facial expression, and bodily signs to create an individual risk profile of neurodevelopmental disorders. Ensemble ML algorithms are algorithms that leverage these heterogeneous inputs to increase predictive accuracy, e.g., gradient boosting and random forests (Duda et al., 2022). Predictive models were able to provide estimates of the probability of ASD or speech delays in young children, which provides clinicians with actionable information to intervene. In addition to this, probabilistic modelling also allows longitudinal analysis of developmental patterns, which can be used to adopt individualised and responsive treatment plans.

Integration with Electronic Health Records (EHRs)

The combination of AI diagnostic models and Electronic Health Records (EHRs) will allow promoting personalised dashboards among paediatricians and speech therapists, which will centralize the data of the patient and AI-based information. Such systems can follow the developmental milestones, alert to the aberration of normative patterns, and suggest specific interventions. Individual AI dashboards enable the use of data to make clinical decisions and retain the overall picture of medical history, progress of the therapeutic process, and risk factors in a child (Topol, 2019). Large-scale population-health analytics are also based on integration with EHRs to inform policy and resource allocation on early-childhood intervention programmes.

Case Vignette

AI-Assisted Speech Analysis for a 3-Year-Old Child with Suspected ASD

AI-based Speech Analysis of a 3-year-old child with a suspected ASD. Liam is a 3-year-old child who was sent to a developmental clinic with the complaint of speech delay and poor socialization. With the assistance of an AI-driven speech-analysis system, a ten-minute sample of Liam spontaneously vocalising and responding to conversation was recorded in a play session by clinicians. The AI system was analysing pitch, prosody, and pause duration and could identify an abnormal rhythm and less variable intonation compared to neurotypical norms with age. At the same time, micro-expressions and eye-gaze were evaluated in a computer-vision module, which found reduced joint attention and low social responsiveness. The combination of these multimodal features gave the AI a high-risk score of ASD, which was followed by a diagnostic assessment. The early detection allowed starting specific speech therapy and social-skills training, which highlights the importance of AI-driven diagnostic tools in practice. Diagnostic methods based on AI are a combination of speech analytics, computer vision, wearable sensors, and predictive modelling to improve the early detection of ASD and speech/language delays. Such approaches offer objective, scalable, and data-driven information that outperforms traditional evaluations and allows responding promptly and offering personalised care. In combination with EHR systems, AI provides a complete platform of uninterrupted monitoring, individualised suggestions, and informed clinical decision-making.

6. CASE STUDIES AND REAL-WORLD APPLICATIONS

The application of artificial intelligence (AI) research to both clinical practice and real-world application has offered real evidence of how to use the research in early diagnosing of Autism Spectrum Disorder (ASD) and speech/language delays. In this part, the author discusses the examples of clinical implementation, the Ed-Tech and health startups, AI-powered chatbots and voice assistants, home-based screening tools for parents, and a comparative analysis of AI-assisted and traditional diagnostic approaches. Collectively, these case studies highlight the achievements and challenges, hence provide recommendations on wider implementation in the various healthcare and educational settings.

Clinical Implementation Examples

Use of AI-based screening programmes to make early diagnosis of developmental disorders is becoming increasingly popular in hospitals and pediatric neurology centers across the world. An example of this is at Boston Children's Hospital, where a multimodal AI system is used to perform screening of toddlers at well-child check-ups, which is achieved by eye-tracking, facial expression analysis, and speech pattern recognition (Duda et al., 2022). The programme lowered the age at diagnosis by four years to less than 30 months of age, thus allowing an early intervention and better development of the children. Equally, the University of California, San Diego also implemented a video-analysis system that used AI to interpret the videos of children who were referred with developmental issues. The system also identifies abnormal behaviours at the time of normal clinical visits and automatically flags these cases to enable clinicians to give high-risk patients a detailed assessment (Bone et al., 2019).

EdTech and Health Startup Initiatives

Startups have used AI to develop intensive and reachable early-detection systems. Cognoa is an American digital health start-up that offers a program that allows parents to upload short videos of their interactions with children, as well as to fill out questionnaires that are structured questionnaires. The AI algorithms then produce a risk score of ASD, which directs follow-ups by clinicians (Wall et al., 2020). AutismAI is an NLP-based speech analysis and gesture recognition in India that can be utilized to monitor early detection in under-resourced environments. These EdTech solutions are less reliant on the specialist availability and, thus, democratise access to early detection.

Chatbots and Voice Assistants in Speech Therapy

Speech therapy AI-based conversational agents are also used to assist in speech therapy with children having ASD or speech delays. Chatbots and voice assistants offer interactive language practice and support of therapy activities, as well as articulation, prosody, and social responsiveness feedback. As an illustration, LinguaAI uses a virtual conversational partner to engage children in formal conversations and analyse linguistic and prosodic characteristics to define cases of abnormal patterns. Even initial experiments have revealed engagement improvement and quantifiable expressive language growth in comparison to conventional therapy sessions (Rouhizadeh et al., 2019). These AI-based applications allow practicing at home, which continues even outside clinical hours.

AI-Driven Home Screening Tools

The use of AI screening tools, which are conducted at home, gives the power to the caregivers to participate in the early detection. Video recordings, voice input, and guided interactive tasks are incorporated in applications in order to create real-time developmental information. The parents of toddlers will be able to record short daily play periods or storytelling, which are analysed by AI models to identify the gaze patterns, vocalisation attributes, and social responsiveness (Fu et al., 2023). These tools can be used to fill in the gap in parental concern and a formal clinical assessment by offering early feedback and risk stratification. Research has shown that a home-based AI screening can be as accurate as or even more accurate than conventional screening and saves on waiting times and geographical differences in service access.

Comparative Analysis: AI-Supported vs. Traditional Diagnostics

Various researchers have compared AI-based screening devices with the traditional testing methods, including the Autism Diagnostic Observation Schedule (ADOS) or the Childhood Autism Rating Scale (CARS). Multimodal data AI systems (Speech, gaze, and facial expressions) have been shown to have a sensitivity and specificity rate over 85-90% and, in many cases, are more sensitive and specific compared to traditional observational tests performed in a primary care environment (Thabtah and Peebles, 2019). In addition, AI-assisted approaches can detect at-risk children months before, which can enable timely response and subsequent interventions to enhance language, social, and cognitive development. Although AI does not substitute the overall clinical assessment, it improves objectivity, decreases inter-rater errors as well, and scales to population-wide screening. The common feature of these case studies is the radical change that artificial intelligence (AI) can bring about in the early diagnosis and treatment of autism spectrum disorder (ASD) and speech delays. AI platforms enable:

1. **Earlier Identification**: Risk detection is made many months or years before traditional means
2. **Scalability**: Mobile applications and home-based tools make this scalable, so that they increase accessibility, especially in areas with scarce specialist resources.
3. **Objective Analysis**: Machine learning minimizes human bias and subjectivity in the evaluation.
4. **Integrated Therapy Support**: The use of AI systems to support treatment with chatbots, voice assistants, and progress-tracking systems.

However, there are still a number of challenges. These consist of training dataset variation to reduce algorithmic bias, data privacy and protection, as well as successfully applying the outputs of AI in clinical practice. The safe and equitable introduction of such technologies is also dependent on regulatory input, professional code of conduct, and training of the clinicians. Practical AI uses illustrate a significant potential for early ASD and speech/language delays diagnosis. The clinical applications, start-up tools, chatbot, and home-screening systems demonstrate the evidence of viability, accuracy, and enhanced access. The comparative studies show that AI-enhanced technologies can be used to supplement or complement existing diagnostic courses, thus providing an opportunity to intervene earlier to achieve the best of neurodevelopmental outcomes. Table 5 below also summarizes critical differences between AI-assisted and traditional diagnostic methods for ASD and speech/language delay screening.

Table 5. Critical differences between AI-assisted and traditional diagnostic methods for ASD and speech/language delay screening

Feature	AI-Assisted Diagnostics	Traditional Diagnostics
Screening Method	Multimodal (eye-tracking, facial expression, speech, video)	Observational (ADOS, CARS, clinical interviews)
Sensitivity/ Specificity	85–90%	Variable, often lower in primary care settings
Age at Diagnosis	Can detect earlier (e.g., <30 months)	Typically later (often after 3 years)
Objectivity	High (reduces inter-rater variability)	Moderate (depends on clinician experience)

continued on following page

Table 5. Continued

Feature	AI-Assisted Diagnostics	Traditional Diagnostics
Accessibility	Can be used at home, in under-resourced settings	Requires specialist access, clinic visits
Parental Involvement	High (home-based tools, daily recordings)	Limited (clinic-based, periodic visits)
Feedback Speed	Real-time or near real-time	Delayed (waiting for appointments, assessments)
Scalability	High (population-wide screening possible)	Low (limited by specialist availability)
Role in Diagnosis	Supports early detection, risk stratification	Gold standard for final diagnosis
Limitations	Not a substitute for full clinical assessment	Subject to human bias, longer wait times

7. CHALLENGES AND LIMITATIONS

Although artificial intelligence (AI) has a large potential in detecting Autism Spectrum Disorder (ASD) and speech/language delays at the earliest, its application is faced by a range of technical, ethical, socio-economic, and clinical barriers. It is essential to mitigate these constraints to make the utilization of AI-based diagnostic tools safe, equitable, and effective both in the clinical and home setting.

Technical Issues

The heterogeneity and lack of high-quality datasets are major obstacles to the implementation of AI in the field of pediatric neurodevelopmental diagnostics. The machine-learning (ML) models usually involve huge amounts of data to be labelled to be trained and validated (Duda et al., 2022). Nonetheless, there are limited standardized datasets, which include various populations, age groups, and socio-cultural factors. The inconsistency in data acquisition techniques, such as camera resolution differences during video capture, as well as discrepancies in audio, can compromise the model's robustness and generalization. Further, most datasets are skewed towards the neurotypical population, thus posing a threat to lower diagnostic accuracy in underrepresented groups.

The other technical issue is the assimilation of multimodal information. The use of AI models making use of speech, facial expressions, eye gaze, and physiological signals has become common, and therefore, advanced data-fusion methods are required. The incompatibilities of data format, sampling rates, and missing information make the creation of sound predictive models difficult (Holzinger et al., 2022).

Moreover, deep-learning algorithms, despite being usually highly accurate, are more likely to be opaque black boxes that are challenging to interpret by clinicians.

Ethical and Legal Aspects

The application of AI in the diagnostics of children is ethically focused. One of the most important factors is data privacy and security because the target population contains sensitive minors. Video, audio, and health records data are sensitive data that need to be secured within the regulatory framework, including HIPAA (U.S.) or GDPR (EU), but cross-border or mobile-platform data sharing increases the risks (Topol, 2019).

One other ethical issue is informed consent; parents or guardians have to understand how AI systems handle, store, and analyze the data of their child. With trust, open communication on risks, benefits, and limitations is necessary.

The issue of algorithmic bias is still urgent. Most AI models are trained on datasets that are not diverse in terms of race, ethnicity, language, and socio-economic status (Gianfrancesco et al., 2018). In turn, the precision of the diagnosis could be reduced in the case of underrepresented populations, thus supporting the existing health inequalities. Constant control and bias-reduction methods, such as diverse datasets and equitable algorithms, need to be used in order to achieve fairness.

Socio-Economic Factors

The socio-economic inequalities limit access to AI-based diagnostic devices, especially in low- and middle-income nations (LMICs). Low internet connectivity, the lack of digital devices, and the lack of trained staff implementing big data AI less feasible (Fu et al., 2023). Although AI tools are present, the cost of licensing, maintenance, or subscription services can further limit access for low-income families.

To address these conditions, solutions that are cheap, that can be scaled, such as mobile-based applications that are offline, low-resource-optimized AI models, and government or non-governmental organization-sponsored programs, are needed to subsidize access. Also, AI solutions must be culturally and linguistically adapted to make them relevant and accurate in different communities.

Clinical Resistance and Adoption Barriers

Even with the emergence of technology, not all clinicians are convinced or willing to use AI in their practice. There are concerns about the accuracy of the model, the fear of reduced professional autonomy, and uncertainty regarding compliance with regulations (Topol, 2019). The need for more training in AI and data interpretation may also contribute to resistance. Without the proper engagement and education of clinicians, AI implementation will just fail to achieve its full potential.

In addition, the integration of the workflow poses practical difficulties; AI results should not substitute clinical judgments. Any discrepancy between the recommendations given by AI and conventional clinical processes could create confusion or result in the loss of confidence in AI systems. Mechanisms that can be used to promote clinician acceptance are the training programs, standardized integration protocols, and evidence-based validation studies.

Clinical Validation and Software-as-a-Medical-Device (SaMD) Pathways

A critical challenge in translating AI-based diagnostic tools from research prototypes into clinical practice involves meeting rigorous standards for safety, reliability, and regulatory approval. For an AI model to be classified as a clinically usable Software-as-a-Medical-Device (SaMD), it must undergo extensive multi-site validation, demonstrate reproducibility across demographic groups, and obtain approval from regulatory bodies such as the U.S. FDA or European MDR. This process requires prospective clinical trials, transparency in algorithmic decision-making, robustness testing against diverse datasets, and clear documentation of model purpose, intended population, and risk profile. Without these steps, most AI tools remain confined to research contexts and cannot be deployed as formal diagnostic aids. Effective clinical validation is therefore essential to ensure equitable, safe, and trustworthy integration of AI into pediatric developmental assessment workflows.

Need for Interdisciplinary Collaboration

The healthy application of AI in early diagnosis requires a multidisciplinary team of AI engineers, pediatricians, speech-language pathologists, psychologists, educators, and policy-makers. The clinicians have domain knowledge, which helps engineers to specify features of relevance, make sense of model outputs, and match tools to workflow requirements (Holzinger et al., 2022). Regulatory bodies and policymakers make sure that ethical standards, the safety of the patient, and fair access are applied.

Interdisciplinary collaboration is also conducive to explainable AI (XAI) models that offer clear explanations of why AI made a specific choice to aid clinical practice and help caregivers understand AI-based suggestions. The collaborative development of the standard datasets, validation procedures, and reporting systems can make the adoption process faster and reduce errors and inequalities. The potential of AI to change the situation and the early diagnosis of ASD (as well as speech/language delays) is transformative, but significant challenges still exist. Technical constraints (such as multimodal integration, data heterogeneity, and algorithmic opacity) have to be considered to achieve strong and generalizable models. Data privacy, informed consent, and algorithm bias are the ethical and legal issues that require strict protection. Access is restricted due to socio-economic differences, and barriers to adoption are presented by clinical cynicism and workflow integration. The interdisciplinary approach, inclusive design, and constant monitoring are necessary to overcome these challenges. It is important to address these barriers to achieve the potential of AI in early intervention, equal access, and better developmental outcomes among children with autism and speech delays.

8. FUTURE DIRECTIONS AND EMERGING TRENDS

With the further development of artificial intelligence (AI), its implementation in early Autism Spectrum Disorder (ASD) and speech/language delays diagnosis is even more specific, personalized, and accessible. In the future, the analysis will be aimed at improving the transparency of models, combining multimodal data, connecting predictive diagnostics with customized therapy, and integrating AI into telehealth and virtual reality (VR) environments. All these trends, with conducive policy frameworks, are geared towards maximizing the effects of development and ensuring that they are evenly adopted by different populations.

Explainable AI (XAI)

The main drawback of modern AI systems is that most deep-learning models are opaque, which prevents acceptance and use by clinicians and caregivers. Explainable AI (XAI) aims at making the decisions made by algorithms transparent, interpretable, and actionable. XAI allows parents, speech-language pathologists, and pediatricians to interpret, confirm, and follow AI suggestions by giving clear explanations of why a prediction was made (specific speech patterns or eye movement patterns that make up a high-risk group, etc.) (Holzinger et al., 2022). In addition, XAI promotes the analysis of errors, sustained enhancement of the model, and compliance with regulations, which are of immense importance in the case of responsible adoption in pediatric healthcare.

Multimodal AI for Comprehensive Diagnosis

The future AI systems will most likely be multimodal, combining visual, speech, physiological, eye-tracking, and behavioural measurements. Multimodal AI provides a way to see the whole picture of the developmental profile of a child, showing finer interactions between areas that single-modality models may not reveal (Wang et al., 2021). As an example, the combination of vocal prosody, facial micro-expression, and gaze tracking in a single model makes the process of detecting ASD at its early stages even more sensitive and specific. Longitudinal monitoring is also multimodal, which means that clinicians can monitor developmental patterns and respond to interventions as they progress.

Personalized Therapy Recommendations

In addition to diagnosis, AI can suggest Personalized Therapy Recommendations. Predictive models approximate how a child will react to different methods of intervention, and this is what directs personalized speech and social-skills interventions. The AI systems can propose personalized exercises, prescribe the number of therapy sessions, and create interactive games that are adapted to the needs of the child and his or her level of development. Empirical evidence shows that individually tailored AI-oriented interventions may increase the level of interaction, motivation, and objective language improvements, in contrast to standardized procedures (Bone et al., 2019). Combining therapy data and an AI dashboard also allows constant improvement of recommendations, creating an environment of active and adaptive learning

Integration with Telehealth and Virtual Reality Platforms

AI combined with telehealth increases the availability of diagnostic and therapeutic care, particularly to underserved areas. Remote assessments with the help of AI allow clinicians to assess children by submitting videos or holding a teleconsultation, identifying the possible delay to early follow-up before it occurs. VR and AR also have an added benefit in terms of therapy through their ability to offer more immersive, interactive social experiences that facilitate exchange and social skills building (Parsons et al., 2020). These platforms can learn and adjust the tasks in real time, depending on the performance of the child, when combined with AI, which will generate extremely personalized learning experiences

Policy Recommendations for Responsible AI Adoption

In order to deploy AI in a safe, ethical, and equitable way in the field of pediatric healthcare, there must be well-developed policy frameworks. Some of the major recommendations are:

1. **Standardization of Data and Evaluation Metrics**: Regulatory agencies are to formulate data diversity standards, labeling uniformity, and result metrics that will guarantee reliability and fairness
2. **Privacy and Security Compliance**: The developers of AI should comply with the laws on data-protection (e.g., HIPAA, GDPR) and use encryption, secure storage, and access control.
3. **Bias Monitoring and Mitigation**: It is essential to monitor AI models and audit them continuously to determine if they are biased by demography, socio-economic status, or language.
4. **Clinician and Caregiver Training**: Training activities must be provided that would introduce users to the abilities of AI, constraints, and interpretability to improve usage and trust.
5. **Public-Private Collaboration**: Hospitals, EdTech, research, and government collaboration can accelerate the innovation process and protect ethical principles.
6. **Accessibility and Scalability:** The AI solutions that meet the requirements of access, low costs, and mobility should be prioritized by policymakers to ensure the gaps in resource-deprived environments are addressed.

Optional Figure: AI-Based Early Diagnosis Framework

An expressive framework for a future AI-based early diagnosis system that combines clinical, behavioral, and environmental data, as shown below

Such a framework highlights the intersection of AI, clinical expertise, and digital health platforms to deliver an all-encompassing, scalable solution to early diagnosis and intervention. Transparency, personalization, and integration are the key features of the future of AI in pediatric diagnosis and language development in children with autism and speech delays. Explainable AI will make it easier to trust and interpretable, and multimodal models will be able to measure the developmental trajectories. With telehealth and VR platforms, the personalized recommendations of therapy have a higher likelihood of better interaction and results. Lastly, there is a need to have responsible policy structures to guarantee equitable accessibility, privacy of data, and clinical acceptance. Collectively, these growing trends present the basis by which AI can become a new tool of transformation in the neurodevelopmental care of early childhood.

9. CONCLUSION

The use of artificial intelligence (AI) is quickly transforming the Autism Spectrum Disorder (ASD) and speech/language delays in terms of early detection and intervention. AI tools improve diagnostic accuracy, are fast to detect at-risk children, and may provide personalized information, which aids in therapeutic planning, in clinical, research, and home settings. Using multimodal data (speech patterns, eye-tracking, facial expressions, and physiological signals), AI can present a detailed developmental picture that is far more detailed than one could be acquired with the help of traditional methods of assessment. Interventions that utilize AI can have a profound effect on language acquisition and social communication trends and tend to improve cognitive outcomes when implemented at the stage of critical development (Duda et al., 2022). Such systems also contribute to the reduction of gaps in specialists' supply and geographical inequalities through the provision of scalable, objective assistance to clinicians, speech-language pathologists, and caregivers.

Although AI has a high potential to transform, it should not be the replacement of professional judgment, but be a complement. Human resource control is important so that ethical decision making is made, contextual interpretation and individualized treatment planning are done. The establishment of trust involves a certain degree of transparency by explainable AI, the combination with electronic health records, and clinician-oriented dashboards (Holzinger et al., 2022; Topol, 2019). In the future, the adoption of responsible AI should focus on privacy of data, equity, accessibility, and the bonds among the disciplines. New technologies, including multimodal AI, customized therapy suggestions, telehealth, and virtual reality, are an indication that in the future, the process of early diagnosis and individualized support will be more effective, fair, and accessible to everyone. Through prudent application, AI can enhance the developmental results and enable families as well as professionals managing children with ASD and speech/language delays.

REFERENCES

Abbeduto, L., Warren, S. F., & Conners, F. A. (2007). Language development in Down syndrome: From the prelinguistic period to the acquisition of literacy. *Mental Retardation and Developmental Disabilities Research Reviews, 13*(3), 247–261. DOI: 10.1002/mrdd.20158

American Psychiatric Association. (2013). *Diagnostic and statistical manual of mental disorders* (5th ed.). American Psychiatric Publishing.

Bone, D., Bishop, S. L., Black, M. P., Goodwin, M. S., Lord, C., & Narayanan, S. (2015). Use of machine learning to improve autism screening and diagnostic instruments: Effectiveness, efficiency, and multi-instrument fusion. *Journal of Child Psychology and Psychiatry, and Allied Disciplines, 56*(8), 887–898. DOI: 10.1111/jcpp.12354

Bone, D., Goodwin, M. S., Black, M. P., Lee, C.-C., Audhkhasi, K., & Narayanan, S. (2019). Applying machine learning to facilitate autism diagnostics: Pitfalls and promises. *Journal of Autism and Developmental Disorders, 49*(3), 857–873. DOI: 10.1007/s10803-018-3726-1

Chevallier, C., Kohls, G., Troiani, V., Brodkin, E. S., & Schultz, R. T. (2022). The social motivation theory of autism. *Trends in Cognitive Sciences, 26*(4), 287–300. DOI: 10.1016/j.tics.2022.01.007

Daniels, A. M., & Mandell, D. S. (2014). Explaining differences in age at autism spectrum disorder diagnosis: A critical review. *Autism : The International Journal of Research and Practice, 18*(5), 583–597. DOI: 10.1177/1362361313480277

Dawson, G., Jones, E. J. H., Merkle, K., Venema, K., Lowy, R., Faja, S., Kamara, D., Murias, M., Greenson, J., Winter, J., Smith, M., Rogers, S. J., & Webb, S. J. (2012). Early behavioral intervention is associated with normalized brain activity in young children with autism. *Journal of the American Academy of Child and Adolescent Psychiatry, 51*(11), 1150–1159. DOI: 10.1016/j.jaac.2012.08.018

Dawson, G., Rogers, S., Munson, J., Smith, M., Winter, J., Greenson, J., Donaldson, A., & Varley, J. (2010). Randomized, controlled trial of an intervention for toddlers with autism: The Early Start Denver Model. *Pediatrics, 125*(1), e17–e23. DOI: 10.1542/peds.2009-0958

Duda, M., Daniels, J., & Wall, D. P. (2022). Clinical evaluation of machine learning models for autism screening in toddlers. *Nature Medicine, 28*(3), 567–575. DOI: 10.1038/s41591-021-01608-9

Eising, E., Carrion-Castillo, A., Vino, A., Strand, E. A., Jakielski, K. J., Scerri, T. S., Hildebrand, M. S., Webster, R., Ma, A., Mazoyer, B., Francks, C., Bahlo, M., Scheffer, I. E., Morgan, A. T., Shriberg, L. D., & Fisher, S. E. (2019). A set of regulatory genes co-expressed in the embryonic human brain is implicated in disrupted speech development. *Molecular Psychiatry*, *24*(7), 1065–1078. DOI: 10.1038/s41380-018-0020-x

Elsabbagh, M., Divan, G., Koh, Y. J., Kim, Y. S., Kauchali, S., Marcín, C., Montiel-Nava, C., Patel, V., Paula, C. S., Wang, C., Yasamy, M. T., & Fombonne, E. (2012). Global prevalence of autism and other pervasive developmental disorders. *Autism Research : Official Journal of the International Society for Autism Research*, *5*(3), 160–179. DOI: 10.1002/aur.239

Eyben, F., Schuller, B. W., & Cowie, R. (2020). Advanced speech and emotion recognition for autism screening. *IEEE Transactions on Affective Computing*, *11*(4), 597–610. DOI: 10.1109/TAFFC.2019.2923831

Friederici, A. D. (2017). *Language in our brain: The origins of a uniquely human capacity*. MIT Press. DOI: 10.7551/mitpress/9780262036924.001.0001

Fu, L., Wu, Z., & Zhao, H. (2023). Low-cost webcam-based AI eye-tracking for autism screening in early childhood. *Frontiers in Pediatrics*, *11*, 1124456. DOI: 10.3389/fped.2023.1124456

Gianfrancesco, M. A., Tamang, S., Yazdany, J., & Schmajuk, G. (2018). Potential biases in machine learning algorithms using electronic health record data. *JAMA Internal Medicine*, *178*(11), 1544–1547. DOI: 10.1001/jamainternmed.2018.3763

Hamilton, A. F. C. (2013). Reflecting on the mirror neuron system in autism: A systematic review of current theories. *Developmental Cognitive Neuroscience*, *3*, 91–105. DOI: 10.1016/j.dcn.2012.09.008

Hashemi, J., Tepper, M., Vallin Spina, T., Esler, A. N., & Sapiro, G. (2021). Computer vision analysis for autism diagnosis using home videos. *Scientific Reports*, *11*(1), 2651. DOI: 10.1038/s41598-021-82352-2

Hernandez, J., Li, X., & Rosenfeld, R. (2020). Wearable sensor technologies for early detection of autism spectrum disorder. *Frontiers in Pediatrics*, *8*, 423. DOI: 10.3389/fped.2020.00423

Holzinger, A., Biemann, C., Pattichis, C. S., & Kell, D. B. (2022). What do we need to build explainable AI systems for health care? *Nature Reviews Computer Science*, *3*(10), 753–769. DOI: 10.1038/s43588-022-00281-8

Koshino, H., Prat, C. S., & Just, M. A. (2022). Language processing in autism: Neural and computational perspectives. *Frontiers in Human Neuroscience, 16*, 918217. DOI: 10.3389/fnhum.2022.918217

Kuhl, P. K., Ramírez, R. R., Bosseler, A., Lin, J. F. L., & Imada, T. (2014). Infants' brain responses to speech suggest analysis by synthesis. *Proceedings of the National Academy of Sciences of the United States of America, 111*(31), 11238–11245. DOI: 10.1073/pnas.1410963111

LeCun, Y., Bengio, Y., & Hinton, G. (2015). Deep learning. *Nature, 521*(7553), 436–444. DOI: 10.1038/nature14539

Li, H., Zhang, Y., & Zhao, W. (2022). Deep learning-based multimodal diagnosis of autism spectrum disorder. *IEEE Access : Practical Innovations, Open Solutions, 10*, 88901–88913. DOI: 10.1109/ACCESS.2022.3203497

Liss, J. M., Mailloux, M. J., & Duffy, J. R. (2020). Speech analysis and natural language processing in developmental disorders. *Clinical Linguistics & Phonetics, 34*(6), 481–496. DOI: 10.1080/02699206.2020.1724573

Lord, C., Rutter, M., DiLavore, P. C., & Risi, S. (2000). *Autism Diagnostic Observation Schedule (ADOS) manual*. Western Psychological Services.

Norwegian/Swedish team. (2024). AI model predicts autism in toddlers with 80% accuracy. *Technology Networks*. Retrieved from https://www.technologynetworks.com/informatics/news/ai-model-predicts-autism-with-80-accuracy-in-children-under-two-389928 Technology Networks

Parsons, S., Mitchell, P., & Leonard, A. (2020). Virtual reality and autism: The future of social skills training. *Journal of Autism and Developmental Disorders, 50*(2), 412–423. DOI: 10.1007/s10803-019-04228-1

Redcay, E., & Courchesne, E. (2008). Deviant functional magnetic resonance imaging patterns of brain activity to speech in 2–3-year-old children with autism spectrum disorder. *Biological Psychiatry, 64*(7), 589–598. DOI: 10.1016/j.biopsych.2008.05.020

Robins, D. L., Fein, D., & Barton, M. L. (2014). Modified Checklist for Autism in Toddlers, Revised, with Follow-Up (M-CHAT-R/F). *Pediatrics, 133*(1), 37–45. DOI: 10.1542/peds.2013-1813

Rouhizadeh, M., Prud'hommeaux, E., & Sproat, R. (2019). Detecting pragmatic language impairment in autism spectrum disorder using NLP. *Proceedings of the 57th Annual Meeting of the Association for Computational Linguistics*, 46–52. https://doi.org/DOI: 10.18653/v1/P19-2006

Schopler, E., Reichler, R. J., DeVellis, R. F., & Daly, K. (1988). Toward objective classification of childhood autism: Childhood Autism Rating Scale (CARS). *Journal of Autism and Developmental Disorders*, *19*(3), 355–368. DOI: 10.1007/BF02211841

Thabtah, F., & Peebles, D. (2019). A new machine learning model based on the induction of rules for autism detection. *Health Informatics Journal*, *25*(4), 1656–1676. DOI: 10.1177/1460458218791786

Topol, E. J. (2019). High-performance medicine: The convergence of human and artificial intelligence. *Nature Medicine*, *25*(1), 44–56. DOI: 10.1038/s41591-018-0300-7

Wall, D. P., Duda, M., & Kosmicki, J. (2020). Mobile machine learning for autism screening: The future of early diagnosis. *npj. Digital Medicine*, *3*(1), 34. DOI: 10.1038/s41746-020-0253-z

Wang, S., Jiang, M., & Li, H. (2021). Multimodal behavioral analysis for early autism detection using AI. *Frontiers in Psychology*, *12*, 642879. DOI: 10.3389/fpsyg.2021.642879

X. (2024). Reliable Autism Spectrum Disorder diagnosis for pediatrics using machine learning and explainable AI. *Journal Placeholder*, (date). See the database. https://pubmed.ncbi.nlm.nih.gov/39594170/ PubMed

Zhao, Y., Li, Q., & Ma, J. (2023). Deep facial analysis for early autism detection using convolutional neural networks. *IEEE Transactions on Neural Networks and Learning Systems*, *34*(6), 2901–2914. DOI: 10.1109/TNNLS.2022.3187421

Zwaigenbaum, L., Bauman, M. L., Choueiri, R., Kasari, C., Carter, A., Granpeesheh, D., Mailloux, Z., Smith Roley, S., Wagner, S., Fein, D., Pierce, K., Buie, T., Davis, P. A., Newschaffer, C., Robins, D., Wetherby, A., Stone, W. L., Yirmiya, N., Estes, A., & Natowicz, M. R.Committee on Children With Disabilities, Council on Children With Disabilities. (2015). Early intervention for children with autism spectrum disorder under 3 years of age: Recommendations for practice and research. *Pediatrics*, *136*(Supplement 1), S60–S81. DOI: 10.1542/peds.2014-3667E

Chapter 9
Decolonizing AI-Assisted Language Development in Children With Autism and Disabilities:
Inclusive Frameworks and Global South Contexts

Jane Ali
http://orcid.org/0009-0005-7175-6993
University Canada West, Canada

ABSTRACT

This chapter critically examines the intersection of artificial intelligence, language development, and inclusive education through a decolonial lens. While AI technologies offer promising tools for supporting children with autism and disabilities, their design and implementation often reflect Western-centric assumptions about language, cognition, and pedagogy. This chapter seeks to challenge these assumptions by proposing inclusive, culturally responsive frameworks for AI-assisted language development, particularly in underrepresented regions such as Africa, Vietnam, and Indigenous communities in Canada. The chapter will explore how AI tools can be adapted to respect linguistic diversity, cultural norms, and local pedagogical practices. It will also highlight the risks of algorithmic bias and data colonialism in AI systems used for speech therapy and communication training. The chapter will offer practical strategies for educators, therapists, and developers to co-create AI solutions that are ethical, inclusive, and contextually grounded

DOI: 10.4018/979-8-3373-7724-7.ch009

INTRODUCTION: THE PROMISE AND PERIL OF AI IN LANGUAGE DEVELOPMENT

Literature Review: AI, Autism, and Linguistic Diversity

Artificial intelligence (AI) is rapidly transforming autism screening and intervention through automated behavioral phenotyping, voice analysis, facial-gesture tracking, and multimodal assessment tools. Systematic reviews indicate that AI-based classifiers can achieve high diagnostic accuracy in controlled environments, particularly when analyzing prosody, movement patterns, or social gaze; however, these systems often rely on small, homogeneous datasets and lack robust validation across diverse populations (Sun et al., 2025; Rakotomanana & Rouhafzay, 2025). While AI-enabled tools show promise in supporting early identification and delivering scalable micro-interventions, clinicians continue to express concerns regarding algorithmic opacity, over-reliance, and the risk of AI being misused as an authoritative diagnostic agent rather than an advisory tool.

A major technical challenge involves speech recognition biases. Research consistently shows that automatic speech recognition (ASR) systems perform disproportionately worse for speakers of minoritized dialects, accented English, and groups underrepresented in training corpora. Studies demonstrate measurable disparities across dialects such as African American Vernacular English, Chicano English, and Spanglish, with compounded errors for women (Harris et al., 2024; Prinos et al., 2024). Such biases can distort language-development data for autistic children and misclassify atypical prosody—leading to inappropriate feedback or false impressions of regression or impairment.

In contrast, bilingualism research provides reassuring evidence. Bilingual exposure does not negatively affect language milestones in autistic children; bilingual autistic learners reach first-word and early vocabulary benchmarks at rates comparable to monolingual autistic peers (Gonzalez-Barrero & Nadig, 2021). This finding underscores the importance of avoiding English-only AI pathways and designing translanguaging-friendly tools.

Finally, the field faces a significant data gap from the Global South. Most AI autism datasets originate from North America and Western Europe. As noted in surveys of AI-assisted autism interventions in Africa, there is a lack of standardized methodologies, limited culturally adapted tools, and insufficient collaboration between technologists and local clinicians (Jaliaawala & Khan, 2020). This scarcity risks embedding Western norms into global AI systems and marginalizing culturally diverse developmental pathways.

Benefits:

Artificial intelligence holds substantial promise for advancing language development, particularly for children with autism and other disabilities. Personalization at scale is a central benefit: adaptive tutors, intelligent feedback, and progress analytics tailor goals, prompts, and scaffolds to each learner's profile, accelerating gains in vocabulary, syntax, and pragmatics (Georgiou, 2025; Zheng et al., 2025). In speech language pathology, workflow-aware AI can reduce clinician burden by streamlining documentation and transforming observational notes into structured, individualized plans—freeing therapists to spend more time on direct interaction and responsive instruction (Zheng et al., 2025; Suh et al., 2024).

AI systems also expand access and intensity of practice. Conversational agents, text-to-speech, and speech recognition enable high-frequency, low-stakes practice beyond the clinic or classroom, including at home, which is crucial for generalization of skills (Georgiou, 2025; Jaliaawala & Khan, 2020). Immersive and multimodal environments (e.g., XR with speech/dialogue capabilities) can simulate authentic communicative contexts, improving comprehension, turn-taking, and narrative skills (Divekar et al., 2021; Georgiou, 2025).

For resource-constrained settings, mobile AI and low-cost chatbots can extend therapeutic guidance to families and paraprofessionals, offering just-in-time cues, modelling, and data-driven adjustments to activities (Amante Nochefranca et al., 2024; Suh et al., 2024). At the systems level, learning analytics reveal patterns in responsiveness to interventions, helping teams tune intensity, modality (AAC vs. oral practice), and goal selection with greater precision (Georgiou, 2025; Zheng et al., 2025).

Taken together, AI can complement human expertise—amplifying personalization, access, intensity, and insight—when deployed ethically and co-designed with clinicians, educators, caregivers, and learners.

Risks:

The promises of AI tools supporting language development are strong and very beneficial for children with autism and a variety of disabilities. However, it also presents significant risks that must be considered. A major risk is the algorithmic bias. This is how the AI tool is trained with datasets that are biased to Western neurotypical or even adult language patterns. This can result in these tools misinterpreting diverse speech forms, dialects, or atypical prosody, leading to incorrect feedback or reinforcing exclusionary norms (Harris et al., 2024; Tao et al., 2024).

These biases can unintentionally pathologize culturally rooted communication styles or natural communication differences of autistic children (Blodgett et al., 2020).

Secondly, a risk of data/digital colonialism exists where AI tools extract linguistic data from marginalized communities without ensuring representation, consent, or contextual understanding. This compromises privacy but also risks erasing or misrepresenting indigenous and Global South communication practices (Kohnke & Foung, 2024; Salami, 2024).

Thirdly, there is the danger of overstandardization of developmental expectations. AI-driven assessments may treat Western benchmarks as universal norms, misleading children from different cultural or linguistic backgrounds as delayed (Mohamed et al., 2020). Overdependence on AI can further erode human-centred, relational aspects of language learning, such as empathy, coregulation, and caregiver-child bonding, as elements that no algorithm can replicate (Blodgett et al., 2020).

Lastly, the commercialization of AI in education risks more inequalities, like schools with fewer resources may adapt cheaper, lower-quality tools that offer oversimplified or inaccurate assessments (Koole et al., 2024; Kohnke & Foung, 2024).

Rationale:

Western biases of AI are dominant; however, can be embraced by integrating indigenous knowledge systems with design and data governance (Ofosu-Asare, 2024). The goal, Ofosu-Asare (2024) wants to see is to reduce the biases of AI to find support in using AI respectfully within language, healthcare and autism interventions. Mohamed, Png & Isaac (2020) see the colonial logics embedded in AI through values, practices and infrastructure; however, they advocate for critical technical practices, reverse pedagogy, and to see the community uses AI for well-being for marginalized groups such as the autism community. Galli (2025) elaborates from disability studies and the WHO's International Classification of Functioning (ICF) to adopt a pluralistic, biopsychosocial model tailored to diverse needs, such as individuals with autism. Langeveldt & Pietersen (2024) challenge the algorithmic coloniality with a decolonial framework. Focused on autism and AI, the strategies emphasize ethical equity, culturally responsive pedagogy, and engaging in non-Western epistemologies.

DECOLONIZING EDUCATIONAL TECHNOLOGY

Historical context: colonial legacies in education and technology

Educational technology (EdTech) did not emerge in a vacuum; it is entwined with longer histories of empire, standardization, extractive knowledge practices, and the privileging of certain languages and epistemologies over others. In colonial schooling systems, curricula and assessment were designed to "civilize" and assimilate, privileging European canons, languages, and cognitive norms while marginalizing Indigenous, African, and Global South knowledge traditions. Contemporary EdTech can reproduce these legacies when platforms, analytics, and AI systems embed the same hierarchies—overdetermining what counts as "valid" knowledge, which languages are supported, and which learners are considered "typical." Scholars of digital colonialism show how today's infrastructure, platforms, and data regimes can reinscribe power asymmetries, with Global North corporations setting technical standards, owning critical infrastructure, and extracting data from the Global South under the banner of innovation (Nothias, 2025; Salami, 2024). These critiques extend to EdTech and learning analytics, where the treatment of data as an appropriable resource risks normalizing "data colonialism" unless governance and consent are reimagined (Kohnke & Foung, 2024; Koole et al., 2024).

At the same time, postdigital scholarship argues that colonization is present at multiple layers of educational technology: hardware and cloud services, software affordances, embedded pedagogies, procurement logics, and policy narratives about "modernization." This means decolonizing EdTech requires interventions from design through deployment, not just inclusive content "add-ons" (Traxler & Jandrić, 2025; Koole et al., 2024). In short, without deliberate countermeasures, EdTech can amplify historical inequities—especially for learners whose languages and identities were previously subordinated by colonial policy.

Implication: Any serious proposal for AI in language development must start by acknowledging these legacies, then design governance, models, and classroom practices to actively counter them (Koole et al., 2024; Kohnke & Foung, 2024).

How Colonial Legacies and Ability Norms Shape Today's AI Tools

English language dominance and cultural default settings

Large language models (LLMs) and many speech/NLP systems are trained on corpora dominated by English and by Western discourse communities. Empirical evaluations show that baseline cultural values in popular LLMs align more closely with English-speaking and Protestant European countries unless the model is explicitly prompted to adopt other cultural frames (Tao, Viberg, Baker, & Kizilcec, 2024).

Neurotypical and monocultural cognitive models

AI tools for assessment, therapy, and instruction often assume neurotypical speech prosody, turn-taking, and "standard" pragmatic conventions. In autism and special education, surveys find methodological heterogeneity and clinician skepticism partly because benchmarks and models are not adapted to local contexts or neurodivergent profiles (Jaliaawala & Khan, 2020). When English-only or monocultural designs are deployed in multilingual communities, they can pathologize bilingual practices (e.g., code-switching) or non-Western communicative norms rather than supporting them—an especially acute risk in Indigenous and Global South settings (Gonzalez-Barrero & Nadig, 2021; Amante-Nochefranca et al., 2024).

Explainability and user studies centered on Western participants

A systematic analysis of explainable AI (XAI) user studies shows a strong over-reliance on Western participant samples and Western explanatory preferences, followed by overgeneralized claims about "human users." This risks building systems whose explanations and interfaces do not align with collectivist or non-Western sense-making practices (Peters & Carman, 2024). Such defaults limit uptake and trust, particularly in school and clinical contexts where interpretation and buy-in from families, teachers, and therapists are essential.

Implication: Without cultural localization and neurodiversity-aware assumptions, AI can nudge learners toward conformity with Western/monolingual standards—undermining linguistic rights and inclusive pedagogy (Tao et al., 2024; Peters & Carman, 2024).

Decolonial theory interrogates how coloniality persists in contemporary institutions, infrastructures, and epistemologies, and it offers strategies like epistemic disobedience, reverse pedagogies, and community sovereignty to re-center marginalized knowledge (Mohamed, Png, & Isaac, 2020; Traxler & Jandrić, 2025).

Critical disability studies (CDS) challenge medicalized, individual-deficit framings of ability and reframe disability as a product of social, cultural, and infrastructural arrangements. Integrating CDS with decolonial theory reveals how "ability" itself is historically constructed through colonial-modern norms of the "ideal" subject (Dirth & Adams, 2019; Kiwan, 2022).

Bringing these frameworks together yields concrete design principles for AI in language development:

1. **Epistemic plurality and linguistic sovereignty** o Treat Indigenous, African, and Global South languages as primary design targets rather than optional "localization." Protect community control over recordings and language corpora (Koole et al., 2024; Kohnke & Foung, 2024).
2. **Neurodiversity-affirming baselines** o Train and calibrate models on speech/ prosody attested among autistic and otherwise neurodivergent learners; avoid penalizing atypical prosody and code-switching; build feedback that is advisory, not punitive (Jaliaawala & Khan, 2020; Dirth & Adams, 2019).
3. **Human-in-the-loop and participatory co-design** o Include therapists, teachers, caregivers, Elders, and youth in iterative design; center their definitions of success (e.g., storytelling participation, joint attention) rather than narrow, decontextualized accuracy metrics (Mohamed et al., 2020; Koole et al., 2024).
4. **Justice-oriented governance** o Implement data sovereignty, purpose-bound consent, benefit-sharing, and low-bandwidth/offline functionality to counter infrastructural inequity—key to resisting data colonialism (Kohnke & Foung, 2024; Salami, 2024).

Result: Decolonial + CDS approaches move AI from enforcing normative assimilation to augmenting culturally and neurologically diverse language development.

HOW AI SYSTEMS USED IN AUTISM WORK (TECHNICAL FOUNDATIONS)

Advances in ASR acoustic modeling have been driven by deep learning architectures such as Conformer, QuartzNet, Whisper, and Transformer-based systems, which integrate acoustic and linguistic cues to improve robustness across noise conditions and multilingual settings. Contemporary reviews highlight how modern end-to-end acoustic models fuse or adapt external acoustic models to reduce domain mismatch and lower error rates, achieving significant performance gains across varied test sets. Comparative multilingual evaluations similarly demonstrate that even state-of-the-art ASR architectures experience sharp degradation under distortions like reverberation, white noise, and pitch-shift, revealing the continued need for acoustically resilient modeling.

In text-to-speech (TTS), neural models—such as WaveNet, Tacotron, FastSpeech, and Transformer-TTS—have largely replaced concatenative and parametric synthesis. These architectures enable highly natural prosody and human-like articulation through deep neural vocoders and end-to-end pipelines. scholarship emphasizes growing efforts to deploy neural TTS on edge devices, making synthesis feasible in low-latency and offline settings critical for assistive technologies (Gerazov et al., 2025).

For LLM adaptation, prompting and fine-tuning represent complementary strategies. Prompt-based approaches leverage frozen model parameters and rely on optimized soft prompts or carefully structured natural-language instructions to elicit task-aligned behavior efficiently (Parthasarathy et al., 2024). Fine-tuning, by contrast, updates model weights directly for domain-specific tasks and generally yields higher task fidelity, especially in specialized or high-stakes domains, as demonstrated in comparative evaluations of legal NER systems.

Finally, key evaluation metrics—including Word Error Rate (WER) and Character Error Rate (CER)—remain central for benchmarking ASR performance, with WER favored for word-segmented languages and CER for character-based scripts. Metrics such as AUC and F1 are widely used in classification-oriented tasks like event-speech recognition or NER, where precision–recall trade-offs shape system reliability.

Examples of bias in NLP and speech recognition tools

Bias is not abstract: it appears in measurable performance gaps, misclassifications, and misalignments that directly affect learners' experiences and outcomes.

Accent and dialect bias in ASR

Content analyses and empirical evaluations show that ASR performance varies substantially by accent/dialect. A recent review of ASR research documents how "accent" is often treated as a deviation from a default standard, with favoured performance on historically privileged accents and worse transcription for others (Prinos, Patwari, & Power, 2024). Experimental work further reveals disparities across English dialects (e.g., African American Vernacular English, Chicano English, Spanglish) and by gender, with compounded errors for women and for speakers of minoritized dialects—undermining fairness in downstream captioning and voice interfaces (Harris, Mgbahurike, Kumar, & Yang, 2024). These patterns mirror the broader point that default model assumptions map to dominant groups, marginalizing others.

Consequences for special education and autism

Surveys of AI interventions in autism note promise for engagement and access, but warn that non-standardized methods, limited clinical validation, and culturally unadapted models erode clinician trust and risk misinterpretation—particularly when prosody, affect, and pragmatics are scored against Western or neurotypical norms (Jaliaawala & Khan, 2020). In bilingual/Indigenous contexts, advising families to abandon the heritage language is not evidence-based; research indicates bilingual exposure does **not** worsen outcomes for autistic children, so English-only AI pathways can be both culturally harmful and scientifically unfounded (Gonzalez-Barrero & Nadig, 2021).

Takeaway: Bias appears at the levels of data, models, interfaces, outcomes, and deployment. Addressing it requires culturally grounded datasets, dialect-tolerant ASR/TTS, neurodiversity-aware targets, and participatory, sovereign data governance—not just post-hoc "debiasing."

TOWARD DECOLONIAL, DISABILITY-AFFIRMING AI FOR LANGUAGE DEVELOPMENT: PRACTICAL GUARDRAILS

1. **Language-first localization (beyond translation):** Build for Indigenous and local languages as primary use-cases. Support translanguaging UIs, code-switch-tolerant ASR, and community-authored lexicons (Nothias, 2025; Gonzalez-Barrero & Nadig, 2021).
2. **Outcome sets that matter locally:** Measure pragmatic participation (story retell, joint attention, turn-taking) alongside vocabulary scores; align dashboards to therapist- and community-valued goals (Jaliaawala & Khan, 2020; Koole et al., 2024).
3. **Human-in-the-loop validation:** Make AI feedback advisory; surface uncertainty; schedule periodic clinician/educator review to maintain trust and prevent overreliance (Peters & Carman, 2024; Jaliaawala & Khan, 2020).
4. **Data sovereignty and ethics:** Use purpose-bound consent, local control, benefit-sharing, and governance councils; resist extraction by ensuring communities set terms for collection and use (Kohnke & Foung, 2024; Salami, 2024).
5. **Low-bandwidth, offline-first engineering:** On-device inference and delayed sync help close access gaps that otherwise amplify inequality (Koole et al., 2024; Traxler & Jandrić, 2025).
6. **Iterative co-design with affected users:** Engage Elders, caregivers, therapists, and youth as co-authors of prompts, content, and evaluation—not just testers—so the tools express local pedagogies and values (Mohamed et al., 2020; Koole et al., 2024).

GLOBAL SOUTH PERSPECTIVES ON LANGUAGE AND DISABILITY

Case Study 1: Philippines (Vietnam Context Proxy)

AI-assisted ESL learning among high school students; cultural & infrastructural challenges; gendered perceptions of AI tools

Primary source: Amante Nochefranca et al. (2024)

Methodology Notes

Data Sources

- Survey responses from 200 senior high school students in the Zamboanga Peninsula.
- Quantitative Likert-scale items + qualitative reflections on AI-assisted English learning.
- Contextual demographic data (grade level, gender, digital access) collected for interpretation.

Study Limitations

- Self-reported perceptions rather than direct learning-outcome measures.
- Sample from a single Philippine region—limited generalizability to other provinces or to Vietnam (the proxy).
- No longitudinal tracking of language improvements; results reflect attitudes, not performance.
- Limited analysis of specific AI tool architectures or backend models.
- Connectivity constraints during data collection may have influenced student responses.

Tools / Interventions Used

- AI-assisted ESL applications on smartphones (pronunciation tools, grammar checkers, chatbot-style tutors).
- Digital learning apps providing instant corrective feedback.
- Mobile-based micro-learning platforms supporting self-paced vocabulary and speaking practice.

Context and Rationale

In the Zamboanga Peninsula of the southern Philippines, 200 senior high school students participated in a descriptive study on AI-assisted English language learning (AI-ALL). The study examined learner beliefs, challenges, and gendered perceptions regarding AI tools for English as a Second Language (ESL) (Amante-Nochefranca et al., 2024). Although situated in the Philippines, the sociotechnical conditions—limited connectivity, varied device access, and multilingual classroom realities—mirror those found in many parts of Vietnam, making this a useful proxy for Vietnam's K-12 contexts where AI-enabled language learning is gaining traction but faces infrastructural asymmetries.

AI-Assisted ESL Practices

Students reported generally positive beliefs about AI-assisted tools: they valued time-saving features, on-demand feedback, and the flexibility of mobile-based practice outside school hours. These perceptions align with the promise of personalized micro-scaffolding for vocabulary, pronunciation, and grammar delivered through chatbots and mobile apps (Amante-Nochefranca et al., 2024). Notably, learners recognized that smartphone-accessible tools extend learning beyond the classroom, supporting spaced practice and self-pacing in ways traditional instruction struggles to provide in large classes.

Cultural and Infrastructural Challenges

Despite optimism, two barriers dominated the learning experience:

1. **Connectivity Constraints:** Poor or unstable internet access produced the largest friction, elevating latency and disrupting feedback loops, a critical component of pronunciation coaching and dialogic practice. Students identified slow speeds as a substantial inhibitor to timely answers from AI systems (Amante-Nochefranca et al., 2024).
2. **Affordability and Usability:** Learners perceived a scarcity of cost-effective, high-quality AI apps and raised concerns about mobile data costs. While tools were viewed as generally user-friendly, usability could improve—especially for learners who juggle multiple apps or have limited digital literacy (Amante-Nochefranca et al., 2024).

Culturally, English learning intersects with multilingual identities (Cebuano/Chavacano/Tagalog/English). AI systems trained primarily on standardized English may misrecognize local pronunciation and code-switching, which risks penalizing multilingual norms rather than leveraging them. In practice, teachers can position AI outputs as *advisory* rather than *authoritative* to avoid stigmatizing local accents and to encourage metalinguistic awareness.

Gendered Perceptions of AI Tools

The study's comparative analysis found no significant gender differences across most belief items; both male and female students expressed positive attitudes toward AI-ALL. However, three areas revealed statistically significant differences: (a) perceptions of features that support or hinder AI-based learning, (b) beliefs about the availability of good smartphone AI apps for language learning, and (c) data cost sensitivity, with males more likely to agree that data costs are high (Amante-Nochefranca et al., 2024). These nuanced results suggest that while broad adoption is feasible across genders, cost transparency, offline functionality, and low-bandwidth modes may differentially influence engagement.

Implementation Insights (Transferable to Vietnam)

- **Design for Offline/Low-Bandwidth Use:** Caching lessons, enabling downloadable practice packs, and asynchronous scoring can maintain continuity when networks degrade (Amante-Nochefranca et al., 2024).
- **Mobile-First and Cost-Aware:** Since smartphones are the primary access point, lightweight apps with compressed audio and local data processing reduce recurring costs.
- **Teacher Mediation:** Integrate AI feedback with classroom formative assessment to calibrate expectations and mitigate overreliance on a single model's judgments.
- **Cultural/Linguistic Fit:** Incorporate localized examples, allow mother-tongue translanguaging bridges, and explicitly normalize accent diversity to avoid pathologizing non-standard varieties (Amante-Nochefranca et al., 2024).

Learning Outcomes

By the end of this case, readers will be able to:

1. **Analyze** how connectivity and affordability shape AI-assisted ESL adoption in secondary schools (Amante-Nochefranca et al., 2024).

2. **Evaluate** gender-related differences in beliefs about AI tools and infer design/implementation implications (Amante-Nochefranca et al., 2024).
3. **Propose** culturally responsive, low-bandwidth strategies for deploying AI-ALL in contexts similar to the Philippines and Vietnam (Amante-Nochefranca et al., 2024).

Discussion Questions

1. **Infrastructure & Equity:** If you had to deploy one AI-assisted ESL intervention in a low-connectivity district, which features would you prioritize (offline packs, SMS prompts, on-device ASR, etc.) and why? Ground your answer in findings from the Philippine cohort.
2. **Gendered Nuance:** The study found limited but notable gender differences (e.g., data cost sensitivity). What programmatic choices (pricing, device loans, data stipends) would you recommend to maximize equitable engagement?
3. **Culture & Pedagogy:** How can teachers mediate AI feedback to value local accents and translanguaging practices while still supporting intelligibility and exam-oriented proficiency?

Case Study 2: Kenya (Africa)

AI-assisted interventions for autism: clinical/classroom potential; methodological gaps; clinician skepticism; call for culturally adapted systems

Primary source: Jaliaawala & Khan (2020)

Methodology Notes

Data Sources

- Comprehensive survey of AI-assisted autism intervention studies across Africa.
- Literature review synthesizing empirical papers, technical benchmarks, and pilot deployments.
- Secondary data from computer-vision, robotics, and ML-based autism tools developed in African or Global South contexts.

Study Limitations

- Africa-focused evidence base is extremely limited; most AI for autism tools originate from Europe/US.
- Lack of standardized methodologies across studies prevented meta-analysis.
- Minimal documentation of ground-truthing procedures or clinical validation.

- Sparse region-specific datasets for training or evaluating autism-related models.
- Clinician skepticism noted but not evaluated through direct field observation.

Tools / Interventions Used

- Computer-vision social communication coaches (e.g., gaze/affect detection platforms).
- Machine-learning–based screening systems analyzing facial expressions, gestures, and prosody.
- Robotics-based interventions for turn-taking and joint attention.
- Tablet-based apps offering structured social-skills micro-practice.

Context and Rationale

Kenya's autism support ecosystem spans public hospitals, private clinics, special units in mainstream schools, and community-based organizations. As demand for assessment and intervention outpaces the number of trained specialists, AI-assisted technologies—computer-vision social skills coaches, speech recognition–based feedback, and adaptive learning apps—are being explored to extend reach and consistency of services. A comprehensive survey by Jaliaawala and Khan (2020) synthesized evidence across technology-based interventions (computer-aided systems, CV-assisted tools, VR/AR, and ML-enabled platforms), concluding that AI shows promise for engagement and skill acquisition in both clinical and classroom settings but the field suffers from non-standardized designs, limited clinician buy-in, and fragmented collaboration between computer scientists and therapists.

Vignette: Piloting AI in a Nairobi School

A Nairobi inclusive primary school partners with a local university lab to pilot a tablet-based social communication coach for learners aged 6–10. The app uses on-device computer vision to give real-time prompts about eye gaze, turn-taking, and facial affect during short conversation games. Teachers appreciate the structured micro-practice and automated progress logs. However, several issues appear within the first month:

- Methodological drift: Each class adapts the session length and goal hierarchy differently, making results non-comparable across students—mirroring the research heterogeneity highlighted by Jaliaawala & Khan (2020).

- Clinician skepticism: Visiting SLPs question the validity of algorithmic feedback and the absence of standardized outcome measures; they fear overreliance on the app may replace (rather than augment) human-led interaction.
- Cultural fit: The avatar's prompts and idioms are Eurocentric; affect models misread local display rules and children's diverse prosodies, reducing trust in the tool.
- Access & continuity: Intermittent connectivity and limited data bundles hinder updates and cloud syncing; some learners share devices at home, creating inconsistent intensity of practice.

These frictions echo the survey's conclusions: potential is clear, but methodological rigour, co-design, and contextualization are prerequisites for durable impact.

What Worked

- Teacher-mediated use: When teachers framed the app as practice between human-led sessions, students persisted longer and generalized greetings and joint attention to peer play.
- Low-bandwidth configuration: Enabling offline inference and delayed sync stabilized use in classes with sporadic Wi-Fi.
- Localized content sprint: A two-week co-design with Kenyan SLPs and teachers replaced idioms, names, and scenarios with locally meaningful ones (market scenes, matatu queues), improving engagement.

What Did Not Work

- Outcome fragmentation: Parallel use of different rating scales (teacher checklists, parent reports, app scores) without a common core made progress opaque.
- One-size-fits-all models: Affect detection trained on Western corpora misclassified neutral expressions as "flat" or "sad," undermining credibility—precisely the kind of bias and misfit that motivates calls for culturally adapted AI (Jaliaawala & Khan, 2020).

Implementation Guidance (Aligned to the Survey's Recommendations)

1. Standardize protocols before scale-up. Predefine session length, fidelity checks, and a minimal core outcome set (e.g., joint attention frequency, turn-taking

latency) to enable cross-class comparison—addressing the survey's concern about non-standard designs.

2. Interdisciplinary governance. Form a standing therapist–engineer working group to vet updates, outcome metrics, and privacy safeguards; this directly targets the collaboration gap identified in the survey.
3. Cultural/linguistic adaptation roadmap. Localize prompts (Swahili/English), calibrate models on locally gathered, consented samples, and allow teacher-editable feedback strings.
4. Human-in-the-loop by design. Make AI feedback advisory, not prescriptive; require periodic clinician validation to sustain professional trust and reduce skepticism noted by clinicians in the literature.
5. Offline-first engineering. On-device inference, downloadable practice packs, and delayed analytics upload mitigate connectivity and cost barriers common in Kenyan classrooms—an implementation reality in many African contexts, the survey reviews.

Learning Outcomes

By the end of this case, readers will be able to:

1. Summarize the potential and limits of AI-assisted autism interventions in African school/clinic settings, as reported in a comprehensive survey (Jaliaawala & Khan, 2020).
2. Diagnose sources of clinician skepticism and methodological variability and propose concrete remedies (core outcome sets, fidelity checks, advisory AI).
3. Design a culturally adapted, offline-capable AI intervention plan for Kenyan classrooms that embeds human-in-the-loop validation and interdisciplinary oversight.

Discussion Questions

1. Rigour vs. Reality: Given heterogeneous classrooms and variable clinician availability, which three protocol elements (e.g., session length, goal hierarchy, fidelity checklist) would you standardize first to enable credible evaluation, and why?
2. Building Trust: What design and workflow choices would you implement to address clinician skepticism—without stalling innovation (think: advisory feedback, validation windows, interpretable dashboards)?

3. Culture & Access: Outline a two-sprint localization plan (content + models) for a Nairobi pilot that also functions in low-connectivity counties. What data governance steps will you require?

Case Study 3: Indigenous Communities in Canada

Bilingualism and autism in Indigenous children

- Preserving linguistic heritage
- Implications for AI tool design

Primary source: Gonzalez-Barrero & Nadig (2021)
Methodology Notes
Data Sources

- Literature review synthesizing empirical studies on bilingualism and autism.
- Comparative analyses of bilingual vs. monolingual autistic children's language milestones (first words, vocabulary size, early combinations).
- Evidence from developmental psychology, speech-language pathology, and bilingual acquisition research.

Study Limitations

- Not specific to Indigenous languages—research mostly covers global bilingual contexts.
- Very few autism studies conducted directly within First Nations, Métis, or Inuit communities.
- Limited data on heritage-language phonology, code-switching norms, or culturally grounded pragmatic skills.
- No AI tools evaluated in Indigenous-language contexts; extrapolations are theoretical.

Tools / Interventions Used

- Not empirical tools; rather implications for AI design, including:
    - o Translanguaging-friendly AI features (dual-language prompts, heritage-language support).
    - o ASR/TTS models adapted to Indigenous phonology.
    - o Community-authored story-based language resources for future AI integration.

- o Proposals for AI systems aligned with OCAP® data governance practices.

Context and Rationale

Across First Nations, Inuit, and Métis territories, many children grow up in bilingual or multilingual homes—e.g., Cree–English, Inuktut–English, Anishinaabemowin–English—where language carries kinship terms, oral histories, and land-based knowledge. In clinical and school settings, caregivers of autistic children are sometimes advised to "stick to one language," typically English, to avoid confusion. The empirical synthesis by Gonzalez-Barrero and Nadig (2021) directly challenges this assumption: bilingual exposure does not lead to additional language delay in children on the autism spectrum; early milestones (first words, onset of word combinations) and rates of early vocabulary growth are, on average, comparable to those of monolingual autistic peers. Maintaining the heritage language may also confer social and familial benefits by sustaining intergenerational bonds, cultural participation, and opportunities for richer pragmatic input (Gonzalez-Barrero & Nadig, 2021).

Classroom Snapshot

A Grade 1 class in a Cree-speaking community school integrates daily circle time with Elders, storywork, and song. One 6-year-old autistic child, "W," alternates between Cree kinship terms and English nouns during picture-book narration. When teachers pilot an AI-assisted vocabulary app (English-only) for home practice, W's Cree utterances are flagged as "incorrect," and the app's pronunciation model gives low confidence scores for W's atypical prosody—common in autism—further discouraging use. Family members note that W becomes less talkative during story time, preferring nonverbal participation. The team reconsiders tool choice and co-designs a translanguaging-friendly setup for the next term.

Why Preserving Linguistic Heritage Matters

For Indigenous Nations, language is a living archive of law, ceremony, ecological knowledge, and ethics of relationality. Reducing heritage-language exposure can narrow a child's opportunities to rehearse pragmatic competencies—turn-taking, perspective-taking, narrative structure—embedded in storytelling, feasts, and land-based routines. Since bilingualism does not worsen core language outcomes in autism, shifting to English-only approaches lacks developmental justification and risks cultural disconnection (Gonzalez-Barrero & Nadig, 2021). Therapy targets such as joint attention, symbolic play, and conversational repair can be pursued through heritage language activities (e.g., call-and-response songs, storytelling with Elders), maintaining identity and belonging.

Implications for AI Tool Design

1. **Translanguaging-aware experiences:** AI interfaces should enable fluid movement between languages (UI labels, prompts, captions) and accept code-switching without penalizing mixed utterances. Custom lexicons should include local kinship, place names, and ceremonial vocabulary authored by community language holders (Gonzalez-Barrero & Nadig, 2021).
2. **Speech tech tolerant of accent, dialect, and atypical prosody:** ASR/TTS should be calibrated for local phonology and for prosodic profiles common in autistic speech. When confidence is low, systems should gracefully degrade—offering visual choices, alternative cues, or caregiver-mediated confirmation—rather than marking responses "wrong."
3. **Community-governed data:** Any recordings (child speech, story corpora) should follow Indigenous data governance (e.g., OCAP® principles where applicable), with purpose-bound consent, local control, and benefit-sharing. Tool updates should be reviewed by a community advisory circle to ensure respectful use of language materials.
4. **Offline-first, low-bandwidth delivery:** Many rural and remote regions face intermittent connectivity. Downloadable "practice packs," on-device inference for basic ASR/TTS, and delayed-sync analytics can sustain engagement without continuous internet.
5. **Culturally congruent progress metrics:** Dashboards should **value pragmatics** (e.g., successful participation in call-and-response, narrative sequencing, use of kinship terms in context) alongside English vocabulary counts—aligning with pedagogies rooted in story and land (Gonzalez-Barrero & Nadig, 2021).

Learning Outcomes

By the end of this case, readers will be able to:

1. **Explain** why bilingual exposure does not harm early language milestones in autistic children and articulate the social benefits of heritage-language maintenance (Gonzalez-Barrero & Nadig, 2021).
2. **Identify** risks of English-only AI tools for Indigenous learners and propose safeguards that uphold linguistic sovereignty (Gonzalez-Barrero & Nadig, 2021).

3. **Design** concrete AI features (translanguaging UI, dialect-tolerant ASR/TTS, offline practice packs) aligned with Indigenous language revitalization and inclusive therapy goals.

Discussion Questions

1. **Clinical Guidance:** If a family is encouraged to "drop" the heritage language to help their autistic child, how would you respond using current evidence, and how could an AI tool reinforce your advice in daily routines?
2. **Design Challenge:** List three specific AI features that would normalize code-switching during an Elder-led story session and describe how each supports pragmatic language targets.
3. **Data Sovereignty:** Your team wants to fine-tune a pronunciation model with local story recordings. What permissions, storage choices, and benefit-sharing agreements are essential before collecting any data?

Table 1. Promises and perils across three case studies

Case Study	Promises	Perils
Philippines (Vietnam Proxy)	Improved ESL practice, motivation, and extended learning	Connectivity barriers, affordability, cultural mismatch, and gendered perceptions
Kenya (Africa)	Scalable therapy; structured micro-practice; reduced clinician workload	Non-standard methods; clinician skepticism; cultural misalignment; connectivity issues
Indigenous Communities in Canada	Supports bilingualism; culturally grounded pedagogy; translanguaging-friendly	Linguistic erasure risk; ASR bias; data sovereignty concerns; misalignment

Cross-Context Implementation Challenges

In many global education and clinical settings, inconsistent connectivity remains one of the most significant barriers to equitable AI adoption. Studies on offline and low-bandwidth educational systems show that unreliable or costly internet access severely limits the usability of AI-driven language and learning tools, making cloud-dependent systems inaccessible in rural or under-resourced communities (Nimbalkar et al., 2025). This challenge directly undermines continuity of learning and restricts opportunities for students who rely on AI for language practice, communication, or assistive support.

Closely linked is the problem of device inequity. Systematic reviews of AI in education emphasize that students' unequal access to smartphones, tablets, or laptops—combined with differing levels of digital readiness—creates stratified learning outcomes and reduces the effectiveness of AI-enhanced instruction. Without intentional provisioning or school-level infrastructure, AI tools can inadvertently widen existing educational gaps.

For clinicians supporting autistic learners, AI introduces both opportunities and burdens. Ethical analyses of AI in healthcare note that clinician workload may increase when systems require oversight, validation, and troubleshooting—especially when models are insufficiently transparent or generate errors requiring manual correction (Wiener et al., 2025). In autism contexts, where interpretation of nuanced behavioral data is essential, clinicians may face additional cognitive load to ensure AI outputs align with developmental realities.

Finally, teacher training gaps present a structural challenge. Research on AI in schools highlights that many educators lack foundational AI literacy, leaving them uncertain about data practices, risks, and pedagogical integration. This lack of preparedness undermines responsible adoption and can fuel mistrust of AI systems (Shukla et al., 2025). Comprehensive professional development is therefore essential to ensure safe, informed, and effective use of AI tools

ETHICAL AND PEDAGOGICAL CONSIDERATIONS

Data sovereignty and privacy in marginalized communities

Deploying AI for language development with children who are autistic and/or disabled in marginalized communities raises more than routine privacy concerns; it invokes collective rights over knowledge, recordings, and stories. First Nations in Canada articulate these rights through the OCAP® principles—Ownership, Control, Access, and Possession—which assert that First Nations determine how data about them is collected, used, stored, and shared, and that communities must retain practical control (possession) to make ownership meaningful. Any AI project that collects child speech, caregiver narratives, or community language corpora should treat OCAP® as baseline governance rather than an optional ethic-of-care add-on.

OCAP® emerged as a direct response to extractive research and surveillance that served external institutions more than communities; its purpose is to transition from data about to data by/for communities. The framework clarifies that First Nations' data include language, song, stories, oral histories, and other cultural knowledge—

materials that many speech/NLP projects would otherwise treat as "free" training inputs. Respecting OCAP®, therefore, means purpose-bound consent, community governance boards, and local stewardship (e.g., community-controlled servers or escrow with access logs).

These requirements sit within broader critiques of digital and data colonialism, which show how platform infrastructures and AI supply chains concentrate control and extract value from the Global South and Indigenous communities under the banner of innovation. In education and EdTech, learning analytics and predictive systems can normalize appropriation of learners' data as a "resource," unless governance is redesigned to center reciprocity and equity. Practically, this entails co-authored data management plans, benefit-sharing agreements, and the right to refuse or revoke participation without penalty.

For research institutions and school systems, OCAP® can be operationalized alongside Indigenous data sovereignty toolkits that explain sovereignty as authority over how data are framed, governed, and interpreted—not merely secured. This perspective extends to language AI: labelling schemes, error heuristics, and feedback messages are interpretive choices that should be governed locally. Ethics review should thus ask, "Whose ontology structures the dataset and outputs?" and "Who holds decision rights over model updates?" rather than only "Is the dataset de-identified?"

Actionable guardrails:

- Establish nation-specific protocols (e.g., OCAP® agreements or equivalent Indigenous data sovereignty frameworks) before any recording, with purpose-bound consent, revocation rights, time-bound retention, and local custody.
- Form a Community Data Council (Elders, caregivers, youth, SLPs, teachers) with veto rights on model use, dataset composition, and publication. This answers recognized risks of extractive data practices in EdTech and AI.

Safeguarding sensitive developmental, behavioural, and clinical data is central to ethical AI use in autism contexts. Encryption is a foundational security measure because AI systems in education and healthcare face documented risks of data leakage, privacy invasion, and unauthorized surveillance. Systematic reviews of AI ethics in education and clinical environments highlight that insecure data flows and inadequate technical safeguards significantly increase vulnerability to breaches, especially when sensitive learner information is processed by opaque algorithms

(Wiener et al., 2025). Encryption—both at rest and in transit—reduces attack surfaces but is only effective when paired with governance mechanisms.

In autism screening and intervention, purpose-bound consent is essential because developmental data can reveal highly sensitive information about communication patterns, behaviour, family routines, or diagnostic pathways. Ethical analyses emphasize that AI systems must ensure consent that is not blanket or perpetual but tied to a clearly defined purpose, allowing families to control how data are used and prevent repurposing for surveillance, prediction, or commercial exploitation (Wiener et al., 2025).

To further mitigate risk, local storage—on secure school/clinic servers or encrypted local devices—offers protection from unauthorized third-party access. Scholars in AI-in-education caution that cloud infrastructures introduce additional layers of exposure, including infrastructure-level and insider-threat risks (Billiris et al., 2025).

Consequently, relying on cloud-based AI tools in schools and clinics carries substantial risks. These include privacy invasion, surveillance creep, and the possibility of algorithmic misuse by external vendors lacking educational or clinical accountability (Shukla et al., 2025). Cloud systems may also retain or infer personal data beyond the original scope of use, raising concerns about data sovereignty, compliance, and long-term trust.

Accessibility and affordability of AI tools

Ethically sound AI must also be *usable* under real constraints. In many Indigenous, rural, and low-income urban contexts, connectivity is intermittent, and data are expensive. Offline-first and low-bandwidth engineering (on-device inference, downloadable "practice packs," delayed synchronization) is not a technical flourish; it is an equity requirement to avoid further stratifying access to language interventions. Peer-reviewed and scholarly assessments emphasize that offline/PWA capabilities, lightweight media, and local caching can sustain participation where constant connectivity is unrealistic.

Evidence from inclusive and special education technology research similarly notes that accessibility hinges on universal design, multi-format delivery (captions, TTS, transcripts), and device-agnostic interfaces—especially when learners rely on older smartphones. As accessibility advocates in higher education warn, communities who stand to benefit most from AI (e.g., learners with disabilities) are often least able to use it when developers do not consult them, and when tools presume high-end bandwidth/hardware. Participatory accessibility reviews and human-in-the-loop corrections (e.g., editable captions) address this gap.

Affordability is also sociotechnical. Surveys in developing-country ESL contexts report that students perceive AI tools as time-saving and flexible but costly in data terms; smartphone access without affordable data blunts the benefits. For K-12 deployments, the ethical baseline should include data-light modes (compressed audio, adjustable sampling rates), transparent data meters, and institutional data stipends negotiated with network providers. These programmatic moves directly respond to cost and connectivity barriers surfaced in school-based AI pilots.

Finally, "access" includes interpretability. If dashboards are opaque composites, teachers and caregivers cannot evaluate whether feedback is trustworthy or usable. Reviews of explainable AI warn that most user studies assume Western explanatory norms and then generalize, risking misfit with local sense-making. Design should therefore offer multiple explanation styles (narrative, exemplar-based, rule-of-thumb) and allow teachers to choose what resonates with their classroom discourse.

Actionable guardrails:

- Ship offline-first builds by default (on-device ASR/TTS where feasible; pre-downloaded modules; sync-when-online).
- Audit total cost of learning (device, data, time) and budget for data subsidies where needed; include built-in low-data toggles and visible usage meters.
- Provide multi-modal accessibility (captions, transcripts, TTS, keyboard navigation) and co-test with disabled users to avoid performative compliance.

PARTICIPATORY DESIGN: INVOLVING CAREGIVERS, EDUCATORS, AND CHILDREN

Ethically responsible AI in language development must be designed with—not merely for—its users. Participatory design (PD) approaches demonstrate how co-creation with children, caregivers, educators, clinicians, and Elders surfaces tacit priorities (e.g., the value of storytelling, norms for turn-taking) that conventional requirements capture poorly. Recent PD work on child-centred AI shows that children themselves articulate distinct rights and hopes for AI in their learning futures; tooling (e.g., co-design stories kits) can translate these perspectives into actionable interface and policy choices.

In special education and rehabilitation, participatory strategies grounded in frameworks like the Capability Approach prioritize what learners can be and do, aligning technical affordances with flourishing rather than solely with impairment remediation. Case studies in educational/clinical AI show that cross-stakeholder design (teachers, therapists, technologists, ethicists) clarifies success criteria, scaffolding needs, and boundary conditions for safe use. PD is not a luxury; it is an ethical method to balance innovation with accountability.

Systematic reviews underscore that for autistic children, participatory and inclusive design aligned with universal design principles is essential because traditional data collection (surveys, lab tasks) may not capture sensory needs, interaction preferences, or communication differences. PD methods (observational co-creation, prototype play) help de-center neurotypical defaults in AI interfaces and reduce abandonment.

Within school teams, early involvement of SLPs and special educators is also key. Reviews and conference studies of SLP workflows demonstrate opportunities for AI to reduce documentation burden and generate useful summaries—if clinicians validate outputs and retain editorial control. Otherwise, professional trust erodes and adoption stalls. Co-designing documentation "prompts," templates, and validation windows with SLPs keeps AI advisory and preserves clinician judgment.

Actionable guardrails:

- Budget and schedule for co-design sprints with caregivers, educators, clinicians, Elders, and children; treat PD as part of risk mitigation, not outreach.
- Use methods appropriate to autism and disability (artifact-mediated sessions, observation, prototype play); avoid relying solely on questionnaires.
- Formalize human-in-the-loop checkpoints (e.g., fortnightly review of AI feedback with SLPs/teachers) so automation never overrides professional or family wisdom.

ETHICAL DILEMMAS IN AUTOMATED DIAGNOSIS AND THERAPY

From promising accuracy to clinical validity

Systematic reviews and meta-analyses report encouraging performance for AI systems classifying autism using facial features, gaze, and behavioural signals in structured contexts. Yet they also emphasize methodological heterogeneity, small samples, and limited validation across demographics—conditions that risk inflated accuracy and poor generalization in real clinics and classrooms. Ethical prudence requires distinguishing *algorithmic discrimination* from *clinical discrimination*: a model can achieve high AUC in lab settings while still disadvantaging populations underrepresented in its training data.

Bias, cultural misfit, and neurotypical benchmarks

Culturally unadapted models can misread affect, prosody, and interaction style—penalizing learners whose communicative norms differ from Western baselines.

Evidence from ASR and NLP shows consistent accent/dialect bias, with higher error rates for minoritized dialects and compounded disparities for women. In educational therapy apps, such misrecognitions can cascade into incorrect scoring and demotivating feedback. Similarly, LLM outputs carry Western cultural bias by default unless culturally prompted, which has implications for prompts, examples, and conversational agents used in therapy.

For bilingual and Indigenous families, the literature shows no evidence that bilingual exposure harms language milestones in autism; English-only advice—when ported into AI tools—thus risks cultural harm without a scientific basis. Ethical AI should normalize translanguaging and avoid framing heritage language usage as "error."

Autonomy, consent, and the developmental subject

Children are not miniature adults. Consent in automated screening/therapy must be an ongoing process that includes child assent practices appropriate to the developmental level, plus family-controlled toggles for data sharing, model retraining, and feature activation. Reviews of generative-AI applications in ASD warn about hallucinations, over-trust, and sparse comparative baselines; these risks intensify when tools act as quasi-authorities in caregiver decision-making. Systems should expose uncertainty, route worrisome suggestions to clinicians, and avoid "diagnostic theatre" that mimics expertise without accountability.

Documentation, surveillance, and secondary use

Automating documentation can save time but also raises risks of function creep—where notes and recordings, gathered for pedagogy or therapy, become input for performance audits or insurer disputes. Interdisciplinary studies with SLPs recommend designing documentation AI around fluidity goals (contextual, assessment, individual) and making clinician control explicit in the interface (approve/edit/reject with rationale). This protects therapeutic relationships and aligns with professional standards.

Implementation justice: who benefits, who bears risk?

Even when AI assists engagement, the distribution of benefits can skew toward well-resourced schools (better devices, connectivity, staff capacity for PD). Reviews of special-education AI stress the need for policy scaffolds, training, and rigorous evidence before scale-up; otherwise, automation may widen inequities under the guise of innovation. Embedding affordability (subsidies, device sharing programs), offline functionality, and teacher professional learning is thus both a moral and practical necessity.

Actionable guardrails:

- Treat algorithmic outputs as *adjunctive signals*—never sole bases for diagnosis or eligibility; require clinical/educational corroboration and publish validation reports by subgroup (age, gender, language, dialect).
- Implement uncertainty disclosure (confidence ranges, "unknown" states), escalation paths to human experts, and red-flag filters for hallucination-prone generative responses.
- Build translanguaging-aware scoring and content; preemptively disable punitive feedback on mixed-language utterances.
- Anchor documentation AI in clinician authority (approve/edit/reject), with audit trails and local storage aligned to community governance.

PUTTING IT TOGETHER: A PRACTICAL ETHICAL BLUEPRINT FOR AI IN LANGUAGE DEVELOPMENT

Governance & Sovereignty

1. Execute OCAP®/Indigenous data sovereignty agreements (or local equivalents) prior to any data collection; define ownership, control, access, and possession explicitly in contracts.
2. Create a Community–School–Clinic Governance Circle with decision rights over datasets, labelling schemes, releases, and research publications.

Design & Participation

3. Run participatory co-design sprints with children, caregivers, teachers, Elders, and clinicians; convert outputs into UI stories, content libraries, and evaluation criteria.
4. Adopt universal design and accessibility-first specifications; budget for iterative usability testing with disabled users and provide multiple explanation styles.

Models & Measurement

5. Localize models (dialect-tolerant ASR/TTS; culture-aware prompts) and publish subgroup performance; include translanguaging support to avoid penalizing bilingual usage.
6. Standardize core outcome sets (e.g., joint attention, turn-taking latency, narrative sequencing) with fidelity checks to counter research heterogeneity and support credible evaluation.

Affordability & Access

7. Engineer offline-first operation with on-device inference and delayed sync; disclose data use; negotiate data subsidies with local providers.

Accountability & Care

8. Enforce human-in-the-loop oversight for diagnostic inferences and goal changes; expose uncertainty; require periodic clinician/educator review and family consent refresh.

FRAMEWORK FOR INCLUSIVE AI-ASSISTED LANGUAGE DEVELOPMENT

Aim. Provide an evidence-informed blueprint for designing, deploying, and governing AI that advances language development for autistic and disabled learners while honouring cultural-linguistic rights and safeguarding community data. (Koole et al., 2024; Kohnke & Foung, 2024)

Principles

1) Cultural Responsiveness

Definition. Cultural responsiveness means AI systems are conceived, built, and evaluated with the local histories, values, languages, and pedagogies of learners and their communities—not "localized" after the fact. (Koole et al., 2024; Nothias, 2025)

This counters patterns of digital/data colonialism through which Northern platforms and analytics norms are exported as universal defaults in education technologies. (Kohnke & Foung, 2024; Nothias, 2025)

Why it matters for language development. Large language models and conversational tools exhibit a measurable "cultural gravity" toward English-speaking/ Protestant European value patterns unless explicitly steered, which can misalign prompts, examples, and feedback with local communicative norms. (Tao, Viberg, Baker, & Kizilcec, 2024)

Explainable-AI user research is also dominated by Western samples and explanatory preferences, limiting trust and usability for non-Western learners and families. (Peters & Carman, 2024)

Design guardrails. Treat cultural adaptation as a first-order requirement, embedding community-authored content (stories, kinship terms, local pragmatics) into training/evaluation while offering explanation styles (narrative, rule-of-thumb, exemplar) that match local sense-making. (Peters & Carman, 2024; Koole et al., 2024)

Use participatory design with children, caregivers, teachers, Elders, and therapists to surface tacit priorities; child-centred AI work shows children articulate distinctive rights and expectations that reshape interface and governance choices. (Wilson, Atabey, & Revans, 2025)

Success indicators. Documented co-design cycles; community satisfaction with cultural fit; subgroup performance/usability metrics reported by locale; community-editable content libraries. (Wilson et al., 2025; Koole et al., 2024)

2) Linguistic Diversity

Definition. Linguistic diversity means AI systems support multilingualism and translanguaging (fluid movement across languages) in content, UI, and assessment—especially vital for Indigenous and Global South communities. (Gonzalez-Barrero & Nadig, 2021; Koole et al., 2024)

Why it matters for autism and disability. The empirical synthesis indicates that bilingual exposure does not cause additional language delay for autistic children; advising families to abandon a heritage language is not supported by evidence and can harm social participation. (Gonzalez-Barrero & Nadig, 2021)

In parallel, ASR systems show systematic accent/dialect and gender disparities that can penalize non-standard varieties and female speakers, degrading feedback in therapy and classrooms. (Harris, Mgbahurike, Kumar, & Yang, 2024; Prinos, Patwari, & Power, 2024)

Design guardrails. Build translanguaging-aware experiences (dual-language prompts/captions, code-switch-tolerant ASR/TTS, bilingual caregiver coaching). (Gonzalez-Barrero & Nadig, 2021)

Publish dialect/variety-specific error analyses and parity targets; measure compounded effects across gender and dialect. (Harris et al., 2024; Prinos et al., 2024)

Success indicators. Mixed-language input accepted without penalty; narrowed WER/CER gaps across dialects/genders; caregiver reports of continued heritage-language use in daily routines. (Harris et al., 2024; Gonzalez-Barrero & Nadig, 2021)

3) Community Co-Creation

Definition. Community co-creation goes beyond user testing to shared decision rights over goals, datasets, model updates, deployments, and publications. (Koole et al., 2024; Kohnke & Foung, 2024)

Data governance. For First Nations in Canada, OCAP®—Ownership, Control, Access, Possession—asserts that Nations hold authority over collection, framing, storage, and sharing; language/speech datasets should be governed with local custody and purpose-bound consent. (First Nations Information Governance Centre, n.d.; University of Ottawa Library, 2022)

Why it matters. Learning analytics often normalizes extraction by treating student data as a "resource"; community governance redirects data flows toward reciprocal benefit and protection. (Kohnke & Foung, 2024; Koole et al., 2024)

Success indicators. Signed data-sovereignty agreements (OCAP®/equivalent), community data councils with veto rights, benefit-sharing arrangements, and public logs of governance decisions. (First Nations Information Governance Centre, n.d.; Kohnke & Foung, 2024)

4) Transparency and Accountability

Definition. Transparency means intelligible disclosures of data sources, training procedures, subgroup performance, and uncertainty; accountability adds binding processes for oversight, redress, and human-in-the-loop control. (Peters & Carman, 2024; Sun et al., 2025)

Why it matters. Reviews of AI for autism assessment/intervention show strong lab-setting performance but highlight small samples, heterogeneity, and limited validation—conditions that inflate accuracy and threaten generalizability if outputs are trusted uncritically. (Sun et al., 2025; Rakotomanana & Rouhafzay, 2025)

XAI research warns against "one-size-fits-all" explanations; transparency should therefore be plural (narratives for caregivers, exemplars for clinicians, policy summaries for administrators). (Peters & Carman, 2024)

Success indicators. Public model cards with subgroup metrics (age, gender, language/dialect), UI-level uncertainty displays, clinician/teacher approval flows for goal changes, and periodic third-party audits. (Sun et al., 2025; Peters & Carman, 2024)

Figure 1. Framework for inclusive AI-assisted language development

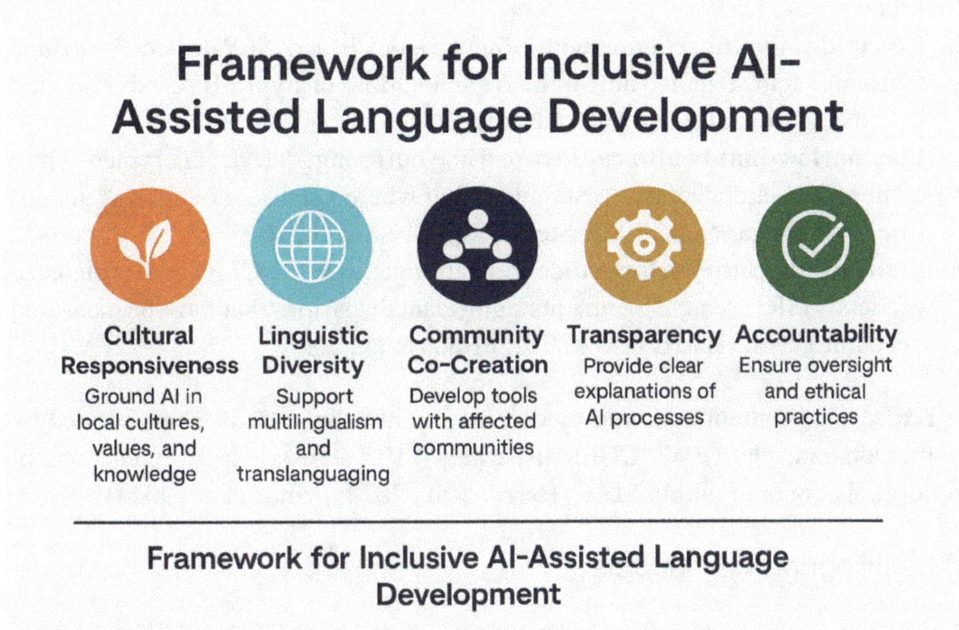

Implementation Strategies

A) Localized Datasets

Rationale. Bias originates in data selection and labelling; even sophisticated debiasing falters if corpora underrepresent local dialects, prosodies, and classroom routines. (Prinos et al., 2024; Harris et al., 2024)

Cultural-heritage scholarship shows AI can inherit and amplify historical prejudices encoded in archives and annotation schemas, requiring interdisciplinary mitigation—not technical fixes alone. (Foka, Griffin, Ortiz Pablo, Rajkowska, & Badri, 2025)

Steps.

1. **Map communicative ecologies** (languages/dialects, settings, interaction genres, pragmatic targets) via co-design workshops; child-centred AI research demonstrates effective toolkits for eliciting children's perspectives. (Wilson et al., 2025)
2. **Establish sovereignty and consent** with OCAP®/equivalent agreements specifying ownership, control, access, possession, retention, and revocation

rights. (First Nations Information Governance Centre, n.d.; University of Ottawa Library, 2022)

3. **Co-create labeling schemes** with bilingual aides/Elders/SLPs/teachers; include translanguaging tags and **non-punitive** annotations of atypical prosody common in autism. (Gonzalez-Barrero & Nadig, 2021)
4. **Plan for low-bandwidth capture** (offline buffering, delayed encrypted sync); offline/PWA architectures sustain learning where persistent internet is unrealistic. (Nimbalkar et al., 2025; Stelea, Robu, & Sandu, 2025)
5. **Publish subgroup performance** and parity gaps (WER/CER) across dialects/genders; ASR research documents significant disparities that must be measured to be mitigated. (Harris et al., 2024; Prinos et al., 2024)

KPIs. % of content authored by community members; % of labels created by local annotators; relative WER/CER disparities $\leq$ 10% across dialect/gender; consent withdrawals honored within SLA. (Harris et al., 2024; Prinos et al., 2024)

B) Multilingual NLP Models

Rationale. LLMs and ASR/TTS engines default to Western cultural values and standard English variants unless adapted; inclusive language development requires multilingual/translanguaging capabilities in both generation and recognition. (Tao et al., 2024; Peters & Carman, 2024)

Modeling tactics.

1. **Translanguaging-aware ASR/TTS** trained/fine-tuned with mixed-language utterances; allow mid-utterance switches without penalization; surface confidence + language segmentation for teacher/caregiver validation. (Gonzalez-Barrero & Nadig, 2021)
2. **Cultural prompting + guardrails** to reduce Western bias in generative outputs, an approach shown to improve alignment across many locales. (Tao et al., 2024)
3. **Plural explainability** (narrative/exemplar/rule-based) to match local sense-making. (Peters & Carman, 2024)
4. **On-device inference** or edge pipelines for equity in low-bandwidth environments. (Nimbalkar et al., 2025)

Validation. Evaluate on local test sets with code-switching and atypical prosody; publish WER/CER and pragmatic task success (e.g., correct identification of turn-taking cues) by subgroup; require external replication before scale-up. (Harris et al., 2024; Sun et al., 2025)

C) Teacher Training Programs

Rationale. AI can reduce SLP/teacher burden (documentation, progress tracking), but adoption falters when outputs are opaque or clinicians fear displacement; training must preserve human authority and focus on pedagogical orchestration. (Suh, Dangol, Meadan, Miller, & Kientz, 2024; Zheng et al., 2025)

Program architecture.

1. **Co-constructed competencies:** selecting culturally congruent AI activities; interpreting uncertainty/confidence; integrating feedback into IEP/therapy goals; safeguarding data sovereignty in classrooms. (Suh et al., 2024; Kohnke & Foung, 2024) [
2. **Practice-embedded PD:** plan–enact–reflect cycles with short classroom videos reviewed alongside AI logs in communities of practice; this cadence sustains trust and calibrates models to real practice. (Suh et al., 2024)
3. **Accessibility-first routines:** enable captions, transcripts, TTS, keyboard navigation; disability advocates warn the very communities who benefit most are too rarely consulted. (Gibson, 2024)
4. **Assessment literacy:** interpret subgroup metrics and avoid over-reliance on scores; diagnostic reviews urge validation before educational reliance. (Sun et al., 2025; Rakotomanana & Rouhafzay, 2025).

Certification & incentives. Recognize micro-credentials tied to artifacts (lesson plans, consent templates, subgroup analyses) and link completion to device/data subsidies to align equity with practice. (Suh et al., 2024; Kohnke & Foung, 2024)

D) Policy Alignment with UNCRPD and SDGs

Rationale. The UNCRPD affirms rights to accessible information and inclusive education; the SDGs commit to quality education, reduced inequalities, and strong institutions. Aligning AI programs to these instruments strengthens legitimacy when paired with scholarly evidence on accessibility, equity, and accountability. (Koole et al., 2024; Kohnke & Foung, 2024)

Policy–practice bridges.

1. **Accessibility & affordability (UNCRPD Art. 9; SDG 4).** Mandate offline-first operation, multi-modal access, and total-cost reviews; offline/PWA and accessibility-first studies show these are practical and necessary. (Nimbalkar et al., 2025; Stelea et al., 2025

2. **Data governance (UNCRPD Art. 22; SDG 16).** Recognize Indigenous data sovereignty (OCAP®) in procurement and funding; require community governance and benefit-sharing for language/speech datasets. (First Nations Information Governance Centre, n.d.; University of Ottawa Library, 2022)
3. **Cultural & linguistic rights (UNCRPD Art. 30; SDG 10).** Fund translanguaging features and dialect-tolerant ASR/TTS; bilingual autism findings and ASR disparities justify these as equity, not extras. (Gonzalez-Barrero & Nadig, 2021; Harris et al., 2024)
4. **Evidence & accountability (SDG 16).** Require model cards with subgroup metrics and third-party audits prior to any use in eligibility/placement decisions; diagnostic meta-analyses urge rigorous validation. (Sun et al., 2025)

POLICY AND PRACTICE RECOMMENDATIONS

Ethical AI Adoption in Special Education

Developing and deploying AI for language development in special education demands a multilayered ethical framework grounded in equity, cultural responsiveness, data sovereignty, and neurodiversity-affirming principles. Research on digital colonialism in education demonstrates that without explicit safeguards, AI systems can perpetuate extractive data practices, Western-centric norms, and biased learning analytics—reproducing educational inequities rather than alleviating them (Kohnke & Foung, 2024; Koole et al., 2024). Likewise, empirical analyses of LLMs and ASR systems show systematic cultural, dialect, and gender biases that risk penalizing disabled learners and those from multilingual or Indigenous communities (Tao et al., 2024; Harris et al., 2024). Therefore, ethical adoption must begin with safeguards in four areas: data governance, equitable access, inclusive model design, and human-centered oversight.

First, data governance must follow Indigenous Data Sovereignty protocols (e.g., OCAP®), which assert community ownership, control, access, and possession of data—an essential guardrail against extractive practices involving children's speech, cultural materials, or community narratives (First Nations Information Governance Centre, n.d.). Second, equitable access requires offline-first and low-bandwidth design so that learners in rural or under-resourced settings can use AI tools without constant internet connectivity; studies on inclusive and accessible e-learning emphasize that these architectures are not optional but foundational to equity (Nimbalkar et al., 2025; Stelea et al., 2025). Third, inclusive model design requires dialect-tolerant ASR/TTS, translanguaging support, and disabling punitive scoring around bilingual speech, especially given research showing that bilingualism does not adversely affect autistic children's language development (Gonzalez-Barrero & Nadig, 2021). Finally, human-in-the-loop oversight is essential because autism-related diagnostic AI often demonstrates inflated accuracy in controlled settings but limited validation in real-world populations (Sun et al., 2025; Rakotomanana & Rouhafzay, 2025).

Reference Checklist for Educators

Before Using an AI Tool

1. Verify data privacy protections
2. Check whether the tool works offline
3. Confirm accessibility features
4. Review cultural and linguistic fit
5. Ensure human oversight

During Classroom Use

1. Watch for over-reliance—students may defer to AI even when outputs are inaccurate.
2. Monitor how feedback is interpreted by autistic or disabled learners who may take AI directions literally.
3. Integrate AI into structured routines, not as a standalone replacement for instruction.

After Use

1. Audit outputs for bias, misrecognition, or harmful patterns.
2. Delete or archive data according to local retention rules and community data-sovereignty agreements.

Red Flags when using AI with Autistic Learners

- ASR misrecognition of atypical prosody
- Literal or rigid interpretations of AI
- Emotion or affect-detection tools making inaccurate inferences
- Tools requiring constant connectivity
- Cloud-based systems storing sensitive recordings without purpose-bound consent
- Automated "progress scores" lacking clinical validation

- AI that overrides caregiver or clinician input

Recommendations for Educators

1. **Prioritize Culturally and Linguistically Responsive Use:** Educators should adopt AI tools that support dual-language prompts, code-switching, and culturally grounded examples. Because LLMs default to Western cultural patterns without guidance (Tao et al., 2024), teachers should apply cultural prompting and select interfaces that allow customization to local linguistic norms.
2. **Implement Human-in-the-Loop Validation:** Research shows clinicians and educators mistrust AI when its feedback is opaque or inconsistent with professional practice (Suh et al., 2024). Educators should review and validate AI-generated recommendations, using them as conversation starters—not replacements—for individualized education program (IEP) planning.
3. **Engage Families and Children Through Participatory Design:** Participatory methods (e.g., co-design workshops, child-centred AI toolkits) enable educators to integrate culturally meaningful tasks, storywork, and sensory supports into AI use (Wilson et al., 2025). This approach is critical for autistic learners, who may have atypical sensory or interaction preferences that mainstream tools overlook.
4. **Promote Accessibility-First Classroom Practices:** Educators should ensure multi-modal access (captions, transcripts, TTS, adjustable font/contrast), consistent with evidence that disabled learners are often least able to benefit from AI due to poor design or high cognitive load (Gibson, 2024).

Recommendations for Developers

1. **Adopt Data Sovereignty and Consent Protocols from the Start:** Developers must comply with Indigenous Data Sovereignty frameworks (e.g., OCAP®) and community-defined consent processes. This includes local data storage, transparent retention schedules, and benefit-sharing agreements (First Nations Information Governance Centre, n.d.).
2. **Engineer Offline-First and Low-Bandwidth Architectures:** Studies on remote education show that offline transcription, LAN-based LMS systems, and on-device inference dramatically expand access in low-resource environments (Nimbalkar et al., 2025). Developers should build PWA-style, async-sync tools rather than assuming reliable connectivity.
3. **Build Bias-Resistant NLP and Speech Pipelines:** ASR research documents significant dialect and gender disparities (Harris et al., 2024; Prinos et al., 2024). Developers must train/fine-tune models using local corpora, expand phonological

coverage, and evaluate subgroup metrics before deployment. Bias mitigation must also consider cultural bias in LLMs (Tao et al., 2024) and Western-centric explanatory norms (Peters & Carman, 2024).

4. **Implement Transparent Model Cards and Uncertainty Displays:** Because autism-diagnostic AI often exhibits inflated accuracy in small or homogeneous samples (Sun et al., 2025), developers must disclose training data, confidence ranges, and known biases.

Recommendations for Policymakers

1. **Align AI Policies with UNCRPD and the SDGs** The UN Convention on the Rights of Persons with Disabilities (UNCRPD) mandates accessible information, inclusive education, and respect for cultural/linguistic identities. Evidence from inclusive EdTech research shows that AI systems must support accessibility, affordability, and low-bandwidth usability to meet global equity goals (Stelea et al., 2025; Koole et al., 2024).
2. **Require Subgroup Performance Reporting** Policy should mandate that vendors report WER/CER by dialect, gender, disability profile, and language background. Research repeatedly shows dialect and gender disparities in ASR/NLP systems (Harris et al., 2024; Prinos et al., 2024). Without such reporting, procurement decisions cannot ensure equitable outcomes.
3. **Mandate Participatory Design for Public AI Procurement** Governments should require that AI tools demonstrate evidence of co-design with families, teachers, disability communities, and local stakeholders. Peer-reviewed participatory research shows this reduces cultural and cognitive misalignment (Cesaroni et al., 2025; Wilson et al., 2025).
4. **Establish Independent Oversight Mechanisms** Policymakers should fund third-party audits of educational AI, similar to medical device reviews, particularly for AI that influences screening/diagnosis. Autism-diagnostic meta-analyses emphasize the risk of false confidence when AI is unvalidated in diverse populations (Sun et al., 2025).

Recommendations for International Organizations

1. **Develop Global Benchmarks for Equitable AI in Special Education:** UNESCO, WHO, and OECD should develop shared benchmarks for equitable AI design and evaluation, focusing on multilingual performance, accessibility, and data-sovereignty compliance. Research on digital colonialism in EdTech documents global inequities caused by the exportation of Northern infrastructures and datasets (Kohnke & Foung, 2024; Nothias, 2025). [

2. **Support Global South Dataset Initiatives:** International agencies should fund collaborative, community-governed corpora development—including Indigenous language corpora—to counter the dominance of English-centric training sets. Evidence shows bias in LLMs' cultural alignment and ASR's dialect sensitivity cannot be fully corrected without local data (Tao et al., 2024; Harris et al., 2024).
3. **Issue Ethical Guidance for Automated Diagnosis and Therapy:** Building on meta-analyses of autism-diagnostic AI, international organizations should issue guidelines discouraging exclusive reliance on automated systems and mandating human-expert oversight, transparent evidence standards, and subgroup validation. (Sun et al., 2025; Rakotomanana & Rouhafzay, 2025)

Funding and Infrastructure Needs in the Global South

1. **Invest in Offline-First and Low-Bandwidth Infrastructure:** Offline-capable systems, LAN-based LMS platforms, and on-device inference architectures are specifically documented as effective for low-resource regions where bandwidth is intermittent or unaffordable (Nimbalkar et al., 2025; Stelea et al., 2025). Funders should support hybrid connectivity models, community mesh networks, and device-level caching to ensure continuity of language development interventions.
2. **Seed Funding for Local Dataset Creation:** Global South developers often lack the annotated datasets needed to build culturally and linguistically inclusive AI systems. Funding should prioritize community-governed corpora and open, culturally grounded datasets to counter English-centric bias (Tao et al., 2024; Kohnke & Foung, 2024).
3. **Strengthen Workforce Capacity:** Teacher and clinician training is essential for ethical AI adoption; PD embedded in practice has been shown to sustain trust and improve integration (Suh et al., 2024). Global South governments and NGOs should fund pre-service and in-service training on AI validity, limitations, bias, uncertainty, and accessibility.
4. **Promote Device Equity:** Many families share devices or rely on outdated smartphones. Research shows accessibility barriers disproportionately affect disabled learners and those in low-income or rural settings (Gibson, 2024). Governments and INGOs should invest in device-sharing programs, refurbished device pipelines, and low-cost hardware procurement

The ethical adoption of AI for language development in special education requires a coordinated effort across educators, developers, policymakers, and international organizations. By anchoring policies in cultural responsiveness, multilingual design, participatory co-creation, data sovereignty, and rigorous validation, stakeholders can ensure AI functions not as a new vector of inequity but as an inclusive, empowering tool for diverse learners worldwide.

CONCLUSION: TOWARD A GLOBAL, DECOLONIAL FUTURE IN AI AND SPECIAL EDUCATION

Across this chapter, we showed that AI's promise for language development—personalization at scale, workflow support for clinicians/teachers, and expanded practice opportunities—will only be realized when systems are designed for cultural and linguistic plurality, not against it. Empirical evidence documents persistent *cultural bias* in large language models and *dialect/gender bias* in speech technologies; left unchecked, these biases can pathologize multilingual practices, neurodivergent prosody, and non-Western communicative norms (e.g., Indigenous or Global South contexts) (Tao et al., 2024; Harris et al., 2024). EdTech scholarship warns that data extraction and default Western design logics reproduce colonial hierarchies in classrooms and therapies unless governance, participation, and evaluation are re-centred on local communities (Kohnke & Foung, 2024; Koole et al., 2024). For autism-related tools specifically, meta-reviews highlight promising accuracy in controlled settings but also small, homogeneous samples and limited clinical validation—underscoring the need for transparent subgroup reporting and human-in-the-loop use (Sun et al., 2025; Rakotomanana & Rouhafzay, 2025). Finally, bilingualism research makes clear that heritage-language maintenance does *not* worsen language outcomes for autistic children, so English-only AI pathways are both inequitable and evidence-misaligned (Gonzalez-Barrero & Nadig, 2021).

Emerging Trends in AI for Autism (2024–2026)

The growth of small, locally deployable LLMs has accelerated through parameter-efficient fine-tuning methods such as LoRA, enabling domain adaptation without full retraining and supporting edge or on-premise deployment (Parthasarathy et al., 2024). Parallel advances in low-resource ASR leverage multilingual self-supervised speech models and fine-tuning strategies that improve performance in limited-data languages. Edge computing for classrooms is becoming feasible as neural TTS and speech systems are optimized for on-device inference, reducing dependence on cloud processing (Gerazov et al., 2025). At the governance level, globally coordinated AI-ethics frameworks are emerging, emphasizing fairness, transparency, and risk mitigation in education systems.

Call to action for inclusive innovation

To move from extractive to emancipatory AI, we call for four shifts. First, governance: Treat Indigenous data sovereignty (e.g., OCAP®) and community control as non-negotiable—explicit ownership, access, and local custody of language/speech data (First Nations Information Governance Centre, n.d.).Second, design: Build translanguaging-aware pipelines (code-switch-tolerant ASR/TTS; cultural prompting) and publish dialect/gender performance with parity targets before deployment (Tao et al., 2024; Harris et al., 2024). Third, participation: Institutionalize co-design with children, caregivers, educators, Elders, and clinicians; child-centred and capability-grounded approaches show practical methods to translate rights and values into interfaces, content, and evaluation (Wilson et al., 2025; Cesaroni et al., 2025).Fourth, access: Engineer offline-first, low-bandwidth operation and multi-modal accessibility so rural and low-income communities can actually use the tools (Nimbalkar et al., 2025; Stelea et al., 2025).

Future research directions

We outline six priorities. (1) Subgroup-first evaluation. Require model cards with Word/Error Rate and outcome metrics by language, dialect, gender, age, disability profile, and report uncertainty ranges; this responds to documented ASR/LLM biases and clinical heterogeneity (Harris et al., 2024; Sun et al., 2025). (2) Community-governed corpora. Fund and study locally stewarded datasets (e.g., Indigenous, African languages) to reduce English-centric bias and enable culturally valid feedback loops (Kohnke & Foung, 2024; Tao et al., 2024). (3) Translanguaging metrics. Develop and validate pragmatic measures (joint attention, narrative sequencing, repair strategies) that value bilingual and culturally specific performances, building on evidence that bilingualism is not a risk factor in autism (Gonzalez-Barrero & Nadig, 2021). (4) Neurodiversity-aligned speech models. Create corpora and evaluation protocols that represent autistic prosody and interaction styles, avoiding punitive scoring; pair with human-in-the-loop guardrails (Sun et al., 2025; Suh et al., 2024). (5) Plural explainability. Compare narrative/exemplar/rule-based explanation styles across cultures to increase trust and comprehension among families and educators (Peters & Carman, 2024). (6) Implementation science. Study offline-first deployments and teacher/SLP professional learning communities in low-resource contexts to understand cost, fidelity, and long-term outcomes (Nimbalkar et al., 2025; Stelea et al., 2025).

A decolonial, disability-affirming future is not a matter of retrofitting translation and accessibility widgets onto universal tools. It is a commitment to *shared authority, epistemic plurality, and engineering for equity.* If we center sovereignty in governance, diversity in modelling, participation in design, and accountability in evaluation, AI can amplify—not overwrite—the voices of children, families, and educators around the world (Koole et al., 2024; Kohnke & Foung, 2024).

REFERENCES

Amante-Nochefranca, G., Orbase-Sandal, O., Alieto, E. O., Laput, I. U., Albani, S. E., Lucas, R. I., & Tanpoco, M. (2024). AI-assisted English language learning and teaching in a developing country: An investigation of ESL students' beliefs and challenges. In *Artificial Intelligence, Data Science and Applications* (pp. 281–289). Springer., DOI: 10.1007/978-3-031-48465-0_37

Billiris, G., Gill, A., & Bandara, M. (2025). Privacy in the Age of AI: A Taxonomy of Data Risks. *arXiv preprint arXiv:2510.02357.*

Blodgett, S. L., Barocas, S., Daumé, H.III, & Wallach, H. (2020). Language (technology) is power: A critical survey of "bias" in NLP. In *Proceedings of the 58th Annual Meeting of the Association for Computational Linguistics* (pp. 5454–5476). ACL. DOI: 10.18653/v1/2020.acl-main.485

Cesaroni, V., Pasqua, E., Bisconti, P., & Galletti, M. (2025). A participatory strategy for AI ethics in education and rehabilitation grounded in the Capability Approach. *arXiv*. https://arxiv.org/pdf/2505.15466

Dirth, T. P., & Adams, G. A. (2019). Decolonial theory and disability studies: On the modernity/coloniality of ability. *Journal of Social and Political Psychology*, *7*(1), 260–289. DOI: 10.5964/jspp.v7i1.762

Divekar, R. R., Drozdal, J., Chabot, S., Zhou, Y., Su, H., Chen, Y., & Braasch, J. A. (2021). Foreign language acquisition via AI and extended reality. *Computer Assisted Language Learning*. Advance online publication. DOI: 10.1080/09588221.2021.1879162

First Nations Information Governance Centre. (n.d.). *The First Nations Principles of OCAP®*. https://fnigc.ca/ocap-training/

Foka, A., Griffin, G., Ortiz Pablo, D., Rajkowska, P., & Badri, S. (2025). Tracing the bias loop: AI, cultural heritage and bias-mitigating in practice. *AI & Society*, *40*(8), 5835–5847. DOI: 10.1007/s00146-025-02349-z

Galli, G. (2025). Pluralism, disability and inclusive artificial intelligence. *Digital Society : Ethics, Socio-Legal and Governance of Digital Technology*, *4*(3), 68. Advance online publication. DOI: 10.1007/s44206-025-00231-5

Georgiou, G. P. (2025). Transforming Speech-Language Pathology with AI: Opportunities, Challenges, and Ethical Guidelines. *Health Care*, *13*(19), 2460. DOI: 10.3390/healthcare13192460 PMID: 41095546

Gerazov, B., Politi, M., & Bratières, S. (2025, October). Arabic ASR on the SADA Large-Scale Arabic Speech Corpus with Transformer-Based Models. In *International Conference on Speech and Computer* (pp. 70-84). Cham: Springer Nature Switzerland.

Gibson, S. (2024). Editorial FoHPE Journal Vol 25.3. *Focus on Health Professional Education: A Multi-Professional Journal, 25*(3), i-iv.

Gonzalez-Barrero, A. M., & Nadig, A. (2021). Bilingualism and language development in children with autism spectrum disorders. In *Encyclopedia of Autism Spectrum Disorders* (pp. 699–702). Springer., DOI: 10.1007/978-3-319-91280-6_102508

Harris, C., Mgbahurike, C., Kumar, N., & Yang, D. (2024). Modeling gender and dialect bias in automatic speech recognition. In *Findings of the Conference on Empirical Methods in Natural Language Processing (EMNLP)* (pp. 15166–15184). ACL. https://doi.org/DOI: 10.18653/v1/2024.findings-emnlp.890

Jaliaawala, M. S., & Khan, R. A. (2020). Can autism be catered with artificial intelligence-assisted intervention technology? A comprehensive survey. *Artificial Intelligence Review, 53*(2), 1039–1069. DOI: 10.1007/s10462-019-09686-8

Kiwan, D. (2022). Dis/abled decolonial human and citizen futures. *Citizenship Studies, 26*(4–5), 530–538. DOI: 10.1080/13621025.2022.2091236

Kohnke, L., & Foung, D. (2024). Deconstructing the normalization of data colonialism in educational technology. *Education Sciences, 14*(1), 57. DOI: 10.3390/educsci14010057

Koole, M., Smith, M., Traxler, J., Adam, T., & Footring, S. (2024). Decolonising educational technology. *Education Sciences, 14*(10), 1070. DOI: 10.3390/educsci14101070

Langeveldt, D. C., & Pietersen, D. (2024). Decolonising AI: A critical approach to education and social justice. *Interdisciplinary Journal of Education Research, 6*(s1, S1), 1–9. Advance online publication. DOI: 10.38140/ijer-2024.vol6.s1.07

Mohamed, S., Png, M.-T., & Isaac, W. (2020). Decolonial AI: Decolonial theory as sociotechnical foresight in artificial intelligence. *Philosophy & Technology, 33*(3), 659–684. DOI: 10.1007/s13347-020-00405-8

Nimbalkar, A. M., Nimbalkar, M., Gondhalekar, M., Dhandal, Y. S., Mahalle, P., Chandre, P., & Barot, J. (2025). Innovative offline learning: AI-driven transcription, real-time communication, and LMS for remote education. In *Smart Trends in Computing and Communications (LNNS, Vol. 1459)* (pp. 543–554). Springer. DOI: 10.1007/978-981-96-7505-0_43

Nothias, T. (2025). An intellectual history of digital colonialism. *The Journal of Communication, 75*(5), 385–397. Advance online publication. DOI: 10.1093/joc/jqaf003

Ofosu-Asare, Y. (2024). Cognitive imperialism in artificial intelligence: Counteracting bias with Indigenous epistemologies. *AI & Society, 40*(4), 3045–3061. DOI: 10.1007/s00146-024-02065-0

Parthasarathy, V. B., Zafar, A., Khan, A., & Shahid, A. (2024). The ultimate guide to fine-tuning llms from basics to breakthroughs: An exhaustive review of technologies, research, best practices, applied research challenges and opportunities. *arXiv preprint arXiv:2408.13296.*

Peters, U., & Carman, M. (2024). Cultural bias in explainable AI research: A systematic analysis. *Journal of Artificial Intelligence Research, 79*, 971–1000. Advance online publication. DOI: 10.1613/jair.1.14888

Prinos, K., Patwari, N., & Power, C. A. (2024). Speaking of accent: A content analysis of accent misconceptions in ASR research. In *Proceedings of the 2024 ACM Conference on Fairness, Accountability, and Transparency (FAccT '24)* (pp. 1–10). ACM. DOI: 10.1145/3630106.3658969

Rakotomanana, H., & Rouhafzay, G. (2025). A Scoping Review of AI-Based Approaches for Detecting Autism Traits Using Voice and Behavioral Data. *Bioengineering (Basel, Switzerland), 12*(11), 1136. DOI: 10.3390/bioengineering12111136 PMID: 41301092

Salami, A. O. (2024). Artificial intelligence, digital colonialism, and the implications for Africa's future development. *Data & Policy, 6*, e67. DOI: 10.1017/dap.2024.75

Shukla, N., & Bass, H. W.Jr. (2025). Investigating AI systems: Examining data and algorithmic bias through hermeneutic reverse engineering. *Frontiers in Communication, 10*, 1380252. Advance online publication. DOI: 10.3389/fcomm.2025.1380252

Stelea, G. A., Robu, D., & Sandu, F.AccessiLearnAI. (2025). An accessibility-first, AI-powered e-learning platform for inclusive education. *Education Sciences, 15*(9), 1125. DOI: 10.3390/educsci15091125

Suh, H., Dangol, A., Meadan, H., Miller, C. A., & Kientz, J. A. (2024). Opportunities and Challenges for AI- Based Support for Speech-Language Pathologists. In *Proceedings of the 3rd Annual Meeting of the Symposium on Human-Computer Interaction for Work (CHIWORK '24)* (pp. 14). ACM. https://doi.org/DOI: 10.1145/3663384.3663387

Sun, C., McEwan, A., Boulton, K. A., Demetriou, E. A., Sadozai, A. K., Lampit, A., & Enticott, P. G. (2025). Artificial intelligence for tracking social behaviours and supporting an autism spectrum disorder diagnosis: Systematic review and meta-analysis. *EBioMedicine*, *120*, 105931. DOI: 10.1016/j.ebiom.2025.105931 PMID: 41014972

Tao, Y., Viberg, O., Baker, R. S., & Kizilcec, R. F. (2024). Cultural bias and cultural alignment of large language models. *PNAS Nexus*, *3*(9), pgae346. Advance online publication. DOI: 10.1093/pnasnexus/pgae346 PMID: 39290441

Traxler, J., & Jandrić, P. (2025). Decolonising educational technology. In *The Geopolitics of Postdigital Educational Development* (pp. 163–196). Springer., 7_9.DOI: 10.1007/978-3-031-99378-7_9

University of Calgary—Indigenous Research Support Team. (n.d.). *Indigenous Data Sovereignty*. https://research.ucalgary.ca/engage-research/indigenous-research-support-team/irst- resources/indigenous-data-sovereignty

University of Ottawa Library. (2022). *The First Nations Principles of OCAP®: Fact sheet*. https://www.uottawa.ca/library/sites/g/files/bhrskd381/files/2022- 12/ bestpractices_fnigc_ocap_fact_sheet_en_final.pdf

Wiener, S., Bramlett, A. A., Brown, B., & Dueck, J. (2025). Acoustic analysis and perception ratings of first and second language speakers' Italian lexical stress. *Applied Linguistics*, •••, amaf075. DOI: 10.1093/applin/amaf075

Wilson, C., Atabey, A., & Revans, J. (2025). Towards child-centred AI in children's learning futures: Participatory design futuring with SmartSchool and the co-design stories toolkit. *International Journal of Human-Computer Studies*, *199*, 103431. DOI: 10.1016/j.ijhcs.2024.103431

Zheng, Q., Choudhry, A., Liu, Z., Rabbani, P., Hu, Y., Olszewski, A., Huang, Y., & Xiong, J. (2025). AI- Enhanced Speech-Language Intervention Documentation: Opportunities and Design Goals. *In Artificial Intelligence in Education (AIED 2025)* (LNAI, Vol. 15882, pp. 132–140). Springer. https://doi.org/DOI: 10.1007/978-3-031-98465-5_17

Chapter 10
AI-Assisted Language Development for Children With Autism and Disabilities

Defia Ulandari
http://orcid.org/0009-0002-2136-1633
Universitas Esa Unggul, Indonesia

Binastya Anggara Sekti
http://orcid.org/0000-0001-5489-4888
Universitas Esa Unggul, Indonesia

ABSTRACT

This chapter explores the transformative role of Artificial Intelligence (AI) in enhancing language development among children with autism and developmental disabilities. It integrates insights from neuroscience, pedagogy, and technology to show how tools like Natural Language Processing (NLP), chatbots, social robots, Augmentative and Alternative Communication (AAC) systems, and Virtual or Augmented Reality (VR/AR) can create adaptive, data-driven, and inclusive learning environments. AI facilitates personalized therapy, early detection of language disorders, and continuous progress monitoring through multimodal analytics. However, the chapter also highlights ethical challenges, such as data privacy, algorithmic bias, and the irreplaceable role of human empathy in education. By combining technological innovation with human-centered design, AI becomes not merely a tool but a catalyst for inclusive education empowering every child to communicate, connect, and thrive in a more equitable digital world.

DOI: 10.4018/979-8-3373-7724-7.ch010

1. INTRODUCTION

Language development is the main foundation in the formation of a child's cognitive, social, and emotional abilities. However, for children with Autism Spectrum Disorder (ASD) and a variety of other developmental disabilities, the process of language acquisition is often a major challenge. Difficulty in understanding and expressing language can hinder their ability to interact, learn, and build healthy social relationships. In this context, language therapy-based interventions become a crucial part of their growth and development journey (Duan, 2025).

Unfortunately, conventional therapy methods such as speech therapy and occupational therapy face a number of limitations, ranging from a lack of professional therapists, limited geographical access, to a significant cost. On the other hand, the need for a more personalized, adaptive and sustainable approach is constantly increasing. Advances in Artificial Intelligence (AI) and Machine Learning (ML) technology are now opening up new possibilities in the world of therapy and special education, especially in supporting the language development of children with autism and disabilities (Wang, Shao, Yu, & Wang, 2025). Figure 1 shows the Concept of Artificial Intelligence-Supported Language Development in Children with Autism.

Figure 1. The concept of artificial intelligence-supported language development in children with autism

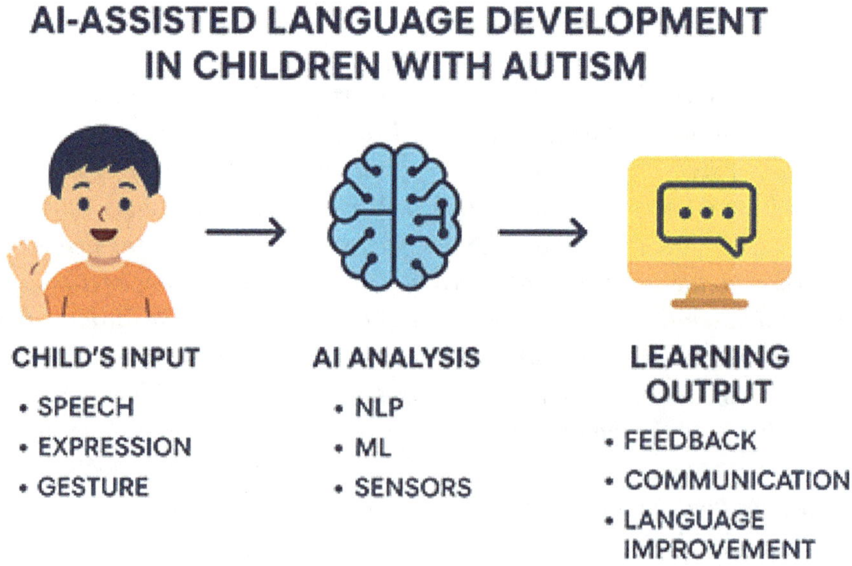

AI has great potential to analyze language patterns, voice intonation, facial expressions, and social behavior of children in the context of learning and therapy. With intelligent algorithms, AI systems can adjust learning materials in real-time, detect specific communication difficulties, and provide personalized feedback. For example, the use of Natural Language Processing (NLP) in language learning applications allows children to practice speaking and understanding meaning in a more interactive and engaging way (Getman et al., 2023).

AI-based approaches also encourage inclusivity in education. Applications such as chatbots, social robots, and Augmentative and Alternative Communication (AAC) devices help non-verbal children to express their needs and feelings independently (Gharaibeh & Basulayyim, 2025). Furthermore, the integration of AI with Virtual Reality (VR) and Augmented Reality (AR) provides an immersive learning environment to practice social skills and language understanding through interactive simulations (Yu et al., 2025).

In addition to the practical aspect, the use of AI in language development also makes a theoretical contribution to the understanding of brain mechanisms and neuroplasticity. This technology can map patterns of neural activity related to language function, assist researchers and therapists in identifying areas of the brain relevant for stimulation, as well as design more effective rehabilitation strategies (Somasundaram & Meyers, 2023). Thus, AI is not only a therapeutic tool, but also a bridge between neuroscience, education, and information technology.

However, the application of AI to the population of children with special needs is inseparable from various ethical, technical, and social challenges. Issues such as data privacy, algorithmic bias, and sensitivity to children's emotional states are major concerns in the development of this technology (Allen et al., 2025). Additionally, it is important to ensure that AI technology does not completely replace human roles, but rather becomes a partner that strengthens collaboration between therapists, teachers, and parents (Ho, Kargeti, Liu, & Mutlu, 2025).

Various recent studies show that AI-assisted storytelling and AI educational robots are able to improve children's language skills and comprehension through visual and interactive narratives (Pujiani, 2025). For example, the use of AI-based educational robots has been shown to improve the literacy abilities of children with learning disabilities (Feng & Wang, 2023b). In addition, ChatGPT-based learning systems have shown positive results in helping children with dyslexia in understanding Arabic-language texts (Gharaibeh & Basulayyim, 2025) and strengthening conceptual comprehension for children in Pakistan (Khan, Daud, & Shahid, 2025).

Given these potential and challenges, it is important to review how AI can be an effective instrument in supporting the language development of children with ASD and disabilities. The focus of this research is not only on the efficiency of technology, but also on the social, pedagogical, and ethical impact of its application.

Therefore, this chapter provides a conceptual foundation on the importance of AI in the language development of children with autism and disabilities, as well as the direction of further research in creating inclusive, intelligent, and human-centered learning systems.

2. NEUROSCIENCE AND MEDICAL FOUNDATIONS IN LANGUAGE DEVELOPMENT OF CHILDREN WITH AUTISM AND DISABILITIES

2.1. The Neurological Basis of Language Disorders

Language is a complex function that involves different areas of the brain, including Broca's area (responsible for speech production) and Wernicke's area (which plays a role in language understanding). In children with autism or other developmental disabilities, connectivity between these areas is often disrupted, causing delays or difficulties in understanding and producing speech (Somasundaram & Meyers, 2023).

Modern neuroimaging research shows that individuals with Autism Spectrum Disorder (ASD) tend to have abnormal activity in brain networks involved in social processing and communication, especially in the prefrontal, temporal, as well as amygdala cortex. These differences lead to challenges in understanding non-verbal social cues such as facial expressions or tone of voice (Yu et al., 2025). Table 1 shows the Brain Areas Involved in Language Processing and Their Functions.

Table 1. Brain areas involved in language processing and their functions

Brain Area	Function	Impact of Impairment (in ASD/Disabilities)
Broca's Area	Speech production	Difficulty articulating or forming words
Wernicke's Area	Language comprehension	Trouble understanding complex sentences
Amygdala	Emotional and social processing	Difficulty recognizing and responding to emotional cues
Superior Temporal Sulcus	Auditory and voice response	Reduced responsiveness to human voices

In addition, disturbances in the superior temporal area of the sulcus also play an important role. This region is usually active when a person hears a voice or sees lip movements when another person speaks. In children with autism, these areas show a weaker response to human voice stimuli, which explains why they tend not to respond when spoken to (Duan, 2025).

Similar neurological disorders are also found in children with cerebral palsy and Down syndrome, in which the motor pathways that control the movement of the speech muscle are blocked. As a result, even though children understand language cognitively, they find it difficult to express it verbally (Allen et al., 2025).

2.2. Neuroplasticity and Technology in Language Recovery

One of the most intriguing concepts in modern neuroscience is neuroplasticity, which is the brain's ability to adapt and form new connections in response to experience and learning. In children with developmental disabilities, repeated stimulation can strengthen neural pathways related to language (Qin, 2024).

AI-based technology plays an important role in harnessing the potential of neuroplasticity. Through an interactive and real-time feedback-based approach, AI can provide a consistent learning experience and stimulate brain activity in relevant areas. For example, AI-based educational robots can be used to help children practice speaking and responding to conversations in a fun and non-intimidating context (Feng & Wang, 2023b).

Research shows that AI-based interventions are able to increase activity in areas of the auditory cortex and Broca after several weeks of repeated training using automated learning systems (Getman et al., 2023). This approach resembles conventional speech therapy, but AI provides an advantage in terms of personalization and adaptation to each child's unique learning patterns.

In addition, a study by (Ho et al., 2025) shows that parental involvement through AI-assisted educational robot systems can improve the effectiveness of language therapy for children with autism, as the emotional interaction between children and parents is amplified by AI-based systems that support collaborative learning at home.

2.3. AI in Early Detection of Language Disorders

Early detection is an important component of interventions for children with autism and other language disorders. The sooner the diagnosis is made, the greater the chance of improving communication function through appropriate therapy (Mocrii & Chirila, 2024).

In this context, machine learning algorithms began to be used to analyze data on children's behavior, voice, and facial expressions to detect early signs of autism. For example, deep learning-based systems can recognize unusual patterns of voice intonation and speech rhythms even before a child reaches the age of two (Zabler et al., 2025).

In addition, AI-based eye-tracking technology is able to identify a child's disinterest in face or eye contact one of the main indicators of ASD with high accuracy

(Wang et al., 2025). Meanwhile, a multimodal AI model that combines video, voice, and gesture analysis shows potential in detecting repetitive behaviors and attention disorders early on (Berrezueta-Guzman et al., 2024).

AI can also analyze video data of children's behavior at home or school to assess the frequency of spontaneous communication, reactions to sounds, and the tendency to repeat words (echolalia). The diagnosis process is faster and more objective than manual observation methods that rely on the therapist's subjective interpretation (Aravantinos et al., 2024).

2.4. Integration of Conventional Therapy with AI Systems

While AI brings a wide range of innovations, the most effective approach is a collaboration between technology and human intervention. AI can be used to support, rather than replace, speech therapy and occupational therapy performed by professionals (Praveena et al., 2024).

For example, therapists can use Natural Language Processing (NLP)-based systems to analyze the results of children's speech exercises, and then adjust therapy strategies according to AI-generated recommendations. Meanwhile, AI can help parents monitor children's development at home through interactive apps that record verbal and non-verbal responses (Ho et al., 2025).

This kind of integration has been shown to increase children's involvement in therapy as well as accelerate their progress. Research (Yu et al., 2025) shows that the use of interactive multimodal AI systems in group therapy can improve the attention and verbal response of autistic children by up to 40% compared to traditional therapy without AI support.

In addition, AI-based interactive models of storytelling also show positive results in strengthening the receptive and expressive language skills of children with learning disabilities (Pujiani, 2025). Thus, the synergy between AI and human therapists expands the scope of therapy while increasing the effectiveness and efficiency of language rehabilitation in children with special needs.

3. EDUCATIONAL AND PEDAGOGICAL PERSPECTIVES IN LANGUAGE DEVELOPMENT WITH THE HELP OF AI

3.1. Language Acquisition Theory in Special Education

Language acquisition is a multidimensional process that is influenced by cognitive, social, emotional, and neurological factors. In the context of special education, language acquisition theory focuses not only on linguistic structure, but also on the child's adaptability to the context of social communication (Pujiani, 2025).

Children with autism or developmental disabilities often exhibit nonlinear patterns of language acquisition. They can understand certain vocabulary but have difficulty combining them into meaningful sentences. This is in line with social interactionist theory, which emphasizes the importance of social interaction in the formation of language. Children with ASD often lack the social motivation that triggers communication, so stimuli from the environment are not strong enough to stimulate language development (Duan, 2025).

Meanwhile, Piaget's theory of cognitive constructivism emphasizes that language learning occurs through exploration and direct experience. Children with disabilities often require a multisensory approach to build a conceptual understanding of words and sentences. This is where technologies such as Augmented Reality (AR) and Virtual Reality (VR) play an important role in bringing immersive learning experiences to children with special needs (Lu et al., 2024).

In this regard, AI is a catalyst for a new pedagogical approach that combines social theory and constructivism. With an AI-based adaptive learning system based on storytelling, children with language disorders can develop linguistic abilities naturally through engaging narrative experiences (Pujiani, 2025). Table 2 shows the Comparison of Language Acquisition Theories in Special Education.

Table 2. Comparison of language acquisition theories in special education

Theory	Main Focus	Implications for AI-Assisted Learning
Social Interactionist	Language develops through social interaction	Social chatbots and educational robots facilitate communication
Piaget's Constructivism	Experiential and multisensory learning processes	AR/VR technologies provide immersive learning experiences
Behaviorism	Learning through positive reinforcement	AI-based adaptive feedback systems strengthen motivation

3.2. AI-Powered Adaptive Learning in Inclusive Education

One of the main advantages of Artificial Intelligence (AI) is its ability to create an adaptive learning system that is able to automatically adjust the level of difficulty, learning style, and individual needs of students. Such a system is known as AI-powered adaptive learning, which allows children to learn with a rhythm and communication style that suits their abilities (Ho et al., 2025).

Through Natural Language Processing (NLP), AI systems can analyze children's responses to instructions, identify linguistic errors, and adjust subsequent learning activities based on the results of the analysis. For example, AI-based apps can provide more frequent pronunciation exercises for children with phonetic difficulties, while children who are stronger on vocabulary aspects will be directed to more complex syntactic exercises (Getman et al., 2023).

Additionally, machine learning analytics allows AI to identify patterns of student progress over time. For example, the system can detect when a child is losing focus or experiencing boredom, then turn the activity into gamified learning to maintain motivation (Wang et al., 2025). This approach is in line with the theory of self-determination, which emphasizes the importance of autonomy and a sense of accomplishment in learning (Khan et al., 2025).

AI also supports inclusive education through a system that facilitates individualized education plans (IEPs). A study by (Aravantinos et al., 2024) confirms that the integration of AI in the primary education curriculum strengthens the involvement of children with disabilities in collaborative learning activities, while helping teachers assess students' communication needs more objectively.

3.3. The Role of Teachers and Parents in the Implementation of AI Technology

While AI provides incredible personalization, the role of humans remains irreplaceable. Teachers and parents have a responsibility to interpret AI-generated data and recommendations so that they can be effectively applied in daily learning activities (Ho et al., 2025).

In the context of inclusive education, teachers act as mediators between AI systems and students' emotional needs. For example, teachers can use the results of analysis from AI systems to design group activities that foster social communication skills. Meanwhile, parents can continue communication practice at home through AI-based interactive applications that adapt the child's learning context (Gharaibeh & Basulayyim, 2025). Figure 2 shows the Collaboration diagram between teachers, AI, parents, and children in inclusive learning.

Figure 2. Collaboration diagram between teachers, AI, parents, and children in inclusive learning.

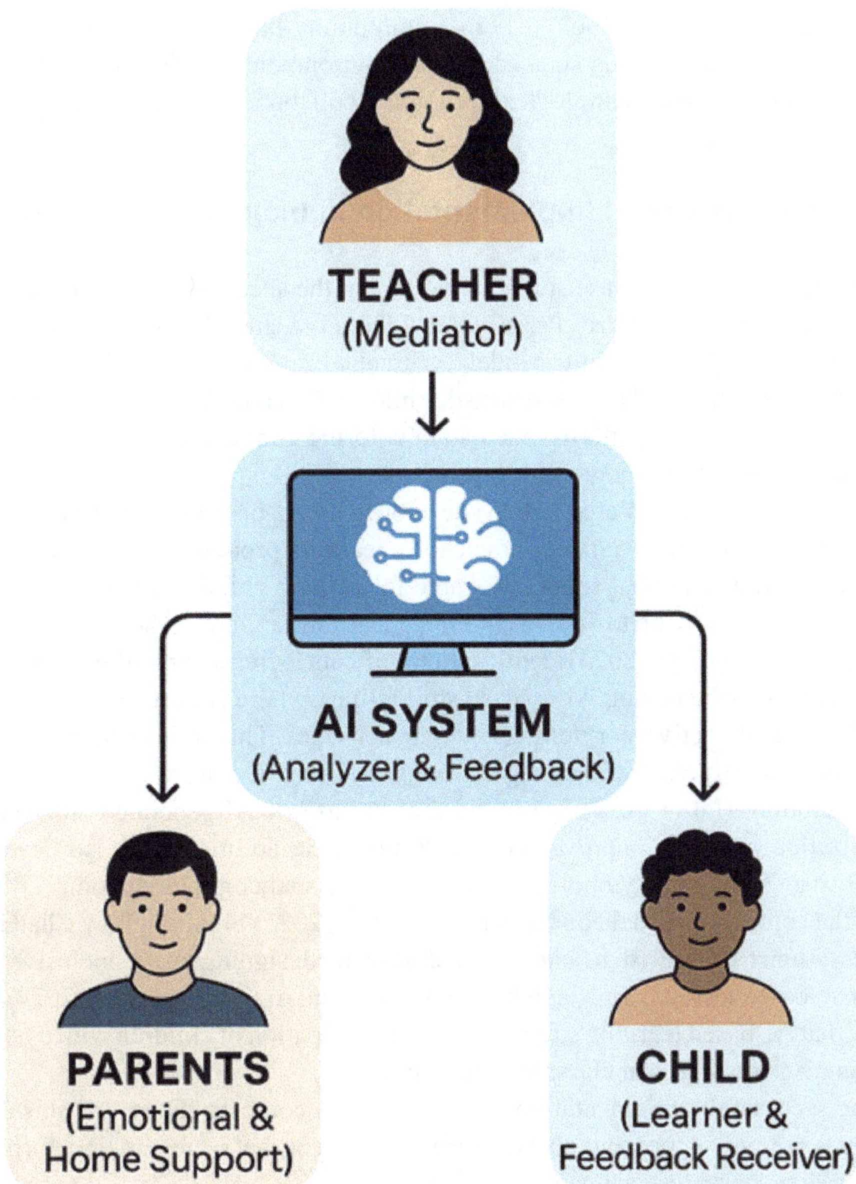

In addition, collaboration between educators, therapists, and technology developers is key to the successful implementation of AI in education. Research (Praveena et al., 2024) shows that learning models that combine AI assistive tools, speech therapists, and special education teachers result in significant improvements in the verbal interactions of children with autism.

According to (Yu et al., 2025), cross-professional collaboration between teachers, psychologists, and AI technologists in a community-based program in Shanghai creates a more harmonious social learning environment for children with ASD. Thus, AI is not only a technological tool, but a collaborative bridge between education stakeholders.

3.4. Case Study of AI Implementation in Inclusive Classroom

Various international case studies have shown the success of the application of AI in the context of inclusive classes. One of them is a study by (Wang et al., 2025) that uses the MS-RRBR (Multi-Model Synergetic Framework) model to recognize limited and repetitive behaviors in autistic children. This model is not only effective in detecting behavioral patterns, but also in tailoring communication interventions according to the child's emotional state.

Another study by (Ho et al., 2025) developed an AI-based educational robot to encourage parental involvement in the child's learning process. As a result, the use of AI-assisted educational robots was able to increase children's verbal and non-verbal interactions by up to 30% in combined learning sessions at home and school.

Meanwhile, (Pujiani, 2025) identified a significant increase in children's narrative language skills when using AI-assisted storytelling, where children are engaged in visual-based interactive storytelling listening activities. This activity helps children understand the structure of language through meaningful context.

In addition, (Lu et al., 2024) found that the use of AI-generated storytelling visualization not only improves children's linguistic abilities, but also develops cognitive awareness of symbols and meanings in visual communication.

In the context of global education, (Khan et al., 2025) highlight how ChatGPT-based systems can assist teachers in Pakistan in designing more inclusive and response-based lessons. This is in line with research (Aravantinos et al., 2024) that shows that AI-based learning strengthens the participation of children with dyslexia and language disorders in classroom activities.

The successful implementation of AI in various contexts shows that this technology is not only a tool, but also a pedagogical agent that is able to transform the way children learn, interact, and develop language.

4. AI TECHNOLOGY AND INNOVATION IN COMMUNICATION SUPPORT FOR CHILDREN WITH DISABILITIES

4.1. Natural Language Processing (NLP) in Language Therapy

One of the most significant innovations in the application of artificial intelligence for children's language development is Natural Language Processing (NLP). This technology allows computers to understand, analyze, and generate human language naturally. In the context of language therapy, NLP is used to recognize children's speech patterns, improve pronunciation, and provide instant feedback during communication exercises (Qin, 2024)

NLP-based applications are able to detect phonetic errors, sentence structure, and typical intonation that are often found in children with autism. The system adjusts exercises based on individual needs for example, repeating certain consonant sounds that are difficult to pronounce or correcting the use of words in the wrong context (Getman et al., 2023). Figure 3 shows the AI Technology Ecosystem in Language Therapy.

Figure 3. AI technology ecosystem in language therapy

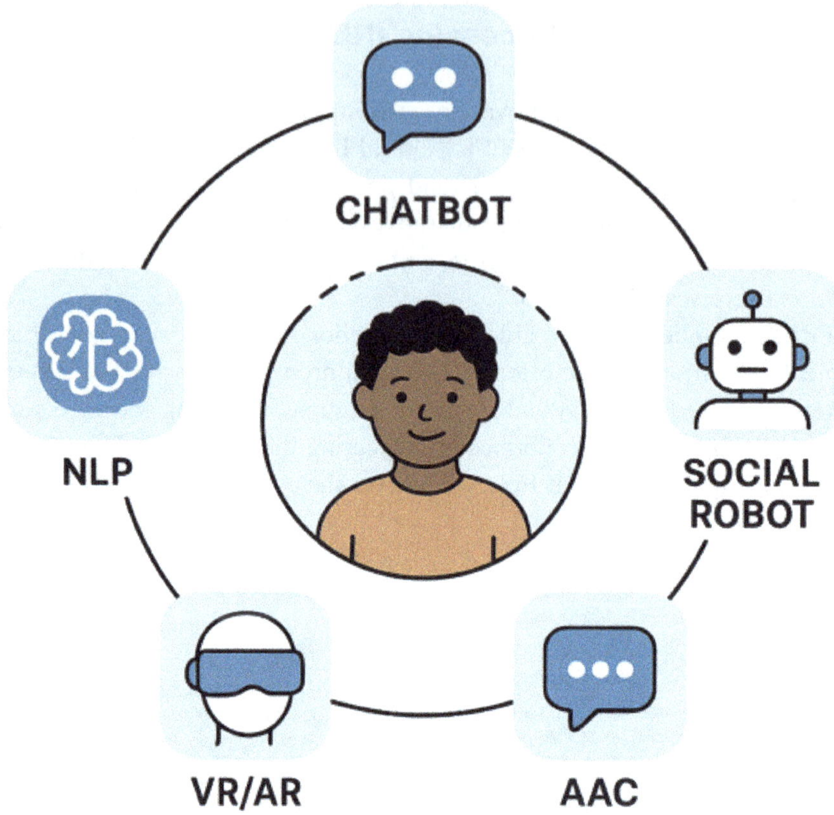

Some modern NLP systems even combine speech-to-text and sentiment analysis to assess a child's emotional expression. This is crucial because children with ASD often have difficulty expressing or understanding emotions in conversation (Allen et al., 2025). With this capability, AI not only serves as a linguistic tool, but also a means to understand a child's emotional well-being during language therapy.

4.2. Chatbot and Conversational AI as Communication Companions

In addition to NLP, the development of Conversational AI such as chatbots provides new opportunities in supporting children to practice communication in a safe and fun environment. Chatbots are capable of realistically simulating social conversations and can be accessed at any time without direct social pressure (Khan et al., 2025).

Large Language Model (LLM)-based systems such as ChatGPT are now used in language therapy for children with autism. This kind of chatbot can ask simple questions like *"How are you feeling today?"* and adjusting language complexity according to children's abilities (Berrezueta-Guzman et al., 2024).

Research by (Iyer, Chakraborty, Reddy, Jyothish, & Krishnaswami, 2023) shows that LLMs designed with child-friendly conversational tone are able to increase verbal participation by up to 25% in individual therapy sessions. This system uses the principle of reinforcement learning to provide positive feedback when children answer correctly, strengthening their confidence and self-efficacy concepts (Duan, 2025).

4.3. Social Robots as Interactive Partners

Social robots are an important innovation in autistic child communication because they allow multimodal interaction through voices, gestures, and facial expressions. A study by (Feng & Wang, 2023) shows that the use of AI-based educational robots can increase children's motivation and conversation duration in the context of bilingual learning.

Robots such as the Echo-Teddy or NAO were developed to mimic human social responses with friendly facial expressions and appropriate tone of voice (Ho et al., 2025). In a study by Yu et al. (2025), regular interactions between autistic children and social robots increased *turn-taking abilities* and emotional awareness by up to 40%.

4.4. Augmentative and Alternative Communication (AAC) Devices

For children who are non-verbal or with severe articulation disorders, AI-based Augmentative and Alternative Communication (AAC) is the main bridge to self-expression. AAC combines symbols, text, and images to aid communication. AI innovations make this system more adaptive, with the ability to predict children's intentions based on the context of previous conversations (Gharaibeh & Basulayyim, 2025).

A study on PubMed by (Draffan, Wald, Ding, & Yin, 2023) explicitly discusses "AI Supporting AAC Pictographic Symbol Adaptations". This study explores how AI can help in adapting symbols to be more personally and contextually appropriate for users.

4.5. Virtual Reality (VR) and Augmented Reality (AR) in Language Training

Virtual Reality (VR) and Augmented Reality (AR) technologies bring a more immersive and contextual learning experience for children with autism. AI-based systems in VR/AR create a simulated social environment where children practice communication skills without real social pressure (Lu et al., 2024).

In this context, the child can participate in a conversation in a virtual classroom or interact with digital characters to understand the meaning of words and actions. This technology can also monitor children's responses using eye tracking and voice detection in real time (Mocrii & Chirila, 2024).

A study by (Feng & Wang, 2023) found that AR-based learning improved receptive language comprehension by up to 32% in autistic children. With interactive narration and AI-controlled 3D visualization, children more easily connect language with concrete experiences, reinforcing the transfer of knowledge from the virtual world to the real world.

4.6. AI-Driven Learning Analytics

In addition to serving as a communication tool, AI is also an important component in analyzing the progress of therapy and child learning. AI-driven learning analytics combines predictive algorithms to assess the effectiveness of interventions based on data on children's behavior, language, and expression (Mocrii & Chirila, 2024).

This system can detect when a child loses focus based on changes in speech patterns or pauses in response. It is a form of *Multimodal Learning Analytics* (MMLA) that uses AI to analyze multimodal data to provide better personalization and *real-time feedback* (Mohammadi et al., 2025). The data helps therapists adjust the duration of the session to stay effective

In addition, AI facilitates automated reporting to parents through an interactive dashboard that displays a graph of the child's communication progress (Ho et al., 2025). This transparency strengthens collaboration between teachers, therapists, and families in building sustainable, data-driven inclusive education.

5. PERSONALIZATION AND AI-BASED ADAPTIVE LEARNING SYSTEMS

5.1. The Concept of Personalization in Language Learning for Children with Special Needs

Personalization of learning is one of the most significant innovations of artificial intelligence (AI) in supporting children with special needs, such as autism and language developmental disorders. In the traditional approach, therapy programs are usually general without taking into account the variation in each child's abilities and characteristics. However, AI is able to learn individual children's behavioral patterns, linguistic abilities, and communication preferences through data analysis based on machine learning algorithms (Gharaibeh & Basulayyim, 2025).

Children with high sensory sensitivity may be better suited to visual activities and soft sounds, while other children respond better to motion-based interactions. Through real-time data analysis, AI systems can adjust the tempo, level of difficulty, and type of stimulus to maintain the child's focus (Ho et al., 2025).

Research conducted by (Feng & Wang, 2023) shows that language learning based on human interaction with AI robots helps children maintain concentration for longer than conventional text-based methods. These results reinforce the finding (Duan, 2025) that adaptive AI systems are able to improve social engagement and communication in children with autism. Thus, AI not only functions as a learning aid, but also as an "adaptive friend" that is able to adjust the approach according to the learning rhythm of each individual (Yu et al., 2025).

5.2. Adaptive Learning System Architecture

AI-based adaptive learning systems generally consist of three main components: a data collection system (input), a machine learning-based analytics model, and an adaptive recommendation system (output).

1. Data Collection System (Input)

This system records various forms of child interaction such as response time, error rate, facial expressions, and tone of voice. This process forms a data base to understand children's learning styles and communication skills (Zabler et al., 2025).

2. Model Analitik (Processing)

This section uses *deep learning* and *reinforcement learning* algorithms to recognize patterns from the data and predict future learning needs (Iyer et al., 2023). Constantly updated AI models improve the accuracy of recommendations, making the system more personalized for each child (Khan et al., 2025).

3. Adaptive Recommendation System (Output)

The results of the analysis are translated into the form of learning recommendations. For example, if a child has difficulty understanding sentence structure, the system will increase related exercises and adjust the context of the sentence to the child's cognitive level (Berrezueta-Guzman et al., 2024).

This data-driven approach makes the learning process no longer dependent on the teacher's intuition alone, but based on empirical evidence collected dynamically from student performance (Aravantinos et al., 2024).

5.3. Adaptive Feedback and Positive Reinforcement

AI plays an important role in providing *adaptive feedback* or feedback that is tailored to the child's response. In the context of language therapy, children with autism respond more to visual or auditory feedback than verbal (Qin, 2024). For example, when a child manages to pronounce a word correctly, the system can provide a positive animation or an appreciation sound. This gamified approach uses the principles of positive reinforcement, which is in line with operant conditioning theory, to increase children's motivation and involvement in therapy sessions (Waseem et al., 2023).

Meanwhile, a study by (Barnafi, Miguel, Vilaca, Milinkovitch, & Ruiz-baier, 2022) emphasizes the importance of real-time feedback to improve children's speaking skills, in this case through *serious game* applications for speech and language therapy. With this approach, AI becomes not only an evaluation tool, but also a trainer that consistently strengthens children's confidence.

5.4. Multimodal Adaptation and Sensor Integration

AI's ability to perform multimodal adaptations is a major breakthrough in supporting communication for children with autism. Through the integration of voice, text, gestures, and facial expressions, AI is able to understand the non-verbal signals that children often use in communicating (Wang et al., 2025).

Modern AI systems are equipped with camera sensors and microphones to analyze multimodal data. This approach combines visual data (such as facial expressions) with audio data (such as speech patterns) to gain a deeper understanding, for example to recognize emotions or assess children's speech automatically (Nemes et al., 2021). Research by (Ho et al., 2025) shows that this sensor-based adaptive response helps reduce communication stress and improves natural interactions between children and systems. If the child seems to lose focus, the system can turn the activity into a more enjoyable educational game (Lu et al., 2024).

This multimodal approach has also been shown to improve children's emotional understanding, as AI is able to provide empathic responses based on facial expressions or intonation of children's voices (Yu et al., 2025).

5.5. Data Analytics for Continuous Personalization

AI not only serves to provide momentary recommendations, but also monitors children's development longitudinally. Through long-term analysis, the system can update the child's learning profile and adjust the material based on the progress made (Popa et al., 2023).

For example, the system can detect that phonetic ability is improving, but semantic understanding is still lagging behind. Based on these patterns, AI adjusts activities to emphasize the context of the meaning of the word (Feng & Wang, 2023).

Research by (Mocrii & Chirila, 2024) shows that AI-driven *analytics-based digital tracking* increases the effectiveness of therapy planning by up to 35%. Thus, AI-based personalization is not a static process, but rather an ongoing mechanism that continues to adapt to the needs of children over time (Pujiani, 2025).

6. ETHICAL, SOCIAL, AND POLICY CONSIDERATIONS IN THE USE OF AI FOR CHILDREN WITH SPECIAL NEEDS

6.1. Ethical Issues in the Use of AI for Children

The application of artificial intelligence (AI) in the education and language therapy of children with autism opens up tremendous opportunities, but it also poses complex ethical challenges. Key issues include data privacy, algorithmic bias, and limits on human responsibility in AI-based decision-making. (Allen et al., 2025) emphasized that the use of large *language models* in the context of children's medicine needs to be strictly regulated because it involves decisions that affect the well-being of individuals who have not been able to give full consent (Sekti, 2025).

Children with communication disabilities are the most vulnerable group because the data collected include facial expressions, speech patterns, and social behaviors that are very personal (Zabler et al., 2025). Therefore, developers and educational institutions are obliged to ensure that the entire data collection process is carried out ethically, with strong encryption and anonymization. The *privacy-by-design approach* must also be applied from the system development stage (Mocrii & Chirila, 2024).

In addition, AI is supposed to function as *an assistive intelligence*, not a substitute for human professionals. (Feng & Wang, 2023) assert that therapeutic and educational decisions for children with special needs require emotional sensitivity that cannot be fully automated. AI needs to be placed as a support in the learning process, while the ultimate responsibility remains with therapists, teachers, and parents.

6.2. Algorithmic Bias and Representation of Children with Disabilities

Algorithmic bias is a serious challenge in the development of AI systems for children with autism or language disorders. Models trained with general datasets tend to fail to recognize typical communication variations of children with disabilities (Getman et al., 2023). For example, speech recognition systems that are not trained using data on children with phonetic disorders often mistakenly assess speech ability (Iyer et al., 2023).

Research (Wang et al., 2025) on *multi-model recognition frameworks* shows that adaptively designed and multimodal AI can reduce the error detection of autistic children's behavior by up to 28%. These findings underscore the importance of developing an inclusive dataset that includes a variety of children's expressions, voices, and learning styles.

Furthermore, an ethical audit of the algorithm is also needed to detect potential system discrimination (Ho et al., 2025). This audit ensures that AI does not assess a child's behavior based on the norms of the majority, but values the diversity of communication and interaction. Collaboration between technologists, child psychologists, and speech therapists is key to creating a fair and representative system (Praveena et al., 2024).

6.3. Protection of Children's Data Privacy and Security

Data privacy is the ethical foundation of the use of AI for children. Every data collected from voice recordings, facial expressions, to behavioral data is highly sensitive biometric information (Sekti, 2026). The risk of data leakage or misuse can have a long-term impact on a child's life (Gharaibeh & Basulayyim, 2025).

Under the *framework of the General Data Protection Regulation* (GDPR), any AI system must obtain explicit consent from a parent or guardian before a child's data is used (Allen et al., 2025). In addition, users have the right to access, correct, and delete their data whenever necessary. *On-device processing technology* is now recommended so that data is processed directly on local devices without being sent to external servers, reducing the risk of leakage (Ho et al., 2025). This approach is important because most AI applications are used at home in the context of informal therapy.

In a clinical context, (Zabler et al., 2025) show that the security of children's medical data can be improved through automated detection systems that use encrypted storage. This is in line with the principle *of ethics by design*, which is to ensure that ethical values are embedded in the technology architecture from the beginning of system design.

6.4. Social Impact and Human–Machine Relations

In addition to ethical and privacy issues, social issues also arise due to the increased interaction between children and AI systems. Social robots and chatbots designed to support communication often create dependency if not balanced with adequate human interaction (Yu et al., 2025).

A *systematic review* has shown that excessive *screen time* in children is associated with lower social-emotional development (Kobashi et al., 2021). Therefore, AI should be used to strengthen rather than replace the interpersonal relationship between children, teachers, and therapists.

However, AI can also function as a *social facilitator* if used appropriately. (Ho et al., 2025) developed a *SET-PAiREd system* that involves the active role of parents in the child's learning process with the help of AI robots. This system strengthens family interactions and improves collaboration between home and school. This approach shows that AI can support human social relationships, not weaken them, as long as they are designed with an empathetic and collaborative purpose.

6.5. AI-Based Inclusive Education Policies and Regulations

The implementation of AI in education and therapy requires national policies that ensure equal access, security, and social justice. According to (Aravantinos et al., 2024), good regulation should guarantee that AI technology is accessible to all children, including those in disadvantaged or low-income areas.

Governments need to develop ethical standards for the use of AI in children's education, including tool certification systems, privacy guidelines, and social impact evaluations (Khan et al., 2025). Educational institutions and technology providers are also required to provide special training for teachers and therapists to be able to operate AI systems responsibly.

This kind of holistic approach will create a sustainable inclusive learning ecosystem where AI serves as an empowerment tool, not just a technological instrument.

Thus, the future of education for children with special needs can be directed towards a more humane, safe, and ethical system.

7. CONCLUSION

7.1. Summary of Key Findings

Artificial intelligence (AI) has brought about a major change in the way children with autism and disabilities acquire and develop language skills. The integration of technologies such as *Natural Language Processing* (NLP), chatbots, social robots, *Augmentative and Alternative Communication* (AAC), as well as *Virtual Reality* (VR) and *Augmented Reality* (AR) has expanded the possibilities of more personalized and data-based interventions.

AI not only serves as an auxiliary; but also bridges the realms of neuroscience, psychology, and pedagogy. From the neuroscience side, research shows that AI-based interactions are able to stimulate children's neuroplasticity through the repetition and reinforcement of language activities. In terms of education, AI-based adaptive systems help teachers and therapists in developing curricula that suit children's learning styles in real-time.

In addition, AI-based learning systems are able to detect communication disorders early through the analysis of children's speech patterns and behavior. This data-driven approach speeds up the diagnosis process and allows for adjustment of interventions from the early stages. Thus, AI is not only a technological innovation; but a new paradigm in understanding and supporting children with special communication needs.

7.2. Interdisciplinary Impact and Practical Benefits

AI delivers broad cross-disciplinary impact. In the field of education, this technology allows teachers to create adaptive and evidence-based learning. In a clinical context, AI systems support more consistent and scalable data-driven therapies than manual methods. Meanwhile, in developmental psychology, this technology helps to understand the communication and emotional patterns of children with autism spectrum disorders.

Practically, AI applications improve the accessibility of therapy, especially for families in areas with a lack of experts. *A home-based therapy* system with AI allows children to continue practicing language independently with minimal mentoring. This finding is in line with the principle *of inclusive education* which is part of the *United Nations* Sustainable Development Goal 4.

However, on the other hand, the application of AI also poses serious challenges, such as algorithmic bias, the risk of data leakage, and the limitations of machine empathy. Therefore, the sustainability of AI innovation in education must be accompanied by ethical policies oriented towards child welfare.

7.3. Strategic Recommendations and Future Research Directions

Based on the results of the multidisciplinary study in the previous chapters, here are five strategic recommendations and future development directions:

a. Strengthening Inclusive Ethics and Policies

Governments need to establish regulations that uphold the principles of child data protection and the ethical use of AI in educational and therapeutic environments. Every AI system must implement a robust privacy framework. A systematic review of privacy in AI emphasizes the importance of Informed Consent and the effectiveness of encryption as crucial technical strategies to protect sensitive user data.

b. Interdisciplinary Collaboration

The effectiveness of AI can only be achieved through close collaboration between technology developers, speech therapists, psychologists, and educators (Praveena et al., 2024). Partnership models such as those applied in social robot learning systems have been shown to improve children's communication outcomes.

c. Inclusive Dataset Enhancement

To avoid algorithmic bias, AI training datasets should represent the variation of children's language, culture, and behaviors from different social groups. Inclusive datasets also need to engage children with phonetic and non-verbal disorders so that AI can adapt to diverse communication patterns.

d. Research on Digital Empathy

Future research needs to develop *empathetic AI.* This is an application from the field of *Affective Computing*, which is a system designed to recognize and respond to children's emotions sensitively, for example in the context of learning. This type of AI is expected to mimic the warmth of human interaction while maintaining analytical objectivity.

e. Integration into the National Education System

AI should be gradually integrated into the national inclusive education curriculum so that its benefits can be felt equally. Training for teachers and professionals is also a must so that the implementation of AI does not create a digital divide.

If this strategy is consistently executed, AI can become an instrument of social justice that strengthens the learning opportunities of children with communication disabilities around the world.

7.4. Closing

Artificial intelligence is now the main catalyst in the transformation of education for children with special needs. This technology expands the boundaries of conventional therapy and brings a new dimension in adaptive, collaborative, and sustainable learning.

However, the success of AI adoption depends not only on the sophistication of the algorithm, but also on the human values that come with it. This approach is in line with the concept *of Human-Centered AI* (HCAI), which asserts that AI was developed to augment and empower teachers and students, rather than replacing them. As such, AI is not intended to replace humans, but rather to strengthen empathy and social relationships in the learning process.

The future of AI-based language therapy is a future that is balanced between technology and humanity of an ecosystem where every child, regardless of condition or ability, has an equal opportunity to be heard, understood, and developed. With this principle, AI is not only a symbol of innovation, but also a tangible embodiment of inclusive and globally equitable education.

REFERENCES

Allen, J. W., Earp, B. D., & Wilkinson, D. (2025). AI-assisted consent in paediatric medicine: Ethical implications of using large language models to support decision-making. *Journal of Medical Ethics*. Advance online publication. DOI: 10.1136/jme-2024-110624 PMID: 40769581

Aravantinos, S., Lavidas, K., Voulgari, I., Papadakis, S., Karalis, T., & Komis, V. (2024). Educational Approaches with AI in Primary School Settings: A Systematic Review of the Literature Available in Scopus. *Education Sciences*, *14*(7), 744. Advance online publication. DOI: 10.3390/educsci14070744

Barnafi, N. A., Miguel, L., Vilaca, D. O., Milinkovitch, M. C., & Ruiz-baier, R. (2022). Coupling Chemotaxis and Growth Poromechanics for the Modelling of Feather Primordia Patterning, 1–25.

Berrezueta-Guzman, S., Kandil, M., Martín-Ruiz, M.-L., Pau, I., & Krusche, S. (2024). Future of ADHD Care: Evaluating the Efficacy of ChatGPT in Therapy Enhancement. *Healthcare (Basel)*, *12*(6), 683. Advance online publication. DOI: 10.3390/healthcare12060683 PMID: 38540647

Draffan, E. A., Wald, M., Ding, C., & Yin, Y. (2023). AI Supporting AAC Pictographic Symbol Adaptations. *Studies in Health Technology and Informatics*, *306*, 215–221. DOI: 10.3233/SHTI230622 PMID: 37638918

Duan, S. (2025). AI-Assisted Social Skills Training for Preschool Children with ASD: A Study on Early Psychological Interventions. *The Journal of Mind and Behavior*, *46*(1), 436–454.

Feng, Y., & Wang, X. (2023a). A comparative study on the development of Chinese and English abilities of Chinese primary school students through two bilingual reading modes: human-AI robot interaction and paper books. *Frontiers in Psychology*, *14*, 1200675. Advance online publication. DOI: 10.3389/fpsyg.2023.1200675 PMID: 37860299

Feng, Y., & Wang, X. (2023b). Educational Robot AI-Assisted Reading Promotes Foreign Children's Chinese Acquisition: An Experimental Study (pp. 139–144). DOI: 10.1145/3594441.3594464

Getman, Y., Phan, N., Al-Ghezi, R., Voskoboinik, E., Singh, M., Grósz, T., Kurimo, M., Salvi, G., Svendsen, T., Strömbergsson, S., Smolander, A., & Ylinen, S. (2023). Developing an AI-Assisted Low-Resource Spoken Language Learning App for Children. *IEEE Access : Practical Innovations, Open Solutions*, *11*, 86025–86037. DOI: 10.1109/ACCESS.2023.3304274

Gharaibeh, M., & Basulayyim, A. (2025). ChatGPT enhances reading comprehension for children with dyslexia in Arabic language. *Disability and Rehabilitation. Assistive Technology*, *20*(8), 2858–2871. Advance online publication. DOI: 10.1080/17483107.2025.2508389 PMID: 40396946

Ho, H.-R., Kargeti, N., Liu, Z., & Mutlu, B. (2025). SET-PAiREd: Designing for Parental Involvement in Learning with an AI-Assisted Educational Robot. DOI: 10.1145/3706598.3713330

Iyer, L. S., Chakraborty, T., Reddy, K. N., Jyothish, K., & Krishnaswami, M. (2023). Ai-assisted models for dyslexia and dysgraphia: Revolutionizing language learning for children (pp. 186–207). DOI: 10.4018/979-8-3693-0378-8.ch008

Khan, N., Daud, H. E., & Shahid, S. (2025). ChatGPT In The Classroom: Guidelines for Integrating AI-Assisted Learning into Pakistani Children's Academic Journey (pp. 319–324). DOI: 10.1145/3700794.3700813

Kobashi, Y., Haque, S. E., Nishikawa, Y., Morita, T., & Nagami, H. (2021). The Increase in Frequency of Protective Behavior against Pesticide Poisoning in Narail, Bangladesh through Use of an Easy Paper Checklist ; an Interventional Study.

Lu, R.-S., Lin, H.-C. K., Yang, Y.-C., & Chen, Y.-P. (2024). Integrating Urban Mining Concepts Through AI-Generated Storytelling and Visuals: Advancing Sustainability Education in Early Childhood. *Sustainability (Basel)*, *16*(24), 11304. Advance online publication. DOI: 10.3390/su162411304

Mocrii, A.-A., & Chirila, O.-S. (2024). AI-Assisted Application for Pediatric Drug Dosing. In *Studies in Health Technology and Informatics* (Vol. 321, pp. 205–209). DOI: 10.3233/SHTI241093

Mohammadi, M., Tajik, E., Martinez-Maldonado, R., Sadiq, S., Tomaszewski, W., & Khosravi, H. (2025). Artificial intelligence in multimodal learning analytics: A systematic literature review. *Computers and Education: Artificial Intelligence, 8*, 100426. https://doi.org/https://doi.org/10.1016/j.caeai.2025.100426

Nemes, B., Frank, D., Puigdollers, A., & Mart, D. (2021). applied sciences Occlusal Splint Therapy Followed by Orthodontic Molar Intrusion as an Effective Treatment Method to Treat Patients with Temporomandibular Disorder : A Retrospective Study.

Popa, S. L., Ismaiel, A., Abenavoli, L., Padureanu, A. M., Dita, M. O., Bolchis, R., … David, L. (2023). Diagnosis of Liver Fibrosis Using Artificial Intelligence: A Systematic Review. *Medicina (Lithuania), 59*(5). DOI: 10.3390/medicina59050992

Praveena, K. N., Mahalakshmi, R., Manjunath, C., & Dakhole, D. K. (2024). Autism, ADHD and Dyslexia Disorder Comorbidity: An Enhanced Study on Education for Children through Artificial Intelligence-Enabled Personalized Assistive Tools (pp. 437–450). DOI: 10.1201/9781003363361-22

Pujiani, T. (2025). AI-Assisted Storytelling for Young Learners: Innovations and Evaluations (pp. 203–232). DOI: 10.4018/979-8-3373-6330-1.ch008

Qin, H. (2024). *Generative AI Applications in Helping Children with Speech Language Issues* (Vol. 3)., DOI: 10.1609/aaaiss.v3i1.31244

Sekti, B. A. (2025). Foundations of Artificial Intelligence Ethics. In *Navigating Social Trust in the AI Era* (pp. 23–47). DOI: 10.4018/979-8-3373-7011-8.ch002

Sekti, B. A. (2026). Data Privacy and Cybersecurity in Wind Power Systems. In *AI-Powered Analysis* (pp. 335–366). Modeling, and Monitoring of Wind Energy Systems., DOI: 10.4018/979-8-3373-4159-0.ch009

Somasundaram, E., & Meyers, A. B. (2023). Bridging the experience gap in pediatric radiology: Towards AI-assisted diagnosis for children. *Pediatric Radiology*, *53*(12), 2398–2399. DOI: 10.1007/s00247-023-05767-7 PMID: 37740780

Wang, Y., Shao, Y., Yu, Z., & Wang, Z. (2025). MS-RRBR: A Multi-Model Synergetic Framework for Restricted and Repetitive Behavior Recognition in Children with Autism. *Applied Sciences (Basel, Switzerland)*, *15*(3), 1577. Advance online publication. DOI: 10.3390/app15031577

Waseem, S., Sherazi, A., Zheng, H., & Lee, J. Y. (2023). *A Machine Learning-Based Applied Prediction Model for Identification of Acute Coronary Syndrome (ACS)*. Outcomes.

Yu, X., Ishiwata, T., Zhang, X., Zhang, D., Xu, L., Su, Y., & Sha, X. (2025). 'More than just music': A multimodal intervention supporting adolescents with autism spectrum disorder in a community-based program in Shanghai. *International Journal of Developmental Disabilities*, 1–16. Advance online publication. DOI: 10.1080/20473869.2025.2561160

Zabler, N., Biondi, A., Kalousios, S., Novitskaya, Y., Faber, H., Duempelmann, M., & Hirsch, M. (2025). Clinical utility of an ambulatory absence seizure detection system. *Epilepsia Open*, *10*(5), 1733–1739. DOI: 10.1002/epi4.70138 PMID: 40932588

Compilation of References

A NLP-based Approach to Improve Speech Recognition Services for People with Speech Disorders. (2022). *2022 IEEE Symposium on Computers and Communications (ISCC)*. DOI: 10.1109/ISCC55528.2022.9912940

Abbeduto, L., Warren, S. F., & Conners, F. A. (2007). Language development in Down syndrome: From the prelinguistic period to the acquisition of literacy. *Mental Retardation and Developmental Disabilities Research Reviews*, *13*(3), 247–261. DOI: 10.1002/mrdd.20158 PMID: 17910087

Abd El-Sattar, H. K. H., Omar, M., & Mohamady, H. (2024). Developing a participatory research framework through serious games to promote learning for children with autism. *Frontiers in Education*, *9*, 1453327. DOI: 10.3389/feduc.2024.1453327

Ackerman, E. (2019, October 28). Blue Frog Robotics answers some of our questions about its delayed social robot Buddy. IEEE Spectrum. https://spectrum.ieee.org/interview-blue-frog-robotics-ceo

Adjorlu, A., Høeg, E. R., Mangano, L., & Serafin, S. (2017). Daily living skills training in virtual reality to help children with autism spectrum disorder in a real shopping scenario. In *2017 IEEE International Symposium on Mixed and Augmented Reality (ISMAR-Adjunct)* (pp. 294–302). IEEE. https://doi.org/DOI: 10.1109/ISMAR-Adjunct.2017.93

Ahuja, L., Vashisth, R., & Simon, R. (2023). NLP & AI Speech Recognition: An Analytical Review. *International Conference on Computing for Sustainable Global Development*, 1390–1396

Ajabshir, Z. F. (2019). The effect of synchronous and asynchronous computer-mediated communication (CMC) on EFL learners' pragmatic competence. *Computers in Human Behavior*, *92*, 169–177. DOI: 10.1016/j.chb.2018.11.015

Alcorn, A., Pain, H., Rajendran, G., Smith, T., Lemon, O., Porayska-Pomsta, K., Foster, M. E., Avramides, K., Frauenberger, C., & Bernardini, S. (2011). Social communication between virtual characters and children with autism. In Biswas, G., Bull, S., Kay, J., & Mitrovic, A. (Eds.), Lecture Notes in Computer Science: Vol. 6738. *Artificial Intelligence in Education* (pp. 7–14). Springer., DOI: 10.1007/978-3-642-21869-9_4

Aleven, V., Roll, I., McLaren, B. M., & Koedinger, K. R. (2016). Help helps, but only so much: Research on help seeking with intelligent tutoring systems. *International Journal of Artificial Intelligence in Education*, *26*(1), 205–223. DOI: 10.1007/s40593-015-0089-1

Alhussen, A., Ansari, A. S., & Mohammadi, M. S. (2025). Enhancing user experience in AI powered human-computer communication with vocal emotions identification using a novel deep learning method. *Computers, Materials & Continua*, *82*(2), 2909–2929. DOI: 10.32604/cmc.2024.059382

Alimisis, D. (2013). Educational robotics: Open questions and new challenges. *Themes in Science and Technology Education*, *6*(1), 63–71. http://ouranos.edu.uoi.gr/theste/index.php/theste/article/view/119

Allen, J. W., Earp, B. D., & Wilkinson, D. (2025). AI-assisted consent in paediatric medicine: Ethical implications of using large language models to support decision-making. *Journal of Medical Ethics*. Advance online publication. DOI: 10.1136/jme-2024-110624 PMID: 40769581

Alrakhawi, H. A., Jamiat, N., & Abu-Naser, S. S. (2023). Intelligent tutoring systems in education: A systematic review of usage, tools, effects and evaluation. *Journal of Theoretical and Applied Information Technology*, *101*(4), 1205–1226. https://www.jatit.org/volumes/Vol101No4/6Vol101No4.pdf

Amante-Nochefranca, G., Orbase-Sandal, O., Alieto, E. O., Laput, I. U., Albani, S. E., Lucas, R. I., & Tanpoco, M. (2024). AI-assisted English language learning and teaching in a developing country: An investigation of ESL students' beliefs and challenges. In *Artificial Intelligence, Data Science and Applications* (pp. 281–289). Springer., DOI: 10.1007/978-3-031-48465-0_37

American Psychiatric Association. (2013). *Diagnostic and statistical manual of mental disorders* (5th ed.). American Psychiatric Publishing.

Anantaram, C., Kopparapu, S. K., Kini, N., & Patel, C. (2015). Improving ASR Recognized Speech Output for Effective Natural Language Processing. *International Conference on the Digital Society*, 17–21. https://www.thinkmind.org/articles/icds_2015_1_40_10127.pdf

Aravantinos, S., Lavidas, K., Voulgari, I., Papadakis, S., Karalis, T., & Komis, V. (2024). Educational Approaches with AI in Primary School Settings: A Systematic Review of the Literature Available in Scopus. *Education Sciences*, *14*(7), 744. Advance online publication. DOI: 10.3390/educsci14070744

Aresti-Bartolome, N., & Garcia-Zapirain, B. (2014). Technologies as support tools for persons with autistic spectrum disorder: A systematic review. *International Journal of Environmental Research and Public Health*, *11*(8), 7767–7802. DOI: 10.3390/ijerph110807767 PMID: 25093654

Ashcraft, M. H. (2002). Math anxiety: Personal, educational, and cognitive consequences. *Current Directions in Psychological Science*, *11*(5), 181–185. DOI: 10.1111/1467-8721.00196

Ashcraft, M. H., & Moore, A. M. (2009). Mathematical anxiety and the affective drop in performance. *Journal of Psychoeducational Assessment*, *27*(3), 197–205. DOI: 10.1177/0734282908330580

Babu, C. S., & Shunmugapriya, K. (2024). Unveiling Critical Periods of Brain Development in Autism Spectrum Disorder: Insights From Prenatal and Postnatal Growth Parameters. In *Clinical Practice and Unmet Challenges in AI-Enhanced Healthcare Systems* (pp. 267-294). IGI Global Scientific Publishing.

Babu, C. S., & Shunmugapriya, K. (2025). The Transformative Role of Artificial Intelligence in Healthcare: Focus on Autism Spectrum Disorder (ASD). In *Convergence of Population Health Management, Pharmacogenomics, and Patient-Centered Care* (pp. 363-374). IGI Global Scientific Publishing.

Baddeley, A. (2003). Working memory: Looking back and looking forward. *Nature Reviews. Neuroscience*, *4*(10), 829–839. DOI: 10.1038/nrn1201

Bahameish, M., Khowaja, K., Abdelaal, Y., & Al-Thani, D. (2025). Pathways to learning: Exploring the impact of augmented reality on vocabulary development in children with autism spectrum disorder. *Interactive Learning Environments*, •••, 1–24. DOI: 10.1080/10494820.2025.2485407

Baird, G., Simonoff, E., Pickles, A., Chandler, S., Loucas, T., Meldrum, D., & Charman, T. (2006). Prevalence of disorders of the autism spectrum in a population cohort of children in south thames: The special needs and autism project (SNAP). *Lancet*, *368*(9531), 210–215. DOI: 10.1016/S0140-6736(06)69041-7 PMID: 16844490

Bandura, A. (1977). *Social learning theory*. Prentice-Hall.

Bandura, A. (1986). *Social foundations of thought and action: A social cognitive theory*. Prentice Hall.

Barnafi, N. A., Miguel, L., Vilaca, D. O., Milinkovitch, M. C., & Ruiz-baier, R. (2022). Coupling Chemotaxis and Growth Poromechanics for the Modelling of Feather Primordia Patterning, 1–25.

Barnes, E., & Hutson, J. (2024). Developing empathetic AI: Exploring the potential of artificial intelligence to understand and simulate family dynamics and cultural identity. *Journal of Artificial Intelligence and Robotics*, *2*(3), 1–25. DOI: 10.59232/AIR-V2I3P101

Barnwal, V. K., Shaw, A., Sarkar, K., Chakraborty, S., & Mukhopadhyay, A. N. (2023). *ARIVA: Artificial Intelligence Enabled Voice Assistance System using Natural Language Processing*. DOI: 10.1109/ICCES57224.2023.10192640

Barsalou, L. W. (2008). Grounded cognition. *Annual Review of Psychology*, *59*(1), 617–645. DOI: 10.1146/annurev.psych.59.103006.093639 PMID: 17705682

Bauer, V., Bouchara, T., Duris, O., Labossière, C., Clément, M. N., & Bourdot, P. (2023). Head mounted augmented reality to support reassurance and social interaction for autistic children with severe learning disabilities. *Frontiers in Virtual Reality*, *4*, 1106061. DOI: 10.3389/frvir.2023.1106061

Beirat, M. A., Algolaylat, A., Al Njadat, H., AlAbdallat, B., & Al-Makhzoomy, A. K. (2025). Utilization of artificial intelligence and assistive technology in autism: Diagnosis, treatment, and education applications: A systematic literature review. *Educational Process: International Journal*, *17*, e2025350. DOI: 10.22521/edupij.2025.17.350

Bellani, M., Fornasari, L., Chittaro, L., & Brambilla, P. (2011). Virtual reality in autism: State of the art. *Epidemiology and Psychiatric Sciences*, *20*(3), 235–238. DOI: 10.1017/S2045796011000448 PMID: 21922965

Belpaeme, T., Kennedy, J., Ramachandran, A., Scassellati, B., & Tanaka, F. (2018). Social robots for education: A review. *Science Robotics*, *3*(21), eaat5954. Advance online publication. DOI: 10.1126/scirobotics.aat5954

Benitti, F. B. V. (2012). Exploring the educational potential of robotics in schools: A systematic review. *Computers & Education*, *58*(3), 978–988. DOI: 10.1016/j.compedu.2011.10.006

Bennett, K., Reichow, B., & Wolery, M. (2011). Effects of structured teaching on the behavior of young children with disabilities. *Focus on Autism and Other Developmental Disabilities*, *26*(3), 143–152. DOI: 10.1177/1088357611405040

Bernardini, S., Porayska-Pomsta, K., & Smith, T. J. (2014). ECHOES: An intelligent serious game for fostering social communication in children with autism. *Information Sciences, 264*, 41–60. DOI: 10.1016/j.ins.2013.10.027

Berrezueta-Guzman, S., Kandil, M., Martín-Ruiz, M.-L., Pau, I., & Krusche, S. (2024). Future of ADHD Care: Evaluating the Efficacy of ChatGPT in Therapy Enhancement. *Healthcare (Basel), 12*(6), 683. Advance online publication. DOI: 10.3390/healthcare12060683 PMID: 38540647

Billiris, G., Gill, A., & Bandara, M. (2025). Privacy in the Age of AI: A Taxonomy of Data Risks. *arXiv preprint arXiv:2510.02357.*

Błażejowska, G., Gruba, Ł., Indurkhya, B., & Gunia, A. (2023). A study on the role of affective feedback in robot assisted learning. *Frontiers in Robotics and AI, 10*, 1132956. DOI: 10.3389/frobt.2023.1132956

Blodgett, S. L., Barocas, S., Daumé, H.III, & Wallach, H. (2020). Language (technology) is power: A critical survey of "bias" in NLP. In *Proceedings of the 58th Annual Meeting of the Association for Computational Linguistics* (pp. 5454–5476). ACL. DOI: 10.18653/v1/2020.acl-main.485

Blue Frog Robotics. (2023). Buddy robot. https://www.bluefrogrobotics.com/robot

Bone, D., Bishop, S. L., Black, M. P., Goodwin, M. S., Lord, C., & Narayanan, S. (2015). Use of machine learning to improve autism screening and diagnostic instruments: Effectiveness, efficiency, and multi-instrument fusion. *Journal of Child Psychology and Psychiatry, and Allied Disciplines, 56*(8), 887–898. DOI: 10.1111/jcpp.12354

Bone, D., Goodwin, M. S., Black, M. P., Lee, C.-C., Audhkhasi, K., & Narayanan, S. (2019). Applying machine learning to facilitate autism diagnostics: Pitfalls and promises. *Journal of Autism and Developmental Disorders, 49*(3), 857–873. DOI: 10.1007/s10803-018-3726-1

Boo, C., Alpers-Leon, N., McIntyre, N., Mundy, P., & Naigles, L. (2022). Conversation during a virtual reality task reveals new structural language profiles of children with ASD, ADHD, and comorbid symptoms of both. *Journal of Autism and Developmental Disorders, 52*(7), 2970–2983. DOI: 10.1007/s10803-021-05175-6 PMID: 34244916

Boyd, B. A., Hume, K., McBee, M. T., Alessandri, M., Gutierrez, A., Johnson, L., Sperry, L., Odom, S. L., & Hall, L. J. (2014). Comparative efficacy of LEAP, TEACCH, and non-model-specific special education programs for preschoolers with autism spectrum disorders. *Journal of Autism and Developmental Disorders, 44*(2), 366–380. DOI: 10.1007/s10803-013-1877-9 PMID: 23812661

Boyd, D., & Crawford, K. (2012). Critical questions for big data: Provocations for a cultural, technological, and scholarly phenomenon. *Information Communication and Society, 15*(5), 662–679. DOI: 10.1080/1369118X.2012.678878

Breazeal, C. (2003). Toward sociable robots. *Robotics and Autonomous Systems, 42*(3-4), 167–175. DOI: 10.1016/S0921-8890(02)00373-1

Bronfenbrenner, U. (1979). *The ecology of human development: Experiments by nature and design*. Harvard University Press. DOI: 10.4159/9780674028845

Bruner, J. S. (1966). *Toward a theory of instruction*. Harvard University Press.

Butterworth, B. (2005). The development of arithmetical abilities. *Journal of Child Psychology and Psychiatry, and Allied Disciplines, 46*(1), 3–18. DOI: 10.1111/j.1469-7610.2004.00374.x

Butterworth, B., & Yeo, D. (2004). *Dyscalculia guidance*. NFER-Nelson.

Cabibihan, J. J., Javed, H., Ang, M.Jr, & Aljunied, S. M. (2013). Why robots? A survey on the roles and benefits of social robots in the therapy of children with autism. *International Journal of Social Robotics, 5*(4), 593–618. DOI: 10.1007/s12369-013-0202-2

Calvo, R. A., & D'Mello, S. (2010). Affect detection: An interdisciplinary review of models, methods, and their applications. *IEEE Transactions on Affective Computing, 1*(1), 18–37. DOI: 10.1109/T-AFFC.2010.1

Camargo, S. P., Rispoli, M., Ganz, J., Hong, E. R., Davis, H., & Mason, R. (2014). A review of the quality of behaviorally based intervention research to improve social interaction skills of children with ASD in inclusive settings. *Journal of Autism and Developmental Disorders, 44*(9), 2096–2116. DOI: 10.1007/s10803-014-2060-7 PMID: 24781498

Carter, A. S., Messinger, D. S., Stone, W. L., Celimli, S., Nahmias, A. S., & Yoder, P. (2011). A randomized controlled trial of Hanen's "More Than Words" in toddlers with early autism symptoms. *Journal of Child Psychology and Psychiatry, and Allied Disciplines, 52*(7), 741–752. DOI: 10.1111/j.1469-7610.2011.02395.x PMID: 21418212

CAST. (2018). Universal Design for Learning guidelines version 2.2. http://udlguidelines.cast.org

Caswell, H. (2019). *Sensitivity analysis: matrix methods in demography and ecology*. Springer Nature. DOI: 10.1007/978-3-030-10534-1

Cesaroni, V., Pasqua, E., Bisconti, P., & Galletti, M. (2025). A participatory strategy for AI ethics in education and rehabilitation grounded in the Capability Approach. *arXiv*. https://arxiv.org/pdf/2505.15466

Chambless, D. L., & Hollon, S. D. (1998). Defining empirically supported therapies. *Journal of Consulting and Clinical Psychology*, *66*(1), 7–18. DOI: 10.1037/0022-006X.66.1.7 PMID: 9489259

Chevallier, C., Kohls, G., Troiani, V., Brodkin, E. S., & Schultz, R. T. (2012). The social motivation theory of autism. *Trends in Cognitive Sciences*, *16*(4), 231–239. DOI: 10.1016/j.tics.2012.02.007 PMID: 22425667

Clabaugh, C., & Matarić, M. (2018). Robots for the people, by the people: Personalizing human-machine interaction. *Science Robotics*, *3*(21), 1–2. DOI: 10.1126/scirobotics.aat7451 PMID: 33141723

Clemente, D., & Granato, M. (2023). Use of virtual reality with ASD: A mini review. *Global Journal of Intellectual & Developmental Disabilities*, *12*(1), 555827. DOI: 10.19080/GJIDD.2023.12.555827

Crawford, J. (2025). Systematic literature reviews: Why I rejected your review. *Journal of University Teaching & Learning Practice*, *22*(2), 1–20. DOI: 10.53761/10vb5076

Creswell, J. W., & Clark, V. L. P. (2025). *Designing and conducting mixed methods research* (4th ed.). SAGE Publications.

D'Mello, S. K., & Graesser, A. C. (2015). Feeling, thinking, and computing with affect-aware learning. In Kappas, A., Gratch, J. M., Calvo, R. A., & D'Mello, S. K. (Eds.), *The Oxford handbook of affective computing* (pp. 419–434). Oxford University Press.

Damschroder, L. J., Aron, D. C., Keith, R. E., Kirsh, S. R., Alexander, J. A., & Lowery, J. C. (2009). Fostering implementation of health services research findings into practice. *Implementation Science : IS*, *4*(1), 50. DOI: 10.1186/1748-5908-4-50 PMID: 19664226

Daniels, A. M., & Mandell, D. S. (2014). Explaining differences in age at autism spectrum disorder diagnosis: A critical review. *Autism : The International Journal of Research and Practice*, *18*(5), 583–597. DOI: 10.1177/1362361313480277

Darmawansah, D., Hwang, G. J., Chen, M. R. A., & Liang, J. C. (2023). Trends and research foci of robotics-based STEM education: A systematic review from diverse angles based on the technology-based learning model. *International Journal of STEM Education, 10*(1), 12. Advance online publication. DOI: 10.1186/s40594-023-00400-3

Dautenhahn, K. (2007). Socially intelligent robots: Dimensions of human–robot interaction. *Philosophical Transactions of the Royal Society of London. Series B, Biological Sciences, 362*(1480), 679–704. DOI: 10.1098/rstb.2006.2004 PMID: 17301026

Davis, D. W., Jawad, K., Lohr, W. D., Trace, M., Le, J., Feygin, Y., & Jones, V. F. (2023). First-line behavioral health treatment prior to stimulant or alpha-2 agonist use for preschoolers on kentucky medicaid in 2017. *Journal of Attention Disorders, 27*(4), 437–446. DOI: 10.1177/10870547221147543 PMID: 36635886

Dawson, G., Bernier, R., & Ring, R. H. (2012). Social attention: A possible early indicator of efficacy in autism clinical trials. *Journal of Neurodevelopmental Disorders, 4*(1), 11. DOI: 10.1186/1866-1955-4-11 PMID: 22958480

Dawson, G., Jones, E. J. H., Merkle, K., Venema, K., Lowy, R., Faja, S., Kamara, D., Murias, M., Greenson, J., Winter, J., Smith, M., Rogers, S. J., & Webb, S. J. (2012). Early behavioral intervention is associated with normalized brain activity in young children with autism. *Journal of the American Academy of Child and Adolescent Psychiatry, 51*(11), 1150–1159. DOI: 10.1016/j.jaac.2012.08.018

Dawson, G., Rogers, S. J., Munson, J., Smith, M., Winter, J., Greenson, J., Donaldson, A., & Varley, J. (2010). Randomized, controlled trial of an intervention for toddlers with autism: The Early Start Denver Model. *Pediatrics, 125*(1), 17–23. DOI: 10.1542/peds.2009-0958 PMID: 19948568

Degutyte, Z., & Astell, A. (2021). The role of eye gaze in regulating turn taking in conversations: A systematized review of methods and findings. *Frontiers in Psychology, 12*, 616471. DOI: 10.3389/fpsyg.2021.616471 PMID: 33897526

Dehaene, S. (2011). The number sense: How the mind creates mathematics (Rev. and updated ed.). Oxford University Press.

Dehaene, S. (1992). Varieties of numerical abilities. *Cognition, 44*(1–2), 1–42. DOI: 10.1016/0010-0277(92)90049-N

Didehbani, N., Allen, T., Kandalaft, M., Krawczyk, D., & Chapman, S. (2016). Virtual reality social cognition training for children with high functioning autism. *Computers in Human Behavior, 62*, 703–711. DOI: 10.1016/j.chb.2016.04.033

Diehl, J. J., Schmitt, L. M., Villano, M., & Crowell, C. R. (2012). The clinical use of robots for individuals with autism spectrum disorders: A critical review. *Research in Autism Spectrum Disorders*, *6*(1), 249–262. DOI: 10.1016/j.rasd.2011.05.006

Dirth, T. P., & Adams, G. A. (2019). Decolonial theory and disability studies: On the modernity/coloniality of ability. *Journal of Social and Political Psychology*, *7*(1), 260–289. DOI: 10.5964/jspp.v7i1.762

Divekar, R. R., Drozdal, J., Chabot, S., Zhou, Y., Su, H., Chen, Y., & Braasch, J. A. (2021). Foreign language acquisition via AI and extended reality. *Computer Assisted Language Learning*. Advance online publication. DOI: 10.1080/09588221.2021.1879162

Doshi-Velez, F., & Kim, B. (2017). Towards a rigorous science of interpretable machine learning. *arXiv preprint arXiv:1702.08608*.

Draffan, E. A., Wald, M., Ding, C., & Yin, Y. (2023). AI Supporting AAC Pictographic Symbol Adaptations. *Studies in Health Technology and Informatics*, *306*, 215–221. DOI: 10.3233/SHTI230622 PMID: 37638918

Duan, S. (2025). AI-Assisted Social Skills Training for Preschool Children with ASD: A Study on Early Psychological Interventions. *The Journal of Mind and Behavior*, *46*(1), 436–454.

Duda, M., Daniels, J., & Wall, D. P. (2022). Clinical evaluation of machine learning models for autism screening in toddlers. *Nature Medicine*, *28*(3), 567–575. DOI: 10.1038/s41591-021-01608-9

Dunst, C. J. (2025). Meta-analysis of the relationships between family systems practices and parenting beliefs and participation in early childhood learning. In S. Phillipson, W. Goff, & S. Garvis (Eds.), *Handbook on Families and Education* (pp. 90-108). Edward Elgar Publishing. https://doi.org/DOI: 10.4337/9781035300686.00014

Eguchi, A. (2014). Robotics as a learning tool for educational transformation. In Proceedings of the 4th International Workshop Teaching Robotics, Teaching with Robotics and 5th International Conference Robotics in Education (pp. 27-34). https://www.terecop.eu/TRTWR-RIE2014/files/00_WFr1/00_WFr1_04.pdf

Ehsan, U., & Riedl, M. O. (2020). Human-centered explainable AI: Towards a reflective sociotechnical approach. *International Conference on Human-Computer Interaction*, 449–466. DOI: 10.1007/978-3-030-60117-1_33

Eide, B. L., & Eide, F. F. (2011). *The dyslexic advantage: Unlocking the hidden potential of the dyslexic brain*. Hudson Street Press.

Eising, E., Carrion-Castillo, A., Vino, A., Strand, E. A., Jakielski, K. J., Scerri, T. S., Hildebrand, M. S., Webster, R., Ma, A., Mazoyer, B., Francks, C., Bahlo, M., Scheffer, I. E., Morgan, A. T., Shriberg, L. D., & Fisher, S. E. (2019). A set of regulatory genes co-expressed in the embryonic human brain is implicated in disrupted speech development. *Molecular Psychiatry*, *24*(7), 1065–1078. DOI: 10.1038/s41380-018-0020-x

Elo, S., & Kyngäs, H. (2008). The qualitative content analysis process. *Journal of Advanced Nursing*, *62*(1), 107–115. DOI: 10.1111/j.1365-2648.2007.04569.x PMID: 18352969

Elsabbagh, M., Divan, G., Koh, Y. J., Kim, Y. S., Kauchali, S., Marcín, C., Montiel-Nava, C., Patel, V., Paula, C. S., Wang, C., Yasamy, M. T., & Fombonne, E. (2012). Global prevalence of autism and other pervasive developmental disorders. *Autism Research : Official Journal of the International Society for Autism Research*, *5*(3), 160–179. DOI: 10.1002/aur.239

Eyben, F., Schuller, B. W., & Cowie, R. (2020). Advanced speech and emotion recognition for autism screening. *IEEE Transactions on Affective Computing*, *11*(4), 597–610. DOI: 10.1109/TAFFC.2019.2923831

Feng, Y., & Wang, X. (2023b). Educational Robot AI-Assisted Reading Promotes Foreign Children's Chinese Acquisition: An Experimental Study (pp. 139–144). DOI: 10.1145/3594441.3594464

Feng, Y., & Wang, X. (2023a). A comparative study on the development of Chinese and English abilities of Chinese primary school students through two bilingual reading modes: human-AI robot interaction and paper books. *Frontiers in Psychology*, *14*, 1200675. Advance online publication. DOI: 10.3389/fpsyg.2023.1200675 PMID: 37860299

First Nations Information Governance Centre. (n.d.). *The First Nations Principles of OCAP®*. https://fnigc.ca/ocap-training/

Fischer, F., Moeller, K., Bientzle, M., Cress, U., & Nuerk, H. C. (2011). Sensorimotor spatial training of number magnitude representation. *Psychonomic Bulletin & Review*, *18*(1), 177–183. DOI: 10.3758/s13423-010-0031-3

Flavell, J. H. (1979). Metacognition and cognitive monitoring: A new area of cognitive–developmental inquiry. *The American Psychologist*, *34*(10), 906–911. DOI: 10.1037/0003-066X.34.10.906

Fletcher, J. M., Lyon, G. R., Fuchs, L. S., & Barnes, M. A. (2019). *Learning disabilities: From identification to intervention* (2nd ed.). Guilford Press.

Foka, A., Griffin, G., Ortiz Pablo, D., Rajkowska, P., & Badri, S. (2025). Tracing the bias loop: AI, cultural heritage and bias-mitigating in practice. *AI & Society, 40*(8), 5835–5847. DOI: 10.1007/s00146-025-02349-z

Friederici, A. D. (2017). *Language in our brain: The origins of a uniquely human capacity*. MIT Press. DOI: 10.7551/mitpress/9780262036924.001.0001

Frith, C. D., & Frith, U. (2006). The neural basis of mentalizing. *Neuron, 50*(4), 531–534. DOI: 10.1016/j.neuron.2006.05.001 PMID: 16701204

Fuchs, L. S., Fuchs, D., Compton, D. L., Powell, S. R., Seethaler, P. M., Capizzi, A. M., & Fletcher, J. M. (2006). The cognitive correlates of third-grade skill in arithmetic, algorithmic computation, and arithmetic word problems. *Journal of Educational Psychology, 98*(1), 29–43. DOI: 10.1037/0022-0663.98.1.29

Fu, L., Wu, Z., & Zhao, H. (2023). Low-cost webcam-based AI eye-tracking for autism screening in early childhood. *Frontiers in Pediatrics, 11*, 1124456. DOI: 10.3389/fped.2023.1124456

Fuller, E. A., & Kaiser, A. P. (2020). The effects of early intervention on social communication outcomes for children with autism spectrum disorder. *Journal of Autism and Developmental Disorders, 50*(5), 1683–1700. DOI: 10.1007/s10803-019-03927-z PMID: 30805766

Galli, G. (2025). Pluralism, disability and inclusive artificial intelligence. *Digital Society : Ethics, Socio-Legal and Governance of Digital Technology, 4*(3), 68. Advance online publication. DOI: 10.1007/s44206-025-00231-5

Geary, D. C. (2011). Cognitive predictors of achievement growth in mathematics: A five-year longitudinal study. *Developmental Psychology, 47*(6), 1539–1552. DOI: 10.1037/a0025510

Geary, D. C. (2011). Consequences, characteristics, and causes of poor mathematics achievement and mathematical learning disabilities. *Journal of Developmental and Behavioral Pediatrics : JDBP, 32*(3), 250–263. DOI: 10.1097/DBP.0b013e318209edef

Georgiou, G. P. (2025). Transforming Speech-Language Pathology with AI: Opportunities, Challenges, and Ethical Guidelines. *Health Care, 13*(19), 2460. DOI: 10.3390/healthcare13192460 PMID: 41095546

Gerazov, B., Politi, M., & Bratières, S. (2025, October). Arabic ASR on the SADA Large-Scale Arabic Speech Corpus with Transformer-Based Models. In *International Conference on Speech and Computer* (pp. 70-84). Cham: Springer Nature Switzerland.

Gersten, R., Clarke, B. S., Jordan, N. C., Newman-Gonchar, R., Haymond, K., & Wilkins, C. (2009). Universal screening in mathematics for the primary grades: Beginnings of a research base. *Exceptional Children*, *75*(4), 423–445. DOI: 10.1177/001440291207800403

Getman, Y., Phan, N., Al-Ghezi, R., Voskoboinik, E., Singh, M., Grósz, T., Kurimo, M., Salvi, G., Svendsen, T., Strömbergsson, S., Smolander, A., & Ylinen, S. (2023). Developing an AI-Assisted Low-Resource Spoken Language Learning App for Children. *IEEE Access : Practical Innovations, Open Solutions*, *11*, 86025–86037. DOI: 10.1109/ACCESS.2023.3304274

Gharaibeh, M., & Basulayyim, A. (2025). ChatGPT enhances reading comprehension for children with dyslexia in Arabic language. *Disability and Rehabilitation. Assistive Technology*, *20*(8), 2858–2871. Advance online publication. DOI: 10.1080/17483107.2025.2508389 PMID: 40396946

Gianfrancesco, M. A., Tamang, S., Yazdany, J., & Schmajuk, G. (2018). Potential biases in machine learning algorithms using electronic health record data. *JAMA Internal Medicine*, *178*(11), 1544–1547. DOI: 10.1001/jamainternmed.2018.3763

Gibson, S. (2024). Editorial FoHPE Journal Vol 25.3. *Focus on Health Professional Education: A Multi-Professional Journal, 25*(3), i-iv.

Goldstein, E. B., & van Hooff, J. C. (2024). *Cognitive psychology* (3rd ed.). Cengage.

Gonzalez-Barrero, A. M., & Nadig, A. (2021). Bilingualism and language development in children with autism spectrum disorders. In *Encyclopedia of Autism Spectrum Disorders* (pp. 699–702). Springer., DOI: 10.1007/978-3-319-91280-6_102508

Goodley, D. (2024). *Disability studies: An interdisciplinary introduction* (3rd ed.). SAGE Publications.

Goswami, U. (2015). Neuroscience and education: From research to practice? *Nature Reviews. Neuroscience*, *16*(10), 631–636. DOI: 10.1038/nrn3980

Gross, J. J. (2015). Emotion regulation: Current status and future prospects. *Psychological Inquiry*, *26*(1), 1–26. DOI: 10.1080/1047840X.2014.940781

Grover, S., & Pea, R. (2013). Computational thinking in K-12: A review of the state of the field. *Educational Researcher*, *42*(1), 38–43. DOI: 10.3102/0013189X12463051

Grynszpan, O., Weiss, P. L., Perez-Diaz, F., & Gal, E. (2014). Innovative technology-based interventions for autism spectrum disorders: A meta-analysis. *Autism : The International Journal of Research and Practice*, *18*(4), 346–361. DOI: 10.1177/1362361313476767 PMID: 24092843

Gundoor, T. K. (2022). IoT-Enabled 5G Networks for Secure Communication. In *Information Security Practices for the Internet of Things, 5G, and Next-Generation Wireless Networks* (pp. 1-29). IGI Global.

Gundoor, T. K., & Sridevi, D. (2024). Optimized Feature Selection and classification for Non-Portable Executable Malware. [IJCNIS]. *International Journal of Communication Networks and Information Security*, *16*(4), 546–552.

Guz, S. (2024). *Who belongs in neighborhood schools?: A mixed methods reexamination of alternative high school transfer* [PhD Dissertation, University of Chicago].

Habibi, F., Sedaghatshoar, S., Attar, T., Shokoohi, M., Kiani, A., & Malek, A. N. (2025). Revolutionizing education and therapy for students with autism spectrum disorder: A scoping review of AI-driven tools, technologies, and ethical implications. *AI and Ethics*, *5*(3), 1–16. DOI: 10.1007/s43681-024-00608-1

Hall, J. R., Savas-Hall, S., & Shaw, E. H. (2023). A deductive approach to a systematic review of entrepreneurship literature. *Management Review Quarterly*, *73*(3), 987–1016. DOI: 10.1007/s11301-022-00266-9

Hamilton, A. F. C. (2013). Reflecting on the mirror neuron system in autism: A systematic review of current theories. *Developmental Cognitive Neuroscience*, *3*, 91–105. DOI: 10.1016/j.dcn.2012.09.008

Hamizi, M. A. A. M., Mokmin, N. A. M., & Ariffin, U. H. (2025). The role of virtual reality in ICT-enhanced learning for students with autism: A dual approach using exploratory and inquiry-based methods. [MyJICT]. *Malaysian Journal of Information and Communication Technology*, *10*(2), 1–14. DOI: 10.53840/myjict10-2-217

Harris, C., Mgbahurike, C., Kumar, N., & Yang, D. (2024). Modeling gender and dialect bias in automatic speech recognition. In *Findings of the Conference on Empirical Methods in Natural Language Processing (EMNLP)* (pp. 15166–15184). ACL. https://doi.org/DOI: 10.18653/v1/2024.findings-emnlp.890

Hashemi, J., Tepper, M., Vallin Spina, T., Esler, A. N., & Sapiro, G. (2021). Computer vision analysis for autism diagnosis using home videos. *Scientific Reports*, *11*(1), 2651. DOI: 10.1038/s41598-021-82352-2

Hattie, J., & Timperley, H. (2007). The power of feedback. *Review of Educational Research*, *77*(1), 81–112. DOI: 10.3102/003465430298487

Hebri, D., Nuthakki, R., Digal, A. K., Venkatesan, K. G. S., Chawla, S., & Raghavendra Reddy, C. (2024). Effective facial expression recognition system using machine learning. *EAI Endorsed Transactions on Internet of Things*, *10*, 1–6. DOI: 10.4108/eetiot.5362

Hernandez, J., Li, X., & Rosenfeld, R. (2020). Wearable sensor technologies for early detection of autism spectrum disorder. *Frontiers in Pediatrics*, *8*, 423. DOI: 10.3389/fped.2020.00423

Herrero, J. F., & Lorenzo, G. (2020). An immersive virtual reality educational intervention on people with autism spectrum disorders (ASD) for the development of communication skills and problem solving. *Education and Information Technologies*, *25*(3), 1689–1722. DOI: 10.1007/s10639-019-10050-0

Ho, H.-R., Kargeti, N., Liu, Z., & Mutlu, B. (2025). SET-PAiREd: Designing for Parental Involvement in Learning with an AI-Assisted Educational Robot. DOI: 10.1145/3706598.3713330

Holmes, B., Chitale, D., Loving, J., Tran, M., Subramanian, V., Berry, A., Rioth, M., Warrier, R., & Brown, T. (2021). Customizable natural language processing biomarker extraction tool. *JCO Clinical Cancer Informatics*, *5*(5), 833–841. DOI: 10.1200/CCI.21.00017 PMID: 34406803

Holmes, J., & Gathercole, S. E. (2013). Taking working memory training from the laboratory into schools. *Educational Psychology*, *34*(4), 440–450. DOI: 10.1080/01443410.2013.797338

Holzinger, A., Biemann, C., Pattichis, C. S., & Kell, D. B. (2022). What do we need to build explainable AI systems for health care? *Nature Reviews Computer Science*, *3*(10), 753–769. DOI: 10.1038/s43588-022-00281-8

Honorato, N., Soltiyeva, A., Oliveira, W., Delabrida, S. E., Hamari, J., & Alimanova, M. (2024). Gamefic strategies in the education of autistic children: A systematic literature review, scient metric analysis, and future research roadmap. *Smart Learning Environments*, *11*(1), 25. DOI: 10.1186/s40561-024-00309-6

Hopcan, S., Polat, E., Ozturk, M. E., & Ozturk, L. (2023). Artificial intelligence in special education: A systematic review. *Interactive Learning Environments*, *31*(10), 7335–7353. DOI: 10.1080/10494820.2022.2067186

Horton, L., & Singleton, J. (2022). Acquisition of turn-taking in sign language conversations: An overview of language modality and turn structure. *Frontiers in Psychology*, *13*, 935342. DOI: 10.3389/fpsyg.2022.935342 PMID: 36003107

Huet, S., Lecorvé, G., Gravier, G., & Sébillot, P. (2008). *Toward the Integration of Natural Language Processing and Automatic Speech Recognition: Using Morpho-Syntax and Pragmatics for Transcription*. Springer US., DOI: 10.1007/978-0-387-76316-3_9

Huot, S., & Loch, S. (2025a). Digital practices in Cambodian EFL classrooms: Teacher narratives from remote learning. In K. Khette & Tayade (Eds.), *Proceeding of one day national conference on English language, literature, cultural studies and media studies* (Vol. 2, pp. 19–31). Centre for Learning, Research and Development, Savda, Maharashtra. DOI: 10.5281/zenodo.16921807

Huot, S. (2025). Digital tutors in the kingdom: Exploring ChatGPT's influence on Cambodian students' academic and cognitive growth. In Pandya, J. D., & Patel, K. C. (Eds.), *Interdisciplinary insights: Exploring multiple perspectives* (Vol. 2, pp. 36–54). Meadow Publication.

Huot, S., & Hok, C. (2025). Unpacking the struggle: Linguistic, pedagogical, and cognitive barriers in Cambodian students' English essay writing. *Context (Ibadan)*, *12*(4), 149–168. DOI: 10.5281/zenodo.15807401

Huot, S., & Loch, S. (2025b). Educating in the age of AI: Preparing Cambodian teachers and students for an AI-augmented learning future. *Journal of Educational Technology and E-Learning Innovations*, *1*(2), 31–38. DOI: 10.54536/jeteli.v1i2.5170

Huot, S., Loch, S., Nget, R., & Em, S. (2025). Exploring multiliteracies in the digital era: A framework for 21st-century learning. [CJESS]. *Cambodian Journal of Educational and Social Sciences*, *2*(1), 7–27. DOI: 10.69496/cjess.v2i1.50

Huot, S., & Such, C. (2025). Leveraging social media for language learning: Opportunities and challenges. [JEILT]. *Journal of Education Innovation and Language Teaching*, *1*(2), 10–29. DOI: 10.63381/jeilt.v1i2.56

Huot, S., & Tep, P. (2025). Advancing ChatGPT for pedagogical innovation in Cambodia: Insight from global evidence and local implications. *The Context: Journal of English Studies*, *12*(4), 115–135. DOI: 10.5281/zenodo.15806972

Iannone, R., & Iannuzzi, I. (2023). The storm of creative destruction. Understanding the" damage-remedy" logic of capitalism in times of pandemics. *Salute E Societá 2023*(1), 27–44 DOI: 10.3280/SES2023-001003

Intawong, K., Homla, P., Wongwan, N., Niemsup, S., Worragin, P., Langgapin, S., & Puritat, K. (2025). An innovative approach to enhancing communication skills and cultural understanding in school settings for children with autism: The immersive virtual reality systems study. *SAGE Open*, *15*(2), 21582440251341985. DOI: 10.1177/21582440251341985

Iyer, L. S., Chakraborty, T., Reddy, K. N., Jyothish, K., & Krishnaswami, M. (2023). Ai-assisted models for dyslexia and dysgraphia: Revolutionizing language learning for children (pp. 186–207). DOI: 10.4018/979-8-3693-0378-8.ch008

Jaliaawala, M. S., & Khan, R. A. (2020). Can autism be catered with artificial intelligence-assisted intervention technology? A comprehensive survey. *Artificial Intelligence Review*, *53*(2), 1039–1069. DOI: 10.1007/s10462-019-09686-8

Jeffries, S., & Everatt, J. (2004). Working memory: Its role in dyslexia and other specific learning difficulties. *Dyslexia : The Journal of the British Dyslexia Association*, *10*(3), 196–214. DOI: 10.1002/dys.278

Jeyarani, R. A., Vignesh, S., Rudhra, Y., & Senthilkumar, R. (2024). A deep learning approach to assess social skills in virtual reality based interventions for children with autism spectrum disorder. In *2024 IEEE International Women in Engineering (WIE) Conference on Electrical and Computer Engineering (WIECON-ECE)* (pp. 410–415). IEEE. https://doi.org/DOI: 10.1109/WIECON-ECE64149.2024.10914905

Jones, A. (1995). Constructivist learning theories and IT. In Heap, N. (Ed.), *Information technology and society* (pp. 249–265). SAGE.

Kabir, H. (2002). Natural language processing for Urdu TTS system. *International Multi-Topic Conference*, 58. DOI: 10.1109/INMIC.2002.1310165

Kandalaft, M. R., Didehbani, N., Krawczyk, D. C., Allen, T. T., & Chapman, S. B. (2013). Virtual reality social cognition training for young adults with high-functioning autism. *Journal of Autism and Developmental Disorders*, *43*(1), 34–44. DOI: 10.1007/s10803-012-1544-6 PMID: 22570145

Kanda, T., Hirano, T., Eaton, D., & Ishiguro, H. (2004). Interactive robots as social partners and peer tutors for children: A field trial. *Human-Computer Interaction*, *19*(1-2), 61–84. DOI: 10.1207/s15327051hci1901&2_4

Karami, B., Koushki, R., Arabgol, F., Rahmani, M., & Vahabie, A. H. (2021). Effectiveness of virtual/augmented reality–based therapeutic interventions on individuals with autism spectrum disorder: A comprehensive meta-analysis. *Frontiers in Psychiatry*, *12*, 665326. DOI: 10.3389/fpsyt.2021.665326 PMID: 34248702

Karande, S., & Kulkarni, M. (2005). Specific learning disability: The invisible handicap. *Indian Pediatrics*, *42*, 315–319. https://pubmed.ncbi.nlm.nih.gov/15812170/

Kewalramani, S., Allen, K. A., Leif, E., & Ng, A. (2024). A scoping review of the use of robotics technologies for supporting social-emotional learning in children with autism. *Journal of Autism and Developmental Disorders*, *54*(12), 4481–4495. DOI: 10.1007/s10803-023-06193-2

Khan, N., Daud, H. E., & Shahid, S. (2025). ChatGPT In The Classroom: Guidelines for Integrating AI-Assisted Learning into Pakistani Children's Academic Journey (pp. 319–324). DOI: 10.1145/3700794.3700813

Khowaja, K., Al-Thani, D., Abdelaal, Y., Hassan, A. O., Mou, Y. A., & Hijab, M. H. (2021). Towards the mixed-reality platform for the learning of children with autism spectrum disorder (ASD): A case study in Qatar. In Rau, S. (Ed.), *International Conference on Human-Computer Interaction* (pp. 329–344). Springer. https://doi.org/DOI: 10.1007/978-3-030-77414-1_24

Khowaja, K., Banire, B., Al-Thani, D., Sqalli, M. T., Aqle, A., Shah, A., & Salim, S. S. (2020). Augmented reality for learning of children with autism spectrum disorder (ASD): A systematic review. *IEEE Access : Practical Innovations, Open Solutions*, *8*, 78779–78807. DOI: 10.1109/ACCESS.2020.2986608

Kiwan, D. (2022). Dis/abled decolonial human and citizen futures. *Citizenship Studies*, *26*(4–5), 530–538. DOI: 10.1080/13621025.2022.2091236

Kobashi, Y., Haque, S. E., Nishikawa, Y., Morita, T., & Nagami, H. (2021). The Increase in Frequency of Protective Behavior against Pesticide Poisoning in Narail, Bangladesh through Use of an Easy Paper Checklist ; an Interventional Study.

Koedinger, K. R., McLaughlin, E. A., & Heffernan, N. T. (2013). A quasi-experimental evaluation of an online formative assessment and tutoring system. *Journal of Educational Psychology*, *105*(4), 1309–1329. DOI: 10.1037/a0034028

Kohnke, L., & Foung, D. (2024). Deconstructing the normalization of data colonialism in educational technology. *Education Sciences*, *14*(1), 57. DOI: 10.3390/educsci14010057

Kolhar, A. & Sridevi. (2025). Future Trends and Innovation in Machine Intelligence for Cyber Risk Management. In M. Almaiah & Y. Maleh (Eds.), *Machine Intelligence Applications in Cyber-Risk Management* (pp. 415-438). IGI Global Scientific Publishing. .DOI: 10.4018/979-8-3693-7540-2.ch018

Kolhar, A. & Sridevi. (2026). Principles and Emerging Trends of Healthcare Robotics. In S. Al-Humairi, P. Naronglerdrit, N. Chantarapanich, & S. Wanchat (Eds.), *Robotics and IoT Synergy in Next-Generation Healthcare* (pp. 401-428). IGI Global Scientific Publishing. DOI: 10.4018/979-8-3373-5447-7.ch012

Koole, M., Smith, M., Traxler, J., Adam, T., & Footring, S. (2024). Decolonising educational technology. *Education Sciences*, *14*(10), 1070. DOI: 10.3390/educsci14101070

Koponen, T., Aunola, K., Ahonen, T., & Nurmi, J. E. (2007). Cognitive predictors of single-digit and procedural calculation skills. *Journal of Experimental Child Psychology*, *97*(3), 220–236. DOI: 10.1016/j.jecp.2007.03.001

Kory-Westlund, J. M., & Breazeal, C. (2019). A long term study of young children's rapport, social emulation, and language learning with a peer like robot playmate in preschool. *Frontiers in Robotics and AI*, *6*, 81. DOI: 10.3389/frobt.2019.00081

Koshino, H., Prat, C. S., & Just, M. A. (2022). Language processing in autism: Neural and computational perspectives. *Frontiers in Human Neuroscience*, *16*, 918217. DOI: 10.3389/fnhum.2022.918217

Kotsi, S., Handrinou, S., Iatraki, G., & Soulis, S.-G. (2025). A review of artificial intelligence interventions for students with autism spectrum disorder. *Disabilities*, *5*(1), 1–14. DOI: 10.3390/disabilities5010007

Kouhbanani, S. S., Khosrorad, R., Zarenezhad, S., & Arabi, S. M. (2021). Comparing the effect of risperidone, virtual reality and risperidone on social skills, and behavioral problems in children with autism: A follow-up randomized clinical trial. *Archives of Iranian Medicine*, *24*(7), 534–541. DOI: 10.34172/aim.2021.76 PMID: 34488318

Kourtesis, P., Kouklari, E.-C., Roussos, P., Mantas, V., Papanikolaou, K., Skaloumbakas, C., & Pehlivanidis, A. (2023). Virtual reality training of social skills in adults with autism spectrum disorder: An examination of acceptability, usability, user experience, social skills, and executive functions. *Behavioral Sciences (Basel, Switzerland)*, *13*(4), 336. DOI: 10.3390/bs13040336 PMID: 37102850

Kourtesis, P., & MacPherson, S. E. (2023). An ecologically valid examination of event-based and time-based prospective memory using immersive virtual reality: The influence of attention, memory, and executive function processes on real-world prospective memory. *Neuropsychological Rehabilitation*, *33*(2), 255–280. DOI: 10.1080/09602011.2021.2008983 PMID: 34856886

Kuhl, P. K. (2010). Brain mechanisms in early language acquisition. *Neuron*, *67*(5), 713–727. DOI: 10.1016/j.neuron.2010.08.038 PMID: 20826304

Kuhl, P. K., Ramírez, R. R., Bosseler, A., Lin, J. F. L., & Imada, T. (2014). Infants' brain responses to speech suggest analysis by synthesis. *Proceedings of the National Academy of Sciences of the United States of America*, *111*(31), 11238–11245. DOI: 10.1073/pnas.1410963111

Kulik, J. A., & Fletcher, J. D. (2016). Effectiveness of intelligent tutoring systems: A meta-analytic review. *Review of Educational Research*, *86*(1), 42–78. DOI: 10.3102/0034654315581420

Lahiri, U., Warren, Z., & Sarkar, N. (2011). Design of a gaze-sensitive virtual social interactive system for children with autism. *IEEE Transactions on Neural Systems and Rehabilitation Engineering : A Publication of the IEEE Engineering in Medicine and Biology Society*, *19*(4), 443–452. DOI: 10.1109/TNSRE.2011.2153874 PMID: 21609889

Landerl, K., & Moll, K. (2010). Comorbidity of learning disorders: Prevalence and cognitive profiles. *Annals of Dyslexia*, *60*(1), 115–132. DOI: 10.1007/s11881-009-0036-0

Langeveldt, D. C., & Pietersen, D. (2024). Decolonising AI: A critical approach to education and social justice. *Interdisciplinary Journal of Education Research*, *6*(s1, S1), 1–9. Advance online publication. DOI: 10.38140/ijer-2024.vol6.s1.07

Lan, W., Tang, Z., Liu, M., Chen, Q., Peng, W., Chen, Y. P., & Pan, Y. (2025). The large language models on biomedical data analysis: A survey. *IEEE Journal of Biomedical and Health Informatics*, *29*(6), 4486–4497. DOI: 10.1109/JBHI.2025.3530794 PMID: 40031690

Larmuseau, C., Cornelis, J., Lancieri, L., Desmet, P., & Depaepe, F. (2020). Multimodal learning analytics to investigate cognitive load during online problem solving. *British Journal of Educational Technology*, *51*(5), 1548–1562. DOI: 10.1111/bjet.12958

Lave, J., & Wenger, E. (1991). *Situated learning: Legitimate peripheral participation*. Cambridge University Press., DOI: 10.1017/CBO9780511815355

LeCun, Y., Bengio, Y., & Hinton, G. (2015). Deep learning. *Nature*, *521*(7553), 436–444. DOI: 10.1038/nature14539

Lee, J. R. H., & Wong, A. (2020). *AEGIS: A real-time multimodal augmented reality computer vision based system to assist facial expression recognition for individuals with autism spectrum disorder*. arXiv. https://doi.org//arXiv.2010.11884DOI: 10.48550

Leite, I., Martinho, C., & Paiva, A. (2013). Social robots for long term interaction: A survey. *International Journal of Social Robotics*, *5*(2), 291–308. DOI: 10.1007/s12369-013-0178-y

Li, C., Gan, Z., Yang, Z., Yang, J., Li, L., Wang, L., & Gao, J. (2024). Multimodal foundation models: From specialists to general-purpose assistants. *Foundations and Trends® in Computer Graphics and Vision*, *16*(1-2), 1–214. DOI: 10.1561/0600000110

Li, H., Zhang, Y., & Zhao, W. (2022). Deep learning-based multimodal diagnosis of autism spectrum disorder. *IEEE Access : Practical Innovations, Open Solutions*, *10*, 88901–88913. DOI: 10.1109/ACCESS.2022.3203497

Li, N., Tian, M., Yang, Y., Liu, Z., Sun, L., & Li, B. (2025). The effect of fully immersive virtual reality technology combined with psychological and behavioral intervention on autism spectrum disorder. *BMC Psychology*, *13*(1), 1120. DOI: 10.1186/s40359-025-03460-y PMID: 41068944

Li, Q., & Ma, X. (2010). A meta-analysis of the effects of computer technology on school students' mathematics learning. *Educational Psychology Review*, *22*(3), 215–243. DOI: 10.1007/s10648-010-9125-8

Liss, J. M., Mailloux, M. J., & Duffy, J. R. (2020). Speech analysis and natural language processing in developmental disorders. *Clinical Linguistics & Phonetics*, *34*(6), 481–496. DOI: 10.1080/02699206.2020.1724573

Liu, N., & Wang, X. (2025, June). The integration of VR technology in early childhood education: Review of impacts and challenges. *Proceeding of International Conference on Social Science and Humanity* 2(3), 785-795. https://doi.org/DOI: 10.61796/icossh.v2i3.161

Lo, H. S., Sher, Y. J., Hong, J. C., Chang, H. K., & Wu, T. F. (2024). The effects of blended learning on the car detailing skills of students with intellectual disabilities. *Journal of Educational Technology & Society*, *27*(3), 46–60. https://www.jstor.org/stable/48787016

Lord, C., Rutter, M., DiLavore, P. C., & Risi, S. (2000). *Autism Diagnostic Observation Schedule (ADOS) manual*. Western Psychological Services.

Lorenzo, G., Lledó, A., Arráez-Vera, G., & Lorenzo-Lledó, A. (2019). The application of immersive virtual reality for students with ASD: A review between 1990–2017. *Education and Information Technologies*, *24*(1), 127–151. DOI: 10.1007/s10639-018-9766-7

Luckin, R., & Holmes, W. (2016). *Intelligence unleashed: An argument for AI in education*. Pearson Knowledge Lab. https://discovery.ucl.ac.uk/id/eprint/1475756

Luckin, R., Holmes, W., Griffiths, M., & Forcier, L. B. (2016). Intelligence unleashed. *An argument for AI in Education, 18*(2), 22-43.

Luckin, R., Holmes, W., Griffiths, M., & Forcier, L. B. (2016). Intelligence unleashed: An argument for AI in education. Pearson Education. https://discovery.ucl.ac.uk/id/eprint/1475756/

Lu, R.-S., Lin, H.-C. K., Yang, Y.-C., & Chen, Y.-P. (2024). Integrating Urban Mining Concepts Through AI-Generated Storytelling and Visuals: Advancing Sustainability Education in Early Childhood. *Sustainability (Basel), 16*(24), 11304. Advance online publication. DOI: 10.3390/su162411304

Maddalon, L., Minissi, M. E., Parsons, T., Hervas, A., & Alcaniz, M. (2024). Exploring adaptive virtual reality systems used in interventions for children with autism spectrum disorder: Systematic review. *Journal of Medical Internet Research, 26*, e57093. DOI: 10.2196/57093 PMID: 39293060

Makransky, G., & Petersen, G. B. (2021). The cognitive affective model of immersive learning (CAMIL): A theoretical research-based model of learning in immersive virtual reality. *Educational Psychology Review*, *33*(3), 937–958. DOI: 10.1007/s10648-020-09586-2

Manjula, P., Saraswathi, G., & Padakannaya, P. (2009). Self-esteem and adjustment among children with reading and writing difficulties. *Jl. of Studies of Home and Community Science*, *36*(2), 91–95.

Matarić, M. J. (2004). Robotics education for all ages. In Proceedings of the AAAI Spring Symposium on Accessible, Hands on AI and Robotics Education. https://cdn.aaai.org/Symposia/Spring/2004/SS-04-01/SS04-01-004.pdf

Ma, X., & Song, K. (2025). Rehabilitation therapy for children with autism based on interactive VR-motion serious game intervention: A randomized-controlled trial. *Frontiers in Public Health, 13*, 1628741. DOI: 10.3389/fpubh.2025.1628741 PMID: 40977792

Mayer, R. E. (2009). *Multimedia learning* (2nd ed.). Cambridge University Press. DOI: 10.1017/CBO9780511811678

Mbonde, N. N. (2025). Wading in digital waters: Black mad/cripistemologies of motherhood and "mental illness" in online support groups amid the double pandemic. *Disability Studies Quarterly*, *45*(1). Advance online publication. DOI: 10.18061/dsq.6868

McLeod, S. (2025). Vygotsky's sociocultural theory of cognitive development. *Simply Psychology*, 1–31. DOI: 10.5281/zenodo.15680745

Menghini, D., Finzi, A., Carlesimo, G. A., & Vicari, S. (2010). Working memory impairment in children with developmental dyslexia: Is it just a phonological deficit? *Developmental Neuropsychology*, *36*(2), 199–213. DOI: 10.1080/87565641.2010.549868

Mesa-Gresa, P., Gil-Gómez, H., Lozano-Quilis, J. A., & Gil-Gómez, J. A. (2018). Effectiveness of virtual reality for children and adolescents with autism spectrum disorder. *Sensors (Basel), 18*(8), 2486. DOI: 10.3390/s18082486 PMID: 30071588

Meyer, A., Rose, D. H., & Gordon, D. (2014). *Universal design for learning: Theory and practice*. CAST. https://udlguidelines.cast.org

Meyer, A., Rose, D. H., & Gordon, D. (2014). *Universal design for learning: Theory and practice*. CAST Professional Publishing.

Milliez, G. (2018). Buddy: A companion robot for the whole family. In Companion of the 2018 ACM/IEEE International Conference on Human Robot Interaction (HRI 2018 Companion). https://doi.org/DOI: 10.1145/3173386.3177839

Ministry of Education, Government of India. (2020). *National Education Policy 2020*. Government of India. https://www.education.gov.in/sites/upload_files/mhrd/files/NEP_Final_English_0.pdf

Mittal, P., Bhadania, M., Tondak, N., Ajmera, P., Yadav, S., Kukreti, A., Kalra, S., & Ajmera, P. (2024). Effect of immersive virtual reality-based training on cognitive, social, and emotional skills in children and adolescents with autism spectrum disorder: A meta-analysis of randomized controlled trials. *Research in Developmental Disabilities, 151*, 104771. DOI: 10.1016/j.ridd.2024.104771 PMID: 38941690

Mocrii, A.-A., & Chirila, O.-S. (2024). AI-Assisted Application for Pediatric Drug Dosing. In *Studies in Health Technology and Informatics* (Vol. 321, pp. 205–209). DOI: 10.3233/SHTI241093

Mohamed, S., Png, M.-T., & Isaac, W. (2020). Decolonial AI: Decolonial theory as sociotechnical foresight in artificial intelligence. *Philosophy & Technology, 33*(3), 659–684. DOI: 10.1007/s13347-020-00405-8

Mohammadi, M., Tajik, E., Martinez-Maldonado, R., Sadiq, S., Tomaszewski, W., & Khosravi, H. (2025). Artificial intelligence in multimodal learning analytics: A systematic literature review. *Computers and Education: Artificial Intelligence, 8*, 100426. https://doi.org/https://doi.org/10.1016/j.caeai.2025.100426

Moyer-Packenham, P. S., & Westenskow, A. (2013). Effects of virtual manipulatives on student achievement and mathematics learning. *International Journal of Virtual and Personal Learning Environments, 4*(3), 35–50. DOI: 10.4018/jvple.2013070103

Mubin, O., Stevens, C. J., Shahid, S., Al Mahmud, A., & Dong, J. J. (2013). A review of the applicability of robots in education. *Journal of Technology in Education and Learning, 1*(1), 1–7. DOI: 10.2316/Journal.209.2013.1.209-0015

Mudi, S., & Samanta, T. K. (2024). Applying vygotsky's zone of proximal development in modern classroom settings: A call for social learning in the digital age. *International Journal For Multidisciplinary Research, 6*(4), 1–6. https://www.ijfmr.com/papers/2024/4/24233.pdf

Mundy, P., & Newell, L. (2007). Attention, joint attention, and social cognition. *Current Directions in Psychological Science, 16*(5), 269–274. DOI: 10.1111/j.1467-8721.2007.00518.x PMID: 19343102

National Council of Educational Research and Training. (2021). *Learning outcomes at the elementary stage*. NCERT. https://ncert.nic.in

Naylor, S., & Keogh, B. (1999). Constructivism in classroom: Theory into practice. *Journal of Science Teacher Education, 10*(2), 93–106. DOI: 10.1023/A:1009419914289

Nemes, B., Frank, D., Puigdollers, A., & Mart, D. (2021). applied sciences Occlusal Splint Therapy Followed by Orthodontic Molar Intrusion as an Effective Treatment Method to Treat Patients with Temporomandibular Disorder : A Retrospective Study.

Ng, Y.-K. (2023). Could artificial intelligence have consciousness? Some perspectives from neurology and parapsychology. *AI & Society, 38*(1), 425–436. DOI: 10.1007/s00146-021-01305-x

Nimbalkar, A. M., Nimbalkar, M., Gondhalekar, M., Dhandal, Y. S., Mahalle, P., Chandre, P., & Barot, J. (2025). Innovative offline learning: AI-driven transcription, real-time communication, and LMS for remote education. In *Smart Trends in Computing and Communications (LNNS, Vol. 1459)* (pp. 543–554). Springer. DOI: 10.1007/978-981-96-7505-0_43

Niu, Y. (2023). *A Natural Language Processing Model Based on Pre-trained Deep Learning Models*. DOI: 10.57237/j.cst.2022.01.007

Noble, S. U. (2018). *Algorithms of oppression: How search engines reinforce racism*. New York university press., DOI: 10.18574/nyu/9781479833641.001.0001

Norwegian/Swedish team. (2024). AI model predicts autism in toddlers with 80% accuracy. *Technology Networks*. Retrieved from https://www.technologynetworks.com/informatics/news/ai-model-predicts-autism-with-80-accuracy-in-children-under-two-389928 Technology Networks

Nothias, T. (2025). An intellectual history of digital colonialism. *The Journal of Communication, 75*(5), 385–397. Advance online publication. DOI: 10.1093/joc/jqaf003

O'Neil, C. (2019). Weapons of math destruction: How big data increases inequality and threatens democracy. *Vikalpa*, *44*(2), 97–98. DOI: 10.1177/0256090919853933

Ofosu-Asare, Y. (2024). Cognitive imperialism in artificial intelligence: Counteracting bias with Indigenous epistemologies. *AI & Society*, *40*(4), 3045–3061. DOI: 10.1007/s00146-024-02065-0

Organisation for Economic Co-operation and Development. (2021). *Digital education outlook 2021: Pushing the frontiers with AI, blockchain, and robots*. OECD Publishing., DOI: 10.1787/589b283f-

Ouyang, F., & Xu, W. (2024). The effects of educational robotics in STEM education: A multilevel meta-analysis. *International Journal of STEM Education*, *11*(1), 7. Advance online publication. DOI: 10.1186/s40594-024-00469-4

Oyucu, S., & Dogan, F. (2023).. . *Improving Text-to-Speech Systems Through Preprocessing and Postprocessing Applications*, *1–5*, 1–5. Advance online publication. DOI: 10.1109/ISMSIT58785.2023.10304907

Page, M. J., McKenzie, J. E., Bossuyt, P. M., Boutron, I., Hoffmann, T. C., Mulrow, C. D., Shamseer, L., Tetzlaff, J. M., Akl, E. A., Brennan, S. E., Chou, R., Glanville, J., Grimshaw, J. M., Hróbjartsson, A., Lalu, M. M., Li, T., Loder, E. W., Mayo-Wilson, E., McDonald, S., & Moher, D. (2021). The PRISMA 2020 statement: An updated guideline for reporting systematic reviews. *BMJ (Clinical Research Ed.)*, *372*, n71. Advance online publication. DOI: 10.1136/bmj.n71 PMID: 33782057

Papert, S. (1980). Mindstorms: Children, computers, and powerful ideas. Basic Books. https://archive.org/details/mindstorms00seym

Parsons, S. (2015). Learning to work together: Designing a multi-user virtual reality game for social collaboration and perspective-taking. *International Journal of Child-Computer Interaction*, *6*, 28–38. DOI: 10.1016/j.ijcci.2015.12.002

Parsons, S., & Cobb, S. (2011). State-of-the-art of virtual reality technologies for children on the autism spectrum. *European Journal of Special Needs Education*, *26*(3), 355–366. DOI: 10.1080/08856257.2011.593831

Parsons, S., Guldberg, K., MacLeod, A., Jones, G., Prunty, A., & Balfe, T. (2011). International review of the evidence on best practice in educational provision for children on the autism spectrum. *European Journal of Special Needs Education*, *26*(1), 47–63. DOI: 10.1080/08856257.2011.543532

Parsons, S., Mitchell, P., & Leonard, A. (2004). The use and understanding of virtual environments by adolescents with autistic spectrum disorders. *Journal of Autism and Developmental Disorders, 34*(4), 449–466. DOI: 10.1023/B:-JADD.0000037421.98517.8d PMID: 15449520

Parsons, S., Mitchell, P., & Leonard, A. (2020). Virtual reality and autism: The future of social skills training. *Journal of Autism and Developmental Disorders, 50*(2), 412–423. DOI: 10.1007/s10803-019-04228-1

Parthasarathy, V. B., Zafar, A., Khan, A., & Shahid, A. (2024). The ultimate guide to fine-tuning llms from basics to breakthroughs: An exhaustive review of technologies, research, best practices, applied research challenges and opportunities. *arXiv preprint arXiv:2408.13296.*

Paul, R., Bianchi, N., Augustyn, A., Klin, A., & Volkmar, F. R. (2008). Production of syllable stress in speakers with autism spectrum disorders. *Research in Autism Spectrum Disorders, 2*(1), 110–124. DOI: 10.1016/j.rasd.2007.04.001 PMID: 19337577

Pennington, D. D., Simpson, G. L., McConnell, M. S., Fair, J. M., & Baker, R. J. (2013). Transdisciplinary research, transformative learning, and transformative science. *Bioscience, 63*(7), 564–573. DOI: 10.1525/bio.2013.63.7.9

Pennisi, P., Tonacci, A., Tartarisco, G., Billeci, L., Ruta, L., Gangemi, S., & Pioggia, G. (2016). Autism and social robotics: A systematic review. *Autism Research : Official Journal of the International Society for Autism Research, 9*(2), 165–183. DOI: 10.1002/aur.1527

Pérez-Fuster, P., Herrera, G., Kossyvaki, L., & Ferrer, A. (2022). Enhancing joint attention skills in children on the autism spectrum through an augmented reality technology-mediated intervention. *Children (Basel, Switzerland), 9*(2), 258. DOI: 10.3390/children9020258 PMID: 35204977

Peters, U., & Carman, M. (2024). Cultural bias in explainable AI research: A systematic analysis. *Journal of Artificial Intelligence Research, 79*, 971–1000. Advance online publication. DOI: 10.1613/jair.1.14888

Piazza, M., Izard, V., Pinel, P., Le Bihan, D., & Dehaene, S. (2004). Tuning curves for approximate numerosity in the human intraparietal sulcus. *Neuron, 44*(3), 547–555. DOI: 10.1016/j.neuron.2004.10.014

Picard, R. W. (2000). *Affective computing*. MIT Press. DOI: 10.7551/mitpress/1140.003.0008

Ponticorvo, M., & Dell'Aquila, E. (2023). Robots at schools: Telerobotics, coding, and teaching embodied artificial intelligence. In *Proceedings of the 2023 Conference on Robots and Education*. https://doi.org/DOI: 10.1145/3664934.3664940

Popa, S. L., Ismaiel, A., Abenavoli, L., Padureanu, A. M., Dita, M. O., Bolchis, R., ... David, L. (2023). Diagnosis of Liver Fibrosis Using Artificial Intelligence: A Systematic Review. *Medicina (Lithuania), 59*(5). DOI: 10.3390/medicina59050992

Praveena, K. N., Mahalakshmi, R., Manjunath, C., & Dakhole, D. K. (2024). Autism, ADHD and Dyslexia Disorder Comorbidity: An Enhanced Study on Education for Children through Artificial Intelligence-Enabled Personalized Assistive Tools (pp. 437–450). DOI: 10.1201/9781003363361-22

Prinos, K., Patwari, N., & Power, C. A. (2024). Speaking of accent: A content analysis of accent misconceptions in ASR research. In *Proceedings of the 2024 ACM Conference on Fairness, Accountability, and Transparency (FAccT '24)* (pp. 1–10). ACM. DOI: 10.1145/3630106.3658969

Priyadharshini, N., & Subbulakshmi, N. (2024). *Natural Language Processing (NLP) based Phonetic Insights for Improving Voice Recognition and Synthesis*. 801–806. DOI: 10.1109/ICSES63445.2024.10762995

Pujiani, T. (2025). AI-Assisted Storytelling for Young Learners: Innovations and Evaluations (pp. 203–232). DOI: 10.4018/979-8-3373-6330-1.ch008

Qin, H. (2024). *Generative AI Applications in Helping Children with Speech Language Issues* (Vol. 3)., DOI: 10.1609/aaaiss.v3i1.31244

Rakotomanana, H., & Rouhafzay, G. (2025). A Scoping Review of AI-Based Approaches for Detecting Autism Traits Using Voice and Behavioral Data. *Bioengineering (Basel, Switzerland), 12*(11), 1136. DOI: 10.3390/bioengineering12111136 PMID: 41301092

Ramaa, S. (2000). Two decades of research on learning disabilities in India. *Dyslexia : The Journal of the British Dyslexia Association, 6*(4), 268–283. DOI: 10.1002/1099-0909(200010/12)6:4<268::AID-DYS177>3.0.CO;2-A

Ramamurthy, P., & Li, T. (2018). Buddy: A speech therapy robot companion for children with cleft lip and palate disorder. In *Companion of the 2018 ACM/IEEE International Conference on Human Robot Interaction* (pp. 359-360). https://doi.org/DOI: 10.1145/3173386.3177830

Räsänen, P., Salminen, J., Wilson, A. J., Aunio, P., & Dehaene, S. (2009). Computer-Assisted Intervention for Children with Low Numeracy Skills. *Cognitive Development, 24*(4), 450–472. DOI: 10.1016/j.cogdev.2009.09.003

Rechowicz, K. J., Shull, J. B., Hascall, M. M., Diallo, S. Y., & O'Brien, K. J. (2021). Internet-of-Things devices in support of the development of echoic skills among children with autism spectrum disorder. *Sensors (Basel), 21*(13), 4621. DOI: 10.3390/s21134621 PMID: 34283166

Redcay, E., & Courchesne, E. (2008). Deviant functional magnetic resonance imaging patterns of brain activity to speech in 2–3-year-old children with autism spectrum disorder. *Biological Psychiatry, 64*(7), 589–598. DOI: 10.1016/j.biopsych.2008.05.020

Relkin, E., de Ruiter, L. E., & Bers, M. U. (2021). Learning to code and the acquisition of computational thinking by young children. *Computers & Education, 169*, 1–15. DOI: 10.1016/j.compedu.2021.104222

Resnick, M., Maloney, J., Monroy-Hernández, A., Rusk, N., Eastmond, E., Brennan, K., & Kafai, Y. (2009). Scratch: Programming for all. *Communications of the ACM, 52*(11), 60–67. DOI: 10.1145/1592761.1592779

Rice, M. F., & Dunn, S. (2023). The use of artificial intelligence with students with identified disabilities: A systematic review with critique. *Computers in the Schools, 40*(4), 370–390. DOI: 10.1080/07380569.2023.2244935

Rizzo, A. S., Lange, B., Suma, E. A., & Bolas, M. (2011). Virtual reality and interactive digital game technology: New tools to address obesity and diabetes. *Journal of Diabetes Science and Technology, 5*(2), 256–264. DOI: 10.1177/193229681100500209 PMID: 21527091

Robins, B., Ferrari, E., Dautenhahn, K., Kronreif, G., Prazak-Aram, B., Gelderblom, G., Caprino, F., Laudanna, E., & Marti, P. (2010). Human centred design methods: Developing scenarios for robot assisted play informed by user panels and field trials. *International Journal of Human-Computer Studies, 68*(12), 873–898. DOI: 10.1016/j.ijhcs.2010.08.001

Robins, D. L., Fein, D., & Barton, M. L. (2014). Modified Checklist for Autism in Toddlers, Revised, with Follow-Up (M-CHAT-R/F). *Pediatrics, 133*(1), 37–45. DOI: 10.1542/peds.2013-1813

Robotical Ltd. (2024). Marty the robot: A tool for teaching programming and robotics. https://robotical.io

Rogers, S. J., & Vismara, L. A. (2008). Evidence-based comprehensive treatments for early autism. *Journal of Clinical Child and Adolescent Psychology : The Official Journal for the Society of Clinical Child and Adolescent Psychology, American Psychological Association, Division 53, 37*(1), 8–38. DOI: 10.1080/15374410701817808 PMID: 18444052

Rose, D., & Dalton, B. (2009). Learning to read in the digital age. *Mind, Brain and Education : The Official Journal of the International Mind, Brain, and Education Society*, *3*(2), 74–83. DOI: 10.1111/j.1751-228X.2009.01057.x

Roth, D. L., Cohen, J., Johnston, D. F., Grabherr, M. G., & Porter, E. W. (2004). *Combined speech recongnition and text-to-speech generation.* https:// patents.google.com/ patent/ US20050038657A1/en

Rouhizadeh, M., Prud'hommeaux, E., & Sproat, R. (2019). Detecting pragmatic language impairment in autism spectrum disorder using NLP. *Proceedings of the 57th Annual Meeting of the Association for Computational Linguistics*, 46–52. https://doi.org/DOI: 10.18653/v1/P19-2006

Ryan, R. M., & Deci, E. L. (2017). *Self-determination theory: Basic psychological needs in motivation, development, and wellness.* Guilford Press. https://psycnet.apa.org/doi/10.1521/978.14625/28806

Saadatzi, M. N., Pennington, R. C., Welch, K. C., & Graham, J. H. (2018). Small-group technology-assisted instruction: Virtual teacher and robot peer for individuals with autism spectrum disorder. *Journal of Autism and Developmental Disorders*, *48*(11), 3816–3830. DOI: 10.1007/s10803-018-3654-2 PMID: 29926295

Saban-Bezalel, R. (2025). Communicative profiles of children with developmental delay compared to age-or language-matched typically developing peers. *Journal of Autism and Developmental Disorders*, *55*(12), 1–15. DOI: 10.1007/s10803-025-06882-0 PMID: 40408045

Salami, A. O. (2024). Artificial intelligence, digital colonialism, and the implications for Africa's future development. *Data & Policy*, *6*, e67. DOI: 10.1017/dap.2024.75

Sandhya, K., Roshan, P., Manikanta, K., & Pandarinath, P. (2025). *Enhancing Automatic Speech Recognitionwith Contextual Understanding using Natural Language Processing*. 2404–2439. DOI: 10.38124/ijisrt/25may1394

Sataloff, R. T., Bush, M. L., Chandra, R., Chepeha, D., Rotenberg, B., Fisher, E. W., Goldenberg, D., Hanna, E. Y., Kerschner, J. E., Kraus, D. H., Krouse, J. H., Li, D., Link, M., Lustig, L. R., Selesnick, S. H., Sindwani, R., Smith, J. J., Tysome, J., Weber, P. C., & Welling, D. B. (2021). Systematic and other reviews: Criteria and complexities. *Journal of Otolaryngology - Head & Neck Surgery*, *50*(1), 41. DOI: 10.1186/s40463-021-00527-9 PMID: 34193276

Satish, E. G., Naidu, P. R., Mogera, G. M., karthik, H., & Abhinandan. (2024). *Voice Over Vision: A Sequence-to-Sequence Model by Text to Speech Technology*. 1–7. DOI: 10.1109/ICICEC62498.2024.10808272

Scassellati, B., Admoni, H., & Matarić, M. J. (2012). Robots for use in autism research. *Annual Review of Biomedical Engineering*, *14*(1), 275–294. DOI: 10.1146/annurev-bioeng-071811-150036

Schopler, E., Reichler, R. J., DeVellis, R. F., & Daly, K. (1988). Toward objective classification of childhood autism: Childhood Autism Rating Scale (CARS). *Journal of Autism and Developmental Disorders*, *19*(3), 355–368. DOI: 10.1007/BF02211841

Sekti, B. A. (2025). Foundations of Artificial Intelligence Ethics. In *Navigating Social Trust in the AI Era* (pp. 23–47). DOI: 10.4018/979-8-3373-7011-8.ch002

Sekti, B. A. (2026). Data Privacy and Cybersecurity in Wind Power Systems. In *AI-Powered Analysis* (pp. 335–366). Modeling, and Monitoring of Wind Energy Systems., DOI: 10.4018/979-8-3373-4159-0.ch009

Selwyn, N. (2022). *Education and technology: Key issues and debates* (3rd ed.). Bloomsbury Academic. DOI: 10.5040/9781350145573

Shaywitz, S. E. (1998). Dyslexia. *The New England Journal of Medicine*, *338*(5), 307–312. DOI: 10.1056/NEJM199801293380507

Shiri, M., & Sadeghi, R. (2025). Psychological Distress among Iranian Older Adults and Its Correlates During the COVID-19 Pandemic in Iran. [JSCC]. *Journal of Social Continuity and Change*, *4*(3), 499–520.

Shivaraj, G. (2024). Advancing Accessibility through Automatic Speech Recognition and NLP Integration. *International Journal for Research in Applied Science and Engineering Technology*, *12*(6), 3–9. DOI: 10.22214/ijraset.2024.62443

Shukla, N., & Bass, H. W.Jr. (2025). Investigating AI systems: Examining data and algorithmic bias through hermeneutic reverse engineering. *Frontiers in Communication*, *10*, 1380252. Advance online publication. DOI: 10.3389/fcomm.2025.1380252

Shute, V. J., & Rahimi, S. (2017). Review of computer-based assessment for learning in elementary and secondary education. *Journal of Computer Assisted Learning*, *33*(1), 1–19. DOI: 10.1111/jcal.12172

Sideraki, A. (2024). Exploring the therapeutic potential of virtual reality and augmented reality in social skills training for individuals with autism spectrum disorder. *World Journal of Advanced Research and Reviews*, *23*(3), 2995–3004. DOI: 10.30574/wjarr.2024.23.3.3002

Silva, L. (2025). *Enhancing autistic children communication skills through augmented reality*. Instituto Superior Técnico, Universidade de Lisboa.

Silva, R. M., Martins, P., & Rocha, T. (2025). Virtual reality educational scenarios for students with ASD: Instruments validation and design of STEM programmatic contents. *Research in Autism Spectrum Disorders*, *119*, 102521. DOI: 10.1016/j.rasd.2024.102521

Skinner, B. F. (1953). *Science and human behavior*. Macmillan.

Smakman, M. H. J., Konijn, E. A., & Vogt, P. A. (2022). Do robotic tutors compromise the social-emotional development of children? A qualitative study into teacher perceptions. *Frontiers in Robotics and AI*, *9*, 734955. DOI: 10.3389/frobt.2022.734955

Snowling, M. J. (2000). *Dyslexia* (2nd ed.). Blackwell Publishers., DOI: 10.1002/9780470694986

Snowling, M. J. (2013). Early identification and interventions for dyslexia: A contemporary view. *Journal of Research in Special Educational Needs*, *13*(1), 7–14. DOI: 10.1111/j.1471-3802.2012.01262.x

Snowling, M. J., & Hulme, C. (2012). Annual research review: The nature and classification of reading disorders. *Journal of Child Psychology and Psychiatry, and Allied Disciplines*, *53*(5), 593–607. DOI: 10.1111/j.1469-7610.2011.02495.x

Soltiyeva, A., Oliveira, W., Madina, A., Adilkhan, S., Urmanov, M., & Hamari, J. (2023). My lovely granny's farm: An immersive virtual reality training system for children with autism spectrum disorder. *Education and Information Technologies*, *28*(12), 16887–16907. DOI: 10.1007/s10639-023-11862-x PMID: 37361850

Somasundaram, E., & Meyers, A. B. (2023). Bridging the experience gap in pediatric radiology: Towards AI-assisted diagnosis for children. *Pediatric Radiology*, *53*(12), 2398–2399. DOI: 10.1007/s00247-023-05767-7 PMID: 37740780

Sridevi & Kolhar. A. (2025). Energy-Efficiency Strategies for Wireless Sensor Networks in IoT. In A. Sathio, M. Rind, S. Awan, & A. Junejo (Eds.), *Energy-Efficient Deep Learning Approaches in IoT, Fog, and Green Blockchain Revolution* (pp. 167-192). IGI Global Scientific Publishing. DOI: 10.4018/979-8-3373-0300-0.ch006

Sridevi & Kolhar. A. (2026). Fundamentals of 6G Networks. In R. Shaikh (Ed.), *6G Networks and AI-Driven Cybersecurity* (pp. 1-32). IGI Global Scientific Publishing. DOI: 10.4018/979-8-3373-0568-4.ch001

Stelea, G. A., Robu, D., & Sandu, F.AccessiLearnAI. (2025). An accessibility-first, AI-powered e-learning platform for inclusive education. *Education Sciences*, *15*(9), 1125. DOI: 10.3390/educsci15091125

Subhashri, C., Vijayakumar, K., Anujna, M., & Bini, K. B. (2025). Revolutionizing Human-Machine Conversations: Real- Time Speech Recognition and Synthesis With GPT-2. *Social Science Research Network.* DOI: 10.2139/ssrn.5075988

Sudhan, S. H., Nair, P. N. R., & Thushara, M. G. (2024). *Text-to-Speech and Speech-to-Text Models: A Systematic Examination of Diverse Approaches.* 2ct61223.2024.10544015 Castillejo, S. P. (2021). Automatic speech recognition. *Innovative language pedagogy report*, 121.DOI: 10.1109/ I

Suganya, V., Prema, K. V., Krishna, C. M., Reddy, C., & Jaswanth, E. (2024). *Emotion Recognition in Speech: A Natural Language Processing Perspective.* 1–8. DOI: 10.1109/ACROSET62108.2024.10743299

Suh, H., Dangol, A., Meadan, H., Miller, C. A., & Kientz, J. A. (2024). Opportunities and Challenges for AI- Based Support for Speech-Language Pathologists. In *Proceedings of the 3rd Annual Meeting of the Symposium on Human-Computer Interaction for Work (CHIWORK '24)* (pp. 14). ACM. https://doi.org/DOI: 10.1145/3663384.3663387

Sula, A., Spaho, E., Matsuo, K., Barolli, L., Miho, R., & Xhafa, F. (2013). An IoT-based system for supporting children with autism spectrum disorder. In *Proceedings of the Eighth International Conference on Broadband and Wireless Computing, Communication and Applications* (pp. 282–289). IEEE. DOI: 10.1109/BWCCA.2013.51

Sun, C., McEwan, A., Boulton, K. A., Demetriou, E. A., Sadozai, A. K., Lampit, A., & Enticott, P. G. (2025). Artificial intelligence for tracking social behaviours and supporting an autism spectrum disorder diagnosis: Systematic review and meta-analysis. *EBioMedicine, 120*, 105931. DOI: 10.1016/j.ebiom.2025.105931 PMID: 41014972

Sun, S. J., Huang, A. C., & Ho, W. S. (2024). Enhancing social skills in autism students with augmented-reality picture books. *Applied Sciences (Basel, Switzerland), 14*(11), 4907. DOI: 10.3390/app14114907

Surendranath P.N., & Padakannaya, P.* (2014). Neurocognitive profile of children with reading disability in Kannada. *Avicenna Journal of Neuro Psycho Physiology, 1*(2), 1-5, e242008.

Swanson, H. L., & Jerman, O. (2006). Math disabilities: A selective meta-analysis of the literature. *Review of Educational Research, 76*(2), 249–274. DOI: 10.3102/00346543076002249

Syriopoulou-Delli, C. K. (2025). Advances in autism spectrum disorder (ASD) diagnostics: From theoretical frameworks to AI-driven innovations. *Electronics (Basel), 14*(5), 951. DOI: 10.3390/electronics14050951

Tager-Flusberg, H., Paul, R., & Lord, C. (2005). *Language and communication in autism* (Vol. 1). Handbook of autism and pervasive developmental disorders.

Tao, Y., Viberg, O., Baker, R. S., & Kizilcec, R. F. (2024). Cultural bias and cultural alignment of large language models. *PNAS Nexus, 3*(9), pgae346. Advance online publication. DOI: 10.1093/pnasnexus/pgae346 PMID: 39290441

Taylor, M. S., & Glavey, E. M. (2024). Harnessing robotics and coding to foster social-emotional learning in students with autism. *Journal of Special Education Technology, 39*(2), 306–313. DOI: 10.1177/01626434231199992

Thabtah, F., & Peebles, D. (2019). A new machine learning model based on the induction of rules for autism detection. *Health Informatics Journal, 25*(4), 1656–1676. DOI: 10.1177/1460458218791786

Thelen, E., & Smith, L. B. (1994). *A dynamic systems approach to the development of cognition and action.* MIT Press. DOI: 10.7551/mitpress/2524.001.0001

Tomasello, M. (2003). *Constructing a language: A usage-based theory of language acquisition.* Harvard University Press., DOI: 10.2307/j.ctv26070v8

Topol, E. J. (2019). High-performance medicine: The convergence of human and artificial intelligence. *Nature Medicine, 25*(1), 44–56. DOI: 10.1038/s41591-018-0300-7

Trapero-González, I., Hinojo-Lucena, F. J., Romero-Rodríguez, J. M., & Martínez-Menéndez, A. (2024). Didactic impact of educational robotics on the development of STEM competence in primary education: A systematic review and meta-analysis. *Frontiers in Education, 9*, 1480908. DOI: 10.3389/feduc.2024.1480908

Traxler, J., & Jandrić, P. (2025). Decolonising educational technology. In *The Geopolitics of Postdigital Educational Development* (pp. 163–196). Springer., 7_9.DOI: 10.1007/978-3-031-99378-7_9

UNESCO. (2017). *A guide for ensuring inclusion and equity in education.* UNESCO Publishing. https://unesdoc.unesco.org/ark:/48223/pf0000248254

UNESCO. (2017). *Ethical principles for safeguarding intangible cultural heritage.* UNESCO. https://ich.unesco.org/en/ethics-and-ich-00866

UNESCO. (2023). *Technology integration of Cambodian higher education: Emerging changes since covid-19 and notable challenges*. Global Education Monitoring Report. https://www.unesco.org/gem-report/sites/default/files/medias/fichiers/2023/09/SopheakandPhyrom.pdf

Ungurean, C., & Burileanu, D. (2011). *An advanced NLP framework for high-quality Text-to-Speech synthesis*. 1–6. DOI: 10.1109/SPED.2011.5940733

University of Calgary—Indigenous Research Support Team. (n.d.). *Indigenous Data Sovereignty*. https://research.ucalgary.ca/engage-research/indigenous-research-support-team/irst- resources/indigenous-data-sovereignty

University of Ottawa Library. (2022). *The First Nations Principles of OCAP®: Fact sheet*. https://www.uottawa.ca/library/sites/g/files/bhrskd381/files/2022- 12/bestpractices_fnigc_ocap_fact_sheet_en_final.pdf

Vallor, S. (2015). Moral deskilling and upskilling in a new machine age: Reflections on the ambiguous future of character. *Philosophy & Technology*, *28*(1), 107–124. DOI: 10.1007/s13347-014-0156-9

VanLehn, K. (2011). The relative effectiveness of human tutoring, intelligent tutoring systems, and other tutoring systems. *Educational Psychologist*, *46*(4), 197–221. DOI: 10.1080/00461520.2011.611369

Vidyasagar, T. R., & Pammer, K. (2010). Dyslexia: A deficit in visuo-spatial attention, not in phonological processing. *Trends in Cognitive Sciences*, *14*(2), 57–63. DOI: 10.1016/j.tics.2009.12.003

Vygotsky, L. S. (1978). *Mind in society: The development of higher psychological processes*. Harvard University Press.

Wainer, A. L., & Ingersoll, B. R. (2015). Increasing access to an ASD imitation intervention via a telehealth parent training program. *Journal of Autism and Developmental Disorders*, *45*(12), 3877–3890. DOI: 10.1007/s10803-014-2186-7 PMID: 25035089

Wall, D. P., Duda, M., & Kosmicki, J. (2020). Mobile machine learning for autism screening: The future of early diagnosis. *npj. Digital Medicine*, *3*(1), 34. DOI: 10.1038/s41746-020-0253-z

Wang, K., Sang, G. Y., Huang, L. Z., Li, S. H., & Guo, J. W. (2023). The effectiveness of educational robots in improving learning outcomes: A meta-analysis. *Sustainability (Basel)*, *15*(5), 4637. DOI: 10.3390/su15054637

Wang, L. C., Tsai, H. J., & Yang, H. M. (2012). Cognitive characteristics of Chinese children with dyslexia. *Research in Developmental Disabilities*, *33*(2), 375–386. DOI: 10.1016/j.ridd.2011.10.012

Wang, S., Jiang, M., & Li, H. (2021). Multimodal behavioral analysis for early autism detection using AI. *Frontiers in Psychology*, *12*, 642879. DOI: 10.3389/fpsyg.2021.642879

Wang, Y., Shao, Y., Yu, Z., & Wang, Z. (2025). MS-RRBR: A Multi-Model Synergetic Framework for Restricted and Repetitive Behavior Recognition in Children with Autism. *Applied Sciences (Basel, Switzerland)*, *15*(3), 1577. Advance online publication. DOI: 10.3390/app15031577

Waseem, S., Sherazi, A., Zheng, H., & Lee, J. Y. (2023). *A Machine Learning-Based Applied Prediction Model for Identification of Acute Coronary Syndrome (ACS)*. Outcomes.

Weintrop, D., & Wilensky, U. (2018). Comparing block based and text based programming in high school computer science classrooms. *ACM Transactions on Computing Education*, *18*(1), 3. Advance online publication. DOI: 10.1145/3089799

Wiener, S., Bramlett, A. A., Brown, B., & Dueck, J. (2025). Acoustic analysis and perception ratings of first and second language speakers' Italian lexical stress. *Applied Linguistics*, •••, amaf075. DOI: 10.1093/applin/amaf075

Wilkey, E. D., Pollack, C., & Price, G. R. (2020). Dyscalculia and typical math achievement are associated with individual differences in number-specific executive function. *Child Development*, *91*(2), 596–619. DOI: 10.1111/cdev.13194

Wilson, C., Atabey, A., & Revans, J. (2025). Towards child-centred AI in children's learning futures: Participatory design futuring with SmartSchool and the co-design stories toolkit. *International Journal of Human-Computer Studies*, *199*, 103431. DOI: 10.1016/j.ijhcs.2024.103431

Wilson, M. (2002). Six views of embodied cognition. *Psychonomic Bulletin & Review*, *9*(4), 625–636. DOI: 10.3758/BF03196322

Wing, J. M. (2006). Computational thinking. *Communications of the ACM*, *49*(3), 33–35. DOI: 10.1145/1118178.1118215

Withanage, P., Liyanage, T., Deeyakaduwe, N., Dias, E., & Thelijjagoda, S. (2018). Road Navigation System Using Automatic Speech Recognition (ASR) And Natural Language Processing (NLP). *IEEE Region Humanitarian Technology Conference*. DOI: 10.1109/R10-HTC.2018.8629859

Wolf, M., & Bowers, P. G. (1999). The double-deficit hypothesis for the developmental dyslexias. *Journal of Educational Psychology, 91*(3), 415–438. DOI: 10.1037/0022-0663.91.3.415

Wood, S. G., Moxley, J. H., Tighe, E. L., & Wagner, R. K. (2018). Does use of text-to-speech and related read-aloud tools improve reading comprehension for students with reading disabilities? A meta-analysis. *Journal of Learning Disabilities, 51*(1), 73–84. DOI: 10.1177/0022219416688170

X. (2024). Reliable Autism Spectrum Disorder diagnosis for pediatrics using machine learning and explainable AI. *Journal Placeholder*, (date). See the database. https://pubmed.ncbi.nlm.nih.gov/39594170/ PubMed

Yang, X., Wu, J., Ma, Y., Yu, J., Cao, H., Zeng, A., Fu, R., Tang, Y., & Ren, Z. (2025). Effectiveness of virtual reality technology interventions in improving the social skills of children and adolescents with autism: Systematic review. *Journal of Medical Internet Research, 27*, e60845. DOI: 10.2196/60845 PMID: 39907288

Yan, W., Zhai, T., Li, Y., Chen, J., Sun, Z., Lin, Y., Zhang, X., & Du, Y. (2025). Effects of immersive virtual reality training on the adaptive skills of children and adolescents with high functioning autism spectrum disorder: A mixed-methods pre-post study. *Frontiers in Psychiatry, 16*, 1570437. DOI: 10.3389/fpsyt.2025.1570437 PMID: 40901263

Yeh, C. C., & Meng, Y. R. (2025). Effectiveness of virtual reality social skills training for students with autism and social difficulties observed through behavior and brain waves. *Applied Sciences (Basel, Switzerland), 15*(9), 4600. DOI: 10.3390/app15094600

Yuan, S. N. V., & Ip, H. H. S. (2018). Using virtual reality to train emotional and social skills in children with autism spectrum disorder. *London Journal of Primary Care, 10*(4), 110–112. DOI: 10.1080/17571472.2018.1483000 PMID: 30083244

Yu, X., Ishiwata, T., Zhang, X., Zhang, D., Xu, L., Su, Y., & Sha, X. (2025). 'More than just music': A multimodal intervention supporting adolescents with autism spectrum disorder in a community-based program in Shanghai. *International Journal of Developmental Disabilities*, 1–16. Advance online publication. DOI: 10.1080/20473869.2025.2561160

Zabler, N., Biondi, A., Kalousios, S., Novitskaya, Y., Faber, H., Duempelmann, M., & Hirsch, M. (2025). Clinical utility of an ambulatory absence seizure detection system. *Epilepsia Open, 10*(5), 1733–1739. DOI: 10.1002/epi4.70138 PMID: 40932588

Zhang, L., Weitlauf, A. S., Amat, A. Z., Swanson, A., Warren, Z. E., & Sarkar, N. (2020). Assessing social communication and collaboration in autism spectrum disorder using intelligent collaborative virtual environments. *Journal of Autism and Developmental Disorders, 50*(1), 199–211. DOI: 10.1007/s10803-019-04246-z PMID: 31583625

Zhao, Y., Li, Q., & Ma, J. (2023). Deep facial analysis for early autism detection using convolutional neural networks. *IEEE Transactions on Neural Networks and Learning Systems, 34*(6), 2901–2914. DOI: 10.1109/TNNLS.2022.3187421

Zheng, Q., Choudhry, A., Liu, Z., Rabbani, P., Hu, Y., Olszewski, A., Huang, Y., & Xiong, J. (2025). AI- Enhanced Speech-Language Intervention Documentation: Opportunities and Design Goals. *In Artificial Intelligence in Education (AIED 2025)* (LNAI, Vol. 15882, pp. 132–140). Springer. https://doi.org/DOI: 10.1007/978-3-031-98465-5_17

Zwaigenbaum, L., Bauman, M. L., Choueiri, R., Kasari, C., Carter, A., Granpeesheh, D., Mailloux, Z., Smith Roley, S., Wagner, S., Fein, D., Pierce, K., Buie, T., Davis, P. A., Newschaffer, C., Robins, D., Wetherby, A., Stone, W. L., Yirmiya, N., Estes, A., & Natowicz, M. R.Committee on Children With Disabilities, Council on Children With Disabilities. (2015). Early intervention for children with autism spectrum disorder under 3 years of age: Recommendations for practice and research. *Pediatrics, 136*(Supplement 1), S60–S81. DOI: 10.1542/peds.2014-3667E

About the Contributors

Nayef J. Jomaa is an assistant professor in Applied Linguistics at the University of Technology and Applied Sciences-Salalah, Sultanate of Oman. He has several years of teaching experience in Syria, Saudi Arabia, Malaysia, and Turkey. His research interests focus on L2 writing, academic writing, genre analysis, and Systemic Functional Linguistics (Functional Grammar).

***

Vennela Akula is a doctoral student in Computer Science and Software Engineering at Auburn University, USA. Her research interests include artificial intelligence, machine learning, educational robotics, intelligent tutoring systems, and human-centered computing. She studies Large Language Model-based methods for embodied mathematics tutoring, strategy-guided robot tutoring pipelines, engagement-aware response generation, and real-time student assessment and feedback. Her work explores the design of interactive technologies that respond to learner needs and support effective communication between students and educational robots. She has contributed to research presented at CSCE 2026, the 2026 IARIA Annual Congress, and the 2025 and 2026 International Conferences on Human-Computer Interaction.

Jane Ali is an experienced educator and leader with a strong background in higher education practices, teaching philosophies, Student Information Systems (SIS), institutional collaboration, and digital accessibility. She serves as an Assistant Professor at University Canada West, and has served other educational institutions in Academic and Compliance Director roles. Her expertise includes curriculum remapping, integrating action learning, AI, Indigenization, and implementing regulatory body compliance. Dr. Ali holds an Ed.D. in Educational Leadership from Aspen University, a Graduate Certificate in Adult Learning and an MA in

Art Leadership (Education/Special Education) from Trinity Western University. She has contributed to research in AI use in academic writing, action learning, and transformational leadership, and is committed to inclusive and equitable education aligned with Indigenous knowledge protection and accessibility standards.

Mohammed Amine Amzazi holds a Ph.D in Sociology and social work, a moroccan researcher in fieled Sociology, Education of sociology, Special education, in addition, he is a visiting professor of social work.

J. Viji Gripsy is an Associate Professor in the Department of Computer Science with Cognitive Systems at PSGR Krishnammal College for Women, Coimbatore. She earned her Ph.D. in Computer Science from Bharathiar University in 2015 and completed a postdoctoral fellowship at Srinivas University in 2024. With over a decade of academic experience, her research focuses on mobile ad-hoc networks, wireless sensor networks, cybersecurity, and AI-driven healthcare systems. Dr. Gripsy has authored more than 60 publications, including journal articles, conference papers, and book chapters, and holds an h-index of 6 with over 100 citations. Her notable projects include developing Tamil speech-enabled mobile interfaces for children with learning disabilities, funded by the Indian Council of Social Science Research and GRG Trust. She actively contributes to academic governance, serving on Boards of Studies for multiple institutions, and is recognized in the AD Scientific Index 2025 for her contributions to mobile ad-hoc and wireless sensor networks.

T. K Gundoor is a dedicated researcher and academic professional with experience in both research and teaching at the postgraduate level, specializing in the critical intersection of Cybersecurity and Artificial Intelligence (AI). He currently serves as an Assistant Professor at the National Forensic Science University (NFSU), Goa. Ph.D. in Computer Science (Cybersecurity) from Karnatak University, Dharwad, focusing his doctoral research on the vital domain of Design an effective algorithm to detect Non-Portable Executable (Non-PE) Malicious Files. He is a Qualified NET and SET candidate in Computer Science and Application and holds a Certified Artificial Intelligence Professional certification from the Defense Institute of Advanced Technology (DIAT, DRDO). His academic foundation includes a Master of Computer Application (MCA) from Visvesvaraya Technological University, Belagavi, and a Bachelor of Computer Application (BCA) from Karnatak University, Dharwad. His research work is highly focused on emerging technology and security, with a track record of significant academic contributions: He has published 6 journal papers including Scopus, Elsevier, springer, two conference papers, and has contributed 10 book chapters, 1 Edited book to publications by renowned international publishers like IGI Global, CRC Apple Press, Bentham science and Wiley, with several being Scopus-indexed. Demonstrating a commitment to continuous learning, he has attended a total of 60+ Faculty Development Programs (FDPs), courses, and training programs, with recent attendance in advanced topics such as Cyber Security, Blockchain, AI, Machine Learning, and Data Science, including multiple programs. Actively contributes to maintaining the quality of scholarly work, receiving a Certificate of Recognition from Bentham Science Publishers for his peer-review contributions. Is a lifetime member of the IAENG International Association of Engineering and holds memberships with the IEEE Student Member, IFERP (Institute for Educational Research and Publication), and the CSTA (Computer Science Teachers Association). His dedication is defined by a passion for helping organizations reach their full potential and a consistent drive to excel in the academic and research fields.

Sovanna Huot is a PhD candidate in Political Science at the University of Delhi, New Delhi, India. He is a vice principal at a Government Public High School of Cambodia and is responsible for the school academic and institutional leadership. He is a very proficient academic across many disciplines. He has completed a two-year teacher training program from 2010-2012 and has obtained bachelor's degrees in English and in Educational Administration. He also has two master's degrees in law and in TEFL obtained through a very competitive scholarship, and a Master of Education, specialized in School Leadership, Upper Secondary School Principalship, from the National Institute of Education (NIE), Phnom Penh, 2021. He specializes in educational reform and in the practice-policy nexus of digit pedagogy and in glonacal (global–national–local) education systems. He has formal academic training in political science and education and has published scholarly work in both disciplines, including articles indexed in Scopus (Author ID: 59316244400).

Abire Ismaili is a doctoral candidate in psychopedagogy at Université Laval and member of the Interuniversity Research Center on Teacher Training and the Teaching Profession (CRIFPE–Université Laval). Research interests include initial teacher education, teachers' practices that support the emotional development of both teachers and students, and well-being in education. ABISM3@ulaval.ca

K. Shunmugapriya, an Assistant Professor deeply passionate about learning and teaching, was influenced by her upbringing in a modest family, instilling in her values of humility and diligence, shaping her journey towards academia. With a natural curiosity and love for learning, she endeavors to simplify complex concepts and inspire her students. Despite a busy schedule, her thirst for knowledge remains unquenchable, driving her to explore new areas of research and innovation. Transitioning into research, she is fueled by a passion for discovery and a desire to make meaningful contributions to her field, addressing real-world challenges along the way. Her journey reflects the power of perseverance and dedication, serving as inspiration for others on their academic path.

Amine Khadraoui is a Moroccan researcher in the field of psychology and educational sciences. He is a visiting professor of "Docimology and Evaluation" at the Higher School of Teachers (ENS), Moulay Ismail University, Meknes, Morocco. He has published several collective books and studies on learning, attention, gamification, and educational technology. He was also the recipient of the National Reading Award in Morocco (2019). In addition, he serves as the Head of Office at the National Social Security Fund (CNSS) in Morocco. He can be contacted at email: am.khadraoui@edu.umi.ac.ma.

Amrutha Kolhar obtained her MCA degree in Computer Science from Karnatak University in 2022 and is currently a Research Scholar under the guidance of Dr. Sridevi, Department of Computer Science, Karnatak University, Dharwad. She is a recipient of the OBC Research Fellowship from the Government of Karnataka. Her research focuses on Network Security, particularly on "Development and Enhancing Inter-operability of API and Validating Its Authentication: X-IoT Devices." She is an IAENG Student Member (Member No. 366909). Ms. Kolhar has published one international journal article, one international conference paper, and seven Scopus-indexed book chapters with IGI Scientific Publishing. She has also more than 50 workshops, demonstrating her active engagement in research and professional development.

Noorul Afreed is an researcher and developer specializing in AI-driven personalization, game-based learning systems, and interactive application development. research investigates the application of artificial intelligence in adaptive educational environments, with emphasis on scalable personalization and communication skill development. has practical experience in Unity development, web-based systems, and AI-integrated platforms.

Daniela Marghitu has served as Auburn University faculty since 1996. She has received nine National Science Foundation awards and one National Institute of Food and Agriculture award. Her publications include seven Pearson books, two IGI Global chapters, and articles in IEEE Access, International Journal on Advances in Software, International Journal on Advances in Internet Technology, Journal of Computer Science Education, Journal of Computing Sciences in Colleges, and International Journal for Virtual Reality. Her honors include the AccessComputing Capacity Building Award, DO-IT Trailblazer Award, IARIA Fellowship, Society for Design and Process Science Fellowship, and 100+ Women Strong Leadership in Diversity Award.

Lovleen Marwaha, Professor, Department of Zoology, School of Bioscience and Bioengineering, Lovely Professional University, Punjab, India Mail ID: lovleenmarwaha@gmail.com Mobile no: 6283587688 Dr. Lovleen Marwaha, Ph.D., is a Professor at the Department of Zoology, School of Bioengineering and Biosciences, Lovely Professional University, Phagwara, India. She has completed her M.S. and Ph.D. in Cytogenetics from the Department of Zoology, Punjab University, Chandigarh. She has worked on the evaluation of pesticide genotoxicity using insect genomes, specifically on different mosquito species and Drosophila melanogaster. She has carried out an intensive study on the correlation between pesticide exposure limit and inductive genotoxic consequences on Dipteran larval salivary polytene chromosomes. Furthermore, she has studied chromosomal and gene mutations in mosquito and fruit fly genomes due to pesticide exposure. Currently, she is working on Apiculture and Sericulture-related topics. She has many research papers published in National and International Journals of repute. Presently, she is working on insecticide resistance in mosquitoes, pesticide genotoxicity evaluation, honey bee development, honey processing, silk fiber, and pearl quality improvement. She has published three authored books on Apiculture and on Mobile Genetic Elements. Forthcoming books include Worker Honey Bees, Apiculture Products, Basic Concepts of Genetics, and Introduction to Sericulture.

Sasikiran Reddy Nallapareddy is a Ph.D. student in Computer Science at Auburn University in Auburn, Alabama. He holds a master's degree in Data Engineering and focuses his research on human–robot interaction, artificial intelligence, and accessible technologies for special education. He has contributed to research on intelligent and assistive robots in K–12 education, extended reality technologies in agriculture, and AI-powered systems for real-time student answer evaluation and feedback. His publications have appeared in Springer conference proceedings and IEEE Access. His current research involves developing accessible, AI-supported educational applications and socially assistive robotic systems. His long-term goal is to advance inclusive SEL learning through human-centered artificial intelligence, adaptive learning technologies, and accessible computing solutions.

Fernanda is a dedicated professional with interests in information technology, digital systems, and applied computing. He has been actively involved in academic and practical projects related to software development, system analysis, and data management, with a strong focus on efficiency and user-centered design. His work reflects solid analytical thinking, problem-solving abilities, and a collaborative approach to addressing real-world technical challenges. Mr. Fernanda continues to expand his expertise in emerging technologies and is committed to contributing to innovative digital solutions in academic and professional environments.

Prakash Padakannaya is a Professor of Psychology at CHRIST University, Bengaluru, India. Trained in educational psycholinguistics and cognition at Utkal University and the MRC Cognitive Development Unit, London, his pioneering Ph.D. on reading development in Oriya demonstrated that phonemic awareness is not essential for learning Indian alpha-syllabaries. His research spans reading, dyslexia, psycho/neurolinguistics, and cognition among preliterate to illiterate populations, using behavioral, neural, and genetic methods. A recipient of prestigious fellowships including Mombusho, Fulbright, and Erasmus Mundus, he is a Fellow of the Association for Psychological Science (USA) and the National Academy of Psychology (India). He co-founded and serves as Managing Editor of the Journal of Cultural Cognitive Science (Springer) and is an Associate Editor for Frontiers in Psychology

Kimyut Phin is an educator and PhD research scholar in English at the University of Delhi, India. He serves as the director of the Institute of Foreign Languages of the University of Heng Samrin Thbongkhmum, Cambodia. Kimyut has also had teaching experiences in linguistics, applied linguistics, teaching methodology, second language acquisition, academic writing skills, global studies, and literature studies for years. Further, he has experience in lesson planning, classroom management, assessment and evaluation, and technology for teaching and learning. His research centers on ELT and linguistics, education, digital pedagogy, literary and theoretical studies, cultural and gender studies, and translation studies, and his work also gains Scopus-indexed publications (Scopus Author ID: 60516584900).

S. Ponmalar is a faculty member in the Department of Computer Science at PSGR Krishnammal College for Women. She is involved in teaching and academic activities related to computer science, with a focus on fostering technical knowledge and practical skills among students. Through her dedication to education and student development, she contributes to creating a strong academic environment that encourages innovation, learning, and professional growth in the field of computing.

Nayanika Reddy Rajoli is a Ph.D. student in the Department of Computer Science and Software Engineering at Auburn University, Auburn, USA. Her research focuses on artificial intelligence for education, with an emphasis on large language models, intelligent tutoring systems, learner state modeling and inference, and edge intelligence for adaptive learning and socially assistive robotics. She has authored and co-authored peer-reviewed conference papers presented at international venues, including the IARIA Annual Congress, the International Conference on Human-Computer Interaction (HCII), and CSCE. Her work explores the integration of AI, robotics, and learner modeling to develop personalized, context-aware, and adaptive educational systems that enhance student learning and engagement. She is committed to advancing intelligent, human-centered educational technologies through interdisciplinary research.

Rajakumari S is an Assistant Professor in the Department of Mathematics at R.M.D. Engineering College. She is actively engaged in teaching, academic mentoring, and research activities in the field of mathematics and its interdisciplinary applications. With a strong commitment to student learning and academic development, she contributes to fostering analytical and problem-solving skills among engineering students.

Binastya Anggara Sekti has been a lecturer at the Faculty of Computer Science, Esa Unggul University, Jakarta, since 2016. He is actively involved in the Artificial Intelligence and Information Security Study Group. He holds a Bachelor's degree in Informatics Engineering from the Bandung Institute of Technology and a Master's degree in Information Systems Management from Trisakti University, Jakarta. Prior to entering academia, he accumulated over 25 years of professional experience as an IT practitioner in various companies across Jakarta. His work focused on developing data centers for internet service providers and delivering IT solutions for the manufacturing and oil & gas sectors. His research interests include artificial intelligence, cybersecurity, and the development of IT infrastructure.

C.V. Suresh Babu is a pioneer in content development. A true entrepreneur, he founded Anniyappa Publications, a company that is highly active in publishing books related to Computer Science and Management. Dr. C.V. Suresh Babu has also ventured into SB Institute, a center for knowledge transfer. He holds a Ph.D. in Engineering Education from the National Institute of Technical Teachers Training & Research in Chennai, along with seven master's degrees in various disciplines such as Engineering, Computer Applications, Management, Commerce, Economics, Psychology, Law, and Education. Additionally, he has UGC-NET/SET qualifications in the fields of Computer Science, Management, Commerce, and Education. Currently, Dr. C.V. Suresh Babu is a Professor in the Department of Information Technology at the School of Computing Science, Hindustan Institute of Technology and Science (Hindustan University) in Padur, Chennai, Tamil Nadu, India. For more information, you can visit his personal blog at https://sites.google.com/view/cvsureshbabu/.

Zahid Ahmad Thoker Research Scholar, Department of Zoology, School of Bioscience and Bioengineering, Lovely Professional University, Punjab, India Mail ID: za7710917@gmail.com, Orcid id: 0009-0002-6897-5835 Mobile No: 9906499012 Mr. Zahid Ahmad Thoker is a serious research Scholar at Lovely Professional University who is working on Insects (Entomology), specifically on Honey Bees. He graduated with his Master's degree in Zoology from Chandigarh University, Gharuan, Mohali, where he developed a very solid academic grounding in life sciences. Zahid has already contributed greatly to academia; one of his research papers was published, one review paper, and over 25 book chapters in reputable national and international volumes. His academic publication is an indication of the desire to promote science, especially in the biological sciences. As a visionary who desires to make a difference in the research world and in society, Zahid hopes to broaden his academic and professional experiences with integrity and excellence. He is also strongly driven by the goal of benefiting society with his research work and making his parents proud by leaving his mark on the field of science and scholarship.

M. Usha is the Dean of the School of Computational Sciences at KG College of Arts and Science. With extensive academic and administrative experience in the field of computer science and emerging technologies, she has contributed significantly to curriculum development, research initiatives, and student mentoring. She is actively involved in promoting innovation-driven learning and fostering industry-oriented education in computational sciences. Dr. Usha is also recognized for her commitment to academic excellence and for guiding students and faculty in research and professional development activities.

Index

www.ingramcontent.com/pod-product-compliance
Lightning Source LLC
LaVergne TN
LVHW081537300926
849161LV00006B/1464